D0467289

American Religious Poems

AMERICAN RELIGIOUS POEMS

AN
ANTHOLOGY
BY

HAROLD
BLOOM

HAROLD BLOOM AND JESSE ZUBA, EDITORS

A Special Publication of
THE LIBRARY OF AMERICA

Introduction, foreword, volume compilation, and notes
© 2006 by Literary Classics of the United States, New York, NY.
All rights reserved. No part of this book may be reproduced
commercially by offset-lithographic or equivalent copying devices
without the permission of the publisher.

Some of the material in this volume is reprinted with
permission of holders of copyright and publication rights.
For acknowledgments, see page 639.

Distributed to the trade by Penguin Putnam, Inc.
Cover and slipcase design by Mark Melnick.

Library of Congress Cataloging in Publication Data:
American religious poems : an anthology / by Harold Bloom.
p. cm.
ISBN 978-1-931082-74-7 (alk. paper)
ISBN 1-931082-74-x
PS595.R4A44 2006
811.008'0382—dc22 2006041031

10 9 8 7 6 5 4 3 2 1

Printed in the United States of America

American Religious Poems
is published with support from
LILLY ENDOWMENT, INC.

Contents

American Indian Songs and Chants

Spirituals and Anonymous Hymns

Introduction

As men's prayers are a disease of the will, so are their creeds a disease of the intellect.
— Emerson, "Self-Reliance"

I

Anyone glancing at the table of contents of this anthology is likely to see that much of it would not be considered religious poetry in Great Britain, or in Britain's American colonies prior to the Declaration of Independence. Walt Whitman proclaims that he can "now and always send sunrise out of me." Is that a religious sentiment? Just nineteen years old, Emily Dickinson wrote a letter to a friend, Jane Humphrey, on 3 April 1850, describing the poet's long, stubborn stand against being saved by the Second Great Awakening in Western Massachusetts:

> Christ is calling everyone here, all my companions have answered, even my darling Vinnie believes she loves and trusts him, and I am standing alone in rebellion, and growing very careless. Abby, Mary, Jane, and farthest of all, my Vinnie have been seeking and they all believe they have found; I can't tell you *what* they have found, but *they* think it is something precious. I wonder if it *is*?

Dickinson's letters seem to me as powerfully *composed* as are her poems. Whitman and Dickinson remain much the strongest of American poets: Frost, Stevens, Eliot, Hart Crane, Elizabeth Bishop, Ammons, Merrill, Ashbery are major figures, but are not of the eminence of the two great American originals. The eight I have just listed include only one Christian believer, the churchwardenly Eliot. Religious poetry, in the United States, has little to do with devotional creeds of the Old World. I suggest that is because the American Jesus and the American Holy Spirit are the deities of what I follow Sidney Ahlstrom in calling "the American Religion":

> The Emersonian message was not a mere softening of traditional doctrines, but a dramatic and drastic demand for a complete re-

> casting of religious life and thought. "Like all puritans, Emerson was an extremist." Some have argued that his was a benign and etherealized form of democratic individualism. Others have pointed to Emerson's parochialism, his puritanic suspicion of the theater, his perennial sermonic tone, his tendency to take the edge off of every sharp romantic insight, his insistence on reducing philosophic discussion to a popular, even pedestrian level. Still others have made of him chiefly a "literary" rather than a speculative figure. There is a great deal of truth in all of these observations. Yet they do not fully account for his obvious importance or explain why he is, with William James, peculiarly America's own philosopher. They fail to recognize that Emerson is in fact the theologian of something we may almost term "the American religion." Most important for our present purpose, none of these deprecations explains why such strident opposition should have arisen against him and those who came to share his outlook.

The strident opposition is still there, though not as prevalent as it was a third of a century ago. T. S. Eliot had proclaimed that the "essays of Emerson are already an encumbrance," and he wondered why Henry James has not carved Emerson up. Robert Penn Warren would assure me at our weekly luncheon together that Waldo was the Devil, thus cheering me on to my graduate seminar on Emerson, which followed directly after. But then, Allen Tate called the American sage "the Lucifer of Concord," and led in the culture war against Emerson that goes on in the South until this day. Emerson, opposing the admission of Texas to the Union, rightly prophesized that Texas would destroy America, though President Bush II goes beyond even Emersonian admonition.

Summarizing Emerson's religion is scarcely possible; he delighted in saying that to be great is to be misunderstood. A good enough starting point is to consider the American Jesus of the "Divinity School Address" with which the sage of Concord scandalized Harvard in 1838:

> Jesus Christ belonged to the true race of prophets. He saw with open eye the mystery of the soul. Drawn by its severe harmony, ravished with its beauty, he lived in it, and had his being there. Alone in all history, he estimated the greatness of man. One man was true to what is in you and me. He saw that God incarnates himself in man, and evermore goes forth anew to take possession of his world. He said, in this jubilee of sublime emotion, 'I am divine. Through me, God

> acts; through me, speaks. Would you see God, see me; or, see thee, when thou also thinkest as I now think.' But what a distortion did his doctrine and memory suffer in the same, in the next, and the following ages! There is no doctrine of the Reason which will bear to be taught by the Understanding. The understanding caught this high chant from the poet's lips, and said, in the next age, 'This was Jehovah come down out of heaven. I will kill you if you say he was a man.' The idioms of his language, and the figures of his rhetoric, have usurped the place of his truth; and churches are not built on his principles, but on his tropes. Christianity became a Mythus, as the poetic teaching of Greece and of Egypt, before. He spoke of miracles; for he felt that man's life was a miracle, and all that man doth, and he knew that this daily miracle shines, as the character ascends. But the word Miracle, as pronounced by Christian churches, gives a false impression; it is Monster. It is not one with the blowing clover and the falling rain.

"See me; or, see thee" is the center; creed and prayer are not even at the circumference. There are three crucial components in Emerson's American religion: the God within; solitude; the best and oldest part of the self, which goes back before creation. What will the poems of that religion have in common with Dante or with the holy George Herbert?

Let me juxtapose Walt Whitman with his contemporary, Gerard Manley Hopkins, who admired the little of the American bard he had read, but declined to read any more because he feared the identity he sensed between Whitman and himself, a bond both homoerotic and rhythmic. Writing to the poet Robert Bridges on 18 October 1882, Hopkins seeks to deny Whitman's influence (rather weakly) and then declares:

> I always knew in my heart Walt Whitman's mind to be more like my own than any other man's living. As he is a very great scoundrel this is not a pleasant confession. And this also makes me the more desirous to read him and the more determined that I will not.

To characterize the ministering angel of the Washington, D.C., hospitals during the Civil War as "a very great scoundrel" is sublimely absurd, even if you are a Jesuit priest and an Oxford gentleman. Our father the old man Walt Whitman was a greater poet than Father Hopkins, and of a religion beyond Hopkins's understanding. G. K. Chesterton, before he converted to the Church of Rome, gave a more accurate sense of the poet of the American religion: ". . . we have not yet begun to get to the beginning of Whitman. The egoism of which men accuse him is that sense of human divinity which no one has felt since Christ."

Hopkins, I suspect, read more widely in Whitman than he cared to admit. "That Nature Is a Heraclitean Fire and of the Comfort of the Resurrection," written in 1888, echoes "The Sleepers," with "heaven-roysterers, in gay-gangs" taking me back to "Onward we move! a gay gang of blackguards," as though the Jesuit renders tribute to the very great scoundrel who was certainly one of his forerunners. After the birth of the United States, we produced no devotional poets of high merit. Emerson's briefly inspired disciple Jones Very celebrates only the God within, and while Eliot, Auden, and Robert Lowell are included in this book because of their confessional stances of devotion, they do not, in my own critical judgment, equal Hopkins and Christina Rossetti, let alone John Donne, George Herbert, Henry Vaughan, and Richard Crashaw.

2

So implicit and universal is the American religion that some of its poets can be unaware that they incarnate and celebrate it. Setting aside Emerson himself and our two grandest voices, Whitman and Dickinson, why should poems by such skeptics as Robert Frost, Wallace Stevens, John Wheelwright, Elizabeth Bishop, and May Swenson be regarded as religious? Hart Crane, who professed no Christian doctrine, became the American equivalent of St. John of the Cross in the proem "To Brooklyn Bridge." A. R. Ammons, John Ashbery, and James Merrill, the strongest poets in my generation, have nothing conventional in their respective spiritualities, but Ammons and Ashbery bring us back to Emerson, Whitman, and Dickinson, while Merrill transmutes Yeats, Stevens, and Auden into creatures largely his own.

Any distinction between sacred and secular literature is finally a political judgment, and therefore irrelevant in the realms of the aesthetic. The United States, already a plutocracy, flickers these days towards theocracy. A theocratic America doubtless will distinguish between sacred and secular utterances, but Whitmanian democracy fuses them in the divinity of the self, which is our native understanding of the Resurrection as an escape from history, that is to say, from European time. The Resurrection is not a mediated event for American Religionists, whether they be Independent Baptists, Mormons, or Emersonians. The ancient Gnostics said that *first* Jesus resurrected, and *then* he died. Our singer of *Song of Myself* records a similar career. William James became the psychologist of the American Religion and found in Whitman the archetype of healthy-mindedness. To recover the Whitman of William James, and of Henry James after *he* had weathered his early savagery against the divine Walt, is to recover not only the greatest American poet but the grandest of American personae, "Walt Whitman, one of the roughs, an American."

Walt Whitman, in his great poetic decade 1855–1865, wrote the authentic literature for the New World. I do not fear being called hyperbolical, since the Critical Sublime is precisely that. How great a writer was Whitman? No one since Whitman, not Henry James nor Marcel Proust, not James Joyce nor Jorge Luis Borges, nor anyone you can hope to name, is nearly as vital and as vitalizing as the visionary poet of *Leaves of Grass*. D. H. Lawrence was fiercely ambivalent toward his crucial precursor, but he at last got it right in the final version of *Studies in Classic American Literature*. Feeling himself to be more Whitman than Whitman himself could be, Lawrence thus took on the role of Christ to Walt's John the Baptist, but actually became St. Paul to Whitman's Christ. Here though is the best and most poignant prose tribute yet made to the artist-seer of *Leaves of Grass*:

> Whitman, the great poet, has meant so much to me. Whitman, the one man breaking a way ahead. Whitman, the one pioneer. And only Whitman. No English pioneers, no French. No European pioneer-poets. In Europe the would-be pioneers are mere innovators. The same in America. Ahead of Whitman, nothing. Ahead of all poets, pioneering into the wilderness of unopened life, Whitman. Beyond him, none. His wide, strange camp at the end of the great high-road. And lots of new little poets camping on Whitman's camping ground now. But none going really beyond. Because Whitman's camp is at the end of the road, and on the edge of the precipice. Over the precipice, blue distances, and the blue hollow of the future. But there is no way down. It is a dead end.
>
> Pisgah. Pisgah sights. And Death. Whitman like a strange, modern, American Moses. Fearfully mistaken. And yet the great leader.

> The essential function of art is moral. Not aesthetic, not decorative, not pastime and recreation. But moral. The essential function of art is moral.
>
> But a passionate, implicit morality, not didactic. A morality which changes the blood, rather than the mind. Changes the blood first. The mind follows later, in the wake.
>
> Now Whitman was the great moralist. He was a great leader. He was a great changer of the blood in the veins of men.

Matching Lawrence's praise of the sublime Walt in eloquence, Wallace Stevens actually was more accurate in giving us Whitman as precisely anti-apocalyptic, rather than Lawrence's proclaimer of finalities:

> In the far South the sun of autumn is passing
> Like Walt Whitman walking along a ruddy shore.
> He is singing and chanting the things that are part of him,
> The worlds that were and will be, death and day.
> Nothing is final, he chants. No man shall see the end.
> His beard is of fire and his staff is a leaping flame.

Our prime shaman of the American Religion affirms the Blessing of more life. Death, for Walt Whitman, was an innocence of the earth, and no false sign or symbol of malice. I do not find it useful to define Whitman's religion apart from his poetry, any more than I trust any social pronouncements in his prose, whether published or not. His sexual orientation, in the poetry, seems to me more Onanistic than homoerotic. It is a paradox that Henry James, massively reticent in his novels, stories, and other writings, particularly in regard to his own homosexuality, may have experienced more actual erotic fulfillment than did the personally shy prophet of "adhesiveness." Still, shamans traditionally have been androgynous, and of Whitman's poetic mastery of archaic techniques of ecstasy I entertain no doubts.

To discover an American achievement equal to Whitman's, I judge you need to fuse two brothers of absolute genius, William and Henry James. Since William composed *The Varieties of Religious Experience* and *The Will to Believe*, no one would dispute his eminence as the prime philosopher-psychologist of our very original national religion. Our greatest American novelist scarcely seems a religious writer, let alone an occultist like the Balzac whom he so vastly admired. Yet the ghostly tales perpetually remind us that the Master excelled at speculative connections, even in his major fictions. Relations, as Frances Wilson has noted, stop nowhere for the James family, who were occultly linked, as befitted the children of a Swedenborgian father. The idea of death is as richly ordered by the James brothers as by Whitman, yet they evade his baroque elaborations, though both of them loved his *Lilacs* elegy for Lincoln.

William James had a less dialectical relation to Emerson than Henry enjoyed, while Whitman's debt to Emerson was so vast that he tried eventually to deny it. Henry James's American heroines are Emersonians, but oddly that was true also in *The Scarlet Letter* and *The Marble Faun*. T. S. Eliot happily praised Henry James for possessing a Vision of Evil that Emerson refused to honor, but Eliot was mistaken in his Christianization of James, just as Eliot's disciple Cleanth Brooks erred in baptizing the fictions of William Faulkner. Eliot's Vision of Evil was gratified best by Christopher Marlowe's *The Jew of Malta*. I wish Eliot had left some comments on Henry James's keenly appreciative account of the Yiddish old East Side in the superb *American Scene*, the Master's return to what had been *his* New York City. In his own way Henry James, like Whitman, contained multitudes.

Again like Whitman, the Master of American prose fiction had a visionary sense of the uncertain borders between the living and the dead, just as both apprehended the wavering line between maleness and femaleness. Emerson had no interest in either demarcation; you can name this healthy-mindedness, though part of my statement is now so politically incorrect as to seem outrageous. Clearly (I would hope) I intend no offense, since Whitman and Henry James merely remain much our greatest imaginative writers. William James, like his father and brother, had something to intimate about a possible life-after-death, but as a psychologist ventured no particular insights into homoeroticism.

Sinuously, Henry did, particularly in *The Sacred Fount*, which shows an affinity with Whitman's distrust of heterosexual marriage. Shamanistic spirituality has little to do with healing marriages, and the author of the grandest American novels and tales was hardly a shaman. Walt Whitman, in an original way, was precisely that during his great decade of 1855 through 1865. He came as medicine, and found himself most truly and most strange in the Civil War hospitals of Washington, D.C. Henry James, consciously imitating Whitman, visited the British wounded of World War I during his closing years, but not very effectively. We cannot think of the Master as the Good Gray Novelist.

3

Books have been written on Whitman's relation to various nineteenth-century American quackeries, but throughout my more than a half-century as a literary critic I have rejected all historicisms, Old or New. No one has ventured to answer my persistent question: "How can any societal over-determination account for the phenomenon of any solitary genius?" Emerson memorably addressed himself to the Question of Genius; all a New Historicist can do is shrug and label Genius a High Romantic myth. In my old age, I refuse to be bored, and what now passes for ongoing scholarly criticism of Walt Whitman is sublimely tiresome. When I teach Robert Browning, a great poet now absurdly neglected, I would feel absurd were I to begin by telling my students that this wonderful dramatic monologist was fiercely heterosexual. What does it matter that Henry James and Walt Whitman were homoerotic, or to use the going lingo, gay or queer? I begin to lose any last shreds of tolerance for anyone who believes that aesthetic splendor, wisdom, and cognitive power cannot be recognized except by criteria of gender, social class, skin pigmentation, ethnic origin, and sexual orientation. The divine Oscar Wilde, who as Borges observed was always right, told us: "All bad poetry is sincere."

Walt Whitman wrote six major great poems, the crown of American literature: *Song of Myself*, "The Sleepers," "Crossing Brooklyn Ferry," "As I Ebb'd with the Ocean of Life," "Out of the Cradle Endlessly Rocking," and "When Lilacs Last in the Dooryard Bloom'd." There are about twenty other shorter poems or fragments of roughly equal eminence, but only three or four of these were composed after 1865, and Whitman died in 1892.

In his strongest poems, Whitman is a new kind of religious bard, virtually indescribable even in his own terms. Discursive contradictions between creeds and creedlessness, God and man, oblivion and immortality melt away in Walt's creative furnace, as they did in William Blake's or Victor Hugo's. I begin to feel that Gershom Scholem was accurate when he told me that Whitman, who certainly never heard of the Kabbalah, conceived of the Divine Reality as the later Kabbalists did. Like the *Ein-Sof*, the Kabbalah's revision of Yahweh, Whitman creates and ruins worlds even as he draws in his breath. John Hollander, describing Whitman's rhetoric, pragmatically invokes Lurianic Kabbalah while perhaps being unaware of the invocation: "When he announces his experiences, containments, and incorporations, he is frequently enacting a contraction and withdrawal." I would add that Walt is most like Yahweh when in effect he warns: "I will be absent wherever and whenever I will be absent." Our great American master of his own real presence, Whitman is endlessly elusive and evasive. Yahweh is not there when you need him, and so I do not trust him or like him, and I wish he would go away, though he won't. Whitman is there on the page, or in my chanting memory, and yet is not his highest art the real absence?

These days we live not in the great poem of Whitmanian democracy, but in an America that fuses plutocracy and theocracy. Tocqueville toured the United States in the 1830s, a generation before *Leaves of Grass*, and concluded that American Christianity, while more democratic than not, nevertheless restrained the national imagination. He could not have anticipated Emerson and Whitman, who freed imagination and discarded Christianity. This American Renaissance, participated in also by Hawthorne, Melville, and Thoreau, flourished from 1850 to 1860, and then yielded to the Civil War, which seems to me is still being fought against the rest of us by the old Confederacy, now the solid Republican South of Reagan and the Bushes. Tocqueville could not have anticipated the Christian Right, whose alliance with Wall Street may be permanent in this ongoing age of worldwide religious warfare. In his cosmic optimism, Whitman also could not foresee our bad time, though he rightly feared that the Union had survived at too high a cost.

What is the center of Whitmanian religion? Clearly, it is Walt Whitman himself as Divine, post-Christian yet a messiah, another son of a carpenter who also is a son of God. There actually was a rather literal-minded Whitman cult, which fortunately ebbed and vanished with the end of World War I in 1919. Though the enterprise was absurd and useless, it serves as another reminder that the reader never can really know what is literal and what is figurative in Whitman. Perhaps nothing in the poetry, including Walt himself, *was* literal, though I suspect the particulars were only sparsely literalized, if at all. You can call Whitman a mythmaker, or merely a liar, but a great poet creates permanent fictions, and "Walt Whitman" remains the largest literary fact we have, reducing to pigmies such fictive entities as the Dr. Doolittle–like pushme-pullyou, the "Ginsberg-Kerouac." Usurpation rarely can be duplicated in a nation's literary history. Like Goethe, Victor Hugo, Shakespeare, Dante, and Homer, Whitman has a way of occupying all of imaginative space. These half-dozen writers are mortal gods, though only Goethe, Hugo, and Whitman seem to have asserted such status.

4

Being a god is rather hard work, though Goethe and Hugo never waned, while Whitman did, but Goethe sensibly did not fight against Napoleon. Victor Hugo gallantly raised the morale of the Paris Commune, particularly devoting himself, despite his advanced years, to gratifying the female communards. Whitman, too middle-aged to fight for the Union, became the heroic ministering angel of the Washington hospitals. By then his divinity had left him, and his magnificent elegy for President Lincoln became implicitly an elegy for his ebbing Incarnation, as poet and as God. I go on judging this as the greatest of American poems, but Whitman himself was irritated whenever anyone called it his best. William and Henry James loved it in part because their preternaturally shared consciousness is echoed by the poem's fusion of Lincoln and Whitman. I suggest that Walt's divine apotheosis lasted five years, from 1854 through 1859, when it attained a crescendo in "Sun-Down Poem," later retitled "Crossing Brooklyn Ferry." In the winter of 1859–60, Whitman evidently suffered a homoerotic crisis, perhaps akin to T. S. Eliot's supposed brief moment with Jean Verdenal: "The awful daring of a moment's surrender / Which an age of prudence can never retract": The Whitmanian debacle gave him the two superb *Sea-Drift* elegies, "Out of the Cradle Endlessly Rocking" and "As I Ebb'd with the Ocean of Life." To find the Divine Walt, we need to center upon *Song of Myself*, the American epic proper, in which the God of the United States achieved decisive self-recognition.

Late in life, Whitman set down in prose notes his recollections of the great Quaker preacher Elias Hicks, who broke with the Philadelphia Quakers in 1829, and led his followers back to the Inner Light vision of George Fox. Walt's paternal grandfather and Walter Whitman Sr. were among these followers, and so in a sense was the American Bard himself, who fused his Emersonian revelations of the God within with Hicksite Quakerism. Of Hicks, Whitman observed: "He is the most *democratic* of the religionists—the prophets." Partly Native American, partly African American, Hicks, like the Whitmans, was working-class and devoted his life to dissident Quaker circuit-riding. Taken first at the age of ten to hear Hicks preach, Walt revived the spirit of Elias in the final passage of *Song of Myself*, section 5:

> Swiftly arose and spread around me the peace and knowledge
> that pass all the argument of the earth,
> And I know that the hand of God is the promise of my own,
> And I know that the spirit of God is the brother of my own,
> And that all the men ever born are also my brothers, and the
> women my sisters and lovers,
> And that a kelson of the creation is love,
> And limitless are leaves stiff or drooping in the fields,
> And brown ants in the little wells beneath them,
> And mossy scabs of the worm fence, heap'd stones, elder,
> mullein and poke-weed.

The directness of this testimony is Hicksite Quakerian, but the final three lines are the purest Whitman, who refuses any hierarchy of being, and who celebrates weeds as though they were flowers. His central metaphor necessarily is "leaves of grass." John Hollander deftly indicated the multiple ambiguities of that "of": are the "leaves" pages of books? Are they figurations for the fresh green of Whitmanian poems? Or are they Sibylline leaves, wind-blown oracles? Primarily they must refer to what Wallace Stevens, with highly conscious belatedness, termed "the fiction of the leaves," sad emblems for the ends of particular human lives in Homer, Virgil, Dante, Milton, Shelley, and Whitman himself. The "grass" then would be that of all flesh harvested by death in the prophet Isaiah, the Psalms of David, and the New Testament. Hollander adds "leavings," departures in song for other realms. I myself suspect, since Whitman learned the printer's trade in a newspaper office, that the leaves are also printer's sheets and the grass throw-away stuff employed to fill up blank pages. This vertigo of metaphor is central to Whitman as the American bardic Christ, self-anointed to strike up the cognitive and spiritual music for the New World.

5

Walt Whitman wrote the poems of our climate, as Stevens ruefully (in certain moods) concluded. How could it have been otherwise? Here was the American Adam, early in the morning, fusing Man, god, and the Gnostic and Hermetic Angel Christ, as he is called by the Sufis. As this amalgam, Walt is like the auroras or Northern Lights described by Wordsworth as "here, there, and everywhere at once." When the daunting illuminations flash upon the beach-walking Stevens in *The Auroras of Autumn*, the aging poet attempts to defend his waning autonomy by unnaming the lights, but they will not be destroyed: "he opens the door of his house / On flames." Whitman, strongest of American bards, met the challenge of dazzling and tremendous sunrise by affirming that, now and always, he could send forth sunrise from himself. There are multitudes of poets contained in the large Walt, and one of them refuses to be subdued by natural appearances.

Angus Fletcher recently has found in Whitman the master of the Environment Poem, an American version of the Picturesque. I would prefer to call *Song of Myself* precisely the Anti-Environment Poem, despite Thoreau's enthusiasm for what in 1856 he knew as the "Sun-Down Poem." What is urgent for Walt is the *crossing*, Emerson's metaphor for darting to a new aim. The shores of America matter most to Whitman as points of departure for the outward voyage. But to where? There is only the grand fourfold: night, death, the mother, and the sea. All of these constitute the unknown nature of which Walt's soul is composed. What the Gnostics called the spark or *pneuma*, the breath of being, Whitman terms the me myself or the real me. That leaves only his supreme fiction, "Walt Whitman, one of the roughs, an American," the prime subject throughout *Song of Myself.*

This psychic cartography is so original that we as yet have not assimilated it, but the study of Whitman's great decade of poetry scarcely has begun, and indeed goes backward at this moment, when even professional scholars of literature have never learned how to read a poem. Whitman hoped to give us chants democratic, but at his strongest he composed chants elitist: esoteric, difficult, evasive, profoundly poignant, and immersed in a new spirituality we only start to notice. He dared to write a New Bible for Americans, who remain obsessed with the old one, though they cannot read it.

6

I will return to Walt Whitman in the final sections of this introduction but cross over now to Emily Dickinson, Whitman's only possible rival in American poetry, not just in the nineteenth century but until now, 2006 and the Age of Ashbery. I have cited an early religious crisis, which culminated in her return to the solitude of her father's house. Emerson and Whitman are American Religionists: Dickinson, distancing herself from Emersonianism as from Calvinism, became a sect of one, like John Milton and William Blake. Her conceptual originality surpassed even theirs, and is dwarfed only by Shakespeare's, of all poets in the language. Shakespeare evades us spiritually, as he does in every regard. We do not know (nor should we) whether the world's supreme writer was Protestant, recusant Catholic, Hermetist, or nihilist (I suggest the latter, on pragmatic grounds). Dickinson, like Whitman, is a major poet of the American Religion, but she does not assume the role of American Christ, as Whitman did. Her private mythology is divulged only by hints. What does it mean to call yourself Empress of Calvary, or Circumference the Bride of Awe? We can speculate but cannot know.

Jesus, to Dickinson, was not the American God we now ken more than too well. I myself regret not following my impulse to employ as epigraph to a recent book I published, *Jesus and Yahweh* (2005), a remark by one Ma Ferguson, governor of the superb state of Texas in the earlier part of the twentieth century. During her rule, Ma Ferguson decreed, no foreign language was to be taught in any state-supported school or college because: "If English was good enough for Jesus, then I suppose it should be good enough for us." The American Jesus is George W. Bush's "favorite philosopher" and loves nine out of ten of us, on a personal and individual basis (Gallup Poll). Dickinson's Jesus did not love her, nor she him: she believed neither in the Resurrection nor the Atonement. Yet she shared in the sufferings of Jesus, and in what she took to be his triumph over them. As Empress of Calvary, she became the bride of the Holy Spirit, its Emperor.

Dickinson's flamboyant exuberance intensifies whenever she challenges received faith. Unlike Whitman, who could identify Christ with himself, Dickinson goes the other way and identifies herself with what she calls the White Election. Her flair acknowledges few bounds in the spiritual realm, where her self-confidence remains startling. Doubtless she derives (knowingly) from the Protestant sense of individual autonomy, and she is a late representative of the Miltonic Inner Light, by which the Bible is read for oneself alone. A. D. Nuttall speaks of Marlowe, Milton, and Blake as the formulators of "alternative Trinities." Dickinson's Trinity comprises Awe (her lover, Judge Otis Lord), the pain-surmounting Jesus (clearly human, not divine), and herself as Empress-Circumference.

Of Dickinson's spirituality, no last word can be spoken, on the fused evidence of poems, poem-like letters, and a life lived as a dark poem anticipatory of Nietzsche's aestheticizing of human pain itself becoming the meaning. My former student, the gifted reader Camille Paglia, insisted there was a sadistic element in Dickinson, but I doubt that. The Amherst visionary might *like* a look of agony because she knew it to be true, but her sense of "Heavenly Hurt" does not assign pain any value as such. I hear no masochism in her proud suffering: she is not Teresa of Avila or John of the Cross. Her greatest disciple, as it has taken scores of years for me to realize, was Hart Crane, whose fusion of erotic and spiritual despair is much like her own, as he came to understand. Their God is an Inquisitor, and their ordeals are difficult for us to apprehend because so much of their travail is experienced cognitively. We have learned to recognize Dickinson's cognitive sovereignty, but criticism has failed badly in estimating the intellectual power of Crane's poems and letters, a power augmented by his experience of reading Dickinson.

I have termed Dickinson a sect of one, akin to Milton and to Blake, and in another way with Emerson. Crane comprehended his affinities with Dickinson, Melville, and Blake, his forerunners in agile believings and disbelievings. In his letters, Hart Crane reminds me of

John Keats, both of them supremely intelligent at exploring the differences between poetry and belief. Dickinson had her own, partly hidden relation to Keats's poetry, since each found her or his most fecund source in Shakespeare, as Crane did also. Shakespeare's father was a recusant Catholic, but *King Lear* and *The Tempest* seem to me neither Christian nor pagan dramas. Crane's still undervalued American epic, *The Bridge*, celebrates what I again would call the American Religion, an extraordinary blend of the spiritual strains of Orphism, Gnosticism, and Enthusiasm. When Crane hymns Brooklyn Bridge he is addressing the Stranger God of our national Gnosis:

> And obscure as that heaven of the Jews,
> Thy guerdon . . . Accolade thou dost bestow
> Of anonymity time cannot raise:
> Vibrant reprieve and pardon thou dost show.
>
> O harp and altar, of the fury fused,
> (How could mere toil align thy choiring strings!)
> Terrific threshold of the prophet's pledge,
> Prayer of pariah, and the lover's cry,—
>
> Again the traffic lights that skim thy swift
> Unfractioned idiom, immaculate sigh of stars,
> Beading thy path—condense eternity:
> And we have seen night lifted in thine arms.
>
> Under thy shadow by the piers I waited;
> Only in darkness is thy shadow clear.
> The City's fiery parcels all undone,
> Already snow submerges an iron year . . .
>
> O Sleepless as the river under thee,
> Vaulting the sea, the prairies' dreaming sod,
> Unto us lowliest sometime sweep, descend
> And of the curveship lend a myth to God.

The heaven of the Jews is totally obscure in the Hebrew Bible or Tanakh, and figures only in Daniel, an apocalyptic work given prophetic status by the Christians, but not by the Jews. Crane confronts a revelation, overwhelming in his knowledge of it, but barely communicated to a reader who has little acquaintance with a peculiarly American mode of transcendence. I hear something of Crane's fervor in his most eloquent elegist, John Brooks Wheelwright, who emulated Crane's mingling of Blake and Whitman in the wonderful rhapsody, "Come Over and Help Us," Pauline only in its title.

Hart Crane, celebrating his ecstatic (yet only momentary) union with the Danish sailor Emil Oppfer (who in his later years of marriage and fatherhood stated that he could not recall Crane), said: "I have seen the Word made flesh." That is the Word of Crane's "Voyages" and *The Bridge*, and is far closer to Emily Dickinson's "loved Philology" than to the Logos of the Gospel of John. Whether Dickinson found the word made flesh in Judge Lord, we cannot know with certainty, but it is clear enough that she found something else in Christ.

7

It is an old maxim that poetry discoursing upon itself can sound more religious than actually it is. Religion, William Blake warned us, is a choosing of forms of worship from poetic tales. The worship of God, Eastern and Western, for most pragmatically must be the awarding of reverence to literary characters, since Yahweh and Jesus, like the Buddha, are known to most of us only through stories. Our greatest American poets—Whitman, Dickinson, Frost, Wallace Stevens, Hart Crane—all were highly cognizant of this character. Our most distinguished Neo-Christian poet, T. S. Eliot, fights against this differently but his triumphs over it, if they come at all, rarely are persuasive. Is *Ash Wednesday* as convincingly devotional as George Herbert or Christina Rossetti?

The Good and Evil of Eternity, Dr. Johnson pungently observed, are too ponderous for the wings of wit. The mind sinks under them, Johnson murmured, content with calm belief and humble adoration. Those admirable states, Johnson implies, do not stimulate poetical composition of the highest order. Eliot, who would not admit it, learned some aspect of that truth. *Murder in the Cathedral* and *Ash Wednesday*, certainly devotional efforts, cultivate the humility of adoration, hardly a Dickinsonian stance. Hart Crane, meditating upon her final harvest, saluted the cognitive strength she demanded of her reader:

> The harvest you descried and understand
> Needs more than wit to gather, love to bind,
> Some reconcilement of remotest mind—

Mind, not spirit: Crane is precise. When, at *The Bridge*'s conclusion, he hymns an "Everpresence, beyond time," his celebration is Gnostic, invoking the Stranger or Alien God, remotely exiled beyond the stars. Like Dickinson, Whitman, Melville, Hart Crane is not a Christian but an American Religionist, more Orphic than his precursors. Emerson had prophesied an American Orphic Poet, and Crane fulfilled the role, metaphorically yet biographically as well. William Empson, a late convert to Crane, told me once that he associated the most desperate of American poets since Edgar Poe with Empson's own "Missing Dates":

> It is the poems you have lost, the ills
> From missing dates, of which the heart expires.

Empson wrote that in 1940, eight years after Hart Crane's drowning, and before the Maoist critic encountered the work of the American poet I still consider to have been our most gifted. Dead at thirty-two, what would Whitman, Dickinson, Frost, Stevens, Eliot have left us? They needed to develop; Hart Crane simply unfolded, until the imperfections of the life destroyed the perfections of the work. A touch of Emersonian Transcendentalism abided in Crane, but was less consequential than an older transcendentalism, the Catholic tradition he refused, even as he rejected Marxism. He sought only the pure purposes of the pure poet, and yet in "To Brooklyn Bridge" and "The Broken Tower" one feels reverberations of St. John of the Cross, whom I doubt Crane ever read. Only in darkness is the shadow of Brooklyn Bridge clear to its lover, and the tower of the closed-down Mexico City cathedral tolls Crane back to the desperation of his sole self. He states no nostalgia for Christ, but his is a soul cut off from T. S. Eliot's Word yet retaining a faithless faith in "the imaged Word," Dickinson's "loved Philology."

8

Like Dr. Johnson, I regard "religious poetry" as an oxymoron in English or Continental tradition. And yet "the American Religion" is the most equivocal of oxymorons, and its poetry is everywhere and nowhere, as this anthology may indicate. The American Jesus, the American God, the American Holy Ghost: these have only spectral traces of European and Middle Eastern dogmas. In the later 1980s, I deliberately invested much energy in wandering about the South and Southwest, ostensibly as a literary lecturer, but more a Seeker than a scholarly critic. A book, *The American Religion* (1992) ensued, but nothing I have published was so weakly misread. That is not a complaint but a confirmation of how little of itself the American spirit recognizes.

That Jesus was an American is no more surprising than the African Jesus or the Asian one. Yet the American Jesus cannot inspire poetry, because he himself is the American Poem, though hardly in any sense compatible with Walt Whitman's declaration that the United States was to be the greatest poem, which now can make us wince, through no fault of Whitman's. Is George W. Bush's Texas a poem, or Bill Clinton's Arkansas?

"American religious poetry" is a coherent phrase, only if we redefine "religious," since "American" defies definition, and "poetry" in the United States long ago ceased to mean John Milton. Verse or prose or more frequently neither, it floods my mail deliveries daily, and I could not read all of it even if I could bear the avalanche. When the sacred Emerson genially observed that all Americans were poets and mystics, he could not foresee the literalization of his remark. God, whatever you take him (or her) to be, presumably prefers good poetry to bad.

A more complete nomination of the strong or prevailing American poets, in my judgment, would be Emerson, Whitman, Melville, Dickinson, E. A. Robinson, Frost, Stevens, W. C. Williams, Marianne Moore, Eliot, and Hart Crane, to list only those born before the twentieth century. Poe and Pound, though esteemed by some critics, do not find me. Now, in these early years of the twenty-first century, we still have no common agreement upon those who were born and died in a crowded twentieth century. A few figures—Elizabeth Bishop, R. P. Warren, Richard Wilbur, James Merrill, John Ashbery, A. R. Ammons—are among the incontrovertible, in my own view, but it will be another generation or two before a saving remnant of common readers guides us to larger and surer judgments. I myself am baffled by our contemporary celebration of Sylvia Plath, who seems to me scarcely a poet at all in comparison with May Swenson or Amy Clampitt. Nor can I understand the neglect of Jay Wright, the only peer of Ralph Ellison in

African-American literature. In such unique artists as the Canadian Anne Carson, the Australian John Kinsella, and the Americans Henri Cole and Rosanna Warren, poetry continues to renew itself.

But can "religious poetry" be renewed, even in the mode I have termed "the American Religion"? If Walt Whitman and Emily Dickinson between them define the Americanness of our poetry, their combined strength fuses itself with Biblical heritage. The Hebraic trope of tropes may be *yeziat*: "get thee out of" Ur of the Chaldees, or out of Egypt, universe of death, into Canaan. Whitman always is getting out of the House of Bondage and always arriving at Emerson's "shores of America," and thus becoming "Walt." Exodus is the thematic center of American religious poetry: how could it be otherwise? America is a scene of trespass: its poets seek singularity, though no one ever may match Whitman and Dickinson in their distinctness. The American Exodus is from Europe into our Evening Land, where Europe has died.

9

The relation of American poetry to its British forerunner has been vexed from Philip Freneau to the present. Edgar Poe, whatever one thinks of his aesthetic eminence or plain badness, found nothing problematic in his reliance upon Coleridge, Byron, and Shelley. Wordsworth, I suspect, so daunted Emerson that the American sage turned to prose as his major quest for achievement. Whitman owed far more to the English Bible than to any particular poet, while I believe we have misunderstood Dickinson's aesthetic heritage; her characteristic quatrains derive from Shakespeare's sonnets, rather than Isaac Watts's hymns. In his sonnets, Shakespeare thinks powerfully through his three quatrains, before finding closure in epigrammatic couplets. No one in the language, not even William Blake, packs as much cognitive force and originality into their quatrains as do Shakespeare and Dickinson.

Except for Robert Frost, Marianne Moore, Elizabeth Bishop, and James Merrill, I cannot think of a crucial twentieth-century American poet who is not haunted by Walt Whitman, though Pound, Eliot, and Wallace Stevens masked their indebtedness, or at least sought to do so. Whitman's stance, rather than his form, is all but inescapable in our later poetry. Exodus, an American version of *yeziat*, is the mode of

Huckleberry Finn, lighting out for the territory, and of Huck's descendants, including Hemingway's Nick Adams. Freedom, in the American Religion, is both the realization that what is best and oldest in one is not part of nature, and also the awareness that not to be alone is itself a House of Bondage.

For almost forty years now, the Counterculture born in 1967 has been our official culture, in the media and the academies alike. Yet even in this era of socially overdetermined standards (to call them that), our poetry, like our spirituality, remains singular and idiosyncratic. I find myself startled by a flood of letters and e-mail, beyond my capacity to respond, that have been provoked by a book called *Jesus and Yahweh: The Names Divine*, that I published about half a year ago. Clergy and lay persons, of all denominations and sects, react to my speculations in ways that initially surprise me, but then my surprise yields to the realization that, Benedictine monks and Mennonite preachers alike, these all are, to one degree or another, American Religionists. Gnosticism, Orphism, and Enthusiasm came together in the Cane Ridge Revival, now more than two centuries ago, and this curious fusion still prevails. The Ebionites, Jewish followers of James the brother of Jesus, are represented in the canonical New Testament only by the Epistle of James, denounced by Luther as "an epistle of straw," because it exalts justification by works, rather than the Pauline salvation by faith alone. A remarkable number of American Christians pragmatically are Ebionites and even more of them identify with the Jesus of the quasi-Gnostic Gospel of Thomas. European Protestantism, like European poetry, undergoes a transmemberment in our Evening Land.

10

So pervasive is the American Religion that it makes obsolete most distinctions between theism, agnosticism, and atheism. My close friend, the late A. R. Ammons, never once referred to God, in our hundreds of conversations and in the correspondence between us. But the Whitmanian Ammons is represented here by six major poems, a fuller selection than that accorded to any other poet since Hart Crane. Robert Frost and Wallace Stevens, both of them Emersonian skeptics (Stevens would have denied this lineage), are anthologized here in their characteristic greatness, as demonstrated by poems untinged by devotional impulses. I cannot conceive of co-editing a volume of British religious poetry on the principles that have governed this book. Great Britain, like the Continent, still distinguishes sharply enough between belief and disbelief, but there is no European equivalent of the American Religion. In Europe, you are a Christian or you are not, but I again cite the Gallup pollsters that here nine out of ten of us are personally loved by God. Americans, who tend to worship either Jesus or the Holy Spirit, rather than God-the-Father, Christianity's diminished version of Yahweh, nevertheless parody Yahweh-like qualities. Walt Whitman, our national poet, authentically manifests such characteristics.

Yahweh, in my speculative judgment, can be said to have (first) come into existence by saying *I Am*. Nietzsche might have ventured to call Yahweh's declaration the grandest insistence of the will's revenge against time, and time's *It Was*. Walt palpably opposes *I Am* to *It Was*. The history of the American Religion and of American poetry seems to me a perpetually strong misreading of Yahweh's initial self-curtailment in the Creation. Whitman proclaims his presence but cultivates absence: he is sly, evasive, self-contradictory. Emerson, in declaring Golgotha "A Great Defeat," went on to say that Americans demanded Victory, a victory to the senses as well as to the soul. One of the sage's mottoes was: "I am defeated all the time but to victory I am born." Whitman, getting off the cross as quickly as John Milton's Christ, says the same.

A breathless Creation is a Great Defeat, and scarcely an American enterprise. Our most fiercely growing denomination now is the Pentecostal, particularly the Assemblies of God. Professional curiosity has drawn me to Pentecostal services (they are hospitable) and I tend to be stunned by outpourings of voice that rush past *I Am* into the self-celebrations of the Holy Spirit, which in itself repudiates divine breathlessness. Whitman, with his Hicksite Quaker upbringing, can be regarded as an American Pentecostalist before the fact. Emily Dickinson, too cognitively speculative to manifest any Enthusiasm, found another way to see the Yahwistic self-contraction, not as a point at the Center, but as a going out upon Circumference.

Hart Crane—more than Eliot, Frost, Stevens—seems to me the Third American Poet. Whitman was our Homer, Dickinson our Shakespearean lyricist, Crane our Pindar, and Emerson our Plato. On that scale, we have to seek our dramatists in our masters of narrative: Hawthorne, Melville, Mark Twain, Henry James, Hemingway, Faulkner. A nation so self-dramatizing cannot have a playwright like Aeschylus or Shakespeare, or even an Ibsen.

Like Whitman and Dickinson, Crane's "Vision of the Voyage" (though his is also Melvillean) surrenders easier pleasures for the difficult pleasures of the American Sublime. Emerson identified "Power" as the most American of attributes, and identified it with *crossing* or *passing*: "the shooting of a gulf, the darting to an aim," where "shooting" and "darting" are more vital than the "aim." Transition, in America, matters more than the destination. Hart Crane's *The Bridge* is the completion or coda to *Song of Myself* as the American epic. A Pindaric epic is an American aesthetic paradox: "One song, one Bridge of Fire." The three central American poets define the pragmatic limits of transcendence in the United States. Whitman is afoot with his vision, and stops somewhere waiting for us. Dickinson navigates from Blank to Blank, giving us the great negative of American vision, culminating in *The Auroras of Autumn*, where Wallace Stevens, the man who is walking the beach, turns *blankly* on the sand. The ruin or blank that we see in nature, Emerson prophesied, is in our own eye, and therefore we behold opacity, and not transparency.

II

I conclude by returning to Walt Whitman, forever the ultimate American even as he is our Adam. Whatever religion and religious poetry is in Europe, or in Africa or Asia, in America it is Whitmanian. Walt is our mythology, the "Appalachian enlargement of our literature" (Emerson's tribute) and our Dante, though Whitman repudiates the Four Last Things. Death is night, the mother and the sea; Judgment is a horrible fiction, and there was never any more Heaven or Hell, than here and now. Endlessly rereading Whitman as I go past three quarters of a century, I find in him the American Scripture. Walt, more even than Emerson or Joseph Smith, is our prophet, seer, and revelator. Except for D. H. Lawrence, whose ambivalence toward Whitman frequently overcame the sanity of seeing Walt plain, we desperately lack accurate critical guides to reading Whitman. He *is* American religious poetry, and he himself is a Christ rather than a Christian. To represent him properly in this anthology, you would have to destroy the volume, by printing everything of supreme aesthetic power in *Leaves of Grass*. With Whitman as with Dickinson, what is printed here is only a synecdoche for what must be sought outside this book.

Defining what truly is American about our condensed encyclicals of an unique spirituality is the burden of this book. Nothing is got for nothing, and that Emersonian (and Shakespearean) admonition is the implicit warning Jesse Zuba and I confront throughout. Much is omitted here that others would desire, but they order these things differently in our Evening Land. The criteria of Political Correctness I dismiss with weary contempt: what they have brought us is George W. Bush, belated monarch of a new Gilded Age.

Always, as a country, we will come back to Walt Whitman, who remains the Bard of the New World, the Western Hemisphere's reply to Europe. Whitman's greatest poetry *is* the death of Europe in our Evening Land. When I was young, I was immersed in William Blake, and then turned to Shakespeare in my middle years. In old age, I read Walt Whitman, discovering more with every fresh visit. Finally, Whitman is the American difference, the herald to the future, if we do not destroy our future. The First Folio of Shakespeare tells us to read him and read him, for everything is in him. We cannot say that of Whitman, and yet everything that altogether is our own is in him.

HAROLD BLOOM

About This Book

This book undertakes two overlapping tasks: to present poems that embody the specifically American religious sensibility whose implications Harold Bloom has explored in the introduction to this volume, in his study *The American Religion*, and elsewhere, and to offer a broad overview of religious poetry in America from its origins until now. In view of the extravagant diversity of American religious poetry, casting a wide net seemed less a choice than a welcome necessity. So it is that some names that may be less well-known to the reader, such as Nicholas Noyes, Emma Hart Willard, Ameen Rihani, Ronald Johnson, Esther Schor, and Brett Foster, join more familiar figures in the table of contents, which brings together poets from dozens of religious traditions, including Catholicism, Islam, Buddhism, Judaism, and Baha'i, among others. To round out our representation of the scope of American religious culture, we have also included a selection of spirituals, hymns, and American Indian songs and chants.

These selections are meant to represent the originality and subtlety with which American poets have rendered experiences, feelings, and thoughts about whatever they consider to be sacred. The book is arranged chronologically, a design that has the virtue of letting the reader see patterns of change in religious and poetic sensibility. While an anthology of American religious poetry is something very different from an overview of American religious thought and practice, the chronological arrangement does reveal what has changed and what has remained the same in the relations between aesthetics and faith. The anthology opens with poems that register the rigorous Calvinism of the Puritans, including works by such prominent figures as Roger Williams, Anne Bradstreet, and Cotton Mather, with a generous selec tion of poems by Edward Taylor, whose language veers between colloquial vigor and learned refinement to give his treatment of even the most reverend themes an unexpectedly freewheeling tone, as in "Meditation Eighteen" (Second Series):

> Mine Heart's a Park or Chase of sins: Mine Head
> 'S a Bowling Alley. Sins play Ninehole here.
> Phansy's a Green: sin Barly break in't led.
> Judgment's a pingle. Blindeman's Buff's plaid there.
> Sin playes at Coursey Parke within my Minde.
> My Wills a Walke in which it aires what's blinde.

The Great Awakening, the massive revival that swept the eastern seaboard beginning in the late 1730s, is reflected in the elegy "On the Death of the Rev. Mr. George Whitefield" by Phillis Wheatley, the first black American to publish a book of poetry. Whitefield was the most celebrated evangelist of the Awakening, known for his privileging of an intensely emotional conversion experience, which he and other "New Lights" preachers presented as the key test of election, rather than the program of gradual spiritual development on which "Old Lights" Congregationalists relied as a guide to their prospects for sainthood. Whitefield was among the first to preach to slaves, and Wheatley, temporarily assuming his voice in the third stanza, pays a tribute to his impartiality which may be heard within the tribute he pays to Christ's:

> ". . . Take him my dear *Americans*, he said,
> Be your complaints on his kind bosom laid:
> Take him, ye *Africans*, he longs for you,
> *Impartial Saviour* is his title due:
> Wash'd in the fountain of redeeming blood,
> You shall be sons, and kings, and priests to God."

Liberalizing trends in the eighteenth century can be discerned in the poetry of Deists such as Joel Barlow and Philip Freneau. "On the Religion of Nature," published in 1815, offers a summation of Freneau's rational religion, which stresses nature's role in human development and suggests an optimism typical of Enlightenment thought:

> Born with ourselves, her early sway
> Inclines the tender mind to take
> The path of right, fair virtue's way
> Its own felicity to make.
> This universally extends
> And leads to no mysterious ends.

Something of the same optimism suffuses Unitarianism, the channel into which the "natural theology" of the Deists coursed during the first half of the nineteenth century. Deriving its name from its adherents' opposition to the orthodox view that God is three distinct persons —Father, Son, and Holy Ghost—in one, its essence resides in the special confidence in individual potential that its leaders championed. It took shape as a denomination in the wake of the controversy that erupted around the appointment of Henry Ware as the Hollis Professor of Divinity at Harvard in 1805, after which the college became a Unitarian stronghold, represented here by the poetry of John Quincy Adams, Henry Wadsworth Longfellow, Oliver Wendell Holmes, and James Russell Lowell. Richard Henry Dana, Julia Ward Howe, and William Cullen Bryant were likewise Unitarians, and most of the members of the Transcendental Club began as Unitarian clergy.

The verse of the Unitarians is characterized by the kind of Romantic turn exemplified by William Cullen Bryant's "To a Waterfowl." Like Freneau, Bryant finds God in nature:

> There is a Power whose care
> Teaches thy way along that pathless coast,—
> The desert and illimitable air,—
> Lone wandering, but not lost.

But Bryant stresses the experience of the "lone wandering" individual and nature's "pathless" wildness, imbuing the prospect of the self's dissolution with a Romantic melancholy.

Even such exaltation of the self as the liberal theology of the Unitarians encouraged was not radical enough for Ralph Waldo Emerson, who described "The Transcendentalist" like this:

> His thought,—that is the Universe. His experience inclines him to behold the procession of facts you call the world, as flowing perpetually outward from an invisible, unsounded centre in himself, centre alike of him and of them, and necessitating him to regard all things as having a subjective or relative existence, relative to that aforesaid Unknown Centre of him.

Refusing to know God at second hand, Emerson broke with the Unitarians. He resigned his pastorate at Boston's Second Church in 1832 and began meeting with the Transcendental Club in 1836, the same year he published *Nature*. In 1838 he delivered his controversial address to the graduating class of the Harvard Divinity School, in which he sought to illuminate "the falsehood of our theology" by condemning "the stationariness of religion," "the assumption that the age of inspiration is past, that the Bible is closed," and "the fear of degrading the character of Jesus by representing him as a man."

Jones Very, America's central devotional poet, limns the kind of unmediated relation to God that Emerson had advocated in *Nature*. For Very, knowing God depended upon a total surrender of the individual will, and he urged this conviction on those around him with such energy that many, including Emerson, doubted his sanity. But Emerson was energetically supportive of Very's work as a poet, in which he must have sensed a kindred desire to awaken the reader to consciousness of a more authentic selfhood, untainted by any mean egotism:

> 'Tis to yourself I speak; you cannot know
> Him whom I call in speaking such an one,
> For thou beneath the earth liest buried low,
> Which he alone as living walks upon;
> Thou mayst at times have heard him speak to you,
> And often wished perchance that you were he;
> And I must ever wish that it were true,
> For then thou couldst hold fellowship with me;
> But now thou hearst us talk as strangers, met
> Above the room wherein thou liest abed; . . .

The Emersonian sense of the higher powers of the self, evidenced in a reciprocity between self and nature, permeates the sensibilities of many of the poets represented here, from Whitman and Dickinson to A. R. Ammons and John Ashbery.

The shifts in religious thought sketched above all took place within the context of American Protestantism. By the middle of the nineteenth century, other traditions began to play a significant role in American culture. To provide some sense of the dramatic changes that began to make themselves felt, one might consider, for example, three very different poets—Catholic, Sufi, and Jewish, respectively—writing at the turn of the century. John Banister Tabb, a Virginian steeped in the regional loyalties of the antebellum South, converted to Roman Catholicism in 1872 and was ordained a priest in 1884. An admirer of

Edgar Allan Poe's billowing sonorities, Tabb nevertheless wrote with an epigrammatic compression typical of Transcendentalist poetry. His "Communion" describes a privileged moment in which "The soul of nature suddenly / Outpoured itself" into his soul. The terms on which he articulates the experience betray Tabb's reading in Emerson:

And for a moment's interval
    The earth, the sky, the sea—
My soul encompassed, each and all,
    As now they compass me.

To one in all, to all in one—
    Since love the work began—
Life's ever-widening circles run,
    Revealing God and man.

Though less familiar to most than his friend Kahlil Gibran, Ameen Rihani pioneered in developing a Lebanese-American literary culture whose representatives in this anthology include Rihani, Gibran, and Mikhail Naimy. Rihani (who was born in 1876 in Lebanon and immigrated at twelve to the United States) was the first Arab to write and publish a novel in English, *The Book of Khalid*, an autobiographical work which, like many of his essays and his collections of poetry, urged a reconciliation between the Judeo-Christian and Islamic traditions. Raised a Maronite Christian, he was excommunicated for his controversial critique of traditional religious thought. His poetry in English often emphasizes the passionate surrender to God as "the Belovéd" characteristic of the tradition of Islamic mysticism known as Sufism:

At eventide the Pilgrim came
    And knocked at the Belovéd's door.
"Who's there!" a voice within, "Thy name?"
    "'T is I," he said. —"Then knock no more.
As well ask thou a lodging of the sea,—
There is no room herein for thee and me."

The Pilgrim went again his way
    And dwelt with Love upon the shore
Of self-oblivion; and one day
    He knocked again at the Belovéd's door.
    "Who's there?" —"It is thyself," he now replied,
And suddenly the door was opened wide.

It is an irony of Rihani's development that he first took a serious interest in Islamic mystical traditions as a result of his reading in Emerson, Thoreau, and other American writers, who had explored the poetry and philosophy of the East, both Near and Far. At the same time, the poem clearly draws on conventions of Sufi poetry; here, for example, is a similar poem by the great Sufi mystic Rumi (translated by Coleman Barks with John Moyne): "I have lived on the lip / of insanity, wanting to know reasons, knocking on a door. It opens. / I've been knocking from the inside!"

Like Rihani, the Yiddish poet H. Leivick was part of the wave of immigration that broke over America in the late nineteenth and early twentieth centuries. Born in Belorussia in 1888, Leivick was arrested in 1906 on account of his membership in the underground Jewish Socialist party and was eventually exiled for life to Siberia. With the help of American political allies he made a dramatic escape in 1912 that took him thousands of miles across the tundra and steppes of Russia to Germany, and he ultimately reached the United States. His literary work expressed a marked sensitivity to human suffering, and his religious beliefs and political ideals sometimes fought for the upper hand in guiding his response to it. Something of that tension comes through in "The Sturdy in Me," in which the speaker recognizes in himself an indestructible spiritual element that he describes as a "song of ancient white bones": hearing it, he knows himself to be "eternal." But he struggles to see in that indestructibility a solution to the immediate sufferings of the poor, whose "fiery eyes" he can only "look into."

The newcomers brought with them their religious traditions, which swelled an already varied pool of paths and creeds even as they bolstered the ranks of established groups. It was on this wave that Hinduism, Buddhism, and Islam rode onto the American scene. The World's Parliament of Religions, convened in Chicago in 1893, allowed many Americans to learn about these traditions for the first time. Swami Vivekananda, presenting Hinduism, urged audiences to "love God for love's sake"; Anagarika Dharmapal made a case for the Buddhist "Middle Path" between sensualism and self-denial; Mohammed Webb distilled the essence of Islam as a resignation to God's will. America's first Vedanta society, dedicated to the advancement of Hinduism, was founded in New York in 1894; the Young Men's Buddhist Association was founded in Hawaii in 1900; and the first American mosque was built by a Lebanese Muslim community in 1930 in North Dakota. The presence in America of Hinduism, Buddhism, and Islam—well-established by the middle of the twentieth century—is reflected here in poems by such contemporaries as Allen Ginsberg, Gary Snyder, Agha Shahid Ali, Arthur Sze, Naomi Shihab Nye, and Khaled Mattawa, among others.

The religious pluralism of twentieth-century America finds expression in a plurality of poetic forms. The sonnet, the prose poem, the verse epistle, the ghazal, and the villanelle are all represented here, as are dozens of stanza shapes and metrical schemes. And poets have also made use of a number of verbal and textual structures—novena, litany, psalm, paternoster, hymn, sermon, sutra, benediction, and obituary, among others—in ways that are sometimes explicitly in the spirit of traditional religious practice, and sometimes more oblique and ironic. The formal and structural range of these poems is commensurate with the variety of occasions that have prompted them: they describe angelic visitations and episodes from history, they commemorate people and places, they narrate creation stories and encounters with death, they express fear, confusion, anger, ecstasy, desire, and much else besides.

Likewise, the modern voices collected here come in many timbres. Listen to three poets who are near contemporaries:

> No, I don't feel death coming.
> I feel death going:
> having thrown up his hands,
> for the moment.

* * *

> The snow falling around the man in the naked woods
> is like the ash of heaven, ash from the cool fire
> of God's mother-of-pearl, moon-stately heart.
> Sympathetic but not merciful. His strictness
> parses us. The discomfort of living this way
> without birds, among maples without leaves, makes
> death and the world visible.

* * *

I have a knocking woodpecker in my heart and I think I have
three souls
One for love one for poetry and one for acting out my insane self
Not insane but boring but perpendicular but untrue but true
The three rarely sing together take my hand it's active
The active ingredient in it is a touch
I am Lord Byron I am Percy Shelley I am Ariosto

The conversational tone of James Baldwin's "Amen" lends his brush-with-death poem a harrowing immediacy, as the swaggering reversal in the opening lines gives way to the grim recognition that death has left him alone "for the moment" only; the spare diction and longer lines of Jack Gilbert's "The White Heart of God" suit the poem's mood of reverie—like the "heart" they describe, the voice of the poem itself seems to burn with "cool fire"; and the dervish-like ecstasy of Kenneth Koch's "Alive for an Instant" comes through in his overloaded, unpunctuated verses, which run on as they fill with multiple, contradictory declarations.

Just as these poems vary with regard to style and topic, so they also vary with regard to the nature and extent of their spiritual commitments. If the poems of earlier centuries display more openly their connections to broader religious trends, those of the twentieth and twenty-first centuries are directed ever more by the imperatives of individual spiritual search. Some poems here affirm religious faith, but we have also made room for some that express doubt, since a poem that articulates uncertainty honors both the reader and her religion by refusing to admit ideas and feelings whose truthfulness or nobility has not yet been proven on the poet's pulse. In fact, the poems collected here are rarely unambiguous in their professions of either faith or doubt. In this they reflect both the nature of poetry—where the play of figures and emphases makes it difficult to think of a poem's meaning as inert and easily pinned down—and that notion of the inscrutability of the divine that informs most religious traditions. If, like the "old sense of a fullness" John Ashbery feels at the end of "By Forced Marches," transcendence in these poems is often "only lightly sketched in," it is not for want of confidence in religious faith, experience, or knowledge. Rather, it is because as poems approach the divine they also approach silence, for words figure at last among the "helps" which, as Emerson claims in "Self-Reliance," "it is vain to seek to interpose," since "the relations of the soul to the divine spirit are so pure."

JESSE ZUBA

The Bay Psalm Book

Psalme 19

The heavens doe declare
   the majesty of God:
also the firmament shews forth
   his handy-work abroad.
Day speaks to day, knowledge
   night hath to night declar'd.
There neither speach nor language is,
   where their voyce is not heard.
Through all the earth their line
   is gone forth, & unto
the utmost end of all the world,
   their speaches reach also:
A Tabernacle hee
   in them pitcht for the Sun.
Who Bridegroom like from's chamber goes
   glad Giants-race to run.
From heavens utmost end,
   his course and compassing;
to ends of it, & from the heat
   thereof is hid nothing.

2

The Lords law perfect is,
   the soule converting back:
Gods testimony faithfull is,
   makes wise who-wisdome-lack.
The statutes of the Lord,
   are right, & glad the heart:
the Lords commandement is pure,
   light doth to eyes impart.
Jehovahs feare is cleane,
   and doth indure for ever:

the judgements of the Lord are true,
    and righteous altogether.
Then gold, then much fine gold,
    more to be prized are,
then hony, & the hony-comb,
    sweeter they are by farre.
Also thy servant is
    admonished from hence:
and in the keeping of the same
    is a full recompence.
Who can his errors know?
    from secret faults cleanse mee.
And from presumptuous-sins, let thou
    kept back thy servant bee:
Let them not beare the rule
    in me, and then shall I
be perfect, and shall cleansed bee
    from much iniquity.
Let the words of my mouth,
    and the thoughts of my heart,
be pleasing with thee, Lord, my Rock
    who my redeemer art.

Thomas Dudley

1576–1653

Dim Eyes, deaf Ears, cold stomack shew
My dissolution is in view.
Eleven times seven near lived have I,
And now God calls, I willing die:
My shuttle's shot, my race is run,
My Sun is set, my Deed is done;
My Span is measur'd, Tale is told,
My Flower is faded and grown old,
My Dream is vanish'd, Shadows fled,
My Soul with Christ, my Body dead.
Farewel dear Wife, Children, and Friends,

Hate Heresie, make blessed ends,
Bear Poverty, live with good men,
So shall we meet with joy agen.

Let men of God in Courts and Churches watch
O'er such as do a Toleration hatch;
Lest that ill Egg bring forth a *Cockatrice*,
To poison all with Heresie and Vice.
If men be left and otherwise combine,
My *Epitaph's, I dy'd no Libertine.*

Roger Williams

c. 1603–1683

God gives them sleep on Ground, on Straw,
  on Sedgie Mats or Boord:
When English softest Beds of Downe,
  sometimes no sleep affoord.

I have knowne them leave their House and Mat
  to lodge a Friend or stranger,
When Jewes and Christians oft have sent
  Christ Jesus to the Manger.

'Fore day they invocate their Gods,
  though Many, False and New:
O how should that God worshipt be,
  who is but One and True?

Bòast not proud *English*, of thy birth & blood,
  Thy brother *Indian* is by birth as Good.
Of one blood God made Him, and Thee & All,
  As wise, as faire, as strong, as personall.

By nature wrath's his portiõ, thine no more
   Till Grace *his* soule and *thine* in Christ restore
Make sure thy second birth, else thou shalt see,
   Heaven ope to *Indians* wild, but shut to thee.

They see Gods wonders that are call'd
   Through dreadfull Seas to passe,
In tearing winds and roaring seas,
   And calmes as smooth as glasse.
I have in *Europes* ships, oft been
   In King of terrours hand;
When all have cri'd, *Now, now we sinck,*
   Yet God brought safe to land.
Alone 'mongst *Indians* in Canoes,
   Sometimes o're-turn'd, I have been
Halfe inch from death, in Ocean deepe,
   Gods wonders I have seene.

The *Indians* prize not *English* gold,
   Nor *English Indians* shell:
Each in his place will passe for ought,
   What ere men buy or sell.

English and *Indians* all passe hence,
   To an eternall place,
Where shels nor finest gold's worth ought,
Where nought's worth ought but Grace.

This Coyne the *Indians* know not of,
   Who knowes how soone they may?
The *English* knowing, prize it not,
   But fling't like drosse away.

Anne Bradstreet

1612–1672

The Flesh and the Spirit

In secret place where once I stood
Close by the Banks of *Lacrim* flood
I heard two sisters reason on
Things that are past, and things to come;
One flesh was call'd, who had her eye
On worldly wealth and vanity;
The other Spirit, who did rear
Her thoughts unto a higher sphere:
Sister, quoth Flesh, what liv'st thou on
Nothing but Meditation?
Doth Contemplation feed thee so
Regardlesly to let earth goe?
Can Speculation satisfy
Notion without Reality?
Dost dream of things beyond the Moon
And dost thou hope to dwell there soon?
Hast treasures there laid up in store
That all in th' world thou count'st but poor?
Art fancy sick, or turn'd a Sot
To catch at shadowes which are not?
Come, come, Ile shew unto thy sence,
Industry hath its recompence.
What canst desire, but thou maist see
True substance in variety?
Dost honour like? acquire the same,
As some to their immortal fame:
And trophyes to thy name erect
Which wearing time shall ne're deject.
For riches dost thou long full sore?
Behold enough of precious store.
Earth hath more silver, pearls and gold,
Then eyes can see, or hands can hold.

Affect's thou pleasure? take thy fill,
Earth hath enough of what you will.
Then let not goe, what thou maist find,
For things unknown, only in mind.
Spir. Be still thou unregenerate part,
Disturb no more my setled heart,
For I have vow'd (and so will doe)
Thee as a foe, still to pursue.
And combate with thee will and must,
Untill I see thee laid in th' dust.
Sisters we are, yea twins we be,
Yet deadly feud 'twixt thee and me;
For from one father are we not,
Thou by old Adam wast begot,
But my arise is from above,
Whence my dear father I do love.
Thou speak'st me fair, but hat'st me sore,
Thy flatt'ring shews Ile trust no more.
How oft thy slave, hast thou me made,
When I believ'd, what thou hast said,
And never had more cause of woe
Then when I did what thou bad'st doe.
Ile stop mine ears at these thy charms,
And count them for my deadly harms.
Thy sinfull pleasures I doe hate,
Thy riches are to me no bait,
Thine honours doe, nor will I love;
For my ambition lyes above.
My greatest honour it shall be
When I am victor over thee,
And triumph shall, with laurel head,
When thou my Captive shalt be led,
How I do live, thou need'st not scoff,
For I have meat thou know'st not off;
The hidden Manna I doe eat,
The word of life it is my meat.
My thoughts do yield me more content
Then can thy hours in pleasure spent.
Nor are they shadows which I catch,

Nor fancies vain at which I snatch,
But reach at things that are so high,
Beyond thy dull Capacity;
Eternal substance I do see,
With which inriched I would be:
Mine Eye doth pierce the heavens, and see
What is Invisible to thee.
My garments are not silk nor gold,
Nor such like trash which Earth doth hold,
But Royal Robes I shall have on,
More glorious then the glistring Sun;
My Crown not Diamonds, Pearls, and gold,
But such as Angels heads infold.
The City where I hope to dwell,
There's none on Earth can parallel;
The stately Walls both high and strong,
Are made of pretious *Jasper* stone;
The Gates of Pearl, both rich and clear,
And Angels are for Porters there;
The Streets thereof transparent gold,
Such as no Eye did e're behold,
A Chrystal River there doth run,
Which doth proceed from the Lambs Throne:
Of Life, there are the waters sure,
Which shall remain for ever pure,
Nor Sun, nor Moon, they have no need,
For glory doth from God proceed:
No Candle there, nor yet Torch light,
For there shall be no darksome night.
From sickness and infirmity,
For evermore they shall be free,
Nor withering age shall e're come there,
But beauty shall be bright and clear;
This City pure is not for thee,
For things unclean there shall not be:
If I of Heaven may have my fill,
Take thou the world, and all that will.

For Delive^{re} from a feaver

When Sorrowes had begyrt me round,
And paines within & out
When in my flesh no part was found
Then didst thou rid me out.
My burning flesh in sweat did boyle
My aking head did break,
From side to side for ease I toyle,
So faint I could not speak.
Beclouded was my Soul wth fear
Of thy Displeasure sore
Nor could I read my Evidence
W^{ch} oft I read before.
Hide not thy face from me I cry'd
From Burnings keep my Soul.
Thou knowst my heart, and hast me try'd
I on thy Mercyes Rowl.
O heal my Soul thou know'st I said,
Tho: flesh consume to nought,
What tho: in dust it shall bee lay'd
To Glory t' shall bee brought.
Thou hear'dst, thy rod thou didst remove
And spar'd by Body frail,
Thou shew'st to me thy tender Love,
My heart no more might quail.
O praises to my mighty God
Praise to my Lord I say,
Who hath redeem'd my Soul from pitt,
Praises to him for Aye.

In silent night when rest I took
For sorrow neer I did not look,
I waken'd was wth thundring nois
And piteous shreiks of dreadfull voice.
That fearfull sound of fire and fire,

Let no man know is my Desire.
I starting up ye light did spye,
And to my God my heart did cry
To strengthen me in my Distresse
And not to leave me succourlesse.
Then coming out beheld a space
The flame consume my dwelling place,
And when I could no longer look
I blest his Name y^t gave + took,
That layd my goods now in ye dvst
Yea so it was, and so 'twas just.
It was his own it was not mine
Far be it y^t I should repine,
He might of All justly bereft,
But yet sufficient for us left.
When by the Ruines oft I past
My sorrowing eyes aside did cast
And here and there ye places spye
Where oft I sate and long did lye,
Here stood that Trunk, and there y^t chest
There lay that store I counted best
My pleasant things in ashes lye
And them behold no more shall I.
Under thy roof no guest shall sitt,
Nor at thy Table eat a bitt.
No pleasant tale shall 'ere be told
Nor things recounted done of old.
No Candle 'ere shall shine in Thee
Nor bridegroom's voice ere heard shall bee.
In silence ever shalt thou lye
Adeiu, Adeiu, All's Vanity.
Then streight I 'gin my heart to chide,
And did thy wealth on earth abide,
Didst fix thy hope on mouldring dust,
The arm of flesh didst make thy trust?
Raise up thy thoughts above the skye
That dunghill mists away may flie.
Thou hast an house on high erect
Fram'd by that mighty Architect,

Wth glory richly furnished
Stands permanent tho: this bee fled.
'Its purchasèd + paid for too
By him who hath Enough to doe.
A prise so vast as is unknown
Yet by his Gift is made thine own.
Ther's wealth enough I need no more,
Farewell my pelf, farewell my Store.
The world no longer let me Love
My hope, and Treasure lyes Above.

As weary pilgrim, now at rest
Hugs wth delight his silent nest
His wasted limbes, now lye full soft
That myrie steps, have troden oft
Blesses himself, to think upon
his dangers past, and travailes done
The burning sun no more shall heat
Nor stormy raines, on him shall beat
The bryars and thornes no more shall scrat
nor hungry wolves at him shall catch
He erring pathes no more shall tread
Nor wild fruits eate, in stead of bread
for waters cold he doth not long
for thirst no more shall parch his tongue
No rugged stones his feet shall gaule
nor stumps nor rocks cause him to fall
All Cares and feares, he bids farwell
and meanes in safity now to dwell.
A pilgrim I, on earth, perplext
Wth sinns wth cares and sorrows vext
By age and paines brought to decay
and my Clay house mouldring away
Oh how I long to be at rest
And soare on high among the blest.
This body shall in silence sleep,

Mine eyes no more shall ever weep
No fainting fits shall me assaile
nor grinding paines, my body fraile.
W^th^ cares and fears ner' cumbred be
Nor losses know, nor sorrowes see.
What tho my flesh shall there consume
it is the bed Christ did perfume
And when a few yeares shall be gone
this mortall shall be cloth'd upon
A Corrupt Carcasse downe it lyes
a glorious body it shall rise
In weaknes and dishonour sowne
in power 'tis rais'd by Christ alone
Then soule and body shall unite
and of their maker have the sight
Such lasting joyes, shall there behold
as eare ner' heard nor tongue ere told
Lord make me ready for that day
then Come deare bridgrome Come away

Aug: 31 69

John Saffin

1626–1710

Consideratus Considerandus

What pleasure can this gaudy world afford?
What true delight does Teeming Nature hoard?
In Her great Store-house, where She lays her Treasure
Alas! tis all the Shaddow of a Pleasure;
No true content in all Her works are found
No solled joys in all Earths Spacious Round
For Labouring Man, who toyles himself in vaine
Eagerly grasping what creates his paine
How false and feeble, Nay scarce worth a Name
Are Riches, Honour Power, and Babling fame
Yet tis for those Men wade through Seas of Blood,

And bold in Mischief, Storm to be withstood
Which when Obtaind breed but Stupendious feare
Strife, jealousies, and Sleep-Disturbing Care;
No Beam of Comfort, not a Ray of Light
Shines thence to guide us thrô Fates Gloomy Night
But lost in Dismall Darkness there we Stay
Bereft of Reason in an Endless way
Vertu's the Souls true good if any bee
Tis that creats us true filicitie
Thô we despise, Contemn, and cast it by
As worthless, or Our fatalst Enemy
Because our Darling Lusts it dare Controule
And bound the Roveings of the wandering Soul.
Therefore in Garments poor it still appears
And sometimes (Naked) it no garment weares
Shun'd by the Great, and worthless deem'd by most
Urg'd to be gone, or wish'd forever Lost
Yet it is Loath to leave our wretched Coast
But in Disguise does here, and there intrude,
Striveing to Conquer base Ingrattitude
And boldly ventures now and then to Shine
So to make known it is of Birth Divine
But clouded oft it like the Lightning plays
Looseing as sone as seen its poynted Rays
Which scarceness makes those that are weak in witt
For vertues Self admire its Counterfiete
With Damned Hipocrites the world Delude
As men on Indians Glass, for Gems obtrude.

Michael Wigglesworth

1631–1705

FROM *The Day of Doom*

VANITY OF VANITIES

Vain, frail, short liv'd, and miserable Man,
Learn what thou art when thine estate is best:
A restless Wave o'th' troubled Ocean,
A Dream, a lifeless Picture finely drest:

A Wind, a Flower, a Vapour, and a Bubble,
A Wheel that stands not still, a trembling Reed,
A rolling Stone, dry Dust, light Chaff, and Stubble,
A Shadow of Something, but nought indeed.

Learn what deceitful toyes, and empty things,
This World, and all its best Enjoyments bee:
Out of the Earth no true Contentment springs,
But all things here are vexing Vanitee.

For what is *Beauty*, but a fading Flower?
Or what is *Pleasure*, but the Devils bait,
Whereby he catcheth whom he would devour,
And multitudes of Souls doth ruinate?

And what are *Friends* but mortal men, as we?
Whom Death from us may quickly separate;
Or else their hearts may quite estranged be,
And all their love be turned into hate.

And what are *Riches* to be doted on?
Uncertain, fickle, and ensnaring things;
They draw Mens Souls into Perdition,
And when most needed, take them to their wings.

Ah foolish Man! that sets his heart upon
Such empty Shadows, such wild Fowl as these,
That being gotten will be quickly gone,
And whilst they stay increase but his disease

As in a Dropsie, drinking draughts begets,
The more he drinks, the more he still requires:
So on this World whoso affection sets,
His Wealths encrease encreaseth his desires.

O happy Man, whose portion is above,
Where Floods, where Flames, where Foes cannot bereave him;
Most wretched man, that fixed hath his love
Upon this World, that surely will deceive him!

For, what is *Honour*? What is *Sov'raignty*,
Whereto mens hearts so restlesly aspire?
Whom have they Crowned with Felicity?
When did they ever satisfie desire?

The Ear of Man with hearing is not fill'd:
To see new sights still coveteth the Eye:
The craving Stomack though it may be still'd,
Yet craves again without a new supply.

All Earthly things, man's Cravings answer not,
Whose little heart would all the World contain,
(If all the World should fall to one man's Lot)
And notwithstanding empty still remain.

The *Eastern Conquerour* was said to weep,
When he the *Indian* Ocean did view,
To see his Conquest bounded by the Deep,
And no more Worlds remaining to subdue.

Who would that man in his Enjoyments bless,
Or envy him, or covet his estate,
Whose gettings do augment his greediness,
And make his wishes more intemperate?

Such is the wonted and the common guise
Of those on Earth that bear the greatest Sway:
If with a few the case be otherwise
They seek a Kingdom that abides for ay.

Moreover they, of all the Sons of men,
That Rule, and are in highest places set,
Are most inclin'd to scorn their Bretheren
And God himself (without great grace) forget.

For as the Sun doth blind the gazer's eyes,
That for a time they nought discern aright:
So Honour doth befool and blind the Wise,
And their own Lustre 'reaves them of their sight.

Great are their Dangers, manifold their Cares,
Thro which, whilst others Sleep, they scarcely Nap;
And yet are oft surprized unawares,
And fall unweeting into Envies Trap.

The mean Mechanick finds his kindly rest,
All void of fear Sleepeth the County Clown,
When greatest Princes often are distrest,
And cannot Sleep upon their Beds of Down.

Could *Strength* or *Valour* men Immortalize,
Could *Wealth* or *Honour* keep them from decay,
There were some cause the same to Idolize,
And give the lye to that which I do say.

But neither can such things themselves endure
Without the hazard of a Change one hour,
Nor such as trust in them can they secure
From dismal dayes, or Deaths prevailing pow'r.

If *Beauty* could the beautiful defend
From Death's dominion, than fair *Absalom*
Had not been brought to such a shameful end;
But fair and foul into the Grave must come.

If *Wealth* or *Scepters* could Immortal make,
Then wealthy *Croesus*, wherefore art thou dead?
If *Warlike force*, which makes the World to quake,
Then why is *Julius Caesar* perished?

Where are the *Scipio's* Thunder-bolts of War?
Renowned *Pompey*, *Caesars* Enemie?
Stout *Hannibal*, *Romes* Terror known so far?
Great *Alexander*, what's become of thee?

If *Gifts* and *Bribes* Death's favour might but win,
If *Power*, if force, or *Threatnings* might it fray,
All these, and more, had still surviving been:
But all are gone, for Death will have no Nay.

Such is this World with all her Pomp and Glory,
Such are the men whom worldly eyes admire:
Cut down by Time, and now become a Story,
That we might after better things aspire.

Go boast thy self of what thy heart enjoyes,
Vain Man! triumph in all thy worldly Bliss:
Thy best enjoyments are but Trash and Toyes:
Delight thy self in that which worthless is.

Omnia praetereunt praeter amare Deum.

Edward Taylor

C. 1642–1729

FROM *Preparatory Meditations: First Series*

8. MEDITATION. JOH. 6.51.
I AM THE LIVING BREAD.

I kening through Astronomy Divine
   The Worlds bright Battlement, wherein I spy
A Golden Path my Pensill cannot line,
   From that bright Throne unto my Threshold ly.
   And while my puzzled thoughts about it pore
   I finde the Bread of Life in't at my doore.

When that this Bird of Paradise put in
   This Wicker Cage (my Corps) to tweedle praise
Had peckt the Fruite forbad: and so did fling
   Away its Food; and lost its golden dayes;
   It fell into Celestiall Famine sore:
   And never could attain a morsell more.

Alas! alas! Poore Bird, what wilt thou doe?
   The Creatures field no food for Souls e're gave.
And if thou knock at Angells dores they show
   An Empty Barrell: they no soul bread have.
   Alas! Poore Bird, the Worlds White Loafe is done.
   And cannot yield thee here the smallest Crumb.

In this sad state, Gods Tender Bowells run
   Out streams of Grace: And he to end all strife
The Purest Wheate in Heaven, his deare-dear Son
   Grinds, and kneads up into this Bread of Life.
   Which Bread of Life from Heaven down came and stands
   Disht on thy Table up by Angells Hands.

Did God mould up this Bread in Heaven, and bake,
Which from his Table came, and to thine goeth?
Doth he bespeake thee thus, This Soule Bread take.
Come Eate thy fill of this thy Gods White Loafe?
Its Food too fine for Angells, yet come, take
And Eate thy fill. Its Heavens Sugar Cake.

What Grace is this knead in this Loafe? This thing
Souls are but petty things it to admire.
Yee Angells, help: This fill would to the brim
Heav'ns whelm'd-down Chrystall meele Bowle, yea and higher.
This Bread of Life dropt in thy mouth, doth Cry.
Eate, Eate me, Soul, and thou shalt never dy.

38. MEDITATION. I JOH. 2.I.

AN ADVOCATE WITH THE FATHER.

Oh! What a thing is Man? Lord, Who am I?
That thou shouldst give him Law (Oh! golden Line)
To regulate his Thoughts, Words, Life thereby.
And judge him Wilt thereby too in thy time.
A Court of justice thou in heaven holdst
To try his Case while he's here housd on mould.

How do thy Angells lay before thine eye
My Deeds both White, and Black I dayly doe?
How doth thy Court thou Pannellst there them try?
But flesh complains. What right for this? let's know.
For right, or wrong I can't appeare unto't.
And shall a sentence Pass on such a suite?

Soft; blemish not this golden Bench, or place.
Here is no Bribe, nor Colourings to hide
Nor Pettifogger to befog the Case
But Justice hath her Glory here well tri'de.
Her spotless Law all spotted Cases tends.
Without Respect or Disrespect them ends.

God's Judge himselfe: and Christ Atturny is,
  The Holy Ghost Regesterer is founde.
Angells the sergeants are, all Creatures kiss
  The booke, and doe as Evidences abounde.
  All Cases pass according to pure Law
  And in the sentence is no Fret, nor flaw.

What saist, my soule? Here all thy Deeds are tri'de.
  Is Christ thy Advocate to pleade thy Cause?
Art thou his Client? Such shall never slide.
  He never lost his Case: he pleads such Laws
  As Carry do the same, nor doth refuse
  The Vilest sinners Case that doth him Choose.

This is his Honour, not Dishonour: nay
  No Habeas-Corpus gainst his Clients came
For all their Fines his Purse doth make down pay.
  He Non-Suites Satan's Suite or Casts the Same.
  He'l plead thy Case, and not accept a Fee.
  He'l plead Sub Forma Pauperis for thee.

My Case is bad. Lord, be my Advocate.
  My sin is red: I'me under Gods Arrest.
Thou hast the Hint of Pleading; plead my State.
  Although it's bad thy Plea will make it best.
  If thou wilt plead my Case before the King:
  I'le Waggon Loads of Love, and Glory bring.

FROM *Preparatory Meditations: Second Series*

12. MEDITATION. EZEK. 37.24.
DAVID MY SERVANT SHALL BE THEIR KING.

Dull, Dull indeed! What shall it e're be thus?
  And why? Are not thy Promises, my Lord,
Rich, Quick'ning things? How should my full Cheeks blush
  To finde mee thus? And those a lifeless Word?

My Heart is heedless: unconcernd hereat:
I finde my Spirits Spiritless, and flat.

Thou Courtst mine Eyes in Sparkling Colours bright,
Most bright indeed, and soul enamoring,
With the most Shining Sun, whose beames did smite
Me with delightfull Smiles to make mee spring.
Embellisht knots of Love assault my minde
Which still is Dull, as if this Sun ne're shin'de.

David in all his gallantry now comes,
Bringing to tende thy Shrine, his Royall Glory,
Rich Prowess, Prudence, Victories, Sweet Songs,
And Piety to Pensill out thy Story;
To draw my Heart to thee in this brave shine
Of typick Beams, most warm. But still I pine.

Shall not this Lovely Beauty, Lord, set out
In Dazzling Shining Flashes 'fore mine Eye,
Enchant my heart, Love's golden mine, till't spout
Out Streames of Love refin'd that on thee lie?
Thy Glory's great: Thou Davids Kingdom shalt
Enjoy for aye. I want and thats my fault.

Spare me, my Lord, spare me, I greatly pray,
Let me thy Gold pass through thy Fire untill
Thy Fire refine, and take my filth away.
That I may shine like Gold, and have my fill
Of Love for thee; untill my Virginall
Chime out in Changes sweet thy Praises shall.

Wipe off my Rust, Lord, with thy wisp me scoure,
And make thy Beams pearch on my Strings their blaze.
My tunes Cloath with thy Shine, and Quavers poure
My Cursing Strings on, loaded with thy Praise.
My Fervent Love with Musick in her hand,
Shall then attend thyselfe, and thy Command.

18. MEDITATION. HEB. 13.10. WEE HAVE AN ALTAR.

A Bran, a Chaff, a very Barly yawn,
An Husk, a Shell, a Nothing, nay yet Worse,
A Thistle, Bryer prickle, pricking Thorn
A Lump of Lewdeness, Pouch of Sin, a purse
Of Naughtiness, I am, yea what not Lord?
And wilt thou be mine Altar? and my bord?

Mine Heart's a Park or Chase of sins: Mine Head
'S a Bowling Alley. Sins play Ninehole here.
Phansy's a Green: sin Barly breaks in't led.
Judgment's a pingle. Blindeman's Buff's plaid there.
Sin playes at Coursey Parke within my Minde.
My Wills a Walke in which it aires what's blinde.

Sure then I lack Atonement. Lord me help.
Thy Shittim Wood ore laid With Wealthy brass
Was an Atoning altar, and sweet smelt:
But if ore laid with pure pure gold it was
It was an Incense Altar, all perfum'd
With Odours, wherein Lord thou thus was bloom'd.

Did this ere during Wood when thus orespread
With these erelasting Metalls altarwise
Type thy Eternall Plank of Godhead, Wed
Unto our Mortall Chip, its sacrifice?
Thy Deity mine Altar. Manhood thine.
Mine Offring on't for all men's Sins, and mine?

This Golden Altar puts such weight into
The sacrifices offer'd on't, that it
Ore weighs the Weight of all the sins that flow
In thine Elect. This Wedge, and beetle split
The knotty Logs of Vengeance too to shivers:
And from their Guilt and shame them cleare delivers.

This Holy Altar by its Heavenly fire
   Refines our Offerings: casts out their dross
And sanctifies their Gold by its rich 'tire
   And all their steams with Holy Odours boss.
   Pillars of Frankincense and rich Perfume
   They 'tone Gods nosthrills with, off from this Loom.

Good News, Good Sirs, more good than comes within
   The Canopy of Angells. Heavens Hall
Allows no better: this atones for sin,
   My Glorious God, Whose Grace here thickest falls.
   May I my Barly yawn, Bran, Bryer Claw,
   Lay on't a Sacrifice? or Chaff or Straw?

Shall I my sin Pouch lay, on thy Gold Bench
   My Offering, Lord, to thee? I've such alone
But have no better. For my sins do drench
   My very best unto their very bone.
   And shall mine Offering by thine Altars fire
   Refin'd, and sanctifi'd to God aspire?

Amen, ev'n so be it. I now will climb
   The stares up to thine Altar, and on't lay
Myselfe, and services, even for its shrine.
   My sacrifice brought thee accept I pray.
   My Morn, and Evning Offerings I'le bring
   And on this Golden Altar Incense fling.

Lord let thy Deity mine Altar bee
   And make thy Manhood, on't my sacrifice.
For mine Atonement: make them both for mee
   My Altar t'sanctify my gifts likewise
   That so myselfe and service on't may bring
   Its worth along with them to thee my king.

The thoughts whereof, do make my tunes as fume,
   From off this Altar rise to thee Most High
And all their steams stufft with thy Altars blooms,
   My Sacrifice of Praise in Melody.
   Let thy bright Angells catch my tune, and sing't.
   That Equalls Davids Michtam which is in't.

Let by rain

Ye Flippering Soule,
Why dost between the Nippers dwell?
Not stay, nor goe. Not yea, nor yet Controle.
Doth this doe well?
Rise journy'ng when the skies fall weeping Showers.
Not o're nor under th'Clouds and Cloudy Powers.

Not yea, nor noe:
On tiptoes thus? Why sit on thorns?
Resolve the matter: Stay thyselfe or goe.
Be n't both wayes born.
Wager thyselfe against thy surplice, see,
And win thy Coate: or let thy Coate Win thee.

Is this th'Effect,
To leaven thus my Spirits all?
To make my heart a Crabtree Cask direct?
A Verjuicte Hall?
As Bottle Ale, whose Spirits prisond nurst
When jog'd, the bung with Violence doth burst?

Shall I be made
A sparkling Wildfire Shop
Where my dull Spirits at the Fireball trade
Do frisk and hop?
And while the Hammer doth the Anvill pay,
The fireball matter sparkles ery way.

One sorry fret,
An anvill Sparke, rose higher
And in thy Temple falling almost set
The house on fire.
Such fireballs droping in the Temple Flame
Burns up the building: Lord forbid the same.

Upon a Spider Catching a Fly

Thou sorrow, venom Elfe.
Is this thy play,
To spin a web out of thyselfe
To Catch a Fly?
For Why?

I saw a pettish wasp
Fall foule therein.
Whom yet thy Whorle pins did not clasp
Lest he should fling
His sting.

But as affraid, remote
Didst stand hereat
And with thy little fingers stroke
And gently tap
His back.

Thus gently him didst treate
Lest he should pet,
And in a froppish, waspish heate
Should greatly fret
Thy net.

Whereas the silly Fly,
Caught by its leg
Thou by the throate tookst hastily
And 'hinde the head
Bite Dead.

This goes to pot, that not
Nature doth call.
Strive not above what strength hath got
Lest in the brawle
Thou fall.

This Frey seems thus to us.
Hells Spider gets

His intrails spun to whip Cords thus
   And wove to nets
      And sets.

To tangle Adams race
   In's stratigems
To their Destructions, spoil'd, made base
   By venom things
      Damn'd Sins.

But mighty, Gracious Lord
   Communicate
Thy Grace to breake the Cord, afford
   Us Glorys Gate
      And State.

We'l Nightingaile sing like
   When pearcht on high
In Glories Cage, thy glory, bright,
   And thankfully,
      For joy.

Upon a Wasp Child with Cold

The Bare that breaths the Northern blast
Did numb, Torpedo like, a Wasp
Whose stiffend limbs encrampt, lay bathing
In Sol's warm breath and shine as saving,
Which with her hands she chafes and stands
Rubbing her Legs, Shanks, Thighs, and hands.
Her petty toes, and fingers ends
Nipt with this breath, she out extends
Unto the Sun, in greate desire
To warm her digits at that fire.
Doth hold her Temples in this state
Where pulse doth beate, and head doth ake.
Doth turn, and stretch her body small,
Doth Comb her velvet Capitall.
As if her little brain pan were

A Volume of Choice precepts cleare.
As if her sattin jacket hot
Contained Apothecaries Shop
Of Natures recepts, that prevails
To remedy all her sad ailes,
As if her velvet helmet high
Did turret rationality.
She fans her wing up to the Winde
As if her Pettycoate were lin'de,
With reasons fleece, and hoises sails
And hu'ming flies in thankfull gails
Unto her dun Curld palace Hall
Her warm thanks offering for all.

Lord cleare my misted sight that I
May hence view thy Divinity.
Some sparkes whereof thou up dost hasp
Within this little downy Wasp
In whose small Corporation wee
A school and a schoolmaster see
Where we may learn, and easily finde
A nimble Spirit bravely minde
Her worke in e'ry limb: and lace
It up neate with a vitall grace,
Acting each part though ne'er so small
Here of this Fustian animall.
Till I enravisht Climb into
The Godhead on this Lather doe.
Where all my pipes inspir'de upraise
An Heavenly musick furrd with praise.

Huswifery

Make me, O Lord, thy Spining Wheele compleate.
Thy Holy Worde my Distaff make for mee.
Make mine Affections thy Swift Flyers neate
And make my Soule thy holy Spoole to bee.
My Conversation make to be thy Reele
And reele the yarn thereon spun of thy Wheele.

Make me thy Loome then, knit therein this Twine:
  And make thy Holy Spirit, Lord, winde quills:
Then weave the Web thyselfe. The yarn is fine.
  Thine Ordinances make my Fulling Mills.
  Then dy the same in Heavenly Colours Choice,
  All pinkt with Varnisht Flowers of Paradise.

Then cloath therewith mine Understanding, Will,
  Affections, Judgment, Conscience, Memory
My Words, and Actions, that their shine may fill
  My wayes with glory and thee glorify.
  Then mine apparell shall display before yee
  That I am Cloathd in Holy robes for glory.

The Ebb and Flow

When first thou on me Lord wrought'st thy Sweet Print,
  My heart was made thy tinder box.
  My 'ffections were thy tinder in't.
    Where fell thy Sparkes by drops.
Those holy Sparks of Heavenly Fire that came
Did ever catch and often out would flame.

But now my Heart is made thy Censar trim,
  Full of thy golden Altars fire,
  To offer up Sweet Incense in
    Unto thyselfe intire:
I finde my tinder scarce thy sparks can feel
That drop out from thy Holy flint and Steel.

Hence doubts out bud for feare thy fire in mee
  'S a mocking Ignis Fatuus
  Or lest thine Altars fire out bee,
    Its hid in ashes thus.
Yet when the bellows of thy Spirit blow
Away mine ashes, then thy fire doth glow.

A Fig for thee Oh! Death

Thou King of Terrours with thy Gastly Eyes
With Butter teeth, bare bones Grim looks likewise.
And Grizzly Hide, and clawing Tallons, fell,
Opning to Sinners Vile, Trap Door of Hell,
That on in Sin impenitently trip
The Downfall art of the infernall Pit,
Thou struckst thy teeth deep in my Lord's blest Side:
Who dasht it out, and all its venom 'stroyde
That now thy Poundrill shall onely dash
My Flesh and bones to bits, and Cask shall clash.
Thou'rt not so frightfull now to me, thy knocks
Do crack my shell. Its Heavenly kernells box
Abides most safe. Thy blows do break its shell,
Thy Teeth its Nut. Cracks are that on it fell.
Thence out its kirnell fair and nut, by worms
Once Viciated out, new formd forth turns
And on the wings of some bright Angell flies
Out to bright glory of Gods blissfull joyes.
Hence thou to mee with all thy Gastly face
Art not so dreadfull unto mee through Grace.
I am resolvde to fight thee, and ne'er yield,
Blood up to th'Ears; and in the battle field
Chasing thee hence: But not for this my flesh,
My Body, my vile harlot, its thy Mess,
Labouring to drown me into Sin, disguise
By Eating and by drinking such evill joyes
Though Grace preserv'd mee that I nere have
Surprised been nor tumbled in such grave.
Hence for my strumpet I'le ne'er draw my Sword
Nor thee restrain at all by Iron Curb
Nor for her safty will I 'gainst thee strive
But let thy frozen gripes take her Captive
And her imprison in thy dungeon Cave
And grinde to powder in thy Mill the grave,
Which powder in thy Van thou'st safely keep
Till she hath slept out quite her fatall Sleep.
When the last Cock shall Crow the last day in
And the Arch Angells Trumpets sound shall ring

Then th'Eye Omniscient seek shall all there round
Each dust death's mill had very finely ground,
Which in death's smoky furnace well refinde
And Each to'ts fellow hath exactly joyn't,
It raised up anew and made all bright
And Christalized; all top full of delight.
And entertains its Soule again in bliss
And Holy Angells waiting all on this,
The Soule and Body now, as two true Lovers
Ery night how do they hug and kiss each other.
And going hand in hand thus through the skies
Up to Eternall glory glorious rise.
Is this the Worst thy terrours then canst, why
Then should this grimace at me terrify?
Why camst thou then so slowly? Mend thy pace.
Thy Slowness me detains from Christ's bright face.
Although thy terrours rise to th'highst degree,
I still am where I was, a Fig for thee.

Benjamin Tompson

1642–1714

A Neighbour's TEARS
Sprinkled on the Dust of the Amiable Virgin,
Mrs. Rebekah Sewall,
Who was born December 30. 1704. and dyed
suddenly, August 3. 1710. AEtatis 6.

Heav'ns only, in dark hours, can Succour send;
And shew a Fountain, where the cisterns end.
I saw this little One but t'other day
With a small flock of Doves, just in my way:
What New-made Creature's this so bright? thought I
Ah! Pity 'tis such Prettiness should die.
Madam, behold the Lamb of GOD; for there's
Your Pretty Lamb, while you dissolve in Tears;
She lies infolded in her Shepherd's Arms,
Whose Bosom's always full of gracious Charms.

Great JESUS claim'd his own; never begrutch
Your Jewels rare into the Hands of Such.
He, with His Righteousness, has better dress'd
Your Babe, than e're you did, when at your breast.
'Tis not your case alone: for thousands have
Follow'd their sweetest Comforts to the Grave.
Seeking the Plat of Immortality,
I saw no Place Secure; but all must dy.
Death, that stern Officer, takes no denial;
I'm griev'd he found your door, to make a trial.
Thus, be it on the Land, or Swelling Seas,
His Sov'raignty doth what His Wisdom please.
Must then the Rulers of this World's affairs,
By Providence be brought thus into Tears?
It is a Lesson hard, I must confess,
For our Proud Wills with Heav'ns to acquiesce.
But when Death goes before; Unseen, behind
There's such a One, as may compose the Mind.
Pray, *Madam*, wipe the tears off your fair eyes;
With your translated Damsel Sympathise:
Could She, from her New School, obtain the leave,
She'd tell you Things would make you cease to grieve.

Nicholas Noyes

1647–1717

A Consolatory POEM Dedicated unto
Mr. COTTON MATHER;
Soon after the Decease of his Excellent and
Vertuous WIFE, that well-accomplished
Gentlewoman, Mrs. Abigail Mather,
Who Changed Earth for Heaven, Dec. 1. 1702,
In the Thirty Third year of her Age.

Sir, After you have wip'd the Eyes
Of *Thousands* in their Miseries,
And oft condol'd the heavy Fates

Of those that have Surviv'd their *Mates*
Its come to length to your own Turn,
To be *One half within an Urn.*
(Your Christ would have it so be done!)
Your *other Self's* torn off, and *Gone.*
Gone! Said I. Yes, and that's the worst:
Your Wife's but *gone to Heaven first.*
  You do *run fast*, but she *out run*,
Hath *Made* her self, not you *Undone*;
Pray, let her *Wear* what she hath *Won!*
Grudge not her *Happiness* above;
You Live by *Faith*, and she by *Love.*
To *Live* is *Christ*, to *Dy* is *Gain*;
Betwixt you *both*, you have the *Twain.*
She was prepar'd for her Release;
And so prepar'd *Departs in Peace.*
And who would *Live*, that God makes fitt
To *Dy*, and then gives a *Permitt*?
And who would choose a World of Fears,
Ready to fall about their Ears,
That might get up above the Spheres?
And leaves the Region of dread Thunder
To them that Love the World that's under:
Where *Canker'd Breasts* with Envy broyle,
And *Smooth Tongues* are but *dipt in Oyle*;
And *Cains* Club only doth ly by,
For want of Opportunity.
Yea, who would Live among *Catarrhes*,
Contagions, *Pains*, and *Strifes*, and *Wars*?
That might go up above the Stars;
And Live in *Health*, and *Peace*, and *Bliss*,
Had in that World; but *Wish'd* in this?
  Disturb not then her precious Dust,
With *Threnodies* that are unjust.
Let not cross'd *Nature* now repine;
Sir, *Grace* hath taught you to resign
To *Christ*, what *Nature* called, *Mine*!
To call for *Mourners* I came not;
There are too many on the Spott.

Already all the Neighbourhood
Have *Wept* as mush as *Weepings* good,
Nor to Embalm her Memory;
She did *That*, e're she came to dy;
'Tis done to long Eternity!
This *Phoenix* built her *Nest of Spice*,
Like to the *Birds of Paradise*;
Which when a *Fiavour* sett on *Fire*,
Her Soul took Wing, and soared higher;
But left choice *Ashes* here behind,
Christ will for *Resurrection* find.
My Muse, pass by her *Out Side Grace*;
Say *nothing* of a Comely Face;
Nor what most Lovely pleasancies
Dwelt Chastly on her Charming Eyes.
These and such *Lilly-Glories* fade,
Absconded all in *Deaths* dark shade.
Yet these again shall Rise and Shine,
Ten Thousand times more bright and fine;
Say *little* of her *Inside Grace*;
For this World is a Spiteful place;
And takes it self for Injured
If Saints are Prais'd, *Alive* or *Dead*:
And they for *Witts* are in Esteem,
That *Heavens Dwellers* do blaspheme.
I hate their Humour, I profess,
It smells of such rank Wickedness.
Yet this Saint shall not go her wayes,
Without a Sprig or two of *Bayes*;
Who well deserv'd far greater Praise.

Her *Maiden Vertues* rendred her,
A *Meet-Help* for a Minister.
For the *Best Women*, the just *Jewes*
(*You* know) this proper phrase would use;
A Woman worthy for to be
Wife to a Priest: And such was She.
Good; Studying that Her Husband too
Nothing but *Good* might always do.

How *Frugal*, yet how *Generous*!
How *Modest*, yet how *Courteous*!
How *Silent*, yet how *Affable*!
How *Wise*, how *Pure*, how *Peaceable*.
As *Child*, her *Parents Joy*; As *Wife*,
Her *Husbands Crown*, and Heart, and Life.
As *Mother* She, a *Fruitful Vine*,
Her *Offspring* of an Holy Line,
By Holy Nurture made them Shine.
More might be said: But lest I vex
And stir the Envy of her Sex,
I'le not proceed in Commendation,
But leave her to their Imitation;
Who having her bright vertue kept
In Lustre; *Thus* at length She slept.
A Sickness full of *Mysteries*,
With Violence did on her Sieze.
She *Thirty Weeks* felt Deaths Attack,
But *Fervent Pray'r* still kept her back.
Her *Faith* and *Patience* t'was to Try,
And Learn *Us* how to *Live* and *Dy*.
At Last, all Thoughts of *Life* were null'd;
For *Earth* by *Heaven* was outpull'd
And She straight way must thither go,
Whether her good Friends would or no.
So with the *Wings* of *Faith* and *Love*,
And feathers of an Holy *Dove*,
She bid this Wretched World adieu,
And Swiftly up to *Heaven* flew;
Yet as She flew, let this Word fall,
Heav'n, Heav'n will make amends for all!

John Norton Jr.

1651–1716

A Funeral Elogy,

Upon that Pattern and Patron of Virtue, the truly pious, peerless & matchless Gentlewoman Mrs. Anne Bradstreet,
right Panaretes,
Mirror of her Age, Glory of her Sex, whose Heaven-born-Soul leaving its earthly Shrine, chose its native home, and was taken to its Rest, upon 16th. Sept. 1672.

Ask not why hearts turn Magazines of passions,
And why that grief is clad in sev'ral fashions;
Why She on progress goes, and doth not borrow
The smallest respite from th'extreams of sorrow,
Her misery is got to such an height,
As makes the earth groan to support its weight,
Such storms of woe, so strongly have beset her,
She hath no place for worse, nor hope for better;
Her comfort is, if any for her be,
That none can shew more cause of grief then she.
Ask not why some in mournfull black are clad;
The sun is set, there needs must be a shade.
Ask not why every face a sadness shrowdes;
The setting Sun ore-cast us hath with Clouds.
Ask not why the great glory of the Skye
That gilds the starrs with heavenly Alchamy,
Which all the world doth lighten with his rayes,
The *Persian* God, the Monarch of the dayes;
Ask not the reason of his extasie,
Paleness of late, in midnoon Majesty,
Why that the palefac'd Empress of the night
Disrob'd her brother of his glorious light.
Did not the language of the starrs foretel

A mournfull Scœne when they with tears did swell?
Did not the glorious people of the Skye
Seem sensible of future misery?
Did not the lowring heavens seem to express
The worlds great lose, and their unhappiness?
Behold how tears flow from the learned hill,
How the bereaved Nine do daily fill
The bosome of the fleeting Air with groans,
And wofull Accents, which witness their Moanes.
How doe the Goddesses of verse, the learned quire,
Lament their rival Quill, which all admire?
Could *Maro*'s Muse but hear her lively strain,
He would condemn his works to fire again.
Methinks I hear the Patron of the Spring,
The unshorn Deity abruptly sing.
Some doe for anguish weep, for anger I
That Ignorance should live, and Art should die.
Black, fatal, dismal, inauspicious day,
Unblest for ever by *Sol*'s precious Ray,
Be it the first of Miseries to all;
Or last of Life, defam'd for Funeral.
When this day yearly comes, let every one,
Cast in their urne, the black and dismal stone,
Succeeding years as they their circuit goe,
Leap o're this day, as a sad time of woe.
Farewell my Muse, since thou hast left thy shrine,
I am unblest in one, but blest in nine.
Fair *Thespian* Ladyes, light your torches all,
Attend your glory to its Funeral,
To court her ashes with a learned tear,
A briny sacrifice, let not a smile appear.
Grave Matron, whoso seeks to blazon thee,
Needs not make use of witts false Heraldry;
Whoso should give thee all thy worth would swell
So high, as 'twould turn the world infidel.
Had he great *Maro*'s Muse, or *Tully*'s tongue,
Or raping numbers like the *Thracian* Song,
In crowning of her merits he would be
Sumptuously poor, low in Hyperbole.

To write is easie; but to write on thee,
Truth would be thought to forfeit modesty.
He'l seem a Poet that shall speak but true;
Hyperbole's in others, are thy due.
Like a most servile flatterer he will show
Though he write truth, and make the Subject, You.
Virtue ne're dies, time will a Poet raise
Born under better Starrs, shall sing thy praise.
Praise her who list, yet he shall be a debtor
For Art ne're feigned, nor Nature fram'd a better.
Her virtues were so great, that they do raise
A work to trouble fame, astonish praise.
When as her Name doth but salute the ear,
Men think that they perfections abstract hear.
Her breast was a brave Pallace, a *Broad-street*,
Where all heroick ample thoughts did meet,
Where nature such a Tenement had tane,
That others souls, to hers, dwelt in a lane.
Beneath her feet, pale envy bites her chain,
And poison Malice, whetts her sting in vain.
Let every Laurel, every Myrtel bough
Be stript for leaves t'adorn and load her brow.
Victorious wreaths, which 'cause they never fade
Wise elder times for Kings and Poets made.
Let not her happy memory e're lack
Its worth in Fame's eternal Almanack,
Which none shall read, but straight their loss deplore,
And blame their Fates they were not born before.
Do not old men rejoyce their Fates did last,
And infants too, that theirs did make such hast,
In such a welcome time to bring them forth,
That they might be a witness to her worth.
Who undertakes this subject to commend
Shall nothing find so hard as how to end.

Finis & non. John Norton.

Omnia Romanæ *sileant Miracula Gentis.*

Cotton Mather

1663–1728

The Rain gasped for

O *Father of the Rain*, Look down
Upon us from on high;
If thy Land be not *Rain'd* upon,
What *Lives* on it will *Dy*.

Lord of the Clouds; In thee we hope;
Thine all the *Bottels* are;
Except Thou open them, a Drop
won't fall upon us here.

If thou make Heav'n as *Brass*, and burn
From thence the groaning Field,
Thy Earth will soon to *Iron* turn,
And no Production yield.

O Let thy Seasonable *Rain*
Drop *Fatness* on our Soyl;
And grant to most unworthy Man
The *Harvest* of his Toil.

But, O my SAVIOUR, in a Showre
Of *Righteousness* descend:
Gifts on me, with thy SPIRIT poure;
And *Life* that cannot End.

Yea, come upon a World forlorn,
And with a Quickening *Dew*,
Make thou Mankind, of *Water* born,
Tho' *Dead*, their *Life* Renew.

In the mean time, thy *Ministers*,
As *Clouds*, how *Fat* and *Bright*!
May they upon *Salvations Heirs*
  Distil Things Good and Right.

Mather Byles

1707–1788

I.

Great GOD, how frail a Thing is Man!
  How swift his Minutes pass!
His Age contracts within a Span;
  He blooms and dies like Grass.

II.

Now in his Breath fresh Spirits dart,
  And vital Vigour reigns:
His Blood pours rapid from his Heart,
  And leaps along his Veins.

III.

His Eyes their sparkling Pleasure speak,
  Joy flutters round his Head;
While Health still blossoms on his Cheek,
  And adds the rosey Red.

IV.

Thus the fond Youth securely stands,
  Nor dreams of a Decay——
At once he feels Death's Iron Hands,
  His Soul is snatch'd away.

V.

Down to the Earth the Body drops,
 Whence it was fram'd at first,
Forgets its former flatt'ring Hopes
 And hastens to its Dust.

VI.

No more we view the wonted Grace;
 The Eye-Balls roll no more:
A livid Horror spreads the Face
 Where Beauty blaz'd before.

VII.

So the young *Spring*, with annual Green,
 Renews the waving Grove;
And Riv'lets thro' the flow'ry Scene
 In Silver Mazes rove.

VIII.

By tuneful Birds of ev'ry Wing,
 Melodious Strains are play'd;
From Tree to Tree their Accents ring,
 Soft-warbling thro' the Shade.

IX.

The painted Meads, and fragrant Fields,
 A sudden Smile bestow:
A golden Gleam each Valley guilds,
 Where numerous Beauties blow.

X.

A Thousand gaudy Colours flush
   Each od'rous Mountain's Side:
Lillies turn fair, and Roses blush,
   And Tulips spread their Pride.

XI.

Thus flourishes the wanton Year,
   In rich Confusion gay,
Till *Autumn* bids the Bloom retire,
   The Verdure fade away.

XII.

Succeeding Cold withers the Woods,
   While hoary *Winter* reigns,
In Fetters binds the frozen Floods,
   And shivers o'er the Plains.

XIII.

And must *my* Moments thus decline?
   And must *I* sink to Death?
To Thee my Spirit I resign,
   Thou SOV'REIGN of my Breath.

XIV.

JESUS my Life has dy'd, has rose:
   I burn to meet his Charms!
Welcome the Pangs, the dying Throes,
   That give me to his Arms.

William Billings

1746–1800

Chester

Let tyrants shake their iron rod,
And Slav'ry clank her galling chains,
We fear them not we trust in God,
New-england's God forever reigns.

Howe and Burgoyne and Clinton too,
With Prescott and Cornwallis join'd,
Together plot our Overthrow,
In one infernal league combin'd.

When God inspir'd us for the fight,
Their ranks were broke their lines were forc'd,
Their ships were shatter'd in our sight,
Or swiftly driven from our Coast.

The Foe comes on with haughty Stride,
Our troops advance with martial noise
Their Vet'rans flee before our Youth,
And Gen'rals yield to beardless Boys.

What grateful Off'ring shall we bring?
What shall we render to the Lord?
Loud Hallelujahs let us Sing,
And praise his name on every Chord.

An Anthem, for Thanksgiving

PSALM 148.

O praise the Lord of heaven, praise him in the height,
Praise him in the depth,
O praise the Lord of heaven,
praise him all ye angels, praise him,
praise him all ye angels, praise,
praise Jehovah, praise Jehovah,
praise him sun and moon and blazing comets,
Praise the Lord, praise the Lord, praise the Lord,
Let them praise the name of the Lord,
For he spake the word and all were made,
he commanded and they were created,
admire, adore, admire adore.

Ye dragons* whose contageous breath,
People the dark abodes of death,
Change your dire hissings into heav'nly songs,
And praise your maker with your forked tongues,
O praise the Lord of heaven fire, hail and snow, wind and storms,
beasts & cattle, creeping insects, flying fowl, kings & princes,
    men & angels praise the Lord,
Jew & Gentile, male & female, bond & free, earth & heaven, land
    & water, praise the Lord,
young men & maids, old men & babes praise the Lord,
join creation, preservation, and redemption join in one;
no exemption, nor dissention, one invention, and intention,
    reigns through the whole,
to praise the Lord, praise the Lord.

*Roscommon

Timothy Dwight

1752–1817

FROM *The Triumph of Infidelity*

There smil'd the Smooth Divine, unus'd to wound
The sinner's heart, with hell's alarming sound.
No terrors on his gentle tongue attend;
No grating truths the nicest ear offend.
That strange new-birth, that methodistic grace,
Nor in his heart, nor sermons, found a place.
Plato's fine tales he clumsily retold,
Trite, fireside, moral seesaws, dull as old;
His Christ, and Bible, plac'd at good remove,
Guilt hell-deserving, and forgiving love.
"'Twas best," he said, "mankind should cease to sin";
Good fame requir'd it; so did peace within:
Their honors, well he knew, would ne'er be driven;
But hop'd they still would please to go to heaven.
Each week, he paid his visitation dues;
Coax'd, jested, laugh'd; rehears'd the private news;
Smok'd with each goody, thought her cheese excell'd;
Her pipe he lighted, and her baby held.
Or plac'd in some great town, with lacquer'd shoes,
Trim wig, and trimmer gown, and glistening hose,
He bow'd, talk'd politics, learn'd manners mild;
Most meekly questioned, and most smoothly smil'd;
At rich men's jests laugh'd loud; their stories prais'd;
Their wives' new patterns gaz'd, and gaz'd, and gaz'd;
Most daintily on pamper'd turkeys din'd;
Nor shrunk with fasting, nor with study pin'd:
Yet from their churches saw his brethren driven,
Who thunder'd truth, and spoke the voice of heaven,
Chill'd trembling guilt, in Satan's headlong path,
Charm'd the feet back, and rous'd the ear of death.
"Let fools," he cried, "starve on, while prudent I
Snug in my nest shall live, and snug shall die."

Philip Freneau

1752–1832

On the Religion of Nature

The power, that gives with liberal hand
The blessings man enjoys, while here,
And scatters through a smiling land
Abundant products of the year;
That power of nature, ever bless'd,
Bestow'd religion with the rest.

Born with ourselves, her early sway
Inclines the tender mind to take
The path of right, fair virtue's way
Its own felicity to make.
This universally extends
And leads to no mysterious ends.

Religion, such as nature taught,
With all divine perfection suits;
Had all mankind this system sought
Sophists would cease their vain disputes,
And from this source would nations know
All that can make their heaven below.

This deals not curses on mankind,
Or dooms them to perpetual grief,
If from its aid no joys they find,
It damns them not for unbelief;
Upon a more exalted plan
Creatress nature dealt with man—

Joy to the day, when all agree
On such grand systems to proceed,
From fraud, design, and error free,
And which to truth and goodness lead:
Then persecution will retreat
And man's religion be complete.

Phillis Wheatley

1753–1784

On the Death of the Rev. Mr. George Whitefield, 1770

Hail, happy saint, on thine immortal throne,
Possest of glory, life, and bliss unknown;
We hear no more the music of thy tongue,
Thy wonted auditories cease to throng.
Thy sermons in unequall'd accents flow'd,
And ev'ry bosom with devotion glow'd;
Thou didst in strains of eloquence refin'd
Inflame the heart, and captivate the mind.
Unhappy we the setting sun deplore,
So glorious once, but ah! it shines no more.

Behold the prophet in his tow'ring flight!
He leaves the earth for heav'n's unmeasur'd height,
And worlds unknown receive him from our sight.
There *Whitefield* wings with rapid course his way,
And sails to *Zion* through vast seas of day.
Thy pray'rs, great saint, and thine incessant cries
Have pierc'd the bosom of thy native skies.
Thou moon hast seen, and all the stars of light,
How he has wrestled with his God by night.
He pray'd that grace in ev'ry heart might dwell,
He long'd to see *America* excel;
He charg'd its youth that ev'ry grace divine
Should with full lustre in their conduct shine;
That Saviour, which his soul did first receive,
The greatest gift that ev'n a God can give,
He freely offer'd to the num'rous throng,
That on his lips with list'ning pleasure hung.

"Take him, ye wretched, for your only good,
Take him ye starving sinners, for your food;
Ye thirsty, come to this life-giving stream,
Ye preachers, take him for your joyful theme;
Take him my dear *Americans*, he said,
Be your complaints on his kind bosom laid:
Take him, ye *Africans*, he longs for you,
Impartial Saviour is his title due:
Wash'd in the fountain of redeeming blood,
You shall be sons, and kings, and priests to God."

Great *Countess*,* we *Americans* revere
Thy name, and mingle in thy grief sincere;
New England deeply feels, the *Orphans* mourn,
Their more than father will no more return.

But, though arrested by the hand of death,
Whitefield no more exerts his lab'ring breath,
Yet let us view him in th'eternal skies,
Let ev'ry heart to this bright vision rise;
While the tomb safe retains its sacred trust,
Till life divine re-animates his dust.

*The Countess of *Huntington*, to whom Mr. *Whitefield* was Chaplain.

To a Lady on the Death of Three Relations

We trace the pow'r of Death from tomb to tomb,
And his are all the ages yet to come.
'Tis his to call the planets from on high,
To blacken *Phoebus*, and dissolve the sky;
His too, when all in his dark realms are hurl'd,
From its firm base to shake the solid world;
His fatal sceptre rules the spacious whole,
And trembling nature rocks from pole to pole.

Awful he moves, and wide his wings are spread:
Behold thy brother number'd with the dead!
From bondage freed, the exulting spirit flies

Beyond *Olympus*, and these starry skies.
Lost in our woe for thee, blest shade, we mourn
In vain; to earth thou never must return.
Thy sisters too, fair mourner, feel the dart
Of Death, and with fresh torture rend thine heart.
Weep not for them, who with thine happy mind
To rise with them, and leave the world behind.

As a young plant by hurricanes up torn,
So near its parent lies the newly born—
But 'midst the bright ethereal train behold
It shines superior on a throne of gold:
Then, mourner, cease; let hope thy tears restrain,
Smile on the tomb, and sooth the raging pain.
On yon blest regions fix thy longing view,
Mindless of sublunary scenes below;
Ascend the sacred mount, in thought arise,
And seek substantial, and immortal joys;
Where hope receives, where faith to vision springs,
And raptur'd seraphs tune th'immortal strings
To strains extatic. Thou the chorus join,
And to thy father tune the praise divine.

John Leland

1754–1841

The day is past and gone,
   The evening shades appear;
O may we all remember well,
   The night of death is near.

We lay our garments by,
   Upon our beds to rest;
So death will soon disrobe us all
   Of what we here possess.

Lord, keep us safe this night,
  Secure from all our fears:
May angels guard us while we sleep,
  Till morning light appears.

And when we early rise,
  And view th'unwearied sun,
May we set out to win the prize,
  And after glory run.

And when our days are past,
  And we from time remove,
O may we in thy bosom rest,
  The bosom of thy love.

Joel Barlow

1755–1812

FROM *The Columbiad*

Hail holy Peace, from thy sublime abode
Mid circling saints that grace the throne of God.
Before his arm, around our embryon earth,
Stretcht the dim void and gave to nature birth,
Ere morning stars his glowing chambers hung,
Or songs of gladness woke an angel's tongue,
Veil'd in the splendors of his beamful mind,
In blest repose thy placid form reclined,
Lived in his life, his inward sapience caught,
And traced and toned his universe of thought.
Borne thro the expanse with his creating voice
Thy presence bade the unfolding worlds rejoice,
Led forth the systems on their bright career,
Shaped all their curves and fashion'd every sphere,
Spaced out their suns, and round each radiant goal,
Orb over orb, compell'd their train to roll,
Bade heaven's own harmony their force combine,

Taught all their host symphonious strains to join,
Gave to seraphic harps their sounding lays,
Their joys to angels and to men their praise.
From scenes of blood, these verdant shores that stain,
From numerous friends in recent battle slain,
From blazing towns that scorch the purple sky,
From houseless hordes, their smoking walls that fly,
From the black prison ships, those groaning graves,
From warring fleets that vex the gory waves,
From a storm'd world, long taught thy flight to mourn,
I rise, delightful Peace, and greet thy glad return.
For now the untuneful trump shall grate no more;
Ye silver streams, no longer swell with gore,
Bear from your war-beat banks the guilty stain
With yon retiring navies to the main.
While other views unfolding on my eyes
And happier themes bid bolder numbers rise;
Bring, bounteous Peace, in thy celestial throng,
Life to my soul and rapture to my song;
Give me to trace, with pure unclouded ray,
The arts and virtues that attend thy sway,
To see thy blissful charms, that here descend,
Thro distant realms and endless years extend.

John Quincy Adams

1767–1848

O Lord, Thy All-Discerning Eyes

O Lord, thy all-discerning eyes
My inmost purpose see;
My deeds, my words, my thoughts, arise
Alike disclosed to thee:
My sitting down, my rising up,
Broad noon, and deepest night,
My path, my pillow, and my cup,
Are open to thy sight.

Before, behind, I meet thine eye,
And feel thy heavy hand:
Such knowledge is for me too high,
To reach or understand:
What of thy wonders can I know?
What of thy purpose see?
Where from thy spirit shall I go?
Where from thy presence flee?

If I ascend to heaven on high,
Or make my bed in hell;
Or take the morning's wings, and fly
O'er ocean's bounds to dwell;
Or seek, from thee, a hiding-place
Amid the gloom of night—
Alike to thee are time and space,
The darkness and the light.

Richard Henry Dana Sr.

1787–1879

The Little Beach-Bird

I.

Thou little bird, thou dweller by the sea,
Why takest thou its melancholy voice,
And with that boding cry
Along the breakers fly?
O, rather, Bird, with me
Through the fair land rejoice!

II.

Thy flitting form comes ghostly dim and pale,
As driven by a beating storm at sea;
Thy cry is weak and scared,

As if thy mates had shared
The doom of us: Thy wail, —
What doth it bring to me?

III.

Thou call'st along the sand, and haunt'st the surge,
Restless and sad; as if, in strange accord
With the motion and the roar
Of waves that drive to shore,
One spirit did ye urge,—
The Mystery,—the Word.

IV.

Of thousands, thou, both sepulchre and pall,
Old Ocean! A requiem o'er the dead,
From out thy gloomy cells,
A tale of mourning tells,—
Tells of man's woe and fall,
His sinless glory fled.

V.

Then turn thee, little Bird, and take thy flight
Where the complaining sea shall sadness bring
Thy spirit never more;
Come, quit with me the shore,
And on the meadows light,
Where birds for gladness sing!

Emma Hart Willard

1787–1870

Rocked in the Cradle of the Deep

Rocked in the cradle of the deep
I lay me down in peace to sleep;
Secure I rest upon the wave,

For thou, O Lord! hast power to save.
I know thou wilt not slight my call,
For Thou dost mark the sparrow's fall;
And calm and peaceful shall I sleep,
Rocked in the cradle of the deep.

When in the dead of night I lie
And gaze upon the trackless sky,
The star-bespangled heavenly scroll,
The boundless waters as they roll,—
I feel thy wondrous power to save
From perils of the stormy wave:
Rocked in the cradle of the deep,
I calmly rest and soundly sleep.

And such the trust that still were mine,
Though stormy winds swept o'er the brine
Or though the tempest's fiery breath
Roused me from sleep to wreck and death
In ocean cave, still safe with Thee
The germ of immortality!
And calm and peaceful shall I sleep,
Rocked in the cradle of the deep.

Lydia Huntley Sigourney

1791–1865

The Coral Insect

Toil on! toil on! ye ephemeral train,
Who build on the tossing and treacherous main;
Toil on! for the wisdom of man ye mock,
With your sand-based structures and domes of rock;
Your columns the fathomless fountains lave,
And your arches spring up through the crested wave;
Ye're a puny race thus boldly to rear
A fabric so vast in a realm so drear.

Ye bind the deep with your secret zone,
The ocean is seal'd, and the surge a stone;
Fresh wreaths from the coral pavement spring,
Like the terraced pride of Assyria's king;
The turf looks green where the breakers roll'd,
O'er the whirlpool ripens the rind of gold,
The sea-snatch'd isle is the home of men,
And mountains exult where the wave hath been.

But why do you plant 'neath the billows dark
The wrecking reef for the gallant bark?
There are snares enough on the tented field;
Mid the blossomed sweets that the valleys yield;
There are serpents to coil ere the flowers are up;
There's a poison drop in man's purest cup;
There are foes that watch for his cradle breath:
And why need ye sow the floods with death?

With mouldering bones the deeps are white,
From the ice-clad pole to the tropics bright;
The mermaid hath twisted her fingers cold
With the mesh of the sea boy's curls of gold;
And the gods of ocean have frown'd to see
The mariner's bed mid their halls of glee:
Hath earth no graves? that ye thus must spread
The boundless sea with the thronging dead?

Ye build! ye build! but ye enter not in,
Like the tribes whom the desert devour'd in their sin;
From the land of promise ye fade and die,
Ere its verdure gleams forth on your wearied eye.
As the cloud-crown'd pyramids' founders sleep
Noteless and lost in oblivion deep,
Ye slumber unmark'd mid the watery plain,
While the wonder and pride of your works remain.

William Cullen Bryant

1794–1878

Thanatopsis

To him who in the love of nature holds
Communion with her visible forms, she speaks
A various language; for his gayer hours
She has a voice of gladness, and a smile
And eloquence of beauty, and she glides
Into his darker musings, with a mild
And gentle sympathy, that steals away
Their sharpness, ere he is aware. When thoughts
Of the last bitter hour come like a blight
Over thy spirit, and sad images
Of the stern agony, and shroud, and pall,
And breathless darkness, and the narrow house,
Make thee to shudder, and grow sick at heart;—
Go forth, under the open sky, and list
To Nature's teachings, while from all around—
Earth and her waters, and the depths of air,—
Comes a still voice—Yet a few days, and thee
The all-beholding sun shall see no more
In all his course; nor yet in the cold ground,
Where thy pale form was laid, with many tears,
Nor in the embrace of ocean shall exist
Thy image. Earth, that nourished thee, shall claim
Thy growth, to be resolved to earth again;
And, lost each human trace, surrendering up
Thine individual being, shalt thou go
To mix forever with the elements,
To be a brother to the insensible rock
And to the sluggish clod, which the rude swain
Turns with his share, and treads upon. The oak
Shall send his roots abroad, and pierce thy mould.
Yet not to thy eternal resting place
Shalt thou retire alone—nor couldst thou wish

Couch more magnificent. Thou shalt lie down
With patriarchs of the infant world—with kings,
The powerful of the earth—the wise, the good,
Fair forms, and hoary seers of ages past,
All in one mighty sepulchre.—The hills
Rock-ribbed and ancient as the sun,—the vales
Stretching in pensive quietness between;
The venerable woods—rivers that move
In majesty, and the complaining brooks
That make the meadows green; and poured round all,
Old ocean's gray and melancholy waste,—
Are but the solemn decorations all
Of the great tomb of man. The golden sun,
The planets, all the infinite host of heaven,
Are shining on the sad abodes of death,
Through the still lapse of ages. All that tread
The globe are but a handful to the tribes
That slumber in its bosom.—Take the wings
Of morning—and the Barcan desert pierce,
Or lose thyself in the continuous woods
Where rolls the Oregan, and hears no sound,
Save his own dashings—yet—the dead are there,
And millions in those solitudes, since first
The flight of years began, have laid them down
In their last sleep—the dead reign there alone.
So shalt thou rest—and what if thou shalt fall
Unheeded by the living—and no friend
Take note of thy departure? All that breathe
Will share thy destiny. The gay will laugh
When thou art gone, the solemn brood of care
Plod on, and each one as before will chase
His favorite phantom; yet all these shall leave
Their mirth and their employments, and shall come,
And make their bed with thee. As the long train
Of ages glide away, the sons of men,
The youth in life's green spring, and he who goes
In the full strength of years, matron, and maid,
And the sweet babe, and the gray-headed man,—
Shall one by one be gathered to thy side,

By those, who in their turn shall follow them.
So live, that when thy summons comes to join
The innumerable caravan, that moves
To that mysterious realm, where each shall take
His chamber in the silent halls of death,
Thou go not, like the quarry-slave at night,
Scourged to his dungeon, but sustained and soothed
By an unfaltering trust, approach thy grave,
Like one who wraps the drapery of his couch
About him, and lies down to pleasant dreams.

To a Waterfowl

Whither, 'midst falling dew,
While glow the heavens with the last steps of day
Far, through their rosy depths, dost thou pursue
Thy solitary way?

Vainly the fowler's eye
Might mark thy distant flight to do thee wrong,
As, darkly painted on the crimson sky,
Thy figure floats along.

Seek'st thou the plashy brink
Of weedy lake, or marge of river wide,
Or where the rocking billows rise and sink
On the chafed ocean side?

There is a Power whose care
Teaches thy way along that pathless coast,—
The desert and illimitable air,—
Lone wandering, but not lost.

All day thy wings have fanned,
At that far height, the cold thin atmosphere,
Yet stoop not, weary, to the welcome land,
Though the dark night is near.

And soon that toil shall end,
Soon shalt thou find a summer home, and rest,
And scream among thy fellows; reeds shall bend,
Soon, o'er thy sheltered nest.

Thou'rt gone, the abyss of heaven
Hath swallow'd up thy form; yet, on my heart
Deeply hath sunk the lesson thou hast given,
And shall not soon depart.

He, who, from zone to zone,
Guides through the boundless sky thy certain flight,
In the long way that I must tread alone,
Will lead my steps aright.

Forest Hymn

The groves were God's first temples. Ere man learned
To hew the shaft, and lay the architrave,
And spread the roof above them,—ere he framed
The lofty vault, to gather and roll back
The sound of anthems; in the darkling wood,
Amidst the cool and silence, he knelt down
And offered to the Mightiest, solemn thanks
And supplication. For his simple heart
Might not resist the sacred influences,
Which, from the stilly twilight of the place,
And from the gray old trunks that high in heaven
Mingled their mossy boughs, and from the sound
Of the invisible breath that swayed at once
All their green tops, stole over him, and bowed
His spirit with the thought of boundless power
And inaccessible majesty. Ah, why
Should we, in the world's riper years, neglect
God's ancient sanctuaries, and adore
Only among the crowd, and under roofs
That our frail hands have raised. Let me, at least,
Here, in the shadow of this aged wood,

Offer one hymn—thrice happy, if it find
Acceptance in his ear.

Father, thy hand
Hath reared these venerable columns, thou
Didst weave this verdant roof. Thou didst look down
Upon the naked earth, and, forthwith, rose
All these fair ranks of trees. They, in thy sun,
Budded, and shook their green leaves in thy breeze,
And shot towards heaven. The century-living crow
Whose birth was in their tops, grew old and died
Among their branches, till, at last, they stood,
As now they stand, massive and tall and dark,
Fit shrine for humble worshipper to hold
Communion with his Maker. Here are seen
No traces of man's pomp or pride;—no silks
Rustle, nor jewels shine, nor envious eyes
Encounter; no fantastic carvings show
The boast of our vain race to change the form
Of thy fair works. But thou art here—thou fill'st
The solitude. Thou art in the soft winds
That run along the summit of these trees
In music;—thou art in the cooler breath,
That from the inmost darkness of the place,
Comes, scarcely felt;—the barky trunks, the ground,
The fresh moist ground, are all instinct with thee.
Here is continual worship;—nature, here,
In the tranquillity that thou dost love,
Enjoys thy presence. Noiselessly, around,
From perch to perch, the solitary bird
Passes; and yon clear spring, that, 'midst its herbs,
Wells softly forth and visits the strong roots
Of half the mighty forest, tells no tale
Of all the good it does. Thou hast not left
Thyself without a witness, in these shades,
Of thy perfections. Grandeur, strength, and grace
Are here to speak of thee. This mighty oak—
By whose immoveable stem I stand and seem
Almost annihilated—not a prince,

In all that proud old world beyond the deep,
E'er wore his crown as loftily as he
Wears the green coronal of leaves with which
Thy hand has graced him. Nestled at his root
Is beauty, such as blooms not in the glare
Of the broad sun. That delicate forest flower,
With scented breath, and look so like a smile,
Seems, as it issues from the shapeless mould,
An emanation of the indwelling Life,
A visible token of the upholding Love,
That are the soul of this wide universe.

My heart is awed within me, when I think
Of the great miracle that still goes on,
In silence, round me—the perpetual work
Of thy creation, finished, yet renewed
Forever. Written on thy works I read
The lesson of thy own eternity.
Lo! all grow old and die—but see, again,
How on the faltering footsteps of decay
Youth presses—ever gay and beautiful youth
In all its beautiful forms. These lofty trees
Wave not less proudly that their ancestors
Moulder beneath them. Oh, there is not lost
One of earth's charms: upon her bosom yet,
After the flight of untold centuries,
The freshness of her far beginning lies
And yet shall lie. Life mocks the idle hate
Of his arch enemy Death—yea—seats himself
Upon the sepulchre, and blooms and smiles,
And of the triumphs of his ghastly foe
Makes his own nourishment. For he came forth
From thine own bosom, and shall have no end.

There have been holy men who hid themselves
Deep in the woody wilderness, and gave
Their lives to thought and prayer, till they outlived
The generation born with them, nor seemed
Less aged than the hoary trees and rocks

Around them;—and there have been holy men
Who deemed it were not well to pass life thus.
But let me often to these solitudes
Retire, and in thy presence re-assure
My feeble virtue. Here its enemies,
The passions, at thy plainer footsteps shrink
And tremble and are still. Oh, God! when thou
Dost scare the world with tempests, set on fire
The heavens with falling thunderbolts, or fill,
With all the waters of the firmament,
The swift dark whirlwind that uproots the woods
And drowns the villages; when, at thy call,
Uprises the great deep and throws himself
Upon the continent and overwhelms
Its cities—who forgets not, at the sight
Of these tremendous tokens of thy power,
His pride, and lays his strifes and follies by?
Oh, from these sterner aspects of thy face
Spare me and mine, nor let us need the wrath
Of the mad unchained elements to teach
Who rules them. Be it ours to meditate
In these calm shades thy milder majesty,
And, to the beautiful order of thy works,
Learn to conform the order of our lives.

Hymn of the Waldenses

Hear, Father, hear thy faint afflicted flock
Cry to thee, from the desert and the rock;
While those, who seek to slay thy children, hold
Blasphemous worship under roofs of gold;
And the broad goodly lands, with pleasant airs
That nurse the grape and wave the grain, are theirs.

Yet better were this mountain wilderness,
And this wild life of danger and distress—
Watchings by night and perilous flight by day,
And meetings in the depths of earth to pray,

Better, far better, than to kneel with them,
And pay the impious rite thy laws condemn.

Thou, Lord, dost hold the thunder; the firm land
Tosses in billows when it feels thy hand;
Thou dashest nation against nation, then
Stillest the angry world to peace again.
Oh, touch their stony hearts who hunt thy sons—
The murderers of our wives and little ones.

Yet, mighty God, yet shall thy frown look forth
Unveiled, and terribly shall shake the earth.
Then the foul power of priestly sin and all
Its long upheld idolatries shall fall.
Thou shalt raise up the trampled and opprest,
And thy delivered saints shall dwell in rest.

George Washington Doane

1799–1859

Evening

Psalm cxli. 2.

Softly now the light of day
Fades upon my sight away;
Free from care, from labour free,
Lord, I would commune with Thee:

Thou, whose all-pervading eye,
  Naught escapes, without, within,
Pardon each infirmity,
  Open fault, and secret sin.

Soon, for me, the light of day
  Shall for ever, pass away;
Then, from sin and sorrow, free,
  Take me, Lord, to dwell with Thee:

Thou, who, sinless, yet hast known
All of man's infirmity;
Then, from Thine eternal throne,
Jesus, look with pitying eye.

Ralph Waldo Emerson

1803–1882

The Problem

I like a church; I like a cowl;
I love a prophet of the soul;
And on my heart monastic aisles
Fall like sweet strains, or pensive smiles;
Yet not for all his faith can see
Would I that cowled churchman be.

Why should the vest on him allure,
Which I could not on me endure?

Not from a vain or shallow thought
His awful Jove young Phidias brought;
Never from lips of cunning fell
The thrilling Delphic oracle;
Out from the heart of nature rolled
The burdens of the Bible old;
The litanies of nations came,
Like the volcano's tongue of flame,
Up from the burning core below,—
The canticles of love and woe;
The hand that rounded Peter's dome,
And groined the aisles of Christian Rome,
Wrought in a sad sincerity;
Himself from God he could not free;
He builded better than he knew;—
The conscious stone to beauty grew.

Know'st thou what wove yon woodbird's nest
Of leaves, and feathers from her breast?
Or how the fish outbuilt her shell,
Painting with morn each annual cell?
Or how the sacred pine-tree adds
To her old leaves new myriads?
Such and so grew these holy piles,
Whilst love and terror laid the tiles.
Earth proudly wears the Parthenon,
As the best gem upon her zone;
And Morning opes with haste her lids,
To gaze upon the Pyramids;
O'er England's abbeys bends the sky,
As on its friends, with kindred eye;
For, out of Thought's interior sphere,
These wonders rose to upper air;
And Nature gladly gave them place,
Adopted them into her race,
And granted them an equal date
With Andes and with Ararat.

These temples grew as grows the grass;
Art might obey, but not surpass.
The passive Master lent his hand
To the vast soul that o'er him planned;
And the same power that reared the shrine,
Bestrode the tribes that knelt within.
Ever the fiery Pentecost
Girds with one flame the countless host,
Trances the heart through chanting choirs,
And through the priest the mind inspires.
The word unto the prophet spoken
Was writ on tables yet unbroken;
The word by seers or sibyls told,
In groves of oak, or fanes of gold,
Still floats upon the morning wind,
Still whispers to the willing mind.
One accent of the Holy Ghost
The heedless world hath never lost.

I know what say the fathers wise,—
The Book itself before me lies,
Old *Chrysostom*, best Augustine,
And he who blent both in his line,
The younger *Golden Lips* or mines,
Taylor, the Shakspeare of divines.
His words are music in my ear,
I see his cowled portrait dear;
And yet, for all his faith could see,
I would not the good bishop be.

The Rhodora

On Being Asked, Whence Is the Flower?

In May, when sea-winds pierced our solitudes,
I found the fresh Rhodora in the woods,
Spreading its leafless blooms in a damp nook,
To please the desert and the sluggish brook.
The purple petals, fallen in the pool,
Made the black water with their beauty gay;
Here might the red-bird come his plumes to cool,
And court the flower that cheapens his array.
Rhodora! if the sages ask thee why
This charm is wasted on the earth and sky,
Tell them, dear, that if eyes were made for seeing,
Then Beauty is its own excuse for being:
Why thou wert there, O rival of the rose!
I never thought to ask, I never knew;
But, in my simple ignorance, suppose
The self-same Power that brought me there brought you.

Dirge

Knows he who tills this lonely field,
  To reap its scanty corn,
What mystic fruit his acres yield
  At midnight and at morn?

In the long sunny afternoon,
  The plain was full of ghosts;
I wandered up, I wandered down,
  Beset by pensive hosts.

The winding Concord gleamed below,
  Pouring as wide a flood
As when my brothers, long ago,
  Came with me to the wood.

But they are gone,—the holy ones
  Who trod with me this lovely vale;
The strong, star-bright companions
  Are silent, low, and pale.

My good, my noble, in their prime,
  Who made this world the feast it was,
Who learned with me the lore of time,
  Who loved this dwelling-place!

They took this valley for their toy,
  They played with it in every mood;
A cell for prayer, a hall for joy,—
  They treated nature as they would.

They colored the horizon round;
  Stars flamed and faded as they bade;
All echoes hearkened for their sound,—
  They made the woodlands glad or mad.

I touch this flower of silken leaf,
  Which once our childhood knew;
Its soft leaves wound me with a grief
  Whose balsam never grew.

Hearken to yon pine-warbler
  Singing aloft in the tree!
Hearest thou, O traveller,
  What he singeth to me?

Not unless God made sharp thine ear
  With sorrow such as mine,
Out of that delicate lay could'st thou
  Its heavy tale divine.

'Go, lonely man,' it saith;
  'They loved thee from their birth;
Their hands were pure, and pure their faith,—
  There are no such hearts on earth.

'Ye drew one mother's milk,
  One chamber held ye all;
A very tender history
  Did in your childhood fall.

'Ye cannot unlock your heart,
  The key is gone with them;
The silent organ loudest chants
  The master's requiem.'

Brahma

If the red slayer think he slays,
  Or if the slain think he is slain,
They know not well the subtle ways
  I keep, and pass, and turn again.

Far or forgot to me is near;
  Shadow and sunlight are the same;
The vanished gods to me appear;
  And one to me are shame and fame.

They reckon ill who leave me out;
  When me they fly, I am the wings;
I am the doubter and the doubt,
  And I the hymn the Brahmin sings.

The strong gods pine for my abode,
  And pine in vain the sacred Seven;
But thou, meek lover of the good!
  Find me, and turn thy back on heaven.

Boston Hymn

Read in Music Hall, January 1, 1863

The word of the Lord by night
To the watching Pilgrims came,
As they sat by the seaside,
And filled their hearts with flame.

God said, I am tired of kings,
I suffer them no more;
Up to my ear the morning brings
The outrage of the poor.

Think ye I made this ball
A field of havoc and war,
Where tyrants great and tyrants small
Might harry the weak and poor?

My angel,—his name is Freedom,—
Choose him to be your king;
He shall cut pathways east and west,
And fend you with his wing.

Lo! I uncover the land
Which I hid of old time in the West,
As the sculptor uncovers the statue
When he has wrought his best;

I show Columbia, of the rocks
Which dip their foot in the seas,
And soar to the air-borne flocks
Of clouds, and the boreal fleece.

I will divide my goods;
Call in the wretch and slave:
None shall rule but the humble,
And none but Toil shall have.

I will have never a noble,
No lineage counted great;
Fishers and choppers and ploughmen
Shall constitute a state.

Go, cut down trees in the forest,
And trim the straightest boughs;
Cut down trees in the forest,
And build me a wooden house.

Call the people together,
The young men and the sires,
The digger in the harvest field,
Hireling, and him that hires;

And here in a pine state-house
They shall choose men to rule
In every needful faculty,
In church, and state, and school.

Lo, now! if these poor men
Can govern the land and sea,
And make just laws below the sun,
As planets faithful be.

And ye shall succor men;
'T is nobleness to serve;
Help them who cannot help again:
Beware from right to swerve.

I break your bonds and masterships,
And I unchain the slave:
Free be his heart and hand henceforth
As wind and wandering wave.

I cause from every creature
His proper good to flow:
As much as he is and doeth,
So much he shall bestow.

But, laying hands on another
To coin his labor and sweat,
He goes in pawn to his victim
For eternal years in debt.

To-day unbind the captive,
So only are ye unbound;
Lift up a people from the dust,
Trump of their rescue, sound!

Pay ransom to the owner,
And fill the bag to the brim.
Who is the owner? The slave is owner,
And ever was. Pay him.

O North! give him beauty for rags,
And honor, O South! for his shame;
Nevada! coin thy golden crags
With Freedom's image and name.

Up! and the dusky race
That sat in darkness long,—
Be swift their feet as antelopes,
And as behemoth strong.

Come, East and West and North,
By races, as snow-flakes,
And carry my purpose forth,
Which neither halts nor shakes.

My will fulfilled shall be,
For, in daylight or in dark,
My thunderbolt has eyes to see
His way home to the mark.

Γνωθι Σεαυτον

If thou canst bear
Strong meat of simple truth
If thou durst my words compare
With what thou thinkest in the soul's free youth

Then take this fact unto thy soul—
God dwells in thee.—
It is no metaphor nor parable
It is unknown to thousands & to thee
Yet there is God.

He is in thy world
But thy world knows him not
He is the mighty Heart
From which life's varied pulses part

Clouded & shrouded there doth sit
The Infinite
Embosomed in a man
And thou art stranger to thy guest
And know'st not what thou dost invest.
The clouds that veil his light within
Are thy thick woven webs of sin
Which his glory struggling through
Darkens to thine evil hue

Then bear thyself, o man!
Up to the scale & compass of thy guest
Soul of thy soul.
Be great as doth beseem
The ambassador who bears
The royal presence where he goes.
Give up to thy soul—
Let it have its way—
It is, I tell thee, God himself,
The selfsame One that rules the Whole
Tho' he speaks thro' thee with a stifled voice
And looks thro' thee shorn of his beams

But if thou listen to his voice
If thou obey the royal thought
It will grow clearer to thine ear
More glorious to thine eye
The clouds will burst that veil him now
And thou shalt see the Lord.

Therefore be great
Not proud, too great to be proud
Let not thine eyes rove
Peep not in corners; let thine eyes
Look straight before thee as befits
The simplicity of Power.
And in thy closet carry state
Filled with light walk therein
And as a King
Would do no treason to his own empire
So do not thou to thine.

This is the reason why thou dost recognize
Things now first revealed
Because in thee resides
The Spirit that lives in all
And thou canst learn the laws of Nature
Because its author is latent in thy breast.
And in the Word
A wise man, Daniel, is the man
In whom the Spirit of the mighty gods abides
His goodness doth permit the deity within
To appear in his own light

Therefore o happy youth
Happy if thou dost know & love this truth
Thou art unto thyself a law
And since the Soul of things is in thee
Thou needest nothing out of thee.
The law, the gospel, & the Providence,
Heaven, Hell, the Judgment, & the stores
Immeasurable of Truth & Good

All these thou must find
Within thy single mind
Or never find.
Thou art the *law*;
The *gospel* has no revelation
Of peace or hope until there is response
From the deep chambers of thy mind thereto
The rest is straw
It can reveal no truth unknown before.
The *Providence*
Thou art thyself that doth dispense
Wealth to thy work Want to thy sloth
Glory to goodness to Neglect the Moth
Thou sow'st the wind, the whirlwind reapest
Thou payest the wages
Of thy own work, through all ages.
The almighty energy within
Crowneth Virtue curseth Sin
Virtue sees by its own light
Stumbleth Sin in selfmade night.

Who approves thee doing right?
God in thee
Who condemns thee doing wrong?
God in thee
Who punishes thine evil deed?
God in thee
What is thine evil meed?
Thy worse mind, with error blind
And more prone to evil
That is, the greater hiding of the God within
The loss of peace
The terrible displeasure of this inmate
And next the consequence
More faintly as more distant wrought
Upon our outward fortunes
Which decay with vice
With virtue rise.

The selfsame God
By the same law
Makes the souls of angels glad
And the souls of devils sad

There is nothing else but God
Where e'er I look
All things hasten back to him
Light is but his shadow dim.

Shall I ask wealth or power of God who gave
An image of himself to be my Soul
As well might swilling Ocean ask a wave
Or the starred firmament a dying coal
For that which is in me lives in the whole

There is in all the sons of men
A love that in the spirit dwells
That panteth after things unseen
And tidings of the Future tells

And God hath built his altar here
To keep this fire of faith alive
And set his priests in holy fear
To speak the truth — for truth to survive.

And hither come the pensive train
Of rich & poor of young & old,
Of ardent youths untouched by pain
Of thoughtful maids & manhood bold

They seek a friend to speak the word
Already trembling on their tongue
To touch with prophet's hand the Chord
Which God in human hearts hath strung

To speak the plain reproof of sin
That sounded in the soul before
And bid them let the angels in
That knock at humble Sorrow's door.

They come to hear of faith & hope
That fill the exulting soul
They come to lift the curtain up
That hides the mortal goal

O thou sole source of hope assured
O give thy servant power
So shall he speak to us the word
Thyself dost give forevermore

I will not live out of me
I will not see with others' eyes
My good is good, my evil ill
I would be free—I cannot be
While I take things as others please to rate them
I dare attempt to lay out my own road
That which myself delights in shall be Good
That which I do not want,—indifferent,
That which I hate is Bad. That's flat
Henceforth, please God, forever I forego
The yoke of men's opinions. I will be
Lighthearted as a bird & live with God.
I find him in the bottom of my heart
I hear continually his Voice therein
And books, & priests, & worlds, I less esteem
Who says the heart's a blind guide? It is not.
My heart did never counsel me to sin
I wonder where it got its wisdom
For in the darkest maze amid the sweetest baits
Or amid horrid dangers never once
Did that gentle Angel fail of his oracle

The little needle always knows the north
The little bird remembereth his note
And this wise Seer never errs
I never taught it what it teaches me
I only follow when I act aright.
Whence then did this Omniscient Spirit come?
From God it came. It is the Deity.

He walked the streets of great New York
Full of men, the men were full of blood
Signs of power, signs of worth,
Yet all seemed trivial
As the ceaseless cry
Of the newsboys in the street
Now men do not listen after
The voice in the breast
Which makes the thunder mean
But the Great God hath departed
And they listen after Scott & Byron
I met no gods—I harboured none,
As I walked by noon & night alone
The crowded ways
And yet I found in the heart of the town
A few children of God nestling in his bosom
Not detached as all the crowd appeared
each one a sutlers boat
Cruising for private gain
But these seemed undetached united
Lovers of Love, of Truth,
And as among Indians they say
The One the One is known
So under the eaves of Wall Street
Brokers had met the Eternal
In the city of surfaces
Where I a swain became a surface
I found & worshipped Him.

Always thus neighbored well
The two contemporaries dwell
The World which by the world is known
And Wisdom seeking still its own
I walked with men
Who seemed as if they were chairs or stools
Tables or shopwindows or champagne baskets
For these they loved & were if truly seen
I walked with others of their wisdom gave me proof
Who brought the starry heaven
As near as the house roof

Shun passion, fold the hands of thrift,
Sit still, and Truth is near;
Suddenly it will uplift
Your eye-lids to the sphere,
Wait a little, you shall see
The portraiture of things to be.

Henry Wadsworth Longfellow

1807–1882

A Psalm of Life

Tell me not, in mournful numbers,
Life is but an empty dream!—
For the soul is dead that slumbers,
And things are not what they seem.

Life is real! Life is earnest!
And the grave is not its goal;
Dust thou art, to dust returnest,
Was not spoken of the soul.

Not enjoyment, and not sorrow,
  Is our destined end or way;
But to act, that each to-morrow
  Find us farther than to-day.

Art is long, and Time is fleeting,
  And our hearts, though stout and brave,
Still, like muffled drums, are beating
  Funeral marches to the grave.

In the world's broad field of battle,
  In the bivouac of Life,
Be not like dumb, driven cattle!
  Be a hero in the strife!

Trust no Future, howe'er pleasant!
  Let the dead Past bury its dead!
Act,—act in the living Present!
  Heart within, and God o'erhead!

Lives of great men all remind us
  We can make our lives sublime,
And, departing, leave behind us
  Footprints on the sands of time;

Footprints, that perhaps another,
  Sailing o'er life's solemn main,
A forlorn and shipwrecked brother,
  Seeing, shall take heart again.

Let us, then, be up and doing,
  With a heart for any fate;
Still achieving, still pursuing,
  Learn to labor and to wait.

The Bridge

I stood on the bridge at midnight,
As the clocks were striking the hour,
And the moon rose o'er the city,
Behind the dark church-tower.

I saw her bright reflection
In the waters under me,
Like a golden goblet falling
And sinking into the sea.

And far in the hazy distance
Of that lovely night in June,
The blaze of the flaming furnace
Gleamed redder than the moon.

Among the long, black rafters
The wavering shadows lay,
And the current that came from the ocean
Seemed to lift and bear them away;

As, sweeping and eddying through them,
Rose the belated tide,
And, streaming into the moonlight,
The seaweed floated wide.

And like those waters rushing
Among the wooden piers,
A flood of thoughts came o'er me
That filled my eyes with tears.

How often, oh how often,
In the days that had gone by,
I had stood on that bridge at midnight
And gazed on that wave and sky!

How often, oh how often,
I had wished that the ebbing tide

Would bear me away on its bosom
   O'er the ocean wild and wide!

For my heart was hot and restless,
   And my life was full of care,
And the burden laid upon me
   Seemed greater than I could bear.

But now it has fallen from me,
   It is buried in the sea;
And only the sorrow of others
   Throws its shadow over me.

Yet whenever I cross the river
   On its bridge with wooden piers,
Like the odor of brine from the ocean
   Comes the thought of other years.

And I think how many thousands
   Of care-encumbered men,
Each bearing his burden of sorrow,
   Have crossed the bridge since then.

I see the long procession
   Still passing to and fro,
The young heart hot and restless,
   And the old subdued and slow!

And forever and forever,
   As long as the river flows,
As long as the heart has passions,
   As long as life has woes;

The moon and its broken reflection
   And its shadows shall appear,
As the symbol of love in heaven,
   And its wavering image here.

The Jewish Cemetery at Newport

How strange it seems! These Hebrews in their graves,
  Close by the street of this fair seaport town,
Silent beside the never-silent waves,
  At rest in all this moving up and down!

The trees are white with dust, that o'er their sleep
  Wave their broad curtains in the south-wind's breath,
While underneath these leafy tents they keep
  The long, mysterious Exodus of Death.

And these sepulchral stones, so old and brown,
  That pave with level flags their burial-place,
Seem like the tablets of the Law, thrown down
  And broken by Moses at the mountain's base.

The very names recorded here are strange,
  Of foreign accent, and of different climes;
Alvares and Rivera interchange
  With Abraham and Jacob of old times.

"Blessed be God! for he created Death!"
  The mourners said, "and Death is rest and peace;"
Then added, in the certainty of faith,
  "And giveth Life that nevermore shall cease."

Closed are the portals of their Synagogue,
  No Psalms of David now the silence break,
No Rabbi reads the ancient Decalogue
  In the grand dialect the Prophets spake.

Gone are the living, but the dead remain,
  And not neglected; for a hand unseen,
Scattering its bounty, like a summer rain,
  Still keeps their graves and their remembrance green.

How came they here? What burst of Christian hate,
  What persecution, merciless and blind,
Drove o'er the sea—that desert desolate—
  These Ishmaels and Hagars of mankind?

They lived in narrow streets and lanes obscure,
  Ghetto and Judenstrass, in mirk and mire;
Taught in the school of patience to endure
  The life of anguish and the death of fire.

All their lives long, with the unleavened bread
  And bitter herbs of exile and its fears,
The wasting famine of the heart they fed,
  And slaked its thirst with marah of their tears.

Anathema maranatha! was the cry
  That rang from town to town, from street to street;
At every gate the accursed Mordecai
  Was mocked and jeered, and spurned by Christian feet.

Pride and humiliation hand in hand
  Walked with them through the world where'er they went;
Trampled and beaten were they as the sand,
  And yet unshaken as the continent.

For in the background figures vague and vast
  Of patriarchs and of prophets rose sublime,
And all the great traditions of the Past
  They saw reflected in the coming time.

And thus forever with reverted look
  The mystic volume of the world they read,
Spelling it backward, like a Hebrew book,
  Till life became a Legend of the Dead.

But ah! what once has been shall be no more!
  The groaning earth in travail and in pain
Brings forth its races, but does not restore,
  And the dead nations never rise again.

Christmas Bells

I heard the bells on Christmas Day
Their old, familiar carols play,
And wild and sweet
The words repeat
Of peace on earth, good-will to men!

And thought how, as the day had come,
The belfries of all Christendom
Had rolled along
The unbroken song
Of peace on earth, good-will to men!

Till, ringing, singing on its way,
The world revolved from night to day,
A voice, a chime,
A chant sublime
Of peace on earth, good-will to men!

Then from each black, accursed mouth
The cannon thundered in the South,
And with the sound
The carols drowned
Of peace on earth, good-will to men!

It was as if an earthquake rent
The hearth-stones of a continent,
And made forlorn
The households born
Of peace on earth, good-will to men!

And in despair I bowed my head;
"There is no peace on earth," I said;
"For hate is strong,
And mocks the song
Of peace on earth, good-will to men!"

Then pealed the bells more loud and deep:
"God is not dead; nor doth he sleep!
    The Wrong shall fail,
    The Right prevail,
With peace on earth, good-will to men!"

My Cathedral

Like two cathedral towers these stately pines
  Uplift their fretted summits tipped with cones;
  The arch beneath them is not built with stones,
  Not Art but Nature traced these lovely lines,
And carved this graceful arabesque of vines;
  No organ but the wind here sighs and moans,
  No sepulchre conceals a martyr's bones,
  No marble bishop on his tomb reclines.
Enter! the pavement, carpeted with leaves,
  Gives back a softened echo to thy tread!
  Listen! the choir is singing; all the birds,
In leafy galleries beneath the eaves,
  Are singing! listen, ere the sound be fled,
  And learn there may be worship without words.

John Greenleaf Whittier

1807–1892

First-Day Thoughts

In calm and cool and silence, once again
  I find my old accustomed place among
  My brethren, where, perchance, no human tongue
  Shall utter words; where never hymn is sung,
  Nor deep-toned organ blown, nor censer swung,
Nor dim light falling through the pictured pane!
There, syllabled by silence, let me hear
The still small voice which reached the prophet's ear;

Read in my heart a still diviner law
Than Israel's leader on his tables saw!
There let me strive with each besetting sin,
   Recall my wandering fancies, and restrain
   The sore disquiet of a restless brain;
   And, as the path of duty is made plain,
May grace be given that I may walk therein,
   Not like the hireling, for his selfish gain,
With backward glances and reluctant tread,
Making a merit of his coward dread,—
   But, cheerful, in the light around me thrown,
   Walking as one to pleasant service led;
   Doing God's will as if it were my own,
Yet trusting not in mine, but in His strength alone!

The Eternal Goodness

O friends! with whom my feet have trod
   The quiet aisles of prayer,
Glad witness to your zeal for God
   And love of man I bear.

I trace your lines of argument;
   Your logic linked and strong
I weigh as one who dreads dissent,
   And fears a doubt as wrong.

But still my human hands are weak
   To hold your iron creeds;
Against the words ye bid me speak
   My heart within me pleads.

Who fathoms the Eternal Thought?
   Who talks of scheme and plan?
The Lord is God! He needeth not
   The poor device of man.

I walk with bare, hushed feet the ground
 Ye tread with boldness shod;
I dare not fix with mete and bound
 The love and power of God.

Ye praise His justice; even such
 His pitying love I deem:
Ye seek a king; I fain would touch
 The robe that hath no seam.

Ye see the curse which overbroods
 A world of pain and loss;
I hear our Lord's beatitudes
 And prayer upon the cross.

More than your schoolmen teach, within
 Myself, alas! I know;
Too dark ye cannot paint the sin,
 Too small the merit show.

I bow my forehead to the dust,
 I veil mine eyes for shame,
And urge, in trembling self-distrust,
 A prayer without a claim.

I see the wrong that round me lies,
 I feel the guilt within;
I hear, with groan and travail-cries,
 The world confess its sin.

Yet, in the maddening maze of things,
 And tossed by storm and flood,
To one fixed stake my spirit clings:
 I know that God is good!

Not mine to look where cherubim
 And seraphs may not see,
But nothing can be good in Him
 Which evil is in me.

The wrong that pains my soul below
   I dare not throne above:
I know not of His hate,—I know
   His goodness and His love.

I dimly guess from blessings known
   Of greater out of sight,
And, with the chastened Psalmist, own
   His judgments too are right.

I long for household voices gone,
   For vanished smiles I long,
But God hath led my dear ones on,
   And He can do no wrong.

I know not what the future hath
   Of marvel or surprise,
Assured alone that life and death
   His mercy underlies.

And if my heart and flesh are weak
   To bear an untried pain,
The bruised reed He will not break,
   But strengthen and sustain.

No offering of my own I have,
   Nor works my faith to prove;
I can but give the gifts He gave,
   And plead His love for love.

And so beside the Silent Sea
   I wait the muffled oar;
No harm from Him can come to me
   On ocean or on shore.

I know not where His islands lift
   Their fronded palms in air;
I only know I cannot drift
   Beyond His love and care.

O brothers! if my faith is vain,
 If hopes like these betray,
Pray for me that my feet may gain
 The sure and safer way.

And Thou, O Lord! by whom are seen
 Thy creatures as they be,
Forgive me if too close I lean
 My human heart on Thee!

Unity

Forgive, O Lord, our severing ways,
The separate altars that we raise,
The varying tongues that speak Thy praise!

Suffice it now. In time to be
Shall one great temple rise to Thee,
Thy church our broad humanity.

White flowers of love its walls shall climb,
Sweet bells of peace shall ring its chime,
Its days shall all be holy time.

The hymn, long sought, shall then be heard,
The music of the world's accord,
Confessing Christ, the inward word!

That song shall swell from shore to shore,
One faith, one love, one hope restore
The seamless garb that Jesus wore!

Oliver Wendell Holmes

1809–1894

The Chambered Nautilus

This is the ship of pearl, which, poets feign,
  Sails the unshadowed main,—
  The venturous bark that flings
On the sweet summer wind its purpled wings
In gulfs enchanted, where the siren sings,
  And coral reefs lie bare,
Where the cold sea-maids rise to sun their streaming hair.

Its webs of living gauze no more unfurl;
  Wrecked is the ship of pearl!
  And every chambered cell,
Where its dim dreaming life was wont to dwell,
As the frail tenant shaped his growing shell,
  Before thee lies revealed,—
Its irised ceiling rent, its sunless crypt unsealed!

Year after year beheld the silent toil
  That spread his lustrous coil;
  Still, as the spiral grew,
He left the past year's dwelling for the new,
Stole with soft step its shining archway through,
  Built up its idle door,
Stretched in his last-found home, and knew the old no more.

Thanks for the heavenly message brought by thee,
  Child of the wandering sea,
  Cast from her lap forlorn!
From thy dead lips a clearer note is born
Than ever Triton blew from wreathèd horn!
  While on mine ear it rings,
Through the deep caves of thought I hear a voice that sings:—

Build thee more stately mansions, O my soul,
As the swift seasons roll!
Leave thy low-vaulted past!
Let each new temple, nobler than the last,
Shut thee from heaven with a dome more vast,
Till thou at length art free,
Leaving thine outgrown shell by life's unresting sea!

The Living Temple

Not in the world of light alone,
Where God has built his blazing throne,
Nor yet alone in earth below,
With belted seas that come and go,
And endless isles of sunlit green,
Is all thy Maker's glory seen:
Look in upon thy wondrous frame,—
Eternal wisdom still the same!

The smooth, soft air with pulse-like waves
Flows murmuring through its hidden caves,
Whose streams of brightening purple rush
Fired with a new and livelier blush,
While all their burden of decay
The ebbing current steals away,
And red with Nature's flame they start
From the warm fountains of the heart.

No rest that throbbing slave may ask,
Forever quivering o'er his task,
While far and wide a crimson jet
Leaps forth to fill the woven net
Which in unnumbered crossing tides
The flood of burning life divides,
Then kindling each decaying part
Creeps back to find the throbbing heart.

But warmed with that unchanging flame
Behold the outward moving frame,
Its living marbles jointed strong
With glistening band and silvery thong,
And linked to reason's guiding reins
By myriad rings in trembling chains,
Each graven with the threaded zone
Which claims it as the master's own.

See how yon beam of seeming white
Is braided out of seven-hued light,
Yet in those lucid globes no ray
By any chance shall break astray.
Hark how the rolling surge of sound,
Arches and spirals circling round,
Wakes the hushed spirit through thine ear
With music it is heaven to hear.

Then mark the cloven sphere that holds
All thought in its mysterious folds,
That feels sensation's faintest thrill
And flashes forth the sovereign will;
Think on the stormy world that dwells
Locked in its dim and clustering cells!
The lightning gleams of power it sheds
Along its hollow glassy threads!

O Father! grant thy love divine
To make these mystic temples thine!
When wasting age and wearying strife
Have sapped the leaning walls of life,
When darkness gathers over all,
And the last tottering pillars fall,
Take the poor dust thy mercy warms
And mould it into heavenly forms!

Edmund Hamilton Sears

1810–1876

It came upon the midnight clear,
  That glorious song of old,
From angels bending near the earth
  To touch their harps of gold;
"Peace on the earth, good will to men
  From heaven's all-gracious King"—
The world in solemn stillness lay
  To hear the angels sing.

Still through the cloven skies they come
  With peaceful wings unfurled,
And still their heavenly music floats
  O'er all the weary world;
Above its sad and lowly plains
  They bend on hovering wing,
And ever o'er its Babel-sounds
  The blessed angels sing.

But with the woes of sin and strife
  The world has suffered long;
Beneath the angel-strain have rolled
  Two thousand years of wrong;
And man, at war with man, hears not
  The love-song which they bring;—
Oh hush the noise, ye men of strife,
  And hear the angels sing!

And ye, beneath life's crushing load,
  Whose forms are bending low,
Who toil along the climbing way
  With painful steps and slow,
Look now! for glad and golden hours
  Come swiftly on the wing;—
Oh, rest beside the weary road
  And hear the angels sing!

For lo! the days are hastening on
  By prophet bards foretold,
When with the ever circling years
  Comes round the age of gold;
When Peace shall over all the earth
  Its ancient splendors fling,
And the whole world give back the song
  Which now the angels sing.

Christopher Pearse Cranch

1813–1892

Correspondences

All things in nature are beautiful types to the soul that can read
  them;
Nothing exists upon earth, but for unspeakable ends,
Every object that speaks to the senses was meant for the spirit;
Nature is but a scroll; God's handwriting thereon.
Ages ago when man was pure, ere the flood overwhelmed him,
While in the image of God every soul yet lived,
Every thing stood as a letter or word of a language familiar,
Telling of truths which now only the angels can read.
Lost to man was the key of those sacred hieroglyphics,
Stolen away by sin, till by heaven restored.
Now with infinite pains we here and there spell out a letter,
Here and there will the sense feebly shine through the dark.
When we perceive the light that breaks through the visible
  symbol,
What exultation is ours! *We* the discovery have made!
Yet is the meaning the same as when Adam lived sinless in Eden,
Only long hidden it slept, and now again is revealed.
Man unconsciously uses figures of speech every moment,
Little dreaming the cause why to such terms he is prone,

Little dreaming that every thing here has its own correspondence
Folded within its form, as in the body the soul.
Gleams of the mystery fall on us still, though much is forgotten,
And through our commonest speech, illumine the path of our
thoughts.

Thus doth the lordly sun shine forth a type of the Godhead;
Wisdom and love the beams that stream on a darkened world.
Thus do the sparkling waters flow, giving joy to the desert,
And the fountain of life opens itself to the thirst.
Thus doth the word of God distil like the rain and the
dew-drops;
Thus doth the warm wind breathe like to the Spirit of God;
And the green grass and the flowers are signs of the
regeneration.

O thou Spirit of Truth, visit our minds once more,
Give us to read in letters of light the language celestial
Written all over the earth, written all over the sky—
Thus may we bring our hearts once more to know our Creator,
Seeing in all things around, types of the Infinite Mind.

Enosis

Thought is deeper than all speech,
Feeling deeper than all thought;
Souls to souls can never teach
What unto themselves was taught.

We are spirits clad in veils;
Man by man was never seen;
All our deep communing fails
To remove the shadowy screen.

Heart to heart was never known;
Mind with mind did never meet;
We are columns left alone,
Of a temple once complete.

Like the stars that gem the sky,
   Far apart, though seeming near,
In our light we scattered lie;
   All is thus but starlight here.

What is social company
   But a babbling summer stream?
What our wise philosophy
   But the glancing of a dream?

Only when the sun of love
   Melts the scattered stars of thought;
Only when we live above
   What the dim-eyed world hath taught;

Only when our souls are fed
   By the Fount which gave them birth,
And by inspiration led,
   Which they never drew from earth,

We like parted drops of rain
   Swelling till they meet and run,
Shall be all absorbed again,
   Melting, flowing into one.

Jones Very

1813–1880

The New Birth

'Tis a new life—thoughts move not as they did
With slow uncertain steps across my mind,
In thronging haste fast pressing on they bid
The portals open to the viewless wind;
That comes not, save when in the dust is laid
The crown of pride that gilds each mortal brow,
And from before man's vision melting fade

The heavens and earth—Their walls are falling now—
Fast crowding on each thought claims utterance strong,
Storm-lifted waves swift rushing to the shore
On from the sea they send their shouts along,
Back through the cave-worn rocks their thunders roar,
And I a child of God by Christ made free
Start from death's slumbers to eternity.

Enoch

I looked to find a man who walked with God,
Like the translated patriarch of old;—
Though gladdened millions on his footstool trod,
Yet none with him did such sweet converse hold;
I heard the wind in low complaint go by
That none his melodies like him could hear;
Day unto day spoke wisdom from on high.
Yet none like David turned a willing ear;
God walked alone unhonored through the earth;
For him no heart-built temple open stood,
The soul forgetful of her nobler birth
Had hewn him lofty shrines of stone and wood,
And left unfinished and in ruins still
The only temple he delights to fill.

The Cup

The bitterness of death is on me now,
Before me stands its dark unclosing door;
Yet to thy will submissive still I bow,
And follow him who for me went before;
The tomb cannot contain me though I die,
For his strong love awakes its sleeping dead;
And bids them through himself ascend on high,
To Him who is of all the living Head;
I gladly enter through the gloomy walls,
Where they have passed who loved their master here;

The voice they heard, to me it onward calls,
And can when faint my sinking spirit cheer;
And from the joy on earth it now has given,
Lead on to joy eternal in the heaven.

The New World

The night that has no star lit up by God,
The day that round men shines who still are blind,
The earth their grave-turned feet for ages trod,
And sea swept over by His mighty wind;
All these have passed away; the melting dream
That flitted o'er the sleeper's half-shut eye,
When touched by morning's golden-darting beam;
And he beholds around the earth and sky
That ever real stands; the rolling spheres,
And heaving billows of the boundless main,
That show though time is past no trace of years,
And earth restored he sees as his again;
The earth that fades not, and the heavens that stand;
Their strong foundations laid by God's right hand!

The Created

There is nought for thee by thy haste to gain;
'Tis not the swift with Me that win the race;
Through long endurance of delaying pain,
Thine opened eye shall see thy Father's face;
Nor here nor there, where now thy feet would turn,
Thou wilt find Him who ever seeks for thee;
But let obedience quench desires that burn,
And where thou art, thy Father too will be!
Behold! as day by day the spirit grows,
Thou see'st by inward light things hid before;
Till what God is, thyself, his image, shows;
And thou dost wear the robe that first thou wore,
When bright with radiance from his forming hand,
He saw thee Lord of all his creatures stand.

Yourself

'Tis to yourself I speak; you cannot know
Him whom I call in speaking such an one,
For thou beneath the earth liest buried low,
Which he alone as living walks upon;
Thou mayst at times have heard him speak to you,
And often wished perchance that you were he;
And I must ever wish that it were true,
For then thou couldst hold fellowship with me;
But now thou hearst us talk as strangers, met
Above the room wherein thou liest abed;
A word perhaps loud spoken thou mayst get,
Or hear our feet when heavily they tread;
But he who speaks, or him who's spoken to,
Must both remain as strangers still to you.

The Cottage

The house my earthly parent left,
My heavenly Father e'er throws down;
For 'tis of air and sun bereft,
Nor stars its roof in beauty crown.

He gave it me, yet gave it not,
As one whose gifts are wise and good:
'Twas but a poor and clay-built cot,
And for a time the storms withstood;

But lengthening years, and frequent rain,
O'ercame its strength, it tottered, fell;
And left me homeless here again,
And where to go I could not tell.

But soon the light and open air,
Received me as a wandering child;
And I soon thought their house more fair,
And was from all my grief beguiled.

Mine was the grove, the pleasant field,
Where dwelt the flowers I daily trod;
And there beside them too I kneeled,
And called their friend, my Father, God.

Autumn Flowers

Still blooming on, when Summer-flowers all fade,
The golden rods and asters fill the glade;
The tokens they of an Exhaustless Love,
That ever to the end doth constant prove.

To one fair tribe another still succeeds,
As still the heart new forms of beauty needs;
Till these, bright children of the waning year!
Its latest born have come our souls to cheer.

They glance upon us from their fringed eyes,
And to their look our own in love replies;
Within our hearts we find for them a place,
As for the flowers, which early Spring-time grace.

Despond not traveller! on life's lengthened way,
When all thy early friends have passed away;
Say not, "No more the beautiful doth live,
And to the earth a bloom and fragrance give."

To every season has our Father given
Some tokens of his love to us from heaven;
Nor leaves us here, uncheered, to walk alone,
When all we loved and prized, in youth, has gone.

Let but thy heart go forth to all around,
Still by thy side the beautiful is found;
Along thy path the Autumn flowers shall smile,
And to its close life's pilgrimage beguile.

The Origin of Man

I.

Man has forgot his Origin; in vain
He searches for the record of his race
In ancient books, or seeks with toil to gain
From the deep cave, or rocks some primal trace.
And some have fancied, from a higher sphere,
Forgetful of his origin he came;
To dwell awhile a wandering exile here
Subject to sense, another, yet the same.

With mind bewildered, weak how should he know
The Source Divine from whom his being springs?
The darkened spirit does its shadow throw
On written record, and on outward things;
That else might plainly to his thought reveal
The wondrous truths, which now they but conceal.

II.

Not suffering for their sins in former state,
As some have taught, their system to explain;
Nor hither sent, as by the sport of fate,
Souls that nor memory, nor love retain,
Do men into this world of nature come;
But born of God; though earthy, frail and weak;
Not all unconscious of a heavenly home,
Which they through trial, suffering, here must seek.
A heavenly Guide has come the way to show,
To lead us to the Father's house above;
From Him he came, to Him, he said, I go;
Oh may we heed the message of his love!
That we no more in darkness, doubt, may roam,
But find while here we dwell our heavenly home.

Night

I thank thee, Father, that the night is near
When I this conscious being may resign;
Whose only task thy words of love to hear,
And in thy acts to find each act of mine;
A task too great to give a child like me,
Thy myriad-handed labors of the day
Too many for my closing eyes to see,
Thy words too frequent for my tongue to say;
Yet when thou see'st me burthened by thy love
Each other gift more lovely then appears,
For dark-robed night comes hovering from above
And all thine other gifts to me endears;
And while within her darkened couch I sleep,
Thine eyes untired above will constant vigils keep.

William Ellery Channing

1818–1901

Hymn of the Earth

My highway is unfeatured air,
My consorts are the sleepless Stars,
And men, my giant arms upbear,
My arms unstained and free from scars.

I rest forever on my way,
Rolling around the happy Sun,
My children love the sunny day,
But noon and night to me are one.

My heart has pulses like their own,
I am their Mother, and my veins
Though built of the enduring stone,
Thrill as do theirs with godlike pains.

The forests and the mountains high,
The foaming ocean and the springs,
The plains,—O pleasant Company,
My voice through all your anthem rings.

Ye are so cheerful in your minds,
Content to smile, content to share,
My being in your Chorus finds
The echo of the spheral air.

No leaf may fall, no pebble roll,
No drop of water lose the road,
The issues of the general Soul
Are mirrored in its round abode.

Henry David Thoreau

1817–1862

Sic Vita

I am a parcel of vain strivings tied
By a chance bond together,
Dangling this way and that, their links
Were made so loose and wide,
Methinks,
For milder weather.

A bunch of violets without their roots,
And sorrel intermixed,
Encircled by a wisp of straw
Once coiled about their shoots,
The law
By which I'm fixed.

A nosegay which Time clutched from out
Those fair Elysian fields,
With weeds and broken stems, in haste,

Doth make the rabble rout
That waste
The day he yields.

And here I bloom for a short hour unseen,
Drinking my juices up,
Which have no root in the land
To keep my branches green,
But stand
In a bare cup.

Some tender buds were left upon my stem
In mimicry of life,
But ah! the children will not know
Till time has withered them,
The woe
With which they're rife.

But now I see I was not plucked for nought,
And after in life's vase
Of glass set while I might survive,
But by a kind hand brought
Alive
To a strange place.

That stock thus thinned will soon redeem its hours,
And by another year
Such as God knows, with freer air,
More fruits and fairer flowers
Will bear,
While I droop here.

Music

Far from this atmosphere that music sounds
Bursting some azure chink in the dull clouds
Of sense that overarch my recent years
And steal his freshness from the noonday sun.

Ah, I have wandered many ways and lost
The boyant step, the whole responsive life
That stood with joy to hear what seemed then
Its echo, its own harmony borne back
Upon its ear. This tells of better space,
Far far beyond the hills the woods the clouds
That bound my low and plodding valley life,
Far from my sin, remote from my distrust,
When first my healthy morning life perchance
Trod lightly as on clouds, and not as yet
My weary and faint hearted noon had sunk
Upon the clod while the bright day went by.
    Lately, I feared my life was empty, now
I know though a frail tenement that it still
Is worth repair, if yet its hollowness
Doth entertain so fine a guest within, and through
Its empty aisles there still doth ring
Though but the echo of so high a strain;
It shall be swept again and cleansed from sin
To be a thoroughfare for celestial airs;
Perchance the God who is proprietor
Will pity take on his poor tenant here
And countenance his efforts to improve
His property and make it worthy to revert,
At some late day Unto himself again.

Inspiration

Whate'er we leave to God, God does,
    And blesses us;
The work we choose should be our own,
    God lets alone.

—

If with light head erect I sing,
Though all the muses lend their force,
From my poor love of anything,
The verse is weak and shallow as its source.

—

But if with bended neck I grope,
Listening behind me for my wit,
With faith superior to hope,
More anxious to keep back than forward it,

—

Making my soul accomplice there
Unto the flame my heart hath lit,
Then will the verse forever wear,
Time cannot bend the line which God hath writ.

—

Always the general show of things
Floats in review before my mind,
And such true love and reverence brings,
That sometimes I forget that I am blind.

—

But soon there comes unsought, unseen,
Some clear divine electuary,
And I, who had but sensual been,
Grow sensible, and as God is am wary.

—

I hearing get who had but ears,
And sight who had but eyes before,
I moments live who lived but years,
And truth discern who knew but learning's lore.

—

I hear beyond the range of sound,
I see beyond the verge of sight,
New earths—new skies—new seas—around,
And in my noon the sun doth pale his light.

—

A clear and ancient harmony
Pierces my soul through all its din,
As through its utmost melody,
Further behind than they, further within.

—

More swift its bolt than lightning is,
Its voice than thunder is more loud,
It doth expand my privacies
To all, and leave me single in the crowd.

—

It speaks with such authority,
With so serene and lofty tone,
That idle Time runs gadding by,
And leaves me with Eternity alone.

—

Then chiefly is my natal hour,
And only then my prime of life,
Of manhood's strength it is the flower,
'T is peace's end and wars beginning strife.

—

'T hath come in summer's broadest noon,
By a grey wall or some chance place,
Unseasoned time, insulted June,
And vexed the day with its presuming face.

—

Such fragrance round my sleep it makes,
More rich than are Arabian drugs,
That my soul scents its life, and wakes
The body up—from 'neath its perfumed rugs.

—

—

Such is the Muse—the heavenly maid,
The star that guides our mortal course,
Which shows where life's true kernel's laid,
Its wheat's fine flower, and its undying force.

—

Who with one breath attunes the spheres,
And also my poor human heart,
With one impulse propels the years
Around, and gives my throbbing pulse its start.

—

I will not doubt forever more,
Nor falter from an iron faith,
For if the system be turned oer,
God takes not back the word which once he saith.

—

I will believe the love untold,
Which not my worth nor want hath bought,
Which wood me young and woos me old,
And call the stars to witness now my thought.

—

My memory I'll educate
To know the one historic truth,
Remembering to the latest date
The only true, and sole immortal youth.

—

Be but thy inspiration given,
No matter through what dangers sought,
I'll fathom hell or climb to heaven,
And yet esteem that cheap which love has bought.

Fame cannot tempt the bard
  Who's famous with his God,
  Nor laurel him reward,
  Who hath his maker's nod.

Julia Ward Howe

1819–1910

Battle-Hymn of the Republic

Mine eyes have seen the glory of the coming of the Lord:
He is trampling out the vintage where the grapes of wrath are
    stored;
He hath loosed the fateful lightning of his terrible swift sword:
        His truth is marching on.

I have seen Him in the watch-fires of a hundred circling camps;
They have builded Him an altar in the evening dews and damps;
I can read His righteous sentence by the dim and flaring lamps.
        His day is marching on.

I have read a fiery gospel, writ in burnished rows of steel:
"As ye deal with my contemners, so with you my grace shall deal;
Let the Hero, born of woman, crush the serpent with his heel,
        Since God is marching on."

He has sounded forth the trumpet that shall never call retreat;
He is sifting out the hearts of men before his judgment-seat:
Oh! be swift, my soul, to answer Him! be jubilant, my feet!
Our God is marching on.

In the beauty of the lilies Christ was born across the sea,
With a glory in his bosom that transfigures you and me:
As he died to make men holy, let us die to make men free,
While God is marching on.

James Russell Lowell

1819–1891

After the Burial

Yes, Faith is a goodly anchor;
When skies are sweet as a psalm,
At the bows it lolls so stalwart,
In bluff, broad-shouldered calm.

And when over breakers to leeward
The tattered surges are hurled,
It may keep our head to the tempest,
With its grip on the base of the world.

But, after the shipwreck, tell me
What help in its iron thews,
Still true to the broken hawser,
Deep down among sea-weed and ooze?

In the breaking gulfs of sorrow,
When the helpless feet stretch out
And find in the deeps of darkness
No footing so solid as doubt,

Then better one spar of Memory,
One broken plank of the Past,
That our human heart may cling to,
Though hopeless of shore at last!

To the spirit its splendid conjectures,
To the flesh its sweet despair,
Its tears o'er the thin-worn locket
With its anguish of deathless hair!

Immortal? I feel it and know it,
Who doubts it of such as she?
But that is the pang's very secret,—
Immortal away from me.

There's a narrow ridge in the graveyard
Would scarce stay a child in his race,
But to me and my thought it is wider
Than the star-sown vague of Space.

Your logic, my friend, is perfect,
Your morals most drearily true;
But, since the earth clashed on *her* coffin,
I keep hearing that, and not you.

Console if you will, I can bear it;
'T is a well-meant alms of breath;
But not all the preaching since Adam
Has made Death other than Death.

It is pagan; but wait till you feel it,—
That jar of our earth, that dull shock
When the ploughshare of deeper passion
Tears down to our primitive rock.

Communion in spirit ! Forgive me,
But I, who am earthy and weak,
Would give all my incomes from dreamland
For a touch of her hand on my cheek.

That little shoe in the corner,
So worn and wrinkled and brown,
With its emptiness confutes you,
And argues your wisdom down.

Herman Melville

1819–1891

FROM *Moby-Dick*

The ribs and terrors in the whale,
  Arched over me a dismal gloom,
While all God's sun-lit waves rolled by,
  And left me deepening down to doom.

I saw the opening maw of hell,
  With endless pains and sorrows there;
Which none but they that feel can tell—
  Oh, I was plunging to despair.

In black distress, I called my God,
  When I could scarce believe him mine,
He bowed his ear to my complaints—
  No more the whale did me confine.

With speed he flew to my relief,
  As on a radiant dolphin borne;
Awful, yet bright, as lightning shone
  The face of my Deliverer God.

My song for ever shall record
  That terrible, that joyful hour;
I give the glory to my God,
  His all the mercy and the power.

FROM *Clarel: A Poem and Pilgrimage in the Holy Land*

EPILOGUE

If Luther's day expand to Darwin's year,
Shall that exclude the hope—foreclose the fear?

Unmoved by all the claims our times avow,
The ancient Sphinx still keeps the porch of shade;
And comes Despair, whom not her calm may cow,
And coldly on that adamantine brow
Scrawls undeterred his bitter pasquinade.
But Faith (who from the scrawl indignant turns)
With blood warm oozing from her wounded trust,
Inscribes even on her shards of broken urns
The sign o' the cross—*the spirit above the dust!*

Yea, ape and angel, strife and old debate—
The harps of heaven and dreary gongs of hell;
Science the feud can only aggravate—
No umpire she betwixt the chimes and knell:
The running battle of the star and clod
Shall run forever—if there be no God.

Degrees we know, unknown in days before;
The light is greater, hence the shadow more;
And tantalized and apprehensive Man
Appealing—Wherefore ripen us to pain?
Seems there the spokesman of dumb Nature's train.
But through such strange illusions have they passed
Who in life's pilgrimage have baffled striven—
Even death may prove unreal at the last,
And stoics be astounded into heaven.

Then keep thy heart, though yet but ill-resigned—
Clarel, thy heart, the issues there but mind;
That like the crocus budding through the snow—
That like a swimmer rising from the deep—
That like a burning secret which doth go

Even from the bosom that would hoard and keep;
Emerge thou mayst from the last whelming sea,
And prove that death but routs life into victory.

Part IV: Bethlehem, Canto 35

The Enthusiast

"Though he slay me yet will I trust in him."

Shall hearts that beat no base retreat
  In youth's magnanimous years—
Ignoble hold it, if discreet
  When interest tames to fears;
Shall spirits that worship light
  Perfidious deem its sacred glow,
  Recant, and trudge where worldlings go,
Conform and own them right?

Shall Time with creeping influence cold
  Unnerve and cow? the heart
Pine for the heartless ones enrolled
  With palterers of the mart?
Shall faith abjure her skies,
  Or pale probation blench her down
  To shrink from Truth so still, so lone
Mid loud gregarious lies?

Each burning boat in Caesar's rear,
  Flames—No return through me!
So put the torch to ties though dear,
  If ties but tempters be.
Nor cringe if come the night:
  Walk through the cloud to meet the pall,
  Though light forsake thee, never fall
From fealty to light.

Fragments of a Lost Gnostic Poem of the 12th Century

* * * *

Found a family, build a state,
The pledged event is still the same:
Matter in end will never abate
His ancient brutal claim.

* * * *

Indolence is heaven's ally here,
And energy the child of hell:
The Good Man pouring from his pitcher clear
But brims the poisoned well.

Pontoosuce

Crowning a bluff where gleams the lake below,
Some pillared pines in well-spaced order stand
And like an open temple show.
And here in best of seasons bland,
Autumnal noon-tide, I look out
From dusk arcades on sunshine all about.

Beyond the Lake, in upland cheer
Fields, pastoral fields, and barns appear,
They skirt the hills where lonely roads
Revealed in links through tiers of woods
Wind up to indistinct abodes
And faery-peopled neighborhoods;
While further fainter mountains keep
Hazed in romance impenetrably deep.

Look, corn in stacks, on many a farm,
And orchards ripe in languorous charm,
As dreamy Nature, feeling sure
Of all her genial labor done,
And the last mellow fruitage won,
Would idle out her term mature;

Reposing like a thing reclined
In kinship with man's meditative mind.

For me, within the brown arcade—
Rich life, methought; sweet here in shade
And pleasant abroad in air!—But, nay,
A counter thought intrusive played,
A thought as old as thought itself,
And who shall lay it on the shelf!—
I felt the beauty bless the day
In opulence of autumn's dower;
But evanescence will not stay!
A year ago was such an hour
As this, which but foreruns the blast
Shall sweep these live leaves to the dead leaves past.

All dies!—
                    I stood in revery long.
Then, to forget death's ancient wrong,
I turned me in the brown arcade,
And there by chance in lateral glade
I saw low tawny mounds in lines
Relics of trunks of stately pines
Ranked erst in colonnades where, lo!
Erect succeeding pillars show!

All dies! and not alone
The aspiring trees and men and grass;
The poet's forms of beauty pass,
And noblest deeds they are undone.
Even truth itself decays, and lo,
From truth's sad ashes fraud and falsehood grow.
All dies!
The workman dies, and, after him, the work;
Like to these pines whose graves I trace,
Statue and statuary fall upon their face:
In very amaranths the worm doth lurk,
Even stars, Chaldæans say, have left their place.
Andes and Apalachee tell

Of havoc ere our Adam fell,
And present Nature as a moss doth show
On the ruins of the Nature of the æons of long ago.

But look—and hark!
                                        Adown the glade,
Where light and shadow sport at will,
Who cometh vocal, and arrayed
As in the first pale tints of morn—
So pure, rose-clear, and fresh and chill!
Some ground-pine sprigs her brow adorn,
The earthy rootlets tangled clinging.
Over tufts of moss which dead things made,
Under vital twigs which danced or swayed,
Along she floats, and lightly singing:

"Dies, all dies!
The grass it dies, but in vernal rain
Up it springs and it lives again;
Over and over, again and again
It lives, it dies and it lives again.
Who sighs that all dies?
Summer and winter, and pleasure and pain
And everything everywhere in God's reign,
They end, and anon they begin again:
Wane and wax, wax and wane:
Over and over and over amain
End, ever end, and begin again—
End, ever end, and forever and ever begin again!"
She ceased, and nearer slid, and hung
In dewy guise; then softlier sung:
"Since light and shade are equal set
And all revolves, nor more ye know;
Ah, why should tears the pale cheek fret
For aught that waneth here below.
Let go, let go!"

With that, her warm lips thrilled me through,
She kissed me, while her chaplet cold

Its rootlets brushed against my brow
With all their humid clinging mould.
She vanished, leaving fragrant breath
And warmth and chill of wedded life and death.

Walt Whitman

1819–1892

In vain were nails driven through my hands.
I remember my crucifixion and bloody coronation
I remember the mockers and the buffeting insults
The sepulchre and the white linen have yielded me up
I am alive in New York and San Francisco,
Again I tread the streets after two thousand years.
Not all the traditions can put vitality in churches
They are not alive, they are cold mortar and brick,
I can easily build as good, and so can you:—
Books are not men—

FROM *Song of Myself*

4

Trippers and askers surround me,
People I meet, the effect upon me of my early life or the ward
    and city I live in, or the nation,
The latest dates, discoveries, inventions, societies, authors old
    and new,
My dinner, dress, associates, looks, compliments, dues,
The real or fancied indifference of some man or woman I love,
The sickness of one of my folks or of myself, or ill-doing or loss
    or lack of money, or depressions or exaltations,
Battles, the horrors of fratricidal war, the fever of doubtful news,
    the fitful events;
These come to me days and nights and go from me again,
But they are not the Me myself.

Apart from the pulling and hauling stands what I am,
Stands amused, complacent, compassionating, idle, unitary,
Looks down, is erect, or bends an arm on an impalpable certain rest,
Looking with side-curved head curious what will come next,
Both in and out of the game and watching and wondering at it.

Backward I see in my own days where I sweated through fog with linguists and contenders,
I have no mockings or arguments, I witness and wait.

5

I believe in you my soul, the other I am must not abase itself to you,
And you must not be abased to the other.

Loafe with me on the grass, loose the stop from your throat,
Not words, not music or rhyme I want, not custom or lecture, not even the best,
Only the lull I like, the hum of your valvèd voice.

I mind how once we lay such a transparent summer morning,
How you settled your head athwart my hips and gently turn'd over upon me,
And parted the shirt from my bosom-bone, and plunged your tongue to my bare-stript heart,
And reach'd till you felt my beard, and reach'd till you held my feet.

Swiftly arose and spread around me the peace and knowledge that pass all the argument of the earth,
And I know that the hand of God is the promise of my own,
And I know that the spirit of God is the brother of my own,
And that all the men ever born are also my brothers, and the women my sisters and lovers,
And that a kelson of the creation is love,
And limitless are leaves stiff or drooping in the fields,

And brown ants in the little wells beneath them,
And mossy scabs of the worm fence, heap'd stones, elder, mullein and poke-weed.

25

Dazzling and tremendous how quick the sun-rise would kill me,
If I could not now and always send sun-rise out of me.

We also ascend dazzling and tremendous as the sun,
We found our own O my soul in the calm and cool of the day-break.

My voice goes after what my eyes cannot reach,
With the twirl of my tongue I encompass worlds and volumes of worlds.

Speech is the twin of my vision, it is unequal to measure itself,
It provokes me forever, it says sarcastically,
Walt you contain enough, why don't you let it out then?

Come now I will not be tantalized, you conceive too much of articulation,
Do you not know O speech how the buds beneath you are folded?
Waiting in gloom, protected by frost,
The dirt receding before my prophetical screams,
I underlying causes to balance them at last,
My knowledge my live parts, it keeping tally with the meaning of all things,
Happiness, (which whoever hears me let him or her set out in search of this day.)

My final merit I refuse you, I refuse putting from me what I really am,
Encompass worlds, but never try to encompass me,
I crowd your sleekest and best by simply looking toward you.

Writing and talk do not prove me,
I carry the plenum of proof and every thing else in my face,
With the hush of my lips I wholly confound the skeptic.

43

I do not despise you priests, all time, the world over,
My faith is the greatest of faiths and the least of faiths,
Enclosing worship ancient and modern and all between ancient and modern,
Believing I shall come again upon the earth after five thousand years,
Waiting responses from oracles, honoring the gods, saluting the sun,
Making a fetich of the first rock or stump, powowing with sticks in the circle of obis,
Helping the llama or brahmin as he trims the lamps of the idols,
Dancing yet through the streets in a phallic procession, rapt and austere in the woods a gymnosophist,
Drinking mead from the skull-cup, to Shastas and Vedas admirant, minding the Koran,
Walking the teokallis, spotted with gore from the stone and knife, beating the serpent-skin drum,
Accepting the Gospels, accepting him that was crucified, knowing assuredly that he is divine,
To the mass kneeling or the puritan's prayer rising, or sitting patiently in a pew,
Ranting and frothing in my insane crisis, or waiting dead-like till my spirit arouses me,
Looking forth on pavement and land, or outside of pavement and land,
Belonging to the winders of the circuit of circuits.

One of that centripetal and centrifugal gang I turn and talk like a man leaving charges before a journey.

Down-hearted doubters dull and excluded,
Frivolous, sullen, moping, angry, affected, dishearten'd, atheistical,

I know every one of you, I know the sea of torment, doubt,
despair and unbelief.

How the flukes splash!
How they contort rapid as lightning, with spasms and spouts of
blood!

Be at peace bloody flukes of doubters and sullen mopers,
I take my place among you as much as among any,
The past is the push of you, me, all, precisely the same,
And what is yet untried and afterward is for you, me, all,
precisely the same.

I do not know what is untried and afterward,
But I know it will in its turn prove sufficient, and cannot fail.

Each who passes is consider'd, each who stops is consider'd, not a
single one can it fail.

It cannot fail the young man who died and was buried,
Nor the young woman who died and was put by his side,
Nor the little child that peep'd in at the door, and then drew back
and was never seen again,
Nor the old man who has lived without purpose, and feels it with
bitterness worse than gall,
Nor him in the poor house tubercled by rum and the bad
disorder,
Nor the numberless slaughter'd and wreck'd, nor the brutish
koboo call'd the ordure of humanity,
Nor the sacs merely floating with open mouths for food to slip
in,
Nor any thing in the earth, or down in the oldest graves of the
earth,
Nor any thing in the myriads of spheres, nor the myriads of
myriads that inhabit them,
Nor the present, nor the least wisp that is known.

52

The spotted hawk swoops by and accuses me, he complains of
 my gab and my loitering.

I too am not a bit tamed, I too am untranslatable,
I sound my barbaric yawp over the roofs of the world.

The last scud of day holds back for me,
It flings my likeness after the rest and true as any on the
 shadow'd wilds,
It coaxes me to the vapor and the dusk.

I depart as air, I shake my white locks at the runaway sun,
I effuse my flesh in eddies, and drift it in lacy jags.

I bequeath myself to the dirt to grow from the grass I love,
If you want me again look for me under your boot-soles.

You will hardly know who I am or what I mean,
But I shall be good health to you nevertheless,
And filter and fibre your blood.

Failing to fetch me at first keep encouraged,
Missing me one place search another,
I stop somewhere waiting for you.

FROM *Crossing Brooklyn Ferry*

9

Flow on, river! flow with the flood-tide, and ebb with the
 ebb-tide!
Frolic on, crested and scallop-edg'd waves!
Gorgeous clouds of the sunset! drench with your splendor me,
 or the men and women generations after me!
Cross from shore to shore, countless crowds of passengers!

Stand up, tall masts of Mannahatta! stand up, beautiful hills of
Brooklyn!
Throb, baffled and curious brain! throw out questions and
answers!
Suspend here and everywhere, eternal float of solution!
Gaze, loving and thirsting eyes, in the house or street or public
assembly!
Sound out, voices of young men! loudly and musically call me by
my nighest name!
Live, old life! play the part that looks back on the actor or actress!
Play the old role, the role that is great or small according as one
makes it!
Consider, you who peruse me, whether I may not in unknown
ways be looking upon you;
Be firm, rail over the river, to support those who lean idly, yet
haste with the hasting current;
Fly on, sea-birds! fly sideways, or wheel in large circles high in
the air;
Receive the summer sky, you water, and faithfully hold it till all
downcast eyes have time to take it from you!
Diverge, fine spokes of light, from the shape of my head, or any
one's head, in the sunlit water!
Come on, ships from the lower bay! pass up or down, white-sail'd
schooners, sloops, lighters!
Flaunt away, flags of all nations! be duly lower'd at sunset!
Burn high your fires, foundry chimneys! cast black shadows at
nightfall! cast red and yellow light over the tops of the
houses!
Appearances, now or henceforth, indicate what you are,
You necessary film, continue to envelop the soul,
About my body for me, and your body for you, be hung out
divinest aromas,
Thrive, cities—bring your freight, bring your shows, ample and
sufficient rivers,
Expand, being than which none else is perhaps more spiritual,
Keep your places, objects than which none else is more lasting.

You have waited, you always wait, you dumb, beautiful ministers,
We receive you with free sense at last, and are insatiate
henceforward,
Not you any more shall be able to foil us, or withhold yourselves
from us,
We use you, and do not cast you aside—we plant you
permanently within us,
We fathom you not—we love you—there is perfection in you
also,
You furnish your parts toward eternity,
Great or small, you furnish your parts toward the soul.

As I Ebb'd with the Ocean of Life

I

As I ebb'd with the ocean of life,
As I wended the shores I know,
As I walk'd where the ripples continually wash you Paumanok,
Where they rustle up hoarse and sibilant,
Where the fierce old mother endlessly cries for her castaways,
I musing late in the autumn day, gazing off southward,
Held by this electric self out of the pride of which I utter poems,
Was seiz'd by the spirit that trails in the lines underfoot,
The rim, the sediment that stands for all the water and all the
land of the globe.

Fascinated, my eyes reverting from the south, dropt, to follow
those slender windrows,
Chaff, straw, splinters of wood, weeds, and the sea-gluten,
Scum, scales from shining rocks, leaves of salt-lettuce, left by the
tide,
Miles walking, the sound of breaking waves the other side of
me,
Paumanok there and then as I thought the old thought of
likenesses,
These you presented to me you fish-shaped island,

As I wended the shores I know,
As I walk'd with that electric self seeking types.

2

As I wend to the shores I know not,
As I list to the dirge, the voices of men and women wreck'd,
As I inhale the impalpable breezes that set in upon me,
As the ocean so mysterious rolls toward me closer and closer,
I too but signify at the utmost a little wash'd-up drift,
A few sands and dead leaves to gather,
Gather, and merge myself as part of the sands and drift.

O baffled, balk'd, bent to the very earth,
Oppress'd with myself that I have dared to open my mouth,
Aware now that amid all that blab whose echoes recoil upon me I have not once had the least idea who or what I am,
But that before all my arrogant poems the real Me stands yet untouch'd, untold, altogether unreach'd,
Withdrawn far, mocking me with mock-congratulatory signs and bows,
With peals of distant ironical laughter at every word I have written,
Pointing in silence to these songs, and then to the sand beneath.

I perceive I have not really understood any thing, not a single object, and that no man ever can,
Nature here in sight of the sea taking advantage of me to dart upon me and sting me,
Because I have dared to open my mouth to sing at all.

3

You oceans both, I close with you,
We murmur alike reproachfully rolling sands and drift, knowing not why,
These little shreds indeed standing for you and me and all.

You friable shore with trails of debris,
You fish-shaped island, I take what is underfoot,
What is yours is mine my father.

I too Paumanok,
I too have bubbled up, floated the measureless float, and been
wash'd on your shores,
I too am but a trail of drift and debris,
I too leave little wrecks upon you, you fish-shaped island.

I throw myself upon your breast my father,
I cling to you so that you cannot unloose me,
I hold you so firm till you answer me something.

Kiss me my father,
Touch me with your lips as I touch those I love,
Breathe to me while I hold you close the secret of the
murmuring I envy.

4

Ebb, ocean of life, (the flow will return,)
Cease not your moaning you fierce old mother,
Endlessly cry for your castaways, but fear not, deny not me,
Rustle not up so hoarse and angry against my feet as I touch you
or gather from you.

I mean tenderly by you and all,
I gather for myself and for this phantom looking down where we
lead, and following me and mine.

Me and mine, loose windrows, little corpses,
Froth, snowy white, and bubbles,
(See, from my dead lips the ooze exuding at last,
See, the prismatic colors glistening and rolling,)
Tufts of straw, sands, fragments,
Buoy'd hither from many moods, one contradicting another,
From the storm, the long calm, the darkness, the swell,
Musing, pondering, a breath, a briny tear, a dab of liquid or soil,

Up just as much out of fathomless workings fermented and
thrown,
A limp blossom or two, torn, just as much over waves floating,
drifted at random,
Just as much for us that sobbing dirge of Nature,
Just as much whence we come that blare of the cloud-trumpets,
We, capricious, brought hither we know not whence, spread out
before you,
You up there walking or sitting,
Whoever you are, we too lie in drifts at your feet.

When Lilacs Last in the Dooryard Bloom'd

1

When lilacs last in the dooryard bloom'd,
And the great star early droop'd in the western sky in the night,
I mourn'd, and yet shall mourn with ever-returning spring.

Ever-returning spring, trinity sure to me you bring,
Lilac blooming perennial and drooping star in the west,
And thought of him I love.

2

O powerful western fallen star!
O shades of night—O moody, tearful night!
O great star disappear'd—O the black murk that hides the star!
O cruel hands that hold me powerless—O helpless soul of me!
O harsh surrounding cloud that will not free my soul.

3

In the dooryard fronting an old farm-house near the white-
wash'd palings,
Stands the lilac-bush tall-growing with heart-shaped leaves of
rich green,

With many a pointed blossom rising delicate, with the perfume
strong I love,
With every leaf a miracle—and from this bush in the dooryard,
With delicate-color'd blossoms and heart-shaped leaves of rich
green,
A sprig with its flower I break.

4

In the swamp in secluded recesses,
A shy and hidden bird is warbling a song.

Solitary the thrush,
The hermit withdrawn to himself, avoiding the settlements,
Sings by himself a song.

Song of the bleeding throat,
Death's outlet song of life, (for well dear brother I know,
If thou wast not granted to sing thou would'st surely die.)

5

Over the breast of the spring, the land, amid cities,
Amid lanes and through old woods, where lately the violets
peep'd from the ground, spotting the gray debris,
Amid the grass in the fields each side of the lanes, passing the
endless grass,
Passing the yellow-spear'd wheat, every grain from its shroud in
the dark-brown fields uprisen,
Passing the apple-tree blows of white and pink in the orchards,
Carrying a corpse to where it shall rest in the grave,
Night and day journeys a coffin.

6

Coffin that passes through lanes and streets,
Through day and night with the great cloud darkening the land,
With the pomp of the inloop'd flags with the cities draped in
black,

With the show of the States themselves as of crape-veil'd women standing,
With processions long and winding and the flambeaus of the night,
With the countless torches lit, with the silent sea of faces and the unbared heads,
With the waiting depot, the arriving coffin, and the sombre faces,
With dirges through the night, with the thousand voices rising strong and solemn,
With all the mournful voices of the dirges pour'd around the coffin,
The dim-lit churches and the shuddering organs—where amid these you journey,
With the tolling tolling bells' perpetual clang,
Here, coffin that slowly passes,
I give you my sprig of lilac.

7

(Nor for you, for one alone,
Blossoms and branches green to coffins all I bring,
For fresh as the morning, thus would I chant a song for you O sane and sacred death.

All over bouquets of roses,
O death, I cover you over with roses and early lilies,
But mostly and now the lilac that blooms the first,
Copious I break, I break the sprigs from the bushes,
With loaded arms I come, pouring for you,
For you and the coffins all of you O death.)

8

O western orb sailing the heaven,
Now I know what you must have meant as a month since I walk'd,
As I walk'd in silence the transparent shadowy night,
As I saw you had something to tell as you bent to me night after night,

As you droop'd from the sky low down as if to my side, (while
the other stars all look'd on,)
As we wander'd together the solemn night, (for something I
know not what kept me from sleep,)
As the night advanced, and I saw on the rim of the west how full
you were of woe,
As I stood on the rising ground in the breeze in the cool
transparent night,
As I watch'd where you pass'd and was lost in the netherward
black of the night,
As my soul in its trouble dissatisfied sank, as where you sad orb,
Concluded, dropt in the night, and was gone.

9

Sing on there in the swamp,
O singer bashful and tender, I hear your notes, I hear your call,
I hear, I come presently, I understand you,
But a moment I linger, for the lustrous star has detain'd me,
The star my departing comrade holds and detains me.

10

O how shall I warble myself for the dead one there I loved?
And how shall I deck my song for the large sweet soul that has
gone?
And what shall my perfume be for the grave of him I love?

Sea-winds blown from east and west,
Blown from the Eastern sea and blown from the Western sea, till
there on the prairies meeting,
These and with these and the breath of my chant,
I'll perfume the grave of him I love.

11

O what shall I hang on the chamber walls?
And what shall the pictures be that I hang on the walls,
To adorn the burial-house of him I love?

Pictures of growing spring and farms and homes,
With the Fourth-month eve at sundown, and the gray smoke lucid and bright,
With floods of the yellow gold of the gorgeous, indolent, sinking sun, burning, expanding the air,
With the fresh sweet herbage under foot, and the pale green leaves of the trees prolific,
In the distance the flowing glaze, the breast of the river, with a wind-dapple here and there,
With ranging hills on the banks, with many a line against the sky, and shadows,
And the city at hand with dwellings so dense, and stacks of chimneys,
And all the scenes of life and the workshops, and the workmen homeward returning.

12

Lo, body and soul—this land,
My own Manhattan with spires, and the sparkling and hurrying tides, and the ships,
The varied and ample land, the South and the North in the light, Ohio's shores and flashing Missouri,
And ever the far-spreading prairies cover'd with grass and corn.

Lo, the most excellent sun so calm and haughty,
The violet and purple morn with just-felt breezes,
The gentle soft-born measureless light,
The miracle spreading bathing all, the fulfill'd noon,
The coming eve delicious, the welcome night and the stars,
Over my cities shining all, enveloping man and land.

13

Sing on, sing on you gray-brown bird,
Sing from the swamps, the recesses, pour your chant from the bushes,
Limitless out of the dusk, out of the cedars and pines.

Sing on dearest brother, warble your reedy song,
Loud human song, with voice of uttermost woe.

O liquid and free and tender!
O wild and loose to my soul—O wondrous singer!
You only I hear—yet the star holds me, (but will soon depart,)
Yet the lilac with mastering odor holds me.

14

Now while I sat in the day and look'd forth,
In the close of the day with its light and the fields of spring, and the farmers preparing their crops,
In the large unconscious scenery of my land with its lakes and forests,
In the heavenly aerial beauty, (after the perturb'd winds and the storms,)
Under the arching heavens of the afternoon swift passing, and the voices of children and women,
The many-moving sea-tides, and I saw the ships how they sail'd,
And the summer approaching with richness, and the fields all busy with labor,
And the infinite separate houses, how they all went on, each with its meals and minutia of daily usages,
And the streets how their throbbings throbb'd, and the cities pent—lo, then and there,
Falling upon them all and among them all, enveloping me with the rest,
Appear'd the cloud, appear'd the long black trail,
And I knew death, its thought, and the sacred knowledge of death.

Then with the knowledge of death as walking one side of me,
And the thought of death close-walking the other side of me,
And I in the middle as with companions, and as holding the hands of companions,
I fled forth to the hiding receiving night that talks not,
Down to the shores of the water, the path by the swamp in the dimness,
To the solemn shadowy cedars and ghostly pines so still.

And the singer so shy to the rest receiv'd me,
The gray-brown bird I know receiv'd us comrades three,
And he sang the carol of death, and a verse for him I love.

From deep secluded recesses,
From the fragrant cedars and the ghostly pines so still,
Came the carol of the bird.

And the charm of the carol rapt me,
As I held as if by their hands my comrades in the night,
And the voice of my spirit tallied the song of the bird.

Come lovely and soothing death,
Undulate round the world, serenely arriving, arriving,
In the day, in the night, to all, to each,
Sooner or later delicate death.

Prais'd be the fathomless universe,
For life and joy, and for objects and knowledge curious,
And for love, sweet love—but praise! praise! praise!
For the sure-enwinding arms of cool-enfolding death.

Dark mother always gliding near with soft feet,
Have none chanted for thee a chant of fullest welcome?
Then I chant it for thee, I glorify thee above all,
I bring thee a song that when thou must indeed come, come
unfalteringly.

Approach strong deliveress,
When it is so, when thou hast taken them I joyously sing the dead,
Lost in the loving floating ocean of thee,
Laved in the flood of thy bliss O death.

From me to thee glad serenades,
Dances for thee I propose saluting thee, adornments and feastings for
thee,
And the sights of the open landscape and the high-spread sky are
fitting,
And life and the fields, and the huge and thoughtful night.

The night in silence under many a star,
The ocean shore and the husky whispering wave whose voice I know,
And the soul turning to thee O vast and well-veil'd death,
And the body gratefully nestling close to thee.

Over the tree-tops I float thee a song,
Over the rising and sinking waves, over the myriad fields and the prairies wide,
Over the dense-pack'd cities all and the teeming wharves and ways,
I float this carol with joy, with joy to thee O death.

15

To the tally of my soul,
Loud and strong kept up the gray-brown bird,
With pure deliberate notes spreading filling the night.

Loud in the pines and cedars dim,
Clear in the freshness moist and the swamp-perfume,
And I with my comrades there in the night.

While my sight that was bound in my eyes unclosed,
As to long panoramas of visions.

And I saw askant the armies,
I saw as in noiseless dreams hundreds of battle-flags,
Borne through the smoke of the battles and pierc'd with missiles I saw them,
And carried hither and yon through the smoke, and torn and bloody,
And at last but a few shreds left on the staffs, (and all in silence,)
And the staffs all splinter'd and broken.

I saw battle-corpses, myriads of them,
And the white skeletons of young men, I saw them,
I saw the debris and debris of all the slain soldiers of the war,
But I saw they were not as was thought,
They themselves were fully at rest, they suffer'd not,

The living remain'd and suffer'd, the mother suffer'd,
And the wife and the child and the musing comrade suffer'd,
And the armies that remain'd suffer'd.

16

Passing the visions, passing the night,
Passing, unloosing the hold of my comrades' hands,
Passing the song of the hermit bird and the tallying song of my
soul,
Victorious song, death's outlet song, yet varying ever-altering
song,
As low and wailing, yet clear the notes, rising and falling,
flooding the night,
Sadly sinking and fainting, as warning and warning, and yet
again bursting with joy,
Covering the earth and filling the spread of the heaven,
As that powerful psalm in the night I heard from recesses,
Passing, I leave thee lilac with heart-shaped leaves,
I leave thee there in the door-yard, blooming, returning with
spring.

I cease from my song for thee,
From my gaze on thee in the west, fronting the west,
communing with thee,
O comrade lustrous with silver face in the night.

Yet each to keep and all, retrievements out of the night,
The song, the wondrous chant of the gray-brown bird,
And the tallying chant, the echo arous'd in my soul,
With the lustrous and drooping star with the countenance full of
woe,
With the holders holding my hand nearing the call of the bird,
Comrades mine and I in the midst, and their memory ever to
keep, for the dead I loved so well,
For the sweetest, wisest soul of all my days and lands—and this
for his dear sake,
Lilac and star and bird twined with the chant of my soul,
There in the fragrant pines and the cedars dusk and dim.

As Adam Early in the Morning

As Adam early in the morning,
Walking forth from the bower refresh'd with sleep,
Behold me where I pass, hear my voice, approach,
Touch me, touch the palm of your hand to my body as I pass,
Be not afraid of my body.

Chanting the Square Deific

1

Chanting the square deific, out of the One advancing, out of the sides,
Out of the old and new, out of the square entirely divine,
Solid, four-sided, (all the sides needed,) from this side Jehovah am I,
Old Brahm I, and I Saturnius am;
Not Time affects me—I am Time, old, modern as any,
Unpersuadable, relentless, executing righteous judgments,
As the Earth, the Father, the brown old Kronos, with laws,
Aged beyond computation, yet ever new, ever with those mighty laws rolling,
Relentless I forgive no man—whoever sins dies—I will have that man's life;
Therefore let none expect mercy—have the seasons, gravitation, the appointed days, mercy? no more have I,
But as the seasons and gravitation, and as all the appointed days that forgive not,
I dispense from this side judgments inexorable without the least remorse.

2

Consolator most mild, the promis'd one advancing,
With gentle hand extended, the mightier God am I,
Foretold by prophets and poets in their most rapt prophecies and poems,

From this side, lo! the Lord Christ gazes—lo! Hermes I—lo! mine
is Hercules' face,
All sorrow, labor, suffering, I, tallying it, absorb in myself,
Many times have I been rejected, taunted, put in prison, and
crucified, and many times shall be again,
All the world have I given up for my dear brothers' and sisters'
sake, for the soul's sake,
Wending my way through the homes of men, rich or poor, with
the kiss of affection,
For I am affection, I am the cheer-bringing God, with hope and
all-enclosing charity,
With indulgent words as to children, with fresh and sane words,
mine only,
Young and strong I pass knowing well I am destin'd myself to an
early death;
But my charity has no death—my wisdom dies not, neither early
nor late,
And my sweet love bequeath'd here and elsewhere never dies.

3

Aloof, dissatisfied, plotting revolt,
Comrade of criminals, brother of slaves,
Crafty, despised, a drudge, ignorant,
With sudra face and worn brow, black, but in the depths of my
heart, proud as any,
Lifted now and always against whoever scorning assumes to rule
me,
Morose, full of guile, full of reminiscences, brooding, with many
wiles,
(Though it was thought I was baffled and dispel'd, and my wiles
done, but that will never be,)
Defiant, I, Satan, still live, still utter words, in new lands duly
appearing, (and old ones also,)
Permanent here from my side, warlike, equal with any, real as
any,
Nor time nor change shall ever change me or my words.

4

Santa Spirita, breather, life,
Beyond the light, lighter than light,
Beyond the flames of hell, joyous, leaping easily above hell,
Beyond Paradise, perfumed solely with mine own perfume,
Including all life on earth, touching, including God, including
Saviour and Satan,
Ethereal, pervading all, (for without me what were all? what
were God?)
Essence of forms, life of the real identities, permanent, positive,
(namely the unseen,)
Life of the great round world, the sun and stars, and of man, I,
the general soul,
Here the square finishing, the solid, I the most solid,
Breathe my breath also through these songs.

A Noiseless Patient Spider

A noiseless patient spider,
I mark'd where on a little promontory it stood isolated,
Mark'd how to explore the vacant vast surrounding,
It launch'd forth filament, filament, filament, out of itself,
Ever unreeling them, ever tirelessly speeding them.

And you O my soul where you stand,
Surrounded, detached, in measureless oceans of space,
Ceaselessly musing, venturing, throwing, seeking the spheres to
connect them,
Till the bridge you will need be form'd, till the ductile anchor
hold,
Till the gossamer thread you fling catch somewhere, O my soul.

Frederick Goddard Tuckerman

1821–1873

Sonnets

I.

The starry flower, the flower-like stars that fade
And brighten with the daylight and the dark,—
The bluet in the green I faintly mark,
And glimmering crags with laurel overlaid,
Even to the Lord of light, the Lamp of shade,
Shine one to me,—the least, still glorious made
As crownèd moon, or heaven's great hierarch.
And, so, dim grassy flower, and night-lit spark,
Still move me on and upward for the True;
Seeking through change, growth, death, in new and old.
The full in few, the statelier in the less,
With patient pain; always remembering this,—
His hand, who touched the sod with showers of gold,
Stippled Orion on the midnight blue.

II.

And so, as this great sphere (now turning slow
Up to the light from that abyss of stars,
Now wheeling into gloom through sunset bars)—
With all its elements of form and flow,
And life in life; where crowned, yet blind, must go
The sensible king,—is but an Unity
Compressed of motes impossible to know;
Which worldlike yet in deep analogy,
Have distance, march, dimension, and degree;
So the round earth—which we the world do call—
Is but a grain in that that mightiest swells,
Whereof the stars of light are particles,
As ultimate atoms of one infinite Ball,
On which God moves, and treads beneath his feet the All!

Not the round natural world, not the deep mind,
The reconcilement holds: the blue abyss
Collects it not; our arrows sink amiss
And but in Him may we our import find.
The agony to know, the grief, the bliss
Of toil, is vain and vain: clots of the sod
Gathered in heat and haste and flung behind
To blind ourselves and others, what but this
Still grasping dust and sowing toward the wind?
No more thy meaning seek, thine anguish plead.
But leaving straining thought and stammering word,
Across the barren azure pass to God:
Shooting the void in silence like a bird,
A bird that shuts his wings for better speed.

Robert Lowry

1826–1899

Beautiful River

"And he showed me a pure River of Water of Life, clear as crystal, proceeding out of the Throne of God and of the Lamb."
—Rev. xxii. 1.

Shall we gather at the river
  Where bright angel feet have trod;
With its crystal tide forever
    Flowing by the throne of God?

Yes, we'll gather at the river,
The beautiful, the beautiful river—
Gather with the saints at the river
That flows by the throne of God.

On the margin of the river,
  Washing up its silver spray,
We will walk and worship ever,
  All the happy, golden day.

Chorus

On the bosom of the river,
  Where the Saviour-king we own,
We shall meet, and sorrow never
  'Neath the glory of the throne.

Chorus

Ere we reach the shining river,
  Lay we every burden down;
Grace our spirits will deliver,
  And provide a robe and crown.

Chorus

At the smiling of the river,
  Rippling with the Saviour's face,
Saints, whom death will never sever,
  Lift their songs of saving grace.

Chorus

Soon we'll reach the shining river,
  Soon our pilgrimage will cease,
Soon our happy hearts will quiver
  With the melody of peace.

Chorus

Emily Dickinson

1830–1886

I got so I could take his name –
Without – Tremendous gain –
That Stop-sensation – on my Soul –
And Thunder – in the Room –

I got so I could walk across
That Angle in the floor,
Where he turned so, and I turned – how –
And all our Sinew tore –

I got so I could stir the Box –
In which his letters grew
Without that forcing, in my breath –
As Staples – driven through –

Could dimly recollect a Grace –
I think, they called it "God" –
Renowned to ease Extremity –
When Formula, had failed –

And shape my Hands –
Petition's way,
Tho' ignorant of a word
That Ordination – utters –

My Business – with the Cloud,
If any Power behind it, be,
Not subject to Despair –
It care – in some remoter way,
For so minute affair
As Misery –
Itself, too vast, for interrupting – more –

I felt a Funeral, in my Brain,
And Mourners to and fro
Kept treading – treading – till it seemed
That Sense was breaking through –

And when they all were seated,
A Service, like a Drum –
Kept beating – beating – till I thought
My mind was going numb –

And then I heard them lift a Box
And creak across my Soul
With those same Boots of Lead, again,
Then Space – began to toll,

As all the Heavens were a Bell,
And Being, but an Ear,
And I, and Silence, some strange Race
Wrecked, solitary, here –

And then a Plank in Reason, broke,
And I dropped down, and down –
And hit a World, at every plunge,
And Finished knowing – then –

I know that He exists.
Somewhere – in silence –
He has hid his rare life
From our gross eyes.

'Tis an instant's play –
'Tis a fond Ambush –
Just to make Bliss
Earn her own surprise!

But – should the play
Prove piercing earnest –
Should the glee – glaze –
In Death's – stiff – stare –

Would not the fun
Look too expensive!
Would not the jest –
Have crawled too far!

After great pain, a formal feeling comes –
The Nerves sit ceremonious, like Tombs –
The stiff Heart questions 'was it He, that bore,'
And 'Yesterday, or Centuries before'?

The Feet, mechanical, go round –
A Wooden way
Of Ground, or Air, or Ought –
Regardless grown,
A Quartz contentment, like a stone –

This is the Hour of Lead –
Remembered, if outlived,
As Freezing persons, recollect the Snow –
First – Chill – then Stupor – then the letting go –

Dare you see a Soul at the "White Heat"?
Then crouch within the door –
Red – is the Fire's common tint –
But when the vivid Ore

Has vanquished Flame's conditions –
It quivers from the Forge

Without a color, but the Light
Of unannointed Blaze –

Least Village, boasts it's Blacksmith –
Whose Anvil's even ring
Stands symbol for the finer Forge
That soundless tugs – within –

Refining these impatient Ores
With Hammer, and with Blaze
Until the designated Light
Repudiate the Forge –

Our journey had advanced –
Our feet were almost come
To that odd Fork in Being's Road –
Eternity – by Term –

Our pace took sudden awe –
Our feet – reluctant – led –
Before – were Cities – but Between –
The Forest of the Dead –

Retreat – was out of Hope –
Behind – a Sealed Route
Eternity's White Flag – Before –
And God – at every Gate –

It might be lonelier
Without the Loneliness –
I'm so accustomed to my Fate –
Perhaps the Other – Peace –

Would interrupt the Dark –
And crowd the little Room –
Too scant – by Cubits – to contain
The Sacrament – of Him –

I am not used to Hope –
It might intrude upon –
It's sweet parade – blaspheme the place –
Ordained to Suffering –

It might be easier
To fail – with Land in Sight –
Than gain – my Blue Peninsula –
To perish – of Delight –

I heard a Fly buzz – when I died –
The Stillness in the Room
Was like the Stillness in the Air –
Between the Heaves of Storm –

The Eyes around – had wrung them dry –
And Breaths were gathering firm
For that last Onset – when the King
Be witnessed – in the Room –

I willed my Keepsakes – Signed away
What portion of me be
Assignable – and then it was
There interposed a Fly –

With Blue – uncertain – stumbling Buzz –
Between the light – and me –
And then the Windows failed – and then
I could not see to see –

To pile like Thunder to it's close
Then crumble grand away
While everything created hid
This – would be Poetry –

Or Love – the two coeval come –
We both and neither prove –
Experience either and consume –
For none see God and live –

"Heavenly Father" – take to thee
The supreme iniquity
Fashioned by thy candid Hand
In a moment contraband –
Though to trust us – seem to us
More respectful – "We are Dust" –
We apologize to thee
For thine own Duplicity –

The Spirit lasts – but in what mode –
Below, the Body speaks,
But as the Spirit furnishes –
Apart, it never talks –
The Music in the Violin
Does not emerge alone
But Arm in Arm with Touch, yet Touch
Alone – is not a Tune –
The Spirit lurks within the Flesh
Like Tides within the Sea
That make the Water live, estranged
What would the Either be?
Does that know – now – or does it cease –
That which to this is done,

Resuming at a mutual date
With every future one?
Instinct pursues the Adamant,
Exacting this Reply,
Adversity if it may be, or wild Prosperity,
The Rumor's Gate was shut so tight
Before my Mind was sown,
Not even a Prognostic's Push
Could make a Dent thereon –

My life closed twice before it's close;
It yet remains to see
If Immortality unveil
A third event to me,

So huge, so hopeless to conceive
As these that twice befell.
Parting is all we know of heaven,
And all we need of hell.

Helen Hunt Jackson

1830–1885

A Last Prayer

Father, I scarcely dare to pray,
So clear I see, now it is done,
That I have wasted half my day,
And left my work but just begun;

So clear I see that things I thought
Were right or harmless were a sin;
So clear I see that I have sought,
Unconscious, selfish aims to win;

So clear I see that I have hurt
  The souls I might have helped to save;
That I have slothful been, inert,
  Deaf to the calls thy leaders gave.

In outskirts of thy kingdoms vast,
  Father, the humblest spot give me;
Set me the lowliest task thou hast;
  Let me repentant work for thee!

Knowles Shaw

1834–1878

Sowing in the Morning

Sowing in the morning, sowing seeds of kindness,
Sowing in the noontide and the dewy eve;
Waiting for the harvest and the time of reaping,
We shall come rejoicing, bringing in the sheaves.

Bringing in the sheaves, bringing in the sheaves,
We shall come rejoicing, bringing in the sheaves;
Bringing in the sheaves, bringing in the sheaves,
We shall come rejoicing, bringing in the sheaves.

Sowing in the sunshine, sowing in the shadows,
Fearing neither clouds nor winter's chilling breeze;
By and by the harvest, and the labor ended,
We shall come rejoicing, bringing in the sheaves.

Chorus

Going forth with weeping, sowing for the Master,
Tho' the loss sustained our spirit often grieves;
When our weeping's over, He will bid us welcome,
We shall come rejoicing, bringing in the sheaves.

Chorus

Phillips Brooks

1835–1893

O Little Town of Bethlehem

O little town of Bethlehem!
How still we see thee lie,
Above thy deep and dreamless sleep,
The silent stars go by;
Yet in thy dark streets shineth
The Everlasting light;
The hopes and fears of all the years,
Are met in thee tonight.

For Christ is born of Mary,
And gathered all above,
While mortals sleep the angels keep
Their watch of wondering love.
O morning stars together
Proclaim the holy birth!
And praises sing to God the King,
And peace to men on earth.

How silently, how silently,
The wondrous gift is given;
So God imparts to human hearts
The blessings of his heaven.
No ear may hear his coming,
But in this world of sin,
Where meek souls will receive him still,
The dear Christ enters in.

O holy child of Bethlehem!
Descend to us, we pray,
Cast out our sin and enter in,
Be born in us to-day.
We hear the Christmas angels,

The great glad tidings tell,
O, come to us, abide with us,
Our Lord Emmanuel!

Sanford F. Bennett

1836–1898

There's a land that is fairer than day,
And by faith we can see it afar;
For the Father waits over the way,
To prepare us a dwelling place there.

In the sweet by and by,
We shall meet on that beautiful shore,
In the sweet by and by
We shall meet on that beautiful shore.

We shall sing on that beautiful shore
The melodious songs of the blest,
And our spirits shall sorrow no more
Not a sigh for the blessing of rest.

Chorus

To our bountiful Father above,
We will offer our tribute of praise,
For the glorious gift of His love,
And the blessings that hallow our days.

Chorus

William Dean Howells

1837–1920

What Shall It Profit?

If I lay waste and wither up with doubt
The blessed fields of heaven where once my faith
Possessed itself serenely safe from death;
If I deny the things past finding out;
Or if I orphan my own soul of One
That seemed a Father, and make void the place
Within me where He dwelt in power and grace,
What do I gain, that am myself undone?

Sidney Lanier

1842–1881

A Ballad of Trees and the Master

Into the woods my Master went,
Clean forspent, forspent.
Into the woods my Master came,
Forspent with love and shame.
But the olives they were not blind to Him,
The little gray leaves were kind to Him:
The thorn-tree had a mind to Him
When into the woods He came.

Out of the woods my Master went,
And He was well content.
Out of the woods my Master came,
Content with death and shame.
When Death and Shame would woo Him last,
From under the trees they drew Him last:
'Twas on a tree they slew Him—last
When out of the woods He came.

John Banister Tabb

1845–1909

Nekros

Lo! all thy glory gone!
God's masterpiece undone!
The last created and the first to fall;
The noblest, frailest, godliest of all.

Death seems the conqueror now,
And yet his victor thou;
The fatal shaft, its venom quenched in thee,
A mortal raised to immortality.

Child of the humble sod,
Wed with the breath of God,
Descend! for with the lowest thou must lie—
Arise! thou hast inherited the sky.

Communion

Once when my heart was passion-free
  To learn of things divine,
The soul of nature suddenly
  Outpoured itself in mine.

I held the secrets of the deep
  And of the heavens above;
I knew the harmonies of sleep,
  The mysteries of love.

And for a moment's interval
  The earth, the sky, the sea—
My soul encompassed, each and all,
  As now they compass me.

To one in all, to all in one—
Since love the work began—
Life's ever-widening circles run,
Revealing God and man.

Tenebrae

Whate'er my darkness be,
'T is not, O Lord, of Thee:
The light is Thine alone;
The shadows, all my own.

Emma Lazarus

1849–1887

In the Jewish Synagogue at Newport

Here, where the noises of the busy town,
The ocean's plunge and roar can enter not,
We stand and gaze around with tearful awe,
And muse upon the consecrated spot.

No signs of life are here: the very prayers
Inscribed around are in a language dead;
The light of the "perpetual lamp" is spent
That an undying radiance was to shed.

What prayers were in this temple offered up,
Wrung from sad hearts that knew no joy on earth,
By these lone exiles of a thousand years,
From the fair sunrise land that gave them birth!

Now as we gaze, in this new world of light,
Upon this relic of the days of old,
The present vanishes, and tropic bloom
And Eastern towns and temples we behold.

Again we see the patriarch with his flocks,
The purple seas, the hot blue sky o'erhead,
The slaves of Egypt,—omens, mysteries,—
Dark fleeing hosts by flaming angels led.

A wondrous light upon a sky-kissed mount,
A man who reads Jehovah's written law,
'Midst blinding glory and effulgence rare,
Unto a people prone with reverent awe.

The pride of luxury's barbaric pomp,
In the rich court of royal Solomon—
Alas! we wake: one scene alone remains,—
The exiles by the streams of Babylon.

Our softened voices send us back again
But mournful echoes through the empty hall;
Our footsteps have a strange unnatural sound,
And with unwonted gentleness they fall.

The weary ones, the sad, the suffering,
All found their comfort in the holy place,
And children's gladness and men's gratitude
Took voice and mingled in the chant of praise.

The funeral and the marriage, now, alas!
We know not which is sadder to recall;
For youth and happiness have followed age,
And green grass lieth gently over all.

Nathless the sacred shrine is holy yet,
With its lone floors where reverent feet once trod.
Take off your shoes as by the burning bush,
Before the mystery of death and God.

The New Ezekiel

What, can these dead bones live, whose sap is dried
  By twenty scorching centuries of wrong?
Is this the House of Israel, whose pride
  Is as a tale that's told, an ancient song?
Are these ignoble relics all that live
  Of psalmist, priest, and prophet? Can the breath
Of very heaven bid these bones revive,
  Open the graves and clothe the ribs of death?

Yea, Prophesy, the Lord hath said. Again
  Say to the wind, Come forth and breathe afresh,
Even that they may live upon these slain,
  And bone to bone shall leap, and flesh to flesh.
The Spirit is not dead, proclaim the word,
  Where lay dead bones, a host of armed men stand!
I ope your graves, my people, saith the Lord,
  And I shall place you living in your land.

Edwin Markham

1852–1940

In Death Valley

There came gray stretches of volcanic plains,
Bare, lone and treeless, then a bleak lone hill,
Like to the dolorous hill that Dobell saw,
Around were heaps of ruins piled between
The Burn o' Sorrow and the Water o' Care;
And from the stillness of the down-crushed walls
One pillar rose up dark against the moon.
There was a nameless Presence everywhere;
In the gray soil there was a purple stain,
And the gray reticent rocks were dyed with blood—
Blood of a vast unknown Calamity.
It was the mark of some ancestral grief—
Grief that began before the ancient Flood.

Lizette Woodworth Reese

1856–1935

Trust

I am Thy grass, O Lord!
   I grow up sweet and tall
But for a day, beneath Thy sword
   To lie at evenfall.

Yet have I not enough
   In that brief day of mine?
The wind, the bees, the wholesome stuff
   The sun pours out like wine.

Behold, this is my crown,—
   Love will not let me be;
Love holds me here; Love cuts me down;
   And it is well with me.

Lord, Love, keep it but so;
   Thy purpose is full plain:
I die that after I may grow
   As tall, as sweet again.

This Very Hour

Master, this very hour,
   Under this village sky,
Between two thieves You go,
   To die.

About our separate work,
   Ever we come and pass;
One Pilate; Andrew one;
   One scarlet Caiaphas.

Peter stoops to his bulbs,
  Under a kitchen pane;
And James halts there to talk
  Of day's luck, field or rain.

Along some brambly wall,
  Where orange haws burn hot,
His thirty coins held fast,
  Goes dark Iscariot.

Edith Wharton

1862–1937

Terminus

Wonderful was the long secret night you gave me, my Lover,
Palm to palm, breast to breast in the gloom. The faint red lamp,
Flushing with magical shadows the common-place room of the
  inn,
With its dull impersonal furniture, kindled a mystic flame
In the heart of the swinging mirror, the glass that has seen
Faces innumerous & vague of the endless travelling automata,
Whirled down the ways of the world like dust-eddies swept
  through a street,
Faces indifferent or weary, frowns of impatience or pain,
Smiles (if such there were ever) like your smile and mine when
  they met
Here, in this self-same glass, while you helped me to loosen my
  dress,
And the shadow-mouths melted to one, like sea-birds that meet
  in a wave—
Such smiles, yes, such smiles the mirror perhaps has reflected;
And the low wide bed, as rutted and worn as a high-road,
The bed with its soot-sodden chintz, the grime of its brasses,
That has borne the weight of fagged bodies, dust-stained,
  averted in sleep,

The hurried, the restless, the aimless—perchance it has also
thrilled
With the pressure of bodies ecstatic, bodies like ours,
Seeking each other's souls in the depths of unfathomed caresses,
And through the long windings of passion emerging again to the
stars . . .
Yes, all this through the room, the passive & featureless room,
Must have flowed with the rise & fall of the human unceasing
current;
And lying there hushed in your arms, as the waves of rapture
receded,
And far down the margin of being we heard the low beat of the
soul,
I was glad as I thought of those others, the nameless, the many,
Who perhaps thus had lain and loved for an hour on the brink of
the world,
Secret and fast in the heart of the whirlwind of travel,
The shaking and shrieking of trains, the night-long shudder of
traffic,
Thus, like us they have lain & felt, breast to breast in the dark,
The fiery rain of possession descend on their limbs while outside
The black rain of midnight pelted the roof of the station;
And thus some woman like me, waking alone before dawn,
While her lover slept, as I woke & heard the calm stir of your
breathing,
Some woman has heard as I heard the farewell shriek of the trains
Crying good-bye to the city & staggering out into darkness,
And shaken at heart has thought: "So must we forth in the
darkness,
Sped down the fixed rail of habit by the hand of implacable fate—
So shall we issue to life, & the rain, & the dull dark dawning;
You to the wide flare of cities, with windy garlands and shouting,
Carrying to populous places the freight of holiday throngs;
I, by waste lands, & stretches of low-skied marsh
To a harbourless wind-bitten shore, where a dull town moulders
& shrinks,
And its roofs fall in, & the sluggish feet of the hours
Are printed in grass in its streets; & between the featureless
houses

Languid the town-folk glide to stare at the entering train,
The train from which no one descends; till one pale evening of
winter,
When it halts on the edge of the town, see, the houses have
turned into grave-stones,
The streets are the grassy paths between the low roofs of the
dead;
And as the train glides in ghosts stand by the doors of the
carriages;
And scarcely the difference is felt—yea, such is the life I return
to . . ."
Thus may another have thought; thus, as I turned may have
turned
To the sleeping lips at her side, to drink, as I drank there,
oblivion. . . .

W.E.B. Du Bois

1868–1963

A Litany at Atlanta

O Silent God, Thou whose voice afar in mist and mystery hath left our ears an-hungered in these fearful days—

Hear us, good Lord!

Listen to us, Thy children: our faces dark with doubt are made a mockery in Thy Sanctuary. With uplifted hands we front Thy Heaven, O God, crying:

We beseech Thee to hear us, good Lord!

We are not better than our fellows, Lord; we are but weak and human men. When our devils do deviltry, curse Thou the doer and the deed,—curse them as we curse them, do to them all and more than ever they have done to innocence and weakness, to womanhood and home.

Have mercy upon us, miserable sinners!

And yet, whose is the deeper guilt? Who made these devils? Who nursed them in crime and fed them on injustice? Who ravished and debauched their mothers and their grandmothers?

Who bought and sold their crime and waxed fat and rich on public iniquity?

Thou knowest, good God!

Is this Thy Justice, O Father, that guile be easier than innocence and the innocent be crucified for the guilt of the untouched guilty?

Justice, O Judge of men!

Wherefore do we pray? Is not the God of the Fathers dead? Have not seers seen in Heaven's halls Thine hearsed and lifeless form stark amidst the black and rolling smoke of sin, where all along bow bitter forms of endless dead?

Awake, Thou that sleepest!

Thou art not dead, but flown afar, up hills of endless light, through blazing corridors of suns, where worlds do swing of good and gentle men, of women strong and free—far from the cozenage, black hypocrisy, and chaste prostitution of this shameful speck of dust!

Turn again, O Lord; leave us not to perish in our sin!

From lust of body and lust of blood,—

Great God, deliver us!

From lust of power and lust of gold,—

Great God, deliver us!

From the leagued lying of despot and of brute,—

Great God, deliver us!

A city lay in travail, God our Lord, and from her loins sprang twin Murder and Black Hate. Red was the midnight; clang, crack, and cry of death and fury filled the air and trembled underneath the stars where church spires pointed silently to Thee. And all this was to sate the greed of greedy men who hide behind the veil of vengeance!

Bend us Thine ear, O Lord!

In the pale, still morning we looked upon the deed. We stopped our ears and held our leaping hands, but they—did they not wag their heads and leer and cry with bloody jaws: *Cease from Crime!* The word was mockery, for thus they train a hundred crimes while we do cure one.

Turn again our captivity, O Lord!

Behold this maimed and broken thing, dear God; it was an humble black man, who toiled and sweat to save a bit from the pittance paid him. They told him: *Work and Rise!* He worked. Did this man sin? Nay, but someone told how someone said another did—one whom he had never seen nor known. Yet for that man's crime this man lieth maimed and murdered, his wife naked to shame, his children to poverty and evil.

Hear us, O heavenly Father!

Doth not this justice of hell stink in Thy nostrils, O God? How long shall the mounting flood of innocent blood roar in Thine ears and pound in our hearts for vengeance? Pile the pale frenzy of blood-crazed brutes, who do such deeds, high on Thine Altar, Jehovah Jireh, and burn it in hell forever and forever!

Forgive us, good Lord; we know not what we say!

Bewildered we are and passion-tossed, mad with the madness of a mobbed and mocked and murdered people; straining at the armposts of Thy throne, we raise our shackled hands and charge Thee, God, by the bones of our stolen fathers, by the tears of our dead mothers, by the very blood of Thy crucified Christ: What meaneth this? Tell us the plan; give us the sign!

Keep not Thou silent, O God!

Sit not longer blind, Lord God, deaf to our prayer and dumb to our dumb suffering. Surely Thou, too, art not white, O Lord, a pale, bloodless, heartless thing!

Ah! Christ of all the Pities!

Forgive the thought! Forgive these wild, blasphemous words! Thou art still the God of our black fathers and in Thy Soul's Soul sit some soft darkenings of the evening, some shadowings of the velvet night.

But whisper—speak—call, great God, for Thy silence is white terror to our hearts! The way, O God, show us the way and point us the path!

Whither? North is greed and South is blood; within, the coward, and without, the liar. Whither? To death?

Amen! Welcome, dark sleep!

Whither? To life? But not this life, dear God, not this. Let the cup pass from us, tempt us not beyond our strength, for there is that clamoring and clawing within, to whose voice we would not listen, yet shudder lest we must,—and it is red. Ah! God! It is a red and awful shape.

Selah!

In yonder East trembles a star.

Vengeance is Mine; I will repay, saith the Lord!
Thy Will, O Lord, be done!
Kyrie Eleison!
Lord, we have done these pleading, wavering words.
We beseech Thee to hear us, good Lord!
We bow our heads and hearken soft to the sobbing of women and little children.
We beseech Thee to hear us, good Lord!
Our voices sink in silence and in night.
Hear us, good Lord!
In night, O God of a godless land!
Amen!
In silence, O Silent God.
Selah!

Edwin Arlington Robinson

1869–1935

The Children of the Night

For those that never know the light,
The darkness is a sullen thing,
And they, the Children of the Night,
Seem lost in Fortune's winnowing.

But some are strong and some are weak,—
And there's the story. House and home
Are shut from countless hearts that seek
World-refuge that will never come.

And if there be no other life,
And if there be no other chance
To weigh their sorrow and their strife
Than in the scales of circumstance,

'T were better, ere the sun go down
Upon the first day we embark,
In life's imbittered sea to drown,
Than sail forever in the dark.

But if there be a soul on earth
So blinded with its own misuse
Of man's revealed, incessant worth,
Or worn with anguish, that it views

No light but for a mortal eye,
No rest but of a mortal sleep,
No God but in a prophet's lie,
No faith for "honest doubt" to keep;

If there be nothing, good or bad,
But chaos for a soul to trust,—
God counts it for a soul gone mad,
And if God be God, He is just.

And if God be God, He is Love;
And though the Dawn be still so dim,
It shows us we have played enough
With creeds that make a fiend of Him.

There is one creed, and only one,
That glorifies God's excellence;
So cherish, that His will be done,
The common creed of common sense.

It is the crimson, not the gray,
That charms the twilight of all time;
It is the promise of the day
That makes the starry sky sublime;

It is the faith within the fear
That holds us to the life we curse;—
So let us in ourselves revere
The Self which is the Universe!

Let us, the Children of the Night,
Put off the cloak that hides the scar!
Let us be Children of the Light,
And tell the ages what we are!

Karma

Christmas was in the air and all was well
With him, but for a few confusing flaws
In divers of God's images. Because
A friend of his would neither buy nor sell,
Was he to answer for the axe that fell?
He pondered; and the reason for it was,
Partly, a slowly freezing Santa Claus
Upon the corner, with his beard and bell.

Acknowledging an improvident surprise,
He magnified a fancy that he wished
The friend whom he had wrecked were here again.
Not sure of that, he found a compromise;
And from the fulness of his heart he fished
A dime for Jesus who had died for men.

James Weldon Johnson

1871–1938

The Creation

And God stepped out on space,
And he looked around and said:
I'm lonely—
I'll make me a world.

And far as the eye of God could see
Darkness covered everything,
Blacker than a hundred midnights
Down in a cypress swamp.

Then God smiled,
And the light broke,
And the darkness rolled up on one side,
And the light stood shining on the other,
And God said: That's good!

Then God reached out and took the light in his hands,
And God rolled the light around in his hands
Until he made the sun;
And he set that sun a-blazing in the heavens.
And the light that was left from making the sun
God gathered it up in a shining ball
And flung it against the darkness,
Spangling the night with the moon and stars.
Then down between
The darkness and the light
He hurled the world;
And God said: That's good!

Then God himself stepped down—
And the sun was on his right hand,
And the moon was on his left;
The stars were clustered about his head,
And the earth was under his feet.
And God walked, and where he trod
His footsteps hollowed the valleys out
And bulged the mountains up.

Then he stopped and looked and saw
That the earth was hot and barren.
So God stepped over to the edge of the world
And he spat out the seven seas—
He batted his eyes, and the lightnings flashed—
He clapped his hands, and the thunders rolled—
And the waters above the earth came down,
The cooling waters came down.

Then the green grass sprouted,
And the little red flowers blossomed,
The pine tree pointed his finger to the sky,
And the oak spread out his arms,
The lakes cuddled down in the hollows of the ground,
And the rivers ran down to the sea;
And God smiled again,
And the rainbow appeared,
And curled itself around his shoulder.

Then God raised his arm and he waved his hand
Over the sea and over the land,
And he said: Bring forth! Bring forth!
And quicker than God could drop his hand,
Fishes and fowls
And beasts and birds
Swam the rivers and the seas,
Roamed the forests and the woods,
And split the air with their wings.
And God said: That's good!

Then God walked around,
And God looked around
On all that he had made.
He looked at his sun,
And he looked at his moon,
And he looked at his little stars;
He looked on his world
With all its living things,
And God said: I'm lonely still.

Then God sat down—
On the side of a hill where he could think;
By a deep, wide river he sat down;
With his head in his hands,
God thought and thought,
Till he thought: I'll make me a man!

Up from the bed of the river
God scooped the clay;
And by the bank of the river
He kneeled him down;
And there the great God Almighty
Who lit the sun and fixed it in the sky,
Who flung the stars to the most far corner of the night,
Who rounded the earth in the middle of his hand;
This Great God,
Like a mammy bending over her baby,

Kneeled down in the dust
Toiling over a lump of clay
Till he shaped it in his own image;

Then into it he blew the breath of life,
And man became a living soul.
Amen. Amen.

Paul Laurence Dunbar

1872–1906

An Ante-Bellum Sermon

We is gathahed hyeah, my brothahs,
   In dis howlin' wildaness,
Fu' to speak some words of comfo't
   To each othah in distress.
An' we chooses fu' ouah subjic'
   Dis—we'll 'splain it by an' by;
"An' de Lawd said, 'Moses, Moses,'
   An' de man said, 'Hyeah am I.'"

Now ole Pher'oh, down in Egypt,
   Was de wuss man evah bo'n,
An' he had de Hebrew chillun
   Down dah wukin' in his co'n;
'T well de Lawd got tiahed o' his foolin',
   An' sez he: "I'll let him know—
Look hyeah, Moses, go tell Pher'oh
   Fu' to let dem chillun go."

"An' ef he refuse to do it,
   I will make him rue de houah,
Fu' I'll empty down on Egypt
   All de vials of my powah."

Yes, he did—an' Pher'oh's ahmy
  Was n't wuth a ha'f a dime;
Fu' de Lawd will he'p his chillun,
  You kin trust him evah time.

An' yo' enemies may 'sail you
  In de back an' in de front;
But de Lawd is all aroun' you,
  Fu' to ba' de battle's brunt.
Dey kin fo'ge yo' chains an' shackles
  F'om de mountains to de sea;
But de Lawd will sen' some Moses
  Fu' to set his chillun free.

An' de lan' shall hyeah his thundah,
  Lak a blas' f'om Gab'el's ho'n,
Fu' de Lawd of hosts is mighty
  When he girds his ahmor on.
But fu' feah some one mistakes me,
  I will pause right hyeah to say,
Dat I'm still a-preachin' ancient,
  I ain't talkin' 'bout to-day.

But I tell you, fellah christuns,
  Things'll happen mighty strange;
Now, de Lawd done dis fu' Isrul,
  An' his ways don't nevah change,
An' de love he showed to Isrul
  Was n't all on Isrul spent;
Now don't run an' tell yo' mastahs
  Dat I's preachin' discontent.

'Cause I isn't; I 'se a-judgin'
  Bible people by deir ac's;
I 'se a-givin' you de Scriptuah,
  I 'se a-handin' you de fac's.
Cose ole Pher'oh b'lieved in slav'ry,
  But de Lawd he let him see,

Dat de people he put bref in,—
  Evah mothah's son was free.

An' dahs othahs thinks lak Pher'oh,
  But dey calls de Scriptuah liar,
Fu' de Bible says "a servant
  Is a-worthy of his hire."
An' you cain't git roun' nor thoo dat,
  An' you cain't git ovah it,
Fu' whatevah place you git in,
  Dis hyeah Bible too'll fit.

So you see de Lawd's intention,
  Evah sence de worl' began,
Was dat His almighty freedom
  Should belong to evah man,
But I think it would be bettah,
  Ef I'd pause agin to say,
Dat I'm talkin' 'bout ouah freedom
  In a Bibleistic way.

But de Moses is a-comin',
  An' he's comin', suah and fas'
We kin hyeah his feet a-trompin',
  We kin hyeah his trumpit blas'.
But I want to wa'n you people,
  Don't you git too brigity;
An' don't you git to braggin'
  'Bout dese things, you wait an' see.

But when Moses wif his powah
  Comes an' sets us chillun free,
We will praise de gracious Mastah
  Dat has gin us liberty;
An' we'll shout ouah halleluyahs,
  On dat mighty reck'nin' day,
When we'se reco'nised ez citiz'—
  Huh uh! Chillun, let us pray!

Religion

I am no priest of crooks nor creeds,
For human wants and human needs
Are more to me than prophets' deeds;
And human tears and human cares
Affect me more than human prayers.

Go, cease your wail, lugubrious saint!
You fret high Heaven with your plaint.
Is this the "Christian's joy" you paint?
Is this the Christian's boasted bliss?
Avails your faith no more than this?

Take up your arms, come out with me,
Let Heav'n alone; humanity
Needs more and Heaven less from thee.
With pity for mankind look 'round;
Help them to rise —and Heaven is found.

Vincent O'Sullivan

1872–1940

Out of the Cloud

That fiend who tricked out like a saint
   Did haunt a most unhappy youth,
And wall it in, and coarsely taint
   Its whiteness with the lees of truth,

And choose for instruments the fools
   Who prate of duty to themselves,
Who fish for virtue in cess-pools,
   And line with lies their mental shelves,—

He is not dead, though Youth is dead,
And Age, Youth's weary son, has smashed
The walls which held his sire and fled !—
He hunts the thing he erewhile lashed.

A scowling ghost with scorching breath
He follows hard, and shall not cease
Till God speaks through the mouth of Death
And smites the sombre silences.

Trumbull Stickney

1874–1904

He said: "If in his image I was made,
I am his equal and across the land
We two should make our journey hand in hand
Like brothers dignified and unafraid."
And God that day was walking in the shade.
To whom he said: "The world is idly planned,
We cross each other, let us understand
Thou who thou art, I who I am," he said.
Darkness came down. And all that night was heard
Tremendous clamour and the broken roar
Of things in turmoil driven down before.
Then silence. Morning broke, and sang a bird.
He lay upon the earth, his bosom stirred;
But God was seen no longer any more.

And, the last day being come, Man stood alone
Ere sunrise on the world's dismantled verge,
Awaiting how from everywhere should urge
The Coming of the Lord. And, behold, none

Did come,—but indistinct from every realm
Of earth and air and water, growing more

And louder, shriller, heavier, a roar
Up the dun atmosphere did overwhelm

His ears; and as he looked affrighted round
Every manner of beast innumerable
All thro' the shadows crying grew, until
The wailing was like grass upon the ground.

Asudden then within his human side
Their anguish, since the goad he wielded first,
And, since he gave them not to drink, their thirst,
Darted compressed and vital.—As he died,

Low in the East now lighting gorgeously
He saw the last sea-serpent iris-mailed
Which, with a spear transfixèd, yet availed
To pluck the sun down into the dead sea.

Anna Hempstead Branch

1875–1937

In the Beginning Was the Word

It took me ten days
To read the Bible through.
Then I saw what I saw,
And I knew what I knew.

I would rise before the dawn,
When the stars were in the sky;
I would go and read the Book,
Till the sun rode high.

In the silence of the noon,
I would read with a will.
I was one who had climbed
To an high, burning hill.

At dusk I fell asleep
With my head on the page.
Then I woke—then I read—
Till it seemed like an age.

For a great wind blows
Through Ezekiel and John,
They are all one flesh
That the Spirit blows upon.

And suddenly the words
Seemed to quicken and to shine;
They glowed like the bread,
They purpled like the wine.

Like bread that had been wheat
In a thousand ample plains,
Sown and harvested by men
From the suns—from the rains.

Like wine that had been grapes
In a thousand vineyards strong—
That was trampled by men's feet
With a shout, with a song.

Like the Bread, like the Wine,
That we eat with one accord—
The body and the blood
Of the supper of the Lord.

And the wine may be old
And the wine may be new—
But it all is the Lord's—
And I knew what I knew.

For a great wind blows
Through Ezekiel and John,
They are all one flesh
That the Spirit blows upon.

And a letter is a power,
And a name is a rune—
And an alphabet, my friends,
Is a strange and ancient tune.

And each letter is a throne
From which fearful splendors stream—
I could see them flash like fire
With an arch-angelic gleam.

And within each word a city
Shone more far than eye could reach—
Where the people shone like stars
With a great new speech.

And each city was an angel,
And they sang with one accord—
Crying, 'Holy, holy, holy,'
In the presence of the Lord.

The Book felt like flesh,
It would breathe—it would sing—
It would throb beneath my hand
Like a breast, like a wing.

It would cry, it would groan,
It would shout and complain—
It would seem to climb a hill
With its solemn stress of pain.

It would grapple with fierce powers,
With a deep interior strife.
It would seem to heave and lift
With a terrible, glad life.

And my flesh was in the Book,
And its blood was in me;
I could feel it throb within,
As plain as it could be

I was filled with its powers,
And I cried all alone,
'The Lord is in the tomb,
And my body is the stone.'

I was anguished, I was dumb,
When the powers began to move,
That shall stir the aching ground,
That shall shake the earth with love.

Then my flesh, which was the stone,
Felt the hills begin to lift.
The seas shook and heaved,
And the stars began to shift.

And the words rushed on
And each letter was a throne.
They swept through my flesh,
Through my brain, through my bone,

With a great, fearful rush,
I felt it clean through.
Oh, I saw what I saw,
And I knew what I knew.

And I swung one side
When the ghostly power began.
Then the Book stood up—
And I saw it was a Man.

For a great wind blows
Through Ezekiel and John.
They are all one flesh
That the Spirit blows upon.

It took me ten days
To read the Bible through—
Then I saw what I saw,
And I knew what I knew.

Robert Frost

1875–1963

A Prayer in Spring

Oh, give us pleasure in the flowers today;
And give us not to think so far away
As the uncertain harvest; keep us here
All simply in the springing of the year.

Oh, give us pleasure in the orchard white,
Like nothing else by day, like ghosts by night;
And make us happy in the happy bees,
The swarm dilating round the perfect trees.

And make us happy in the darting bird
That suddenly above the bees is heard,
The meteor that thrusts in with needle bill,
And off a blossom in mid air stands still.

Bereft

Where had I heard this wind before
Change like this to a deeper roar?
What would it take my standing there for,
Holding open a restive door,
Looking down hill to a frothy shore?
Summer was past and day was past.
Somber clouds in the west were massed.
Out in the porch's sagging floor,
Leaves got up in a coil and hissed,
Blindly struck at my knee and missed.
Something sinister in the tone
Told me my secret must be known:
Word I was in the house alone
Somehow must have gotten abroad,
Word I was in my life alone,
Word I had no one left but God.

Design

I found a dimpled spider, fat and white,
On a white heal-all, holding up a moth
Like a white piece of rigid satin cloth—
Assorted characters of death and blight
Mixed ready to begin the morning right,
Like the ingredients of a witches' broth—
A snow-drop spider, a flower like a froth,
And dead wings carried like a paper kite.

What had that flower to do with being white,
The wayside blue and innocent heal-all?
What brought the kindred spider to that height,
Then steered the white moth thither in the night?
What but design of darkness to appall?—
If design govern in a thing so small.

Once by the Pacific

The shattered water made a misty din.
Great waves looked over others coming in,
And thought of doing something to the shore
That water never did to land before.
The clouds were low and hairy in the skies,
Like locks blown forward in the gleam of eyes.
You could not tell, and yet it looked as if
The shore was lucky in being backed by cliff,
The cliff in being backed by continent;
It looked as if a night of dark intent
Was coming, and not only a night, an age.
Someone had better be prepared for rage.
There would be more than ocean-water broken
Before God's last *Put out the Light* was spoken.

Directive

Back out of all this now too much for us,
Back in a time made simple by the loss
Of detail, burned, dissolved, and broken off
Like graveyard marble sculpture in the weather,
There is a house that is no more a house
Upon a farm that is no more a farm
And in a town that is no more a town.
The road there, if you'll let a guide direct you
Who only has at heart your getting lost,
May seem as if it should have been a quarry—
Great monolithic knees the former town
Long since gave up pretense of keeping covered.
And there's a story in a book about it:
Besides the wear of iron wagon wheels
The ledges show lines ruled southeast northwest,
The chisel work of an enormous Glacier
That braced his feet against the Arctic Pole.
You must not mind a certain coolness from him
Still said to haunt this side of Panther Mountain.
Nor need you mind the serial ordeal
Of being watched from forty cellar holes
As if by eye pairs out of forty firkins.
As for the woods' excitement over you
That sends light rustle rushes to their leaves,
Charge that to upstart inexperience.
Where were they all not twenty years ago?
They think too much of having shaded out
A few old pecker-fretted apple trees.
Make yourself up a cheering song of how
Someone's road home from work this once was,
Who may be just ahead of you on foot
Or creaking with a buggy load of grain.
The height of the adventure is the height
Of country where two village cultures faded
Into each other. Both of them are lost.
And if you're lost enough to find yourself
By now, pull in your ladder road behind you

And put a sign up CLOSED to all but me.
Then make yourself at home. The only field
Now left's no bigger than a harness gall.
First there's the children's house of make believe,
Some shattered dishes underneath a pine,
The playthings in the playhouse of the children.
Weep for what little things could make them glad.
Then for the house that is no more a house,
But only a belilaced cellar hole,
Now slowly closing like a dent in dough.
This was no playhouse but a house in earnest.
Your destination and your destiny's
A brook that was the water of the house,
Cold as a spring as yet so near its source,
Too lofty and original to rage.
(We know the valley streams that when aroused
Will leave their tatters hung on barb and thorn.)
I have kept hidden in the instep arch
Of an old cedar at the waterside
A broken drinking goblet like the Grail
Under a spell so the wrong ones can't find it,
So can't get saved, as Saint Mark says they mustn't.
(I stole the goblet from the children's playhouse.)
Here are your waters and your watering place.
Drink and be whole again beyond confusion.

Ameen Rihani

1876–1940

The Song of Siva

'T is Night; all the Sirens are silent,
All the Vultures asleep;
And the horns of the Tempest are stirring
Under the Deep;
'T is Night; all the snow-burdened Mountains
Dream of the Sea,
And down in the Wadi the River
Is calling to me.

'T is Night; all the Caves of the Spirit
Shake with desire,
And the Orient Heaven 's essaying
Its lances of fire;
They hear, in the stillness that covers
The land and the sea,
The River, in the heart of the Wadi,
Calling to me.

'T is night, but a night of great joyance,
A night of unrest:—
The night of the birth of the spirit
Of the East and the West;
And the Caves and the Mountains are dancing
On the Foam of the Sea,
For the River inundant is calling,
Calling to me.

Renunciation

At eventide the Pilgrim came
  And knocked at the Belovéd's door.
"Who's there!" a voice within, "Thy name?"
  "'T is I," he said.—"Then knock no more.
As well ask thou a lodging of the sea,—
There is no room herein for thee and me."

The Pilgrim went again his way
  And dwelt with Love upon the shore
Of self-oblivion; and one day
  He knocked again at the Belovéd's door.
  "Who's there?"—"It is thyself," he now replied,
And suddenly the door was opened wide.

A Sufi Song

My heart 's the field I sow for thee,
For thee to water and to reap;
My heart 's the house I ope for thee,
For thee to air and dust and sweep;
My heart 's the rug I spread for thee,
For thee to dance or pray or sleep;
My heart 's the pearls I thread for thee,
For thee to wear or break or keep;
My heart 's a sack of magic things—
Magic carpets, caps and rings—
To bring thee treasures from afar
And from the Deep.

Carl Sandburg

1878–1967

Our Prayer of Thanks

For the gladness here where the sun is shining at evening on the
weeds at the river,
Our prayer of thanks.

For the laughter of children who tumble barefooted and
bareheaded in the summer grass,
Our prayer of thanks.

For the sunset and the stars, the women and the white arms that
hold us,
Our prayer of thanks.

God,
If you are deaf and blind, if this is all lost to you,
God, if the dead in their coffins amid the silver handles on the
edge of town, or the reckless dead of war days thrown
unknown in pits, if these dead are forever deaf and blind and
lost,
Our prayer of thanks.

God,
The game is all your way, the secrets and the signals and the
system; and so for the break of the game and the first play
and the last.
Our prayer of thanks.

For You

The peace of great doors be for you.
Wait at the knobs, at the panel oblongs.
Wait for the great hinges.

The peace of great churches be for you,
Where the players of loft pipe organs
Practice old lovely fragments, alone.

The peace of great books be for you,
Stains of pressed clover leaves on pages,
Bleach of the light of years held in leather.

The peace of great prairies be for you.
Listen among windplayers in cornfields,
The wind learning over its oldest music.

The peace of great seas be for you.
Wait on a hook of land, a rock footing
For you, wait in the salt wash.

The peace of great mountains be for you,
The sleep and the eyesight of eagles,
Sheet mist shadows and the long look across.

The peace of great hearts be for you,
Valves of the blood of the sun,
Pumps of the strongest wants we cry.

The peace of great silhouettes be for you,
Shadow dancers alive in your blood now,
Alive and crying, "Let us out, let us out."

The peace of great changes be for you.
Whisper, Oh beginners in the hills.
Tumble, Oh cubs—tomorrow belongs to you.

The peace of great loves be for you.
Rain, soak these roots; wind, shatter the dry rot.
Bars of sunlight, grips of the earth, hug these.

The peace of great ghosts be for you,
Phantoms of night-gray eyes, ready to go
To the fog-star dumps, to the fire-white doors.

Yes, the peace of great phantoms be for you,
Phantom iron men, mothers of bronze,
Keepers of the lean clean breeds.

William Stanley Braithwaite

1878–1962

The Eternal Self

To Vere Goldthwaite

This earth is but a semblance and a form—
An apparition poised in boundless space;
This life we live so sensible and warm,
Is but a dreaming in a sleep that stays
About us from the cradle to the grave.
Things seen are as inconstant as a wave
That must obey the impulse of the wind;
So in this strange communicable being
There is a higher consciousness confined—
But separate and divine, and foreseeing.

Our bodies are but garments made of clay
That is a smothering weight upon the soul—
But as the sun, conquering a cloudy day,
Our spirits penetrate to Source and Goal.
That intimate and hidden quickening
Bestowing sense and color with the Spring,
Is felt and known and seen in the design
By unsubstantial Self within the portal
Of this household of flesh, that doth confine
Part of the universally immortal.

Beyond the prison of our hopes and fears,
Beyond the undertow of passion's sea —
And stronger than the strength earth holds in years,
Lives man's subconscious personality.
O world withheld! seen through the hazy drift

Of this twilight of flesh, when sleep shall lift
I shall go forth my own true self at last,
And glory in the triumph of my winning
The road that joins the Future and the Past,
Where I can reach the Ending and Beginning!

Vachel Lindsay

1879–1931

General William Booth Enters Into Heaven

(To be sung to the tune of The Blood of the Lamb *with indicated instrument)*

I

[*Bass drum beaten loudly.*]
Booth led boldly with his big bass drum—
(Are you washed in the blood of the Lamb?)
The Saints smiled gravely and they said: "He's come."
(Are you washed in the blood of the Lamb?)
Walking lepers followed, rank on rank,
Lurching bravoes from the ditches dank,
Drabs from the alleyways and drug fiends pale—
Minds still passion-ridden, soul-powers frail:—
Vermin-eaten saints with mouldy breath,
Unwashed legions with the ways of Death—
(Are you washed in the blood of the Lamb?)

[*Banjos.*]
Every slum had sent its half-a-score
The round world over. (Booth had groaned for more.)
Every banner that the wide world flies
Bloomed with glory and transcendent dyes.
Big-voiced lasses made their banjos bang,
Tranced, fanatical they shrieked and sang:—
"Are you washed in the blood of the Lamb?"
Hallelujah! It was queer to see

Bull-necked convicts with that land make free.
Loons with trumpets blowed a blare, blare, blare
On, on upward thro' the golden air!
(Are you washed in the blood of the Lamb?)

II

[*Bass drum slower and softer.*]
Booth died blind and still by Faith he trod,
Eyes still dazzled by the ways of God.
Booth led boldly, and he looked the chief
Eagle countenance in sharp relief,
Beard a-flying, air of high command
Unabated in that holy land.

[*Sweet flute music.*]
Jesus came from out the court-house door,
Stretched his hands above the passing poor.
Booth saw not, but led his queer ones there
Round and round the mighty court-house square.
Yet in an instant all that blear review
Marched on spotless, clad in raiment new.
The lame were straightened, withered limbs uncurled
And blind eyes opened on a new, sweet world.

[*Bass drum louder.*]
Drabs and vixens in a flash made whole!
Gone was the weasel-head, the snout, the jowl!
Sages and sibyls now, and athletes clean,
Rulers of empires, and of forests green!

[*Grand chorus of all instruments. Tambourines to the foreground.*]
The hosts were sandalled, and their wings were fire!
(Are you washed in the blood of the Lamb?)
But their noise played havoc with the angel-choir.
(Are you washed in the blood of the Lamb?)
O, shout Salvation! It was good to see
Kings and Princes by the Lamb set free.
The banjos rattled and the tambourines
Jing-jing-jingled in the hands of Queens.

[*Reverently sung, no instruments.*]
And when Booth halted by the curb for prayer
He saw his Master thro' the flag-filled air.
Christ came gently with a robe and crown
For Booth the soldier, while the throng knelt down.
He saw King Jesus. They were face to face,
And he knelt a-weeping in that holy place.
Are you washed in the blood of the Lamb?

The Unpardonable Sin

This is the sin against the Holy Ghost:—
To speak of bloody power as right divine,
And call on God to guard each vile chief's house,
And for such chiefs, turn men to wolves and swine:—

To go forth killing in White Mercy's name,
Making the trenches stink with spattered brains,
Tearing the nerves and arteries apart,
Sowing with flesh the unreaped golden plains.

In any Church's name, to sack fair towns,
And turn each home into a screaming sty,
To make the little children fugitive,
And have their mothers for a quick death cry,—

This is the sin against the Holy Ghost:
This is the sin no purging can atone:—
To send forth rapine in the name of Christ:—
To set the face, and make the heart a stone.

Wallace Stevens

1879–1955

Tea at the Palaz of Hoon

Not less because in purple I descended
The western day through what you called
The loneliest air, not less was I myself.

What was the ointment sprinkled on my beard?
What were the hymns that buzzed beside my ears?
What was the sea whose tide swept through me there?

Out of my mind the golden ointment rained,
And my ears made the blowing hymns they heard.
I was myself the compass of that sea:

I was the world in which I walked, and what I saw
Or heard or felt came not but from myself;
And there I found myself more truly and more strange.

Sunday Morning

I

Complacencies of the peignoir, and late
Coffee and oranges in a sunny chair,
And the green freedom of a cockatoo
Upon a rug mingle to dissipate
The holy hush of ancient sacrifice.
She dreams a little, and she feels the dark
Encroachment of that old catastrophe,
As a calm darkens among water-lights.
The pungent oranges and bright, green wings
Seem things in some procession of the dead,
Winding across wide water, without sound.

The day is like wide water, without sound,
Stilled for the passing of her dreaming feet
Over the seas, to silent Palestine,
Dominion of the blood and sepulchre.

II

Why should she give her bounty to the dead?
What is divinity if it can come
Only in silent shadows and in dreams?
Shall she not find in comforts of the sun,
In pungent fruit and bright, green wings, or else
In any balm or beauty of the earth,
Things to be cherished like the thought of heaven?
Divinity must live within herself:
Passions of rain, or moods in falling snow;
Grievings in loneliness, or unsubdued
Elations when the forest blooms; gusty
Emotions on wet roads on autumn nights;
All pleasures and all pains, remembering
The bough of summer and the winter branch.
These are the measures destined for her soul.

III

Jove in the clouds had his inhuman birth.
No mother suckled him, no sweet land gave
Large-mannered motions to his mythy mind.
He moved among us, as a muttering king,
Magnificent, would move among his hinds,
Until our blood, commingling, virginal,
With heaven, brought such requital to desire
The very hinds discerned it, in a star.
Shall our blood fail? Or shall it come to be
The blood of paradise? And shall the earth
Seem all of paradise that we shall know?
The sky will be much friendlier then than now,
A part of labor and a part of pain,
And next in glory to enduring love,
Not this dividing and indifferent blue.

IV

She says, "I am content when wakened birds,
Before they fly, test the reality
Of misty fields, by their sweet questionings;
But when the birds are gone, and their warm fields
Return no more, where, then, is paradise?"
There is not any haunt of prophesy,
Nor any old chimera of the grave,
Neither the golden underground, nor isle
Melodious, where spirits gat them home,
Nor visionary south, nor cloudy palm
Remote on heaven's hill, that has endured
As April's green endures; or will endure
Like her remembrance of awakened birds,
Or her desire for June and evening, tipped
By the consummation of the swallow's wings.

V

She says, "But in contentment I still feel
The need of some imperishable bliss."
Death is the mother of beauty; hence from her,
Alone, shall come fulfilment to our dreams
And our desires. Although she strews the leaves
Of sure obliteration on our paths,
The path sick sorrow took, the many paths
Where triumph rang its brassy phrase, or love
Whispered a little out of tenderness,
She makes the willow shiver in the sun
For maidens who were wont to sit and gaze
Upon the grass, relinquished to their feet.
She causes boys to pile new plums and pears
On disregarded plate. The maidens taste
And stray impassioned in the littering leaves.

VI

Is there no change of death in paradise?
Does ripe fruit never fall? Or do the boughs
Hang always heavy in that perfect sky,
Unchanging, yet so like our perishing earth,
With rivers like our own that seek for seas
They never find, the same receding shores
That never touch with inarticulate pang?
Why set the pear upon those river-banks
Or spice the shores with odors of the plum?
Alas, that they should wear our colors there,
The silken weavings of our afternoons,
And pick the strings of our insipid lutes!
Death is the mother of beauty, mystical,
Within whose burning bosom we devise
Our earthly mothers waiting, sleeplessly.

VII

Supple and turbulent, a ring of men
Shall chant in orgy on a summer morn
Their boisterous devotion to the sun,
Not as a god, but as a god might be,
Naked among them, like a savage source.
Their chant shall be a chant of paradise,
Out of their blood, returning to the sky;
And in their chant shall enter, voice by voice,
The windy lake wherein their lord delights,
The trees, like serafin, and echoing hills,
That choir among themselves long afterward.
They shall know well the heavenly fellowship
Of men that perish and of summer morn.
And whence they came and whither they shall go
The dew upon their feet shall manifest.

VIII

She hears, upon that water without sound,
A voice that cries, "The tomb in Palestine
Is not the porch of spirits lingering.
It is the grave of Jesus, where he lay."
We live in an old chaos of the sun,
Or old dependency of day and night,
Or island solitude, unsponsored, free,
Of that wide water, inescapable.
Deer walk upon our mountains, and the quail
Whistle about us their spontaneous cries;
Sweet berries ripen in the wilderness;
And, in the isolation of the sky,
At evening, casual flocks of pigeons make
Ambiguous undulations as they sink,
Downward to darkness, on extended wings.

God Is Good. It Is a Beautiful Night

Look round, brown moon, brown bird, as you rise to fly,
Look round at the head and zither
On the ground.

Look round you as you start to rise, brown moon,
At the book and shoe, the rotted rose
At the door.

This was the place to which you came last night,
Flew close to, flew to without rising away.
Now, again,

In your light, the head is speaking. It reads the book.
It becomes the scholar again, seeking celestial
Rendezvous,

Picking thin music on the rustiest string,
Squeezing the reddest fragrance from the stump
Of summer.

The venerable song falls from your fiery wings.
The song of the great space of your age pierces
The fresh night.

Less and Less Human, O Savage Spirit

If there must be a god in the house, must be,
Saying things in the rooms and on the stair,

Let him move as the sunlight moves on the floor,
Or moonlight, silently, as Plato's ghost

Or Aristotle's skeleton. Let him hang out
His stars on the wall. He must dwell quietly.

He must be incapable of speaking, closed,
As those are: as light, for all its motion, is;

As color, even the closest to us, is;
As shapes, though they portend us, are.

It is the human that is the alien,
The human that has no cousin in the moon.

It is the human that demands his speech
From beasts or from the incommunicable mass.

If there must be a god in the house, let him be one
That will not hear us when we speak: a coolness,

A vermilioned nothingness, any stick of the mass
Of which we are too distantly a part.

Angel Surrounded by Paysans

One of the countrymen:

There is
A welcome at the door to which no one comes?
The angel:
I am the angel of reality,
Seen for a moment standing in the door.

I have neither ashen wing nor wear of ore
And live without a tepid aureole,

Or stars that follow me, not to attend,
But, of my being and its knowing, part.

I am one of you and being one of you
Is being and knowing what I am and know.

Yet I am the necessary angel of earth,
Since, in my sight, you see the earth again,

Cleared of its stiff and stubborn, man-locked set,
And, in my hearing, you hear its tragic drone

Rise liquidly in liquid lingerings,
Like watery words awash; like meanings said

By repetitions of half-meanings. Am I not,
Myself, only half of a figure of a sort,

A figure half seen, or seen for a moment, a man
Of the mind, an apparition apparelled in

Apparels of such lightest look that a turn
Of my shoulder and quickly, too quickly, I am gone?

Final Soliloquy of the Interior Paramour

Light the first light of evening, as in a room
In which we rest and, for small reason, think
The world imagined is the ultimate good.

This is, therefore, the intensest rendezvous.
It is in that thought that we collect ourselves,
Out of all the indifferences, into one thing:

Within a single thing, a single shawl
Wrapped tightly round us, since we are poor, a warmth,
A light, a power, the miraculous influence.

Here, now, we forget each other and ourselves.
We feel the obscurity of an order, a whole,
A knowledge, that which arranged the rendezvous,

Within its vital boundary, in the mind.
We say God and the imagination are one . . .
How high that highest candle lights the dark.

Out of this same light, out of the central mind,
We make a dwelling in the evening air,
In which being there together is enough.

Of Mere Being

The palm at the end of the mind,
Beyond the last thought, rises
In the bronze decor,

A gold-feathered bird
Sings in the palm, without human meaning,
Without human feeling, a foreign song.

You know then that it is not the reason
That makes us happy or unhappy.
The bird sings. Its feathers shine.

The palm stands on the edge of space.
The wind moves slowly in the branches.
The bird's fire-fangled feathers dangle down.

Kahlil Gibran

1883–1931

O Soul

Were it not my ambition to find eternity,
I would not have learnt the melody sung by the ages.
I would have been forced, rather, to end my life,
so that my visible self would have secretly withered and died.

O soul, had I not cleansed myself with tears,
had not my lids been shadowed with sorrows,
I would have lived with scales upon my eyes,
like a blind man, seeing only the face of darkness,

O soul, what is life if not a night
fading until it ends in the dawn; and the dawn endures.
And in the thirst of my heart is a sign, proclaiming the existence
of a celestial river in the urn of death, womb of clemency.

O soul, some madman may tell you: 'The soul dies like the body,
and whatever passes from life to death surely does not return.'
Then make this answer: 'Flowers die, but the seeds remain.
And within them dwells the very essence of eternity.'

William Carlos Williams

1883–1963

Burning the Christmas Greens

Their time past, pulled down
cracked and flung to the fire
—go up in a roar

All recognition lost, burnt clean
clean in the flame, the green
dispersed, a living red,
flame red, red as blood wakes
on the ash—

and ebbs to a steady burning
the rekindled bed become
a landscape of flame

At the winter's midnight
we went to the trees, the coarse
holly, the balsam and
the hemlock for their green

At the thick of the dark
the moment of the cold's
deepest plunge we brought branches
cut from the green trees

to fill our need, and over
doorways, about paper Christmas
bells covered with tinfoil
and fastened by red ribbons

we stuck the green prongs
in the windows hung
woven wreaths and above pictures
the living green. On the

mantle we built a green forest
and among those hemlock
sprays put a herd of small
white deer as if they

were walking there. All this!
and it seemed gentle and good
to us. Their time past,
relief! The room bare. We

stuffed the dead grate
with them upon the half burntout
log's smoldering eye, opening
red and closing under them

and we stood there looking down.
Green is a solace
a promise of peace, a fort
against the cold (though we

did not say so) a challenge
above the snow's
hard shell. Green (we might
have said) that, where

small birds hide and dodge
and lift their plaintive
rallying cries, blocks for them
and knocks down

the unseeing bullets of
the storm. Green spruce boughs
pulled down by a weight of
snow—Transformed!

Violence leaped and appeared.
Recreant! roared to life
as the flame rose through and
our eyes recoiled from it.

In the jagged flames green
to red, instant and alive. Green!
those sure abutments . . . Gone!
lost to mind

and quick in the contracting
tunnel of the grate
appeared a world! Black
mountains, black and red—as

yet uncolored—and ash white,
an infant landscape of shimmering
ash and flame and we, in
that instant, lost,

breathless to be witnesses,
as if we stood
ourselves refreshed among
the shining fauna of that fire.

The Gift

As the wise men of old brought gifts
        guided by a star
                to the humble birthplace

of the god of love,
        the devils
                as an old print shows
retreated in confusion.

        What could a baby know
                of gold ornaments
or frankincense and myrrh,
        of priestly robes
                and devout genuflections?

But the imagination
        knows all stories
                before they are told
and knows the truth of this one
        past all defection

The rich gifts
        so unsuitable for a child
                though devoutly proffered,
stood for all that love can bring.

The men were old
how could they know
of a mother's needs
or a child's
appetite?

But as they kneeled
the child was fed.

They saw it
and
gave praise!

A miracle
had taken place,
hard gold to love,
a mother's milk!
before
their wondering eyes.

The ass brayed
the cattle lowed.
It was their nature.

All men by their nature give praise.
It is all
they can do.

The very devils
by their flight give praise.
What is death,
beside this?

Nothing. The wise men
came with gifts
and bowed down
to worship
this perfection.

Sara Teasdale

1884–1933

The Sanctuary

If I could keep my innermost Me
Fearless, aloof and free
Of the least breath of love or hate,
And not disconsolate
At the sick load of sorrow laid on men;
If I could keep a sanctuary there
Free even of prayer,
If I could do this, then,
With quiet candor as I grew more wise
I could look even at God with grave forgiving eyes.

H.D.

1886–1961

FROM *The Walls Do Not Fall*

I

An incident here and there,
and rails gone (for guns)
from your (and my) old town square:

mist and mist-grey, no colour,
still the Luxor bee, chick and hare
pursue unalterable purpose

in green, rose-red, lapis;
they continue to prophesy
from the stone papyrus:

there, as here, ruin opens
the tomb, the temple; enter,
there as here, there are no doors:

the shrine lies open to the sky,
the rain falls, here, there
sand drifts; eternity endures:

ruin everywhere, yet as the fallen roof
leaves the sealed room
open to the air,

so, through our desolation,
thoughts stir, inspiration stalks us
through gloom:

unaware, Spirit announces the Presence;
shivering overtakes us,
as of old, Samuel:

trembling at a known street-corner,
we know not nor are known;
the Pythian pronounces—we pass on

to another cellar, to another sliced wall
where poor utensils show
like rare objects in a museum;

Pompeii has nothing to teach us,
we know crack of volcanic fissure,
slow flow of terrible lava,

pressure on heart, lungs, the brain
about to burst its brittle case
(what the skull can endure!):

over us, Apocryphal fire,
under us, the earth sway, dip of a floor,
slope of a pavement

where men roll, drunk
with a new bewilderment,
sorcery, bedevilment:

the bone-frame was made for
no such shock knit within terror,
yet the skeleton stood up to it:

the flesh? it was melted away,
the heart burnt out, dead ember,
tendons, muscles shattered, outer husk dismembered,

yet the frame held:
we passed the flame: we wonder
what saved us? what for?

FROM *The Flowering of the Rod*

III

In resurrection, there is confusion
if we start to argue; if we stand and stare,

we do not know where to go;
in resurrection, there is simple affirmation

but do not delay to round up the others,
up and down the street; your going

in a moment like this, is the best proof
that you know the way;

does the first wild-goose stop to explain
to the others? no—he is off;

they follow or not,
that is their affair;

does the first wild-goose care
whether the others follow or not?

I don't think so—he is so happy to be off—
he knows where he is going;

so we must be drawn or we must fly,
like the snow-geese of the Arctic circle,

to the Carolinas or to Florida,
or like those migratory flocks

who still (they say) hover
over the lost island, Atlantis;

seeking what we once knew,
we know ultimately we will find

happiness; *to-day shalt thou be*
with me in Paradise.

VI

So I would rather drown, remembering—
than bask on tropic atolls

in the coral-seas; I would rather drown,
remembering—than rest on pine or fir-branch

where great stars pour down
their generating strength, Arcturus

or the sapphires of the Northern Crown;
I would rather beat in the wind, crying to these others:

yours is the more foolish circling,
yours is the senseless wheeling

round and round—yours has no reason—
I am seeking heaven;

yours has no vision,
I see what is beneath me, what is above me,

what men say is-not—I remember,
I remember, I remember—you have forgot:

you think, even before it is half-over,
that your cycle is at an end,

but you repeat your foolish circling—again, again, again;
again, the steel sharpened on the stone;

again, the pyramid of skulls;
I gave pity to the dead,

O blasphemy, pity is a stone for bread,
only love is holy and love's ecstasy

that turns and turns and turns about one centre,
reckless, regardless, blind to reality,

that knows the Islands of the Blest are there,
for *many waters can not quench love's fire*.

VII

Yet resurrection is a sense of direction,
resurrection is a bee-line,

straight to the horde and plunder,
the treasure, the store-room,

the honeycomb;
resurrection is remuneration,

food, shelter, fragrance
of myrrh and balm.

Moyshe-Leyb Halpern

1886–1932

Memento Mori

And if Moyshe-Leyb, Poet, recounted how
He's glimpsed Death in the breaking waves, the way
You catch that sight of yourself in the mirror
At about 10 A.M. on some actual day,
Who would be able to believe Moyshe-Leybl?

And if Moyshe-Leyb greeted Death from afar,
With a wave of his hand, asking, "Things all right?"
At the moment when many a thousand people
Lived there in the water, wild with delight,
Who would be able to believe Moyshe-Leybl?

And if Moyshe-Leyb were to swear
That he was drawn to Death in the way
An exiled lover is to the casement
Of his worshipped one, at the end of the day,
Who would be able to believe Moyshe-Leybl?

And if Moyshe-Leyb were to paint them Death
Not gray, dark, but color-drenched, as it shone
At around 10 A.M. there, distantly,
Between the sky and the breakers, alone,
Who would be able to believe Moyshe-Leybl?

translated from Yiddish
by John Hollander

The Will

Now this is how I did myself in:
No sooner did the sun begin
To shine, when I was up and away,

Gathering goat-shit for my tune
—The one I wrote just yesterday
About the moonlight and the moon—
And then I put with these also
Some poems from my portfolio
In re the bible's sanctity
(Just thinking of them sickens me)
And these I wrapped up in my rag
Of an old coat, packed up like a bag,
After which, I took the whole shebang
Put up a nail, and let it hang
Outside my window, on a tray.
Adults and children passed my way
And asked what that mess up there could be,
So I answered them, on bended knee:
These are all my years; I think
They went all rotten with infection
By wisdom, and its ancient stink,
From my precious book collection.
But when my son, the little boy,
(In my sea of sorrow and cup of joy
He's just turned four) strained his eyes to see
Those summits of sublimity,
Well—I put him on my knee
And spake thus: Harken thou to me,
My son and heir, I swear that, just
As none disturb the dead in their rest,
So, when you have finally grown,
I'll leave you thoroughly alone.
Want to be a loan-shark, a bagel-lifter?
Be one, my child.
Want to murder, set fires, or be a grifter?
Be one, my child.
Want to change off girls with the speed that those
Same girls keep changing their own clothes?
Change away, my child.
But one thing, child, I have to say:
If once ambition leads you to try
To make some kind of big display

Of yourself with what's hanging up there in the sky;
If you dare (but may that time not come soon!)
To write about moonlight and the moon,
Or some poem of the bible, poisoning the world,
Then, my dear,
If I'm worth something then by way of any
Money, so much as a single penny,
I'll make my will, leaving everything
To my *Landsman*, the future Polish King.
Though we've both stopped calling each other "thou",
I'll chop up, like a miser shredding
Cake for beggars at a wedding,
All the ties that yet bind us now.
Poppa-chopper   Son-schmon
And so   help me   God in Heaven
This
Will
Be
Done.

translated from Yiddish
by John Hollander

Robinson Jeffers

1887–1962

Shine, Perishing Republic

While this America settles in the mould of its vulgarity, heavily thickening to empire,
And protest, only a bubble in the molten mass, pops and sighs out, and the mass hardens,

I sadly smiling remember that the flower fades to make fruit, the fruit rots to make earth.
Out of the mother; and through the spring exultances, ripeness and decadence; and home to the mother.

You making haste haste on decay: not blameworthy; life is good, be it stubbornly long or suddenly
A mortal splendor: meteors are not needed less than mountains: shine, perishing republic.

But for my children, I would have them keep their distance from the thickening center; corruption
Never has been compulsory, when the cities lie at the monster's feet there are left the mountains.

And boys, be in nothing so moderate as in love of man, a clever servant, insufferable master.
There is the trap that catches noblest spirits, that caught—they say—God, when he walked on earth.

Apology for Bad Dreams

I

In the purple light, heavy with redwood, the slopes drop seaward,
Headlong convexities of forest, drawn in together to the steep ravine. Below, on the sea-cliff,
A lonely clearing; a little field of corn by the streamside; a roof under spared trees. Then the ocean
Like a great stone someone has cut to a sharp edge and polished to shining. Beyond it, the fountain
And furnace of incredible light flowing up from the sunk sun. In the little clearing a woman
Is punishing a horse; she had tied the halter to a sapling at the edge of the wood, but when the great whip
Clung to the flanks the creature kicked so hard she feared he would snap the halter; she called from the house
The young man her son; who fetched a chain tie-rope, they working together
Noosed the small rusty links round the horse's tongue
And tied him by the swollen tongue to the tree.
Seen from this height they are shrunk to insect size,

Out of all human relation. You cannot distinguish
The blood dripping from where the chain is fastened,
The beast shuddering; but the thrust neck and the legs
Far apart. You can see the whip fall on the flanks . . .
The gesture of the arm. You cannot see the face of the woman.
The enormous light beats up out of the west across the cloud-
bars of the trade-wind. The ocean
Darkens, the high clouds brighten, the hills darken together.
Unbridled and unbelievable beauty
Covers the evening world . . . not covers, grows apparent out of
it, as Venus down there grows out
From the lit sky. What said the prophet? "I create good: and I
create evil: I am the Lord."

II

This coast crying out for tragedy like all beautiful places,
(The quiet ones ask for quieter suffering: but here the granite cliff
the gaunt cypresses crown
Demands what victim? The dykes of red lava and black what
Titan? The hills like pointed flames
Beyond Soberanes, the terrible peaks of the bare hills under the
sun, what immolation?)
This coast crying out for tragedy like all beautiful places: and like
the passionate spirit of humanity
Pain for its bread: God's, many victims', the painful deaths, the
horrible transfigurements: I said in my heart,
"Better invent than suffer: imagine victims
Lest your own flesh be chosen the agonist, or you
Martyr some creature to the beauty of the place." And I said,
"Burn sacrifices once a year to magic
Horror away from the house, this little house here
You have built over the ocean with your own hands
Beside the standing boulders: for what are we,
The beast that walks upright, with speaking lips
And little hair, to think we should always be fed,
Sheltered, intact, and self-controlled? We sooner more liable
Than the other animals. Pain and terror, the insanities of desire;
not accidents but essential,

And crowd up from the core": I imagined victims for those
wolves, I made them phantoms to follow,
They have hunted the phantoms and missed the house. It is not
good to forget over what gulfs the spirit
Of the beauty of humanity, the petal of a lost flower blown
seaward by the night-wind, floats to its quietness.

III

Boulders blunted like an old bear's teeth break up from the
headland; below them
All the soil is thick with shells, the tide-rock feasts of a dead
people.
Here the granite flanks are scarred with ancient fire, the ghosts
of the tribe
Crouch in the nights beside the ghost of a fire, they try to
remember the sunlight,
Light has died out of their skies. These have paid something for
the future
Luck of the country, while we living keep old griefs in memory:
though God's
Envy is not a likely fountain of ruin, to forget evils calls down
Sudden reminders from the cloud: remembered deaths be our
redeemers;
Imagined victims our salvation: white as the half moon at
midnight
Someone flamelike passed me, saying, "I am Tamar Cauldwell, I
have my desire,"
Then the voice of the sea returned, when she had gone by, the
stars to their towers.
. . . Beautiful country burn again, Point Pinos down to the Sur
Rivers
Burn as before with bitter wonders, land and ocean and the
Carmel water.

IV

He brays humanity in a mortar to bring the savor
From the bruised root: a man having bad dreams, who invents
victims, is only the ape of that God.
He washes it out with tears and many waters, calcines it with fire
in the red crucible,
Deforms it, makes it horrible to itself: the spirit flies out and
stands naked, he sees the spirit,
He takes it in the naked ecstasy; it breaks in his hand, the atom is
broken, the power that massed it
Cries to the power that moves the stars, "I have come home to
myself, behold me.
I bruised myself in the flint mortar and burnt me
In the red shell, I tortured myself, I flew forth,
Stood naked of myself and broke me in fragments,
And here am I moving the stars that are me."
I have seen these ways of God: I know of no reason
For fire and change and torture and the old returnings.
He being sufficient might be still. I think they admit no reason;
they are the ways of my love.
Unmeasured power, incredible passion, enormous craft: no
thought apparent but burns darkly
Smothered with its own smoke in the human brain-vault: no
thought outside: a certain measure in phenomena:
The fountains of the boiling stars, the flowers on the foreland,
the ever-returning roses of dawn.

Hurt Hawks

I

The broken pillar of the wing jags from the clotted shoulder,
The wing trails like a banner in defeat,
No more to use the sky forever but live with famine
And pain a few days: cat nor coyote
Will shorten the week of waiting for death, there is game
without talons.

He stands under the oak-bush and waits
The lame feet of salvation; at night he remembers freedom
And flies in a dream, the dawns ruin it.
He is strong and pain is worse to the strong, incapacity is worse.
The curs of the day come and torment him
At distance, no one but death the redeemer will humble that head,
The intrepid readiness, the terrible eyes.
The wild God of the world is sometimes merciful to those
That ask mercy, not often to the arrogant.
You do not know him, you communal people, or you have
forgotten him;
Intemperate and savage, the hawk remembers him;
Beautiful and wild, the hawks, and men that are dying,
remember him.

II

I'd sooner, except the penalties, kill a man than a hawk; but the
great redtail
Had nothing left but unable misery
From the bones too shattered for mending, the wing that trailed
under his talons when he moved.
We had fed him six weeks, I gave him freedom,
He wandered over the foreland hill and returned in the evening,
asking for death,
Not like a beggar, still eyed with the old
Implacable arrogance. I gave him the lead gift in the twilight.
What fell was relaxed,
Owl-downy, soft feminine feathers; but what
Soared: the fierce rush: the night-herons by the flooded river
cried fear at its rising
Before it was quite unsheathed from reality.

The Treasure

Mountains, a moment's earth-waves rising and hollowing; the
earth too's an ephemerid; the stars—
Short-lived as grass the stars quicken in the nebula and dry in
their summer, they spiral

Blind up space, scattered black seeds of a future; nothing lives
long, the whole sky's
Recurrences tick the seconds of the hours of the ages of the gulf
before birth, and the gulf
After death is like dated: to labor eighty years in a notch of
eternity is nothing too tiresome,
Enormous repose after, enormous repose before, the flash of
activity.
Surely you never have dreamed the incredible depths were
prologue and epilogue merely
To the surface play in the sun, the instant of life, what is called
life? I fancy
That silence is the thing, this noise a found word for it;
interjection, a jump of the breath at that silence;
Stars burn, grass grows, men breathe: as a man finding treasure
says "Ah!" but the treasure's the essence;
Before the man spoke it was there, and after he has spoken he
gathers it, inexhaustible treasure.

Marianne Moore

1887–1972

The Steeple-Jack

Dürer would have seen a reason for living
in a town like this, with eight stranded whales
to look at; with the sweet sea air coming into your house
on a fine day, from water etched
with waves as formal as the scales
on a fish.

One by one in two's and three's, the seagulls keep
flying back and forth over the town clock,
or sailing around the lighthouse without moving their wings—
rising steadily with a slight
quiver of the body—or flock
mewing where

a sea the purple of the peacock's neck is
paled to greenish azure as Dürer changed
the pine green of the Tyrol to peacock blue and guinea
gray. You can see a twenty-five-
pound lobster; and fish nets arranged
to dry. The

whirlwind fife-and-drum of the storm bends the salt
marsh grass, disturbs stars in the sky and the
star on the steeple; it is a privilege to see so
much confusion. Disguised by what
might seem the opposite, the sea-
side flowers and

trees are favored by the fog so that you have
the tropics at first hand: the trumpet-vine,
fox-glove, giant snap-dragon, a salpiglossis that has
spots and stripes; morning-glories, gourds,
or moon-vines trained on fishing-twine
at the back door;

cat-tails, flags, blueberries and spiderwort,
striped grass, lichens, sunflowers, asters, daisies—
yellow and crab-claw ragged sailors with green bracts—
toad-plant,
petunias, ferns; pink lilies, blue
ones, tigers; poppies; black sweet-peas.
The climate

is not right for the banyan, frangipani, or
jack-fruit trees; or for exotic serpent
life. Ring lizard and snake-skin for the foot, if you see fit;
but here they've cats, not cobras, to
keep down the rats. The diffident
little newt

with white pin-dots on black horizontal spaced-
out bands lives here; yet there is nothing that
ambition can buy or take away. The college student

named Ambrose sits on the hillside
with his not-native books and hat
and sees boats

at sea progress white and rigid as if in
a groove. Liking an elegance of which
the source is not bravado, he knows by heart the antique
sugar-bowl shaped summer-house of
interlacing slats, and the pitch
of the church

spire, not true, from which a man in scarlet lets
down a rope as a spider spins a thread;
he might be part of a novel, but on the sidewalk a
sign says C. J. Poole, Steeple-Jack,
in black and white; and one in red
and white says

Danger. The church portico has four fluted
columns, each a single piece of stone, made
modester by white-wash. This would be a fit haven for
waifs, children, animals, prisoners,
and presidents who have repaid
sin-driven

senators by not thinking about them. The
place has a school-house, a post-office in a
store, fish-houses, hen-houses, a three masted
schooner on
the stocks. The hero, the student,
the steeple-jack, each in his way,
is at home.

It could not be dangerous to be living
in a town like this, of simple people,
who have a steeple-jack placing danger signs by the church
while he is gilding the solid-
pointed star, which on a steeple
stands for hope.

Elinor Wylie

1887–1928

Address to My Soul

My soul, be not disturbed
By planetary war;
Remain securely orbed
In this contracted star.

Fear not, pathetic flame;
Your sustenance is doubt:
Glassed in translucent dream
They cannot snuff you out.

Wear water, or a mask
Of unapparent cloud;
Be brave and never ask
A more defunctive shroud.

The universal points
Are shrunk into a flower;
Between its delicate joints
Chaos keeps no power.

The pure integral form,
Austere and silver-dark,
Is balanced on the storm
In its predestined arc.

Small as a sphere of rain
It slides along the groove
Whose path is furrowed plain
Among the suns that move.

The shapes of April buds
Outlive the phantom year:
Upon the void at odds
The dewdrop falls severe.

Five-petalled flame, be cold:
Be firm, dissolving star:
Accept the stricter mould
That makes you singular.

T. S. Eliot

1888–1965

The Hippopotamus

Similiter et omnes revereantur Diaconos, ut mandatum Jesu Christi; et Episcopum, ut Jesum Christum, existentem filium Patris; Presbyteros autem, ut concilium Dei et conjunctionem Apostolorum. Sine his Ecclesia non vocatur; de quibus suadeo vos sic habeo. S. Ignatii Ad Trallianos.

And when this epistle is read among you, cause that it be read also in the church of the Laodiceans.

The broad-backed hippopotamus
Rests on his belly in the mud;
Although he seems so firm to us
He is merely flesh and blood.

Flesh and blood is weak and frail,
Susceptible to nervous shock;
While the True Church can never fail
For it is based upon a rock.

The hippo's feeble steps may err
In compassing material ends,
While the True Church need never stir
To gather in its dividends.

The 'potamus can never reach
The mango on the mango-tree;
But fruits of pomegranate and peach
Refresh the Church from over sea.

At mating time the hippo's voice
Betrays inflexions hoarse and odd,
But every week we hear rejoice
The Church, at being one with God.

The hippopotamus's day
Is passed in sleep; at night he hunts;
God works in a mysterious way—
The Church can sleep and feed at once.

I saw the 'potamus take wing
Ascending from the damp savannas,
And quiring angels round him sing
The praise of God, in loud hosannas.

Blood of the Lamb shall wash him clean
And him shall heavenly arms enfold,
Among the saints he shall be seen
Performing on a harp of gold.

He shall be washed as white as snow,
By all the martyr'd virgins kist,
While the True Church remains below
Wrapt in the old miasmal mist.

Ash-Wednesday

I

Because I do not hope to turn again
Because I do not hope
Because I do not hope to turn
Desiring this man's gift and that man's scope
I no longer strive to strive towards such things
(Why should the agèd eagle stretch its wings?)
Why should I mourn
The vanished power of the usual reign?

Because I do not hope to know again
The infirm glory of the positive hour
Because I do not think
Because I know I shall not know
The one veritable transitory power
Because I cannot drink
There, where trees flower, and springs flow, for there is nothing
again

Because I know that time is always time
And place is always and only place
And what is actual is actual only for one time
And only for one place
I rejoice that things are as they are and
I renounce the blessèd face
And renounce the voice
Because I cannot hope to turn again
Consequently I rejoice, having to construct something
Upon which to rejoice

And pray to God to have mercy upon us
And I pray that I may forget
These matters that with myself I too much discuss
Too much explain
Because I do not hope to turn again
Let these words answer
For what is done, not to be done again
May the judgement not be too heavy upon us

Because these winks are no longer wings to fly
But merely vans to beat the air
The air which is now thoroughly small and dry
Smaller and dryer than the will
Teach us to care and not to care
Teach us to sit still.

Pray for us sinners now and at the hour of our death
Pray for us now and at the hour of our death.

II

Lady, three white leopards sat under a juniper-tree
In the cool of the day, having fed to satiety
On my legs my heart my liver and that which had been
    contained
In the hollow round of my skull. And God said
Shall these bones live? shall these
Bones live? And that which had been contained
In the bones (which were already dry) said chirping:
Because of the goodness of this Lady
And because of her loveliness, and because
She honours the Virgin in meditation,
We shine with brightness. And I who am here dissembled
Proffer my deeds to oblivion, and my love
To the posterity of the desert and the fruit of the gourd.
It is this which recovers
My guts the strings of my eyes and the indigestible portions
Which the leopards reject. The Lady is withdrawn
In a white gown, to contemplation, in a white gown.
Let the whiteness of bones atone to forgetfulness.
There is no life in them. As I am forgotten
And would be forgotten, so I would forget
Thus devoted, concentrated in purpose. And God said
Prophesy to the wind, to the wind only for only
The wind will listen. And the bones sang chirping
With the burden of the grasshopper, saying

Lady of silences
Calm and distressed
Torn and most whole
Rose of memory
Rose of forgetfulness
Exhausted and life-giving
Worried reposeful
The single Rose
Is now the Garden
Where all loves end
Terminate torment

Of love unsatisfied
The greater torment
Of love satisfied
End of the endless
Journey to no end
Conclusion of all that
Is inconclusible
Speech without word and
Word of no speech
Grace to the Mother
For the Garden
Where all love ends.

Under a juniper-tree the bones sang, scattered and shining
We are glad to be scattered, we did little good to each other,
Under a tree in the cool of the day, with the blessing of sand,
Forgetting themselves and each other, united
In the quiet of the desert. This is the land which ye
Shall divide by lot. And neither division nor unity
Matters. This is the land. We have our inheritance.

III

At the first turning of the second stair
I turned and saw below
The same shape twisted on the banister
Under the vapour in the fetid air
Struggling with the devil of the stairs who wears
The deceitful face of hope and of despair.

At the second turning of the second stair
I left them twisting, turning below;
There were no more faces and the stair was dark,
Damp, jaggèd, like an old man's mouth drivelling, beyond repair,
Or the toothed gullet of an agèd shark.

At the first turning of the third stair
Was a slotted window bellied like the fig's fruit

And beyond the hawthorn blossom and a pasture scene
The broadbacked figure drest in blue and green
Enchanted the maytime with an antique flute.
Blown hair is sweet, brown hair over the mouth blown,
Lilac and brown hair;
Distraction, music of the flute, stops and steps of the mind over
the third stair,
Fading, fading; strength beyond hope and despair
Climbing the third stair.

Lord, I am not worthy
Lord, I am not worthy

but speak the word only.

IV

Who walked between the violet and the violet
Who walked between
The various ranks of varied green
Going in white and blue, in Mary's colour,
Talking of trivial things
In ignorance and in knowledge of eternal dolour
Who moved among the others as they walked,
Who then made strong the fountains and made fresh the springs

Made cool the dry rock and made firm the sand
In blue of larkspur, blue of Mary's colour,
Sovegna vos

Here are the years that walk between, bearing
Away the fiddles and the flutes, restoring
One who moves in the time between sleep and waking, wearing

White light folded, sheathed about her, folded.
The new years walk, restoring
Through a bright cloud of tears, the years, restoring
With a new verse the ancient rhyme. Redeem
The time. Redeem

The unread vision in the higher dream
While jewelled unicorns draw by the gilded hearse.

The silent sister veiled in white and blue
Between the yews, behind the garden god,
Whose flute is breathless, bent her head and signed but spoke no
word

But the fountain sprang up and the bird sang down
Redeem the time, redeem the dream
The token of the word unheard, unspoken

Till the wind shake a thousand whispers from the yew

And after this our exile

V

If the lost word is lost, if the spent word is spent
If the unheard, unspoken
Word is unspoken, unheard;
Still is the unspoken word, the Word unheard,
The Word without a word, the Word within
The world and for the world;
And the light shone in darkness and
Against the Word the unstilled world still whirled
About the centre of the silent Word.

O my people, what have I done unto thee.

Where shall the word be found, where will the word
Resound? Not here, there is not enough silence
Not on the sea or on the islands, not
On the mainland, in the desert or the rain land,
For those who walk in darkness
Both in the day time and in the night time
The right time and the right place are not here
No place of grace for those who avoid the face
No time to rejoice for those who walk among noise and deny the
voice

Will the veiled sister pray for
Those who walk in darkness, who chose thee and oppose thee,
Those who are torn on the horn between season and season,
    time and time, between
Hour and hour, word and word, power and power, those who
    wait
In darkness? Will the veiled sister pray
For children at the gate
Who will not go away and cannot pray:
Pray for those who chose and oppose

O my people, what have I done unto thee.

Will the veiled sister between the slender
Yew trees pray for those who offend her
And are terrified and cannot surrender
And affirm before the world and deny between the rocks
In the last desert between the last blue rocks
The desert in the garden the garden in the desert
Of drouth, spitting from the mouth the withered apple-seed.

O my people.

VI

Although I do not hope to turn again
Although I do not hope
Although I do not hope to turn

Wavering between the profit and the loss
In this brief transit where the dreams cross
The dreamcrossed twilight between birth and dying
(Bless me father) though I do not wish to wish these things
From the wide window towards the granite shore
The white sails still fly seaward, seaward flying
Unbroken wings

And the lost heart stiffens and rejoices
In the lost lilac and the lost sea voices
And the weak spirit quickens to rebel
For the bent golden-rod and the lost sea smell
Quickens to recover
The cry of quail and the whirling plover
And the blind eye creates
The empty forms between the ivory gates
And smell renews the salt savour of the sandy earth

This is the time of tension between dying and birth
The place of solitude where three dreams cross
Between blue rocks
But when the voices shaken from the yew-tree drift away
Let the other yew be shaken and reply.

Blessèd sister, holy mother, spirit of the fountain, spirit of the
garden,
Suffer us not to mock ourselves with falsehood
Teach us to care and not to care
Teach us to sit still
Even among these rocks,
Our peace in His will
And even among these rocks
Sister, mother
And spirit of the river, spirit of the sea,
Suffer me not to be separated

And let my cry come unto Thee.

Journey of the Magi

'A cold coming we had of it,
Just the worst time of the year
For a journey, and such a long journey:
The ways deep and the weather sharp,
The very dead of winter.'
And the camels galled, sore-footed, refractory,

Lying down in the melting snow.
There were times we regretted
The summer palaces on slopes, the terraces,
And the silken girls bringing sherbet.
Then the camel men cursing and grumbling
And running away, and wanting their liquor and women,
And the night-fires going out, and the lack of shelters,
And the cities hostile and the towns unfriendly
And the villages dirty and charging high prices:
A hard time we had of it.
At the end we preferred to travel all night,
Sleeping in snatches,
With the voices singing in our ears, saying
That this was all folly.

Then at dawn we came down to a temperate valley,
Wet, below the snow line, smelling of vegetation;
With a running stream and a water-mill beating the darkness,
And three trees on the low sky,
And an old white horse galloped away in the meadow.
Then we came to a tavern with vine-leaves over the lintel,
Six hands at an open door dicing for pieces of silver,
And feet kicking the empty wine-skins.
But there was no information, and so we continued
And arrived at evening, not a moment too soon
Finding the place; it was (you may say) satisfactory.

All this was a long time ago, I remember,
And I would do it again, but set down
This set down
This: were we led all that way for
Birth or Death? There was a Birth, certainly,
We had evidence and no doubt. I had seen birth and death,
But had thought they were different; this Birth was
Hard and bitter agony for us, like Death, our death.
We returned to our places, these Kingdoms,
But no longer at ease here, in the old dispensation,
With an alien people clutching their gods.
I should be glad of another death.

A Song for Simeon

Lord, the Roman hyacinths are blooming in bowls and
The winter sun creeps by the snow hills;
The stubborn season has made stand.
My life is light, waiting for the death wind,
Like a feather on the back of my hand.
Dust in sunlight and memory in corners
Wait for the wind that chills towards the dead land.

Grant us thy peace.
I have walked many years in this city,
Kept faith and fast, provided for the poor,
Have given and taken honour and ease.
There went never any rejected from my door.
Who shall remember my house, where shall live my children's
children
When the time of sorrow is come?
They will take to the goat's path, and the fox's home,
Fleeing from the foreign faces and the foreign swords.

Before the time of cords and scourges and lamentation
Grant us thy peace.
Before the stations of the mountain of desolation,
Before the certain hour of maternal sorrow,
Now at this birth season of decease,
Let the Infant, the still unspeaking and unspoken Word,
Grant Israel's consolation
To one who has eighty years and no to-morrow.

According to thy word.
They shall praise Thee and suffer in every generation
With glory and derision,
Light upon light, mounting the saints' stair.
Not for me the martyrdom, the ecstasy of thought and prayer,
Not for me the ultimate vision.
Grant me thy peace.
(And a sword shall pierce thy heart,
Thine also.)

I am tired with my own life and the lives of those after me,
I am dying in my own death and the deaths of those after me.
Let thy servant depart,
Having seen thy salvation.

Little Gidding

I

Midwinter spring is its own season
Sempiternal though sodden towards sundown,
Suspended in time, between pole and tropic.
When the short day is brightest, with frost and fire,
The brief sun flames the ice, on pond and ditches,
In windless cold that is the heart's heat,
Reflecting in a watery mirror
A glare that is blindness in the early afternoon.
And glow more intense than blaze of branch, or brazier,
Stirs the dumb spirit: no wind, but pentecostal fire
In the dark time of the year. Between melting and freezing
The soul's sap quivers. There is no earth smell
Or smell of living thing. This is the spring time
But not in time's covenant. Now the hedgerow
Is blanched for an hour with transitory blossom
Of snow, a bloom more sudden
Than that of summer, neither budding nor fading,
Not in the scheme of generation.
Where is the summer, the unimaginable
Zero summer?

If you came this way,
Taking the route you would be likely to take
From the place you would be likely to come from,
If you came this way in may time, you would find the hedges
White again, in May, with voluptuary sweetness.
It would be the same at the end of the journey,
If you came at night like a broken king,
If you came by day not knowing what you came for,

It would be the same, when you leave the rough road
And turn behind the pig-sty to the dull façade
And the tombstone. And what you thought you came for
Is only a shell, a husk of meaning
From which the purpose breaks only when it is fulfilled
If at all. Either you had no purpose
Or the purpose is beyond the end you figured
And is altered in fulfilment. There are other places
Which also are the world's end, some at the sea jaws,
Or over a dark lake, in a desert or a city—
But this is the nearest, in place and time,
Now and in England.

If you came this way,
Taking any route, starting from anywhere,
At any time or at any season,
It would always be the same: you would have to put off
Sense and notion. You are not here to verify,
Instruct yourself, or inform curiosity
Or carry report. You are here to kneel
Where prayer has been valid. And prayer is more
Than an order of words, the conscious occupation
Of the praying mind, or the sound of the voice praying.
And what the dead had no speech for, when living,
They can tell you, being dead: the communication
Of the dead is tongued with fire beyond the language of the living.
Here, the intersection of the timeless moment
Is England and nowhere. Never and always.

II

Ash on an old man's sleeve
Is all the ash the burnt roses leave.
Dust in the air suspended
Marks the place where a story ended.
Dust inbreathed was a house—
The wall, the wainscot and the mouse.
The death of hope and despair,
This is the death of air.

There are flood and drouth
Over the eyes and in the mouth,
Dead water and dead sand
Contending for the upper hand.
The parched eviscerate soil
Gapes at the vanity of toil,
Laughs without mirth.
This is the death of earth.

Water and fire succeed
The town, the pasture and the weed.
Water and fire deride
The sacrifice that we denied.
Water and fire shall rot
The marred foundations we forgot,
Of sanctuary and choir.
This is the death of water and fire.

In the uncertain hour before the morning
Near the ending of interminable night
At the recurrent end of the unending
After the dark dove with the flickering tongue
Had passed below the horizon of his homing
While the dead leaves still rattled on like tin
Over the asphalt where no other sound was
Between three districts whence the smoke arose
I met one walking, loitering and hurried
As if blown towards me like the metal leaves
Before the urban dawn wind unresisting.
And as I fixed upon the down-turned face
That pointed scrutiny with which we challenge
The first-met stranger in the waning dusk
I caught the sudden look of some dead master
Whom I had known, forgotten, half recalled
Both one and many; in the brown baked features
The eyes of a familiar compound ghost
Both intimate and unidentifiable.
So I assumed a double part, and cried

And heard another's voice cry: 'What! are *you* here?'
Although we were not. I was still the same,
Knowing myself yet being someone other—
And he a face still forming; yet the words sufficed
To compel the recognition they preceded.
And so, compliant to the common wind,
Too strange to each other for misunderstanding,
In concord at this intersection time
Of meeting nowhere, no before and after,
We trod the pavement in a dead patrol.
I said: 'The wonder that I feel is easy,
Yet ease is cause of wonder. Therefore speak:
I may not comprehend, may not remember.'
And he: 'I am not eager to rehearse
My thought and theory which you have forgotten.
These things have served their purpose: let them be.
So with your own, and pray they be forgiven
By others, as I pray you to forgive
Both bad and good. Last season's fruit is eaten
And the fullfed beast shall kick the empty pail.
For last year's words belong to last year's language
And next year's words await another voice.
But, as the passage now presents no hindrance
To the spirit unappeased and peregrine
Between two worlds become much like each other,
So I find words I never thought to speak
In streets I never thought I should revisit
When I left my body on a distant shore.
Since our concern was speech, and speech impelled us
To purify the dialect of the tribe
And urge the mind to aftersight and foresight,
Let me disclose the gifts reserved for age
To set a crown upon your lifetime's effort.
First, the cold friction of expiring sense
Without enchantment, offering no promise
But bitter tastelessness of shadow fruit
As body and soul begin to fall asunder.
Second, the conscious impotence of rage
At human folly, and the laceration

Of laughter at what ceases to amuse.
And last, the rending pain of re-enactment
Of all that you have done, and been; the shame
Of motives late revealed, and the awareness
Of things ill done and done to others' harm
Which once you took for exercise of virtue.
Then fools' approval stings, and honour stains.
From wrong to wrong the exasperated spirit
Proceeds, unless restored by that refining fire
Where you must move in measure, like a dancer.'
The day was breaking. In the disfigured street
He left me, with a kind of valediction,
And faded on the blowing of the horn.

III

There are three conditions which often look alike
Yet differ completely, flourish in the same hedgerow:
Attachment to self and to things and to persons, detachment
From self and from things and from persons; and, growing
between them, indifference
Which resembles the others as death resembles life,
Being between two lives—unflowering, between
The live and the dead nettle. This is the use of memory:
For liberation—not less of love but expanding
Of love beyond desire, and so liberation
From the future as well as the past. Thus, love of a country
Begins as attachment to our own field of action
And comes to find that action of little importance
Though never indifferent. History may be servitude,
History may be freedom. See, now they vanish,
The faces and places, with the self which, as it could, loved them,
To become renewed, transfigured, in another pattern.

Sin is Behovely, but
All shall be well, and
All manner of thing shall be well.
If I think, again, of this place,
And of people, not wholly commendable,

Of no immediate kin or kindness,
But some of peculiar genius,
All touched by a common genius,
United in the strife which divided them;
If I think of a king at nightfall,
Of three men, and more, on the scaffold
And a few who died forgotten
In other places, here and abroad,
And of one who died blind and quiet,
Why should we celebrate
These dead men more than the dying?
It is not to ring the bell backward
Nor is it an incantation
To summon the spectre of a Rose.
We cannot revive old factions
We cannot restore old policies
Or follow an antique drum.
These men, and those who opposed them
And those whom they opposed
Accept the constitution of silence
And are folded in a single party.
Whatever we inherit from the fortunate
We have taken from the defeated
What they had to leave us—a symbol:
A symbol perfected in death.
And all shall be well and
All manner of thing shall be well
By the purification of the motive
In the ground of our beseeching.

IV

The dove descending breaks the air
With flame of incandescent terror
Of which the tongues declare
The one discharge from sin and error.
The only hope, or else despair
    Lies in the choice of pyre or pyre—
    To be redeemed from fire by fire.

Who then devised the torment? Love.
Love is the unfamiliar Name
Behind the hands that wove
The intolerable shirt of flame
Which human power cannot remove.
We only live, only suspire
Consumed by either fire or fire.

V

What we call the beginning is often the end
And to make an end is to make a beginning.
The end is where we start from. And every phrase
And sentence that is right (where every word is at home,
Taking its place to support the others,
The word neither diffident nor ostentatious,
An easy commerce of the old and the new,
The common word exact without vulgarity,
The formal word precise but not pedantic,
The complete consort dancing together)
Every phrase and every sentence is an end and a beginning,
Every poem an epitaph. And any action
Is a step to the block, to the fire, down the sea's throat
Or to an illegible stone: and that is where we start.
We die with the dying:
See, they depart, and we go with them.
We are born with the dead:
See, they return, and bring us with them.
The moment of the rose and the moment of the yew-tree
Are of equal duration. A people without history
Is not redeemed from time, for history is a pattern
Of timeless moments. So, while the light fails
On a winter's afternoon, in a secluded chapel
History is now and England.
With the drawing of this Love and the voice of this Calling

We shall not cease from exploration
And the end of all our exploring

Will be to arrive where we started
And know the place for the first time.
Through the unknown, remembered gate
When the last of earth left to discover
Is that which was the beginning;
At the source of the longest river
The voice of the hidden waterfall
And the children in the apple-tree
Not known, because not looked for
But heard, half-heard, in the stillness
Between two waves of the sea.
Quick now, here, now, always—
A condition of complete simplicity
(Costing not less than everything)
And all shall be well and
All manner of thing shall be well
When the tongues of flame are in-folded
Into the crowned knot of fire
And the fire and the rose are one.

H. Leivick

1888–1962

The Sturdy in Me

The sturdy in me—song of ancient white bones,
I am in the thrall of the bony whiteness.
Smaller than the smallest I am, but older—eternal,
Intimate with the lord of hidden life.

Where is my beginning that I began?
Where is my end that I will end?
Yet, see: my eyes stray over Hester Park
And my heart rises in a great light.

What am I doing here, in New York's Hester Park?
I shall come again, I shall come again.
To look into the radiant eyes of the poor
And to hear the song of ancient white bones.

My father's grave—near an old mill
In a small town in a Russian field,
My mother's grave—near the same mill—
Old mill,
Old mill—
Light up in the glow of New York's Hester Park.

Hester Park is full of hands, toiling trusting hands,
And toiling hands carry on their palms
Measure and weight, judgment and verdict, and final destiny.

What am I doing here, in New York's Hester Park—
I shall come again and come again—
To look into the fiery eyes of the poor
And to hear the song of ancient white bones.

John Crowe Ransom

1888–1974

Armageddon

Antichrist, playing his lissome flute and merry
As was his wont, debouched upon the plain;
Then came a swirl of dust, and Christ drew rein,
Brooding upon his frugal breviary.

Now which shall die, the roundel, rose, and hall,
Or else the tonsured beadsman's monkery?
For Christ and Antichrist arm cap-a-pie,
The prospect charms the soul of the lean jackal.

But Antichrist got down from the Barbary beast
And doffed his plume in courteous prostration;
Christ left his jennet's back in deprecation
And raised him, his own hand about the waist.

Then they must finger chivalry's quaint page,
Of precedence discoursing by the letter.
The oratory of Antichrist was better,
He invested Christ with the elder lineage.

He set Christ on his own Mahomet's back
Where Christ sat fortressed up like Diomede;
The cynical jennet was the other steed,
Obtuse, and most indifferent to attack.

The lordings measured lances and stood still,
And each was loath to let the other's blood;
Originally they were one brotherhood;
There stood the white pavilion on the hill.

To the pavilion went then the hierarchs,
If they might truce their honorable dispute;
Firm was the Christian's chin and he was mute,
And Antichrist ejected scant remarks.

Antichrist tendered a spray of rosemary
To serve his brother for a buttonhole,
Then Christ about his adversary's poll
Wrapped a dry palm that grew on Calvary.

Christ wore a dusty cassock, and the knight
Did him the honors of his tiring-hall,
Whence Christ did not come forth too finical
In his egregious beauty richly dight.

With feasting they concluded every day,
And when the other shaped his phrases thicker
Christ, introducing water in the liquor,
Made wine of more ethereal bouquet.

At wassail Antichrist would pitch the strain
For unison of all the retinue;
Christ beat the time, and hummed a stave or two,
But did not say the words, which were profane.

Perruquiers were privily presented,
Till, knowing his need extreme and his heart pure,
Christ let them dress him his thick chevelure,
And soon his beard was glozed and sweetly scented.

And so the Wolf said Brother to the Lamb,
The True Heir keeping with the poor Impostor,
The rubric and the holy paternoster
Were jangled strangely with the dithyramb.

It could not be. There was a patriarch,
A godly liege of old malignant brood
Who could not fathom the new brotherhood
Between the children of the light and dark.

He sought the ear of Christ on these doings
But in the white pavilion when he stood
And saw them favored and dressed like twins at food,
Profound and mad became his misgivings.

The voices, and their burdens, he must hear,
But equal between the pleasant Princes flew
Theology, art, the old customs and new;
Hoarsely he ran and hissed—in the wrong ear!

He was discomfited, but Christ much more.
Christ sheds unmannerly his devil's pelf,
Takes ashes from the hearth and smears himself,
Calls for his smock and jennet as before.

His trump recalls his own to right opinions,
With scourge they mortify their carnal selves,
With stone they whet the ax-heads on the helves
And seek the Prince Beelzebub and minions.

Christ and his myrmidons, Christ at the head,
Chanted of death and glory and no complaisance;
Antichrist and the armies of malfeasance
Made songs of innocence and no bloodshed.

The immortal Adversary shook his head;
If now they fought too long, why, he would famish;
And if much blood was shed he would be squeamish.
"These Armageddons!" he said; and later bled.

Conrad Aiken

1889–1973

Tetélestai

I

How shall we praise the magnificence of the dead,
The great man humbled, the haughty brought to dust?
Is there a horn we should not blow as proudly
For the meanest of us all, who creeps his days,
Guarding his heart from blows, to die obscurely?
I am no king, have laid no kingdoms waste,
Taken no princes captive, led no triumphs
Of weeping women through long walls of trumpets;
Say rather, I am no one, or an atom;
Say rather, two great gods, in a vault of starlight,
Play ponderingly at chess, and at the game's end
One of the pieces, shaken, falls to the floor
And runs to the darkest corner; and that piece
Forgotten there, left motionless, is I. . . .
Say that I have no name, no gifts, no power,
Am only one of millions, mostly silent;
One who came with eyes and hands and a heart,
Looked on beauty, and loved it, and then left it.
Say that the fates of time and space obscured me,
Led me a thousand ways to pain, bemused me,

Wrapped me in ugliness; and like great spiders
Dispatched me at their leisure. . . . Well, what then?
Should I not hear, as I lie down in dust,
The horns of glory blowing above my burial?

II

Morning and evening opened and closed above me:
Houses were built above me; trees let fall
Yellowing leaves upon me, hands of ghosts;
Rain has showered its arrows of silver upon me
Seeking my heart; winds have roared and tossed me;
Music in long blue waves of sound has borne me
A helpless weed to shores of unthought silence;
Time, above me, within me, crashed its gongs
Of terrible warning, sifting the dust of death;
And here I lie. Blow now your horns of glory
Harshly over my flesh, you trees, you waters!
You stars and suns, Canopus, Deneb, Rigel,
Let me, as I lie down, here in this dust,
Hear, far off, your whispered salutation!
Roar now above my decaying flesh, you winds,
Whirl out your earth-scents over this body, tell me
Of ferns and stagnant pools, wild roses, hillsides!
Anoint me, rain, let crash your silver arrows
On this hard flesh! I am the one who named you,
I lived in you, and now I die in you.
I your son, your daughter, treader of music,
Lie broken, conquered . . . Let me not fall in silence.

III

I, the restless one; the circler of circles;
Herdsman and roper of stars, who could not capture
The secret of self; I who was tyrant to weaklings,
Striker of children; destroyer of women; corrupter
Of innocent dreamers, and laugher at beauty; I,
Too easily brought to tears and weakness by music,
Baffled and broken by love, the helpless beholder

Of the war in my heart of desire with desire, the struggle
Of hatred with love, terror with hunger; I
Who laughed without knowing the cause of my laughter, who
grew
Without wishing to grow, a servant to my own body;
Loved without reason the laughter and flesh of a woman,
Enduring such torments to find her! I who at last
Grow weaker, struggle more feebly, relent in my purpose,
Choose for my triumph an easier end, look backward
At earlier conquests; or, caught in the web, cry out
In a sudden and empty despair, 'Tetélestai!'
Pity me, now! I, who was arrogant, beg you!
Tell me, as I lie down, that I was courageous.
Blow horns of victory now, as I reel and am vanquished.
Shatter the sky with trumpets above my grave.

IV

. . . Look! this flesh how it crumbles to dust and is blown!
These bones, how they grind in the granite of frost and are
nothing!
This skull, how it yawns for a flicker of time in the darkness,
Yet laughs not and sees not! It is crushed by a hammer of
sunlight,
And the hands are destroyed. . . . Press down through the
leaves of the jasmine,
Dig through the interlaced roots—nevermore will you find me;
I was no better than dust, yet you cannot replace me. . . .
Take the soft dust in your hand—does it stir: does it sing?
Has it lips and a heart? Does it open its eyes to the sun?
Does it run, does it dream, does it burn with a secret, or tremble
In terror of death? Or ache with tremendous decisions? . . .
Listen! . . . It says: 'I lean by the river. The willows
Are yellowed with bud. White clouds roar up from the south
And darken the ripples; but they cannot darken my heart,
Nor the face like a star in my heart! . . . Rain falls on the water
And pelts it, and rings it with silver. The willow trees glisten,
The sparrows chirp under the eaves; but the face in my heart
Is a secret of music. . . . I wait in the rain and am silent.'

Listen again! . . . It says: 'I have worked, I am tired,
The pencil dulls in my hand: I see through the window
Walls upon walls of windows with faces behind them,
Smoke floating up to the sky, an ascension of sea-gulls.
I am tired. I have struggled in vain, my decision was fruitless,
Why then do I wait? with darkness, so easy, at hand! . . .
But tomorrow, perhaps . . . I will wait and endure till
    tomorrow!' . . .
Or again: 'It is dark. The decision is made. I am vanquished
By terror of life. The walls mount slowly about me
In coldness. I had not the courage. I was forsaken.
I cried out, was answered by silence . . . Tetélestai! . . .'

V

Hear how it babbles!—Blow the dust out of your hand,
With its voices and visions, tread on it, forget it, turn homeward
With dreams in your brain. . . . This, then, is the humble, the
    nameless,—
The lover, the husband and father, the struggler with shadows,
The one who went down under shoutings of chaos, the weakling
Who cried his 'forsaken!' like Christ on the darkening
    hilltop! . . .
This, then, is the one who implores, as he dwindles to silence,
A fanfare of glory. . . . And which of us dares to deny him?

Mikhail Naimy

1889–1988

Autumn Leaves

Spread over the earth!
O joy of the eye
ballroom of sun, O
swing of the moon
O organ of night and O
guitar of dawn!

Sign of the restless,
art of the wayward,
memory's total glory—
the trees have cast you off.

Dress our earth!
Touch, leaf to leaf,
the shadows of the lost,
then raise your head to the vast blue:
the past will not return.

And once you leave old friends behind
dance your heart to the caravan
of Fate. Touch, leaf to leaf.
Cast no blame on branch, wind, or cloud.
They cannot soothe; they cannot reply.

Time is ripe with wonders
spreads a wake of ruins
stills desire, and does not heed a plea.
Go on—blame no one—

back to the arms of the earth.
Turn the Wheel once more,
Forget your faded beauty:
the past will not return.

How many roses before you bloomed
and how many did fade!

Do not be afraid; Fate is not at fault.
The jewel we have lost
we will find again in the grave.

Go back to the arms of the earth.

Translated from Arabic by
Sharif S. Elmusa with Gregory Orfalea

Claude McKay

1890–1948

I Know My Soul

I plucked my soul out of its secret place,
And held it to the mirror of my eye,
To see it like a star against the sky,
A twitching body quivering in space,
A spark of passion shining on my face.
And I explored it to determine why
This awful key to my infinity
Conspires to rob me of sweet joy and grace.
And if the sign may not be fully read,
If I can comprehend but not control,
I need not gloom my days with futile dread,
Because I see a part and not the whole.
Contemplating the strange, I'm comforted
By this narcotic thought: I know my soul.

Russian Cathedral

Bow down my soul in worship very low
And in the holy silences be lost.
Bow down before the marble man of woe,
Bow down before the singing angel host.
What jewelled glory fills my spirit's eye!
What golden grandeur moves the depths of me!
The soaring arches lift me up on high
Taking my breath with their rare symmetry.

Bow down my soul and let the wondrous light
Of Beauty bathe thee from her lofty throne,
Bow down before the wonder of man's might.
Bow down in worship, humble and alone;
Bow lowly down before the sacred sight
Of man's divinity alive in stone.

Edna St. Vincent Millay

1892–1950

God's World

O world, I cannot hold thee close enough!
  Thy winds, thy wide grey skies!
  Thy mists, that roll and rise!
Thy woods, this autumn day, that ache and sag
And all but cry with colour! That gaunt crag
To crush! To lift the lean of that black bluff!
World, World, I cannot get thee close enough!

Long have I known a glory in it all,
      But never knew I this;
      Here such a passion is
As stretcheth me apart,—Lord, I do fear
Thou'st made the world too beautiful this year;
My soul is all but out of me,—let fall
No burning leaf; prithee, let no bird call.

Samuel Greenberg

1893–1917

God

I followed and breathed in silence.
What of its task is beheld?
My feeding thee has lent all
Which broke the current thread breeze
That kept the sprout of pregnant seas
Of weathered promising call.

The filing shades he only changes,
Tells the logos, its unearned dew
Not to feed, as if from cages,
His cloak that perfumes fragrant hew;
What of all the bulging mountains,
Sordid earth and rotting clays?
If then sense is suction fountains,
That same thought is but its ways.

E. E. Cummings

1894–1962

i thank You God for most this amazing
day:for the leaping greenly spirits of trees
and a blue true dream of sky;and for everything
which is natural which is infinite which is yes

(i who have died am alive again today,
and this is the sun's birthday;this is the birth
day of life and of love and wings:and of the gay
great happening illimitably earth)

how should tasting touching hearing seeing
breathing any—lifted from the no
of all nothing—human merely being
doubt unimaginable You?

(now the ears of my ears awake and
now the eyes of my eyes are opened)

Charles Reznikoff

1894–1976

Luzzato

Padua 1727

The sentences we studied are rungs upon the ladder Jacob saw;
the law itself is nothing but the road;
I have become impatient of what the rabbis said,
and try to listen to what the angels say.
I have left Padua and am in Jerusalem at last, my friend;
for, as our God was never of wood or bone,
our land is not of stones or earth.

Spinoza

He is the stars,
multitudinous as the drops of rain,
and the worm at our feet,
leaving only a blot on the stone;
except God there is nothing.

God neither hates nor loves, has neither pleasure nor pain;
were God to hate or love, He would not be God;
He is not a hero to fight our enemies,
nor like a king to be angry or pleased at us,
nor even a father to give us our daily bread, forgive us our
trespasses;
nothing is but as He wishes,
nothing was but as He willed it;
as He wills it, so it will be.

There is nobody in the street
of those who crowded about David
to watch me
as I dance before the Lord:
alone in my unimportance
to do as I like.

Jean Toomer

1894–1967

Prayer

My body is opaque to the soul.
Driven of the spirit, long have I sought to temper it unto the
spirit's longing,
But my mind, too, is opaque to the soul.
A closed lid is my soul's flesh-eye.
O Spirits of whom my soul is but a little finger,
Direct it to the lid of its flesh-eye.
I am weak with much giving.
I am weak with the desire to give more.
(How strong a thing is the little finger!)
So weak that I have confused the body with the soul,
And the body with its little finger.
(How frail is the little finger.)
My voice could not carry to you did you dwell in stars,
O Spirits of whom my soul is but a little finger . .

The Gods Are Here

This is no mountain
But a house,
No rock of solitude
But a family chair,
No wilds
But life appearing

As life anywhere domesticated,
Yet I know the gods are here,
And that if I touch them
I will arise
And take majesty into the kitchen.

Jacob Glatshteyn

1896–1971

Without Offerings

I am poor. I don't bring you
Any more offerings.
I come near you, empty-handed.
The phrases with their explained-away heads
I threw out long ago.
I know how you always rejoiced
In symbols.

As to sad synagogues,
To doorsteps of belief—
How hard to come back
To old words.
I know well their places.
I hear their humming.
At times I get close, I look longingly
Through the windowpanes.

But you, still resting in the shadows of biblical trees,
Oh sing me chilly consolation
Of all that you remember, all that you know.

Louise Bogan

1897–1970

Night

The cold remote islands
And the blue estuaries
Where what breathes, breathes
The restless wind of the inlets,
And what drinks, drinks
The incoming tide;

Where shell and weed
Wait upon the salt wash of the sea,
And the clear nights of stars
Swing their lights westward
To set behind the land;

Where the pulse clinging to the rocks
Renews itself forever;
Where, again on cloudless nights,
The water reflects
The firmament's partial setting;

—O remember
In your narrowing dark hours
That more things move
Than blood in the heart.

John Wheelwright

1897–1940

Fish Food

An Obituary to Hart Crane

As you drank deep as Thor, did you think of milk or wine?
Did you drink blood, while you drank the salt deep?
Or see through the film of light, that sharpened your rage with
 its stare,
a shark, dolphin, turtle? Did you not see the Cat
who, when Thor lifted her, unbased the cubic ground?
You would drain fathomless flagons to be slaked with vacuum—
The sea's teats have suckled you, and you are sunk far
in bubble-dreams, under swaying translucent vines
of thundering interior wonder. Eagles can never now
carry parts of your body, over cupped mountains
as emblems of their anger, embers to fire self-hate
to other wonders, unfolding white, flaming vistas.

Fishes now look upon you, with eyes which do not gossip.
Fishes are never shocked. Fishes will kiss you, each
fish tweak you; every kiss take bits of you away,
till your bones alone will roll, with the Gulf Stream's swell.
So has it been already, so have the carpers and puffers
nibbled your carcass of fame, each to his liking. Now
in tides of noon, the bones of your thought-suspended structures
gleam as you intended. Noon pulled your eyes with small
magnetic headaches; the will seeped from your blood. Seeds
of meaning popped from the pods of thought. And you fall. And
 the unseen
churn of Time changes the pearl-hued ocean;
like a pearl-shaped drop, in a huge water-clock
falling; from *came* to *go*, from *come* to *went*. And you fell.

Waters received you. Waters of our Birth in Death dissolve you.
Now you have willed it, may the Great Wash take you.

As the Mother-Lover takes your woe away, and cleansing
grief and you away, you sleep, you do not snore.
Lie still. Your rage is gone on a bright flood
away; as, when a bad friend held out his hand
you said, "Do not talk any more. I know you meant no harm."
What was the soil whence your anger sprang, who are deaf
as the stones to the whispering flight of the Mississippi's rivers?
What did you see as you fell? What did you hear as you sank?
Did it make you drunken with hearing?
I will not ask any more. You saw or heard no evil.

Come Over and Help Us

A Rhapsody

I

Our masks are gauze / and screen our faces for those unlike us
only,
Who are easily deceived. / Pierce through these masks to our
unhidden tongues
And watch us scold, / scold with intellectual lust; / scold
Ourselves, our foes, our friends; / Europe, America, Boston; and
all that is not
Boston; / till we reach a purity, fierce as the love of God;— / Hate.
Hate, still fed by the shadowed source; / but fallen, stagnant
fallen;
Sunk low between thin channels; rises, rises; / swells to burst
Its walls; and rolls out deep and wide. / Hate rules our drowning
Race.
Any freed from our Tyrant; / abandon their farms, forsake their
Country, *become American.*

We, the least subtle of Peoples, / lead each only one life at a
time,—
Being never, never anything but sincere; / yet we trust our
honesty
So little that we dare not depart from it,— / knowing it to need
habitual stimulation.

And living amid a world of Spooks, / we summon another to us
Who is (in some sort) our Clown,— / as he affords us amusement.
O! sweet tormentor, Doubt! longed-for and human, / leave us some plausible
Evil motive, however incredible. / The Hate in the World outside our World
(Envious, malicious, vindictive) / makes our Hate gleam in the splendor
Of a Castrate / who with tongue plucked out; / arms, legs sawed off;
Eyes and ears, pierced through; / still thinks / thinks
By means of all his nutriment, / with intense, exacting Energy, terrible, consuming.
Madness, we so politely placate / as an every-day inconvenience
We shun in secret. / Madness is sumptuous; Hate, ascetic.
Those only who remain sane, / taste the flavor of Hate.
Strong Joy, we forbid ourselves / and deny large pleasurable objects,
But, too shrewd to forego amusement, / we enjoy all joys which, dying, leave us teased.
So spare us, sweet Doubt, our tormentor, / the Arts, our concerts, and novels;
The theater, sports, the exotic Past; / to use to stave off Madness,
To use as breathing spells, / that our drug's tang may not die.
We are not tireless; / distract us from thin ecstasy, that we may hate
If with less conviction, / with some result, some end,—
So pure ourselves; so clear our passion; / *pure, clear, alone.*

II

The New Englander leaves New England / to flaunt his drab person
Before Latin decors / and Asiatic back-drops.
Wearies. / Returns to life,—life tried for a little while.
A poor sort of thing / (filling the stomach; emptying the bowels;
Bothering to speak to friends on the street; / filling the stomach again;

Dancing, drinking, whoring) / forms the tissue of this fabric.—
(Marriage; society; business; charity;— / *Life, and life refused*.)

The New Englander appraises sins, / finds them beyond his means, / and hoards.
Likewise, he seldom spends his goodness / on someone ignoble as he,
But, to make an occasion, he proves himself / that he is equally ignoble.
Then he breaks his fast! / Then he ends his thirsting!
He censors the Judge. / He passes judgment on the Censor. / No language is left.
His lone faculty, Condemnation,—condemned. / Nothing is left to say.
Proclaim an Armistice / Through Existence, livid, void, / *let silence flood*.

Ask the Silent One your question. / (He is stupid in misery
No more than the talkative man, who talks through his hat.) / Ask the question.
If he replied at all, / it would be to remark that he never could despise
Anyone so much as himself / should he once give way to Self-pity.
A different act of faith is his,— / the white gesture of Humility.
He knows his weakness. / He is well-schooled / and he never forgets the shortest
Title of his Knowledge. / The jailer of his Soul sees Pride. / He sees
Tears, never. / The Silent One is so eaten away
He cannot make that little effort / which surrender to external Fact
Requires, / but looks out always only with one wish,— / *to realize he exists*.

Lo! a Desire! / A Faint motive! / A motive (however faint) beyond disinterestedness.
Faint. / It is faint. / But the boundary is clear. / Desire, oh desire further!
Past that boundary lies Annihilation / where the Soul

Breaks the monotonous familiar / and man wakes to the
shocking
Unastounded company of other men. / But the Silent One
would not pass
Where the Redmen have gone. / He would live without end.
That,— / *the ultimate nature of Hell.*

Bread-Word Giver

For John, unborn

John, founder of towns,—dweller in none;
Wheelwright, schismatic,— schismatic from schismatics;
friend of great men whom these great feared greatly;
Saint, whose name and business I bear with me;
rebel New England's rebel against dominion;
who made bread-giving words for bread makers;
whose blood floods me with purgatorial fire;
I, and my unliving son, adjure you:
keep us alive with your ghostly disputation
make our renunciation of dominion
mark not the escape, but the permanent of rebellion.

Speak! immigrant ancestor in blood; brain
ancestor of all immigrants I like. Speak,
who unsealed sealed wells with a flame and sword:
'The springs that we dug clean must be kept flowing.
If Philistines choke wells with dirt,—open
'em up clear. And we have a flaming flare
whose light is the flare that flames up in the people.

'The way we take (who will not fire and water
taken away) is this: prepare to fight. If we
fight not for fear in the night, we shall be surprised.
Wherever we live, who want present abundance
take care to show ourselves brave. If *we* do not try
they prevail. Come out,—get ready for war;
stalwart men, out and fight. Cursed
are all who'll come not against strong wrong.

First steel your swordarm and first sword.
But the second way to go? and deed to do?

'That is this: Take hold upon our foes and kill.
We are they whose power underneath a nation
breaks it in bits as shivered by iron bars.
What iron bars are these but working wills?
Toothed as spiked threshing flails we beat
hills into chaff. Wherefore, handle our second
swords with awe. They are two-edged. They cut their
  wielders' hearts.'

Melvin B. Tolson

1898–1966

A Song for Myself

I judge
My soul
Eagle
Nor mole:
A man
Is what
He saves
From rot.

The corn
Will fat
A hog
Or rat:
Are these
Dry bones
A hut's
Or throne's?

Who filled
The moat

'Twixt sheep
And goat?
Let Death,
The twin
Of Life,
Slip in?

Prophets
Arise,
Mask-hid,
Unwise,
Divide
The earth
By class
And birth.

Caesars
Without,
The People
Shall rout;
Caesars
Within,
Crush flat
As tin.

Who makes
A noose
Envies
The goose.
Who digs
A pit
Dices
For it.

Shall tears
Be shed
For those
Whose bread
Is thieved

Headlong?
Tears right
No wrong.

Prophets
Shall teach
The meek
To reach.
Leave not
To God
The boot
And rod.

The straight
Lines curve?
Failure
Of nerve?
Blind-spots
Assail?
Times have
Their Braille.

If hue
Of skin
Trademark
A sin,
Blame not
The *make*
For God's
Mistake.

Since flesh
And bone
Turn dust
And stone,
With life
So brief,
Why add
To grief?

I sift
The chaff
From wheat
And laugh.
No curse
Can stop
The tick
Of clock.

Those who
Wall in
Themselves
And grin
Commit
Incest
And spawn
A pest.

What's writ
In vice
Is writ
In ice.
The truth
Is not
Of fruits
That rot.

A sponge,
The mind
Soaks in
The kind
Of stuff
That fate's
Milieu
Dictates.

Jesus,
Mozart,
Shakespeare,

Descartes,
Lenin,
Chladni,
Have lodged
With me.

I snatch
From hooks
The meat
Of books.
I seek
Frontiers,
Not worlds
On biers.

The snake
Entoils
The pig
With coils.
The pig's
Skewed wail
Does not
Prevail.

Old men
Grow worse
With prayer
Or curse:
Their staffs
Thwack youth
Starved thin
For truth.

Today
The Few
Yield poets
Their due;
Tomorrow
The Mass

Judgment
Shall pass.

I harbor
One fear
If death
Crouch near:
Does my
Creed span
The Gulf
Of Man?

And when
I go
In calm
Or blow
From mice
And men,
Selah!
What . . . then?

Léonie Adams

1899–1988

Bell Tower

I have seen, desolate one, the voice has its tower;
The voice also, builded at secret cost,
Its temple of precious tissue. Not silent then
Forever—casting silence in your hour.

There marble boys are leant from the light throat,
Thick locks that hang with dew and eyes dewlashed,
Dazzled with morning, angels of the wind,
With ear a-point for the enchanted note.

And these at length shall tip the hanging bell,
And first the sound must gather in deep bronze,
Till, clearer than ice, purer than a bubble of gold,
It beat in the sky and the air and the ear's remorseless well.

Hart Crane

1899–1932

Lachrymae Christi

Whitely, while benzine
Rinsings from the moon
Dissolve all but the windows of the mills
(Inside the sure machinery
Is still
And curdled only where a sill
Sluices its one unyielding smile)

Immaculate venom binds
The fox's teeth, and swart
Thorns freshen on the year's
First blood. From flanks unfended,
Twanged red perfidies of spring
Are trillion on the hill.

And the nights opening
Chant pyramids,—
Anoint with innocence,—recall
To music and retrieve what perjuries
Had galvanized the eyes.

While chime
Beneath and all around
Distilling clemencies,—worms'
Inaudible whistle, tunneling
Not penitence
But song, as these
Perpetual fountains, vines,—

Thy Nazarene and tinder eyes.

(Let sphinxes from the ripe
Borage of death have cleared my tongue
Once and again; vermin and rod
No longer bind. Some sentient cloud
Of tears flocks through the tendoned loam:
Betrayed stones slowly speak.)

Names peeling from Thine eyes
And their undimming lattices of flame,
Spell out in palm and pain
Compulsion of the year, O Nazarene.

Lean long from sable, slender boughs,
Unstanched and luminous. And as the nights
Strike from Thee perfect spheres,
Lift up in lilac-emerald breath the grail
Of earth again—

Thy face
From charred and riven stakes, O
Dionysus, Thy
Unmangled target smile.

FROM *Voyages*

—And yet this great wink of eternity,
Of rimless floods, unfettered leewardings,
Samite sheeted and processioned where
Her undinal vast belly moonward bends,
Laughing the wrapt inflections of our love;

Take this Sea, whose diapason knells
On scrolls of silver snowy sentences,
The sceptred terror of whose sessions rends
As her demeanors motion well or ill,
All but the pieties of lovers' hands.

And onward, as bells off San Salvador
Salute the crocus lustres of the stars,
In these poinsettia meadows of her tides,—
Adagios of islands, O my Prodigal,
Complete the dark confessions her veins spell.

Mark how her turning shoulders wind the hours,
And hasten while her penniless rich palms
Pass superscription of bent foam and wave,—
Hasten, while they are true,—sleep, death, desire,
Close round one instant in one floating flower.

Bind us in time, O Seasons clear, and awe.
O minstrel galleons of Carib fire,
Bequeath us to no earthly shore until
Is answered in the vortex of our grave
The seal's wide spindrift gaze toward paradise.

FROM *The Bridge*

From going to and fro in the earth,
and from walking up and down in it.
THE BOOK OF JOB

TO BROOKLYN BRIDGE

How many dawns, chill from his rippling rest
The seagull's wings shall dip and pivot him,
Shedding white rings of tumult, building high
Over the chained bay waters Liberty—

Then, with inviolate curve, forsake our eyes
As apparitional as sails that cross
Some page of figures to be filed away;
—Till elevators drop us front our day . . .

I think of cinemas, panoramic sleights
With multitudes bent toward some flashing scene
Never disclosed, but hastened to again,
Foretold to other eyes on the same screen;

And Thee, across the harbor, silver-paced
As though the sun took step of thee, yet left
Some motion ever unspent in thy stride,—
Implicitly thy freedom staying thee!

Out of some subway scuttle, cell or loft
A bedlamite speeds to thy parapets,
Tilting there momently, shrill shirt ballooning,
A jest falls from the speechless caravan.

Down Wall, from girder into street noon leaks,
A rip-tooth of the sky's acetylene;
All afternoon the cloud-flown derricks turn . . .
Thy cables breathe the North Atlantic still.

And obscure as that heaven of the Jews,
Thy guerdon . . . Accolade thou dost bestow
Of anonymity time cannot raise:
Vibrant reprieve and pardon thou dost show.

O harp and altar, of the fury fused,
(How could mere toil align thy choiring strings!)
Terrific threshold of the prophet's pledge,
Prayer of pariah, and the lover's cry,—

Again the traffic lights that skim thy swift
Unfractioned idiom, immaculate sigh of stars,
Beading thy path—condense eternity:
And we have seen night lifted in thine arms.

Under thy shadow by the piers I waited;
Only in darkness is thy shadow clear.
The City's fiery parcels all undone,
Already snow submerges an iron year . . .

O Sleepless as the river under thee,
Vaulting the sea, the prairies' dreaming sod,
Unto us lowliest sometime sweep, descend
And of the curveship lend a myth to God.

I. AVE MARIA

Venient annis, saecula seris,
Quibus Oceanus vincula rerum
Laxet et ingens pateat tellus
Tethysque novos detegat orbes
Nec sit terris ultima Thule.
—SENECA

Columbus, alone, gazing toward Spain, invokes the presence of two faithful partisans of his quest . . .

Be with me, Luis de San Angel, now—
Witness before the tides can wrest away
The word I bring, O you who reined my suit
Into the Queen's great heart that doubtful day;
For I have seen now what no perjured breath
Of clown nor sage can riddle or gainsay;—
To you, too, Juan Perez, whose counsel fear
And greed adjourned,—I bring you back Cathay!

Here waves climb into dusk on gleaming mail;
Invisible valves of the sea,—locks, tendons
Crested and creeping, troughing corridors
That fall back yawning to another plunge.
Slowly the sun's red caravel drops light
Once more behind us. . . . It is morning there—
O where our Indian emperies lie revealed,
Yet lost, all, let this keel one instant yield!

I thought of Genoa; and this truth, now proved,
That made me exile in her streets, stood me
More absolute than ever—biding the moon
Till dawn should clear that dim frontier, first seen
—The Chan's great continent. . . . Then faith, not fear
Nigh surged me witless. . . . Hearing the surf near—
I, wonder-breathing, kept the watch,—saw
The first palm chevron the first lighted hill.

And lowered. And they came out to us crying,
"The Great White Birds!" (O Madre Maria, still
One ship of these thou grantest safe returning;
Assure us through thy mantle's ageless blue!)
And record of more, floating in a casque,
Was tumbled from us under bare poles scudding;
And later hurricanes may claim more pawn. . . .
For here between two worlds, another, harsh,

This third, of water, tests the word; lo, here
Bewilderment and mutiny heap whelming
Laughter, and shadow cuts sleep from the heart
Almost as though the Moor's flung scimitar
Found more than flesh to fathom in its fall.
Yet under tempest-lash and surfeitings
Some inmost sob, half-heard, dissuades the abyss,
Merges the wind in measure to the waves,

Series on series, infinite,—till eyes
Starved wide on blackened tides, accrete—enclose
This turning rondure whole, this crescent ring
Sun-cusped and zoned with modulated fire
Like pearls that whisper through the Doge's hands
—Yet no delirium of jewels! O Fernando,
Take of that eastern shore, this western sea,
Yet yield thy God's, thy Virgin's charity!

—Rush down the plenitude, and you shall see
Isaiah counting famine on this lee!

. . .

An herb, a stray branch among salty teeth,
The jellied weeds that drag the shore,—perhaps
Tomorrow's moon will grant us Saltes Bar—
Palos again,—a land cleared of long war.
Some Angelus environs the cordage tree;
Dark waters onward shake the dark prow free.

. . .

O Thou who sleepest on Thyself, apart
Like ocean athwart lanes of death and birth,

And all the eddying breath between dost search
Cruelly with love thy parable of man,—
Inquisitor! incognizable Word
Of Eden and the enchained Sepulchre,
Into thy steep savannahs, burning blue,
Utter to loneliness the sail is true.

Who grindest oar, and arguing the mast
Subscribest holocaust of ships, O Thou
Within whose primal scan consummately
The glistening seignories of Ganges swim;—
Who sendest greeting by the corposant,
And Teneriffe's garnet—flamed it in a cloud,
Urging through night our passage to the Chan;—
Te Deum laudamus, for thy teeming span!

Of all that amplitude that time explores,
A needle in the sight, suspended north,—
Yielding by inference and discard, faith
And true appointment from the hidden shoal:
This disposition that thy night relates
From Moon to Saturn in one sapphire wheel:
The orbic wake of thy once whirling feet,
Elohim, still I hear thy sounding heel!

White toil of heaven's cordons, mustering
In holy rings all sails charged to the far
Hushed gleaming fields and pendant seething wheat
Of knowledge,—round thy brows unhooded now
—The kindled Crown! acceded of the poles
And biassed by full sails, meridians reel
Thy purpose—still one shore beyond desire!
The sea's green crying towers a-sway, Beyond

And kingdoms
        naked in the
               trembling heart—
   Te Deum laudamus
              O Thou Hand of Fire

VII. THE TUNNEL

To Find the Western path
Right thro' the Gates of Wrath.
—BLAKE

Performances, assortments, résumés—
Up Times Square to Columbus Circle lights
Channel the congresses, nightly sessions,
Refractions of the thousand theatres, faces—
Mysterious kitchens. . . . You shall search them all.
Someday by heart you'll learn each famous sight
And watch the curtain lift in hell's despite;
You'll find the garden in the third act dead,
Finger your knees—and wish yourself in bed
With tabloid crime-sheets perched in easy sight.

Then let you reach your hat
and go.
As usual, let you—also
walking down—exclaim
to twelve upward leaving
a subscription praise
for what time slays.

Or can't you quite make up your mind to ride;
A walk is better underneath the L a brisk
Ten blocks or so before? But you find yourself
Preparing penguin flexions of the arms,—
As usual you will meet the scuttle yawn:
The subway yawns the quickest promise home.

Be minimum, then, to swim the hiving swarms
Out of the Square, the Circle burning bright—
Avoid the glass doors gyring at your right,
Where boxed alone a second, eyes take fright
—Quite unprepared rush naked back to light:
And down beside the turnstile press the coin
Into the slot. The gongs already rattle.

And so
of cities you bespeak
subways, rivered under streets
and rivers. . . . In the car
the overtone of motion
underground, the monotone
of motion is the sound
of other faces, also underground—

"Let's have a pencil Jimmy—living now
at Floral Park
Flatbush—on the fourth of July—
like a pigeon's muddy dream—potatoes
to dig in the field—travlin the town—too—
night after night—the Culver line—the
girls all shaping up—it used to be—"

Our tongues recant like beaten weather vanes.
This answer lives like verdigris, like hair
Beyond extinction, surcease of the bone;
And repetition freezes—"What

"what do you want? getting weak on the links?
fandaddle daddy don't ask for change—IS THIS
FOURTEENTH? it's half past six she said—if
you don't like my gate why did you
swing on it, why *didja*
swing on it
anyhow—"

And somehow anyhow swing—

The phonographs of hades in the brain
Are tunnels that re-wind themselves, and love
A burnt match skating in a urinal—
Somewhere above Fourteenth TAKE THE EXPRESS
To brush some new presentiment of pain—

"But I want service in this office SERVICE
I said—after
the show she cried a little afterwards but—"

Whose head is swinging from the swollen strap?
Whose body smokes along the bitten rails,
Bursts from a smoldering bundle far behind
In back forks of the chasms of the brain,—
Puffs from a riven stump far out behind
In interborough fissures of the mind . . . ?

And why do I often meet your visage here,
Your eyes like agate lanterns—on and on
Below the toothpaste and the dandruff ads?
—And did their riding eyes right through your side,
And did their eyes like unwashed platters ride?
And Death, aloft,—gigantically down
Probing through you—toward me, O evermore!
And when they dragged your retching flesh,
Your trembling hands that night through Baltimore—
That last night on the ballot rounds, did you,
Shaking, did you deny the ticket, Poe?

For Gravesend Manor change at Chambers Street.
The platform hurries along to a dead stop.

The intent escalator lifts a serenade
Stilly
Of shoes, umbrellas, each eye attending its shoe, then
Bolting outright somewhere above where streets
Burst suddenly in rain. . . . The gongs recur:
Elbows and levers, guard and hissing door.
Thunder is galvothermic here below. . . . The car
Wheels off. The train rounds, bending to a scream,
Taking the final level for the dive
Under the river—
And somewhat emptier than before,
Demented, for a hitching second, humps; then
Lets go. . . . Toward corners of the floor

Newspapers wing, revolve and wing.
Blank windows gargle signals through the roar.

And does the Daemon take you home, also,
Wop washerwoman, with the bandaged hair?
After the corridors are swept, the cuspidors—
The gaunt sky-barracks cleanly now, and bare,
O Genoese, do you bring mother eyes and hands
Back home to children and to golden hair?

Daemon, demurring and eventful yawn!
Whose hideous laughter is a bellows mirth
—Or the muffled slaughter of a day in birth—
O cruelly to inoculate the brinking dawn
With antennae toward worlds that glow and sink;—
To spoon us out more liquid than the dim
Locution of the eldest star, and pack
The conscience navelled in the plunging wind,
Umbilical to call—and straightway die!

O caught like pennies beneath soot and steam,
Kiss of our agony thou gatherest;
Condensed, thou takest all—shrill ganglia
Impassioned with some song we fail to keep.
And yet, like Lazarus, to feel the slope,
The sod and billow breaking,—lifting ground,
—A sound of waters bending astride the sky
Unceasing with some Word that will not die . . . !

. . . . .

A tugboat, wheezing wreaths of steam,
Lunged past, with one galvanic blare stove up the River.
I counted the echoes assembling, one after one,
Searching, thumbing the midnight on the piers.
Lights, coasting, left the oily tympanum of waters;
The blackness somewhere gouged glass on a sky.
And this thy harbor, O my City, I have driven under,
Tossed from the coil of ticking towers. . . . Tomorrow,
And to be. . . . Here by the River that is East—
Here at the waters' edge the hands drop memory;

Shadowless in that abyss they unaccounting lie.
How far away the star has pooled the sea—
Or shall the hands be drawn away, to die?

Kiss of our agony Thou gatherest,
O Hand of Fire
gatherest—

VIII. ATLANTIS

Music is then the knowledge of that which
relates to love in harmony and system.
—PLATO

Through the bound cable strands, the arching path
Upward, veering with light, the flight of strings,—
Taut miles of shuttling moonlight syncopate
The whispered rush, telepathy of wires.
Up the index of night, granite and steel—
Transparent meshes—fleckless the gleaming staves—
Sibylline voices flicker, waveringly stream
As though a god were issue of the strings. . . .

And through that cordage, threading with its call
One arc synoptic of all tides below—
Their labyrinthine mouths of history
Pouring reply as though all ships at sea
Complighted in one vibrant breath made cry,—
"Make thy love sure—to weave whose song we ply!"
—From black embankments, moveless soundings hailed,
So seven oceans answer from their dream.

And on, obliquely up bright carrier bars
New octaves trestle the twin monoliths
Beyond whose frosted capes the moon bequeaths
Two worlds of sleep (O arching strands of song!)—
Onward and up the crystal-flooded aisle
White tempest nets file upward, upward ring
With silver terraces the humming spars,
The loft of vision, palladium helm of stars.

Sheerly the eyes, like seagulls stung with rime—
Slit and propelled by glistening fins of light—
Pick biting way up towering looms that press
Sidelong with flight of blade on tendon blade
—Tomorrows into yesteryear—and link
What cipher-script of time no traveller reads
But who, through smoking pyres of love and death,
Searches the timeless laugh of mythic spears.

Like hails, farewells—up planet-sequined heights
Some trillion whispering hammers glimmer Tyre:
Serenely, sharply up the long anvil cry
Of inchling aeons silence rivets Troy.
And you, aloft there—Jason! hesting Shout!
Still wrapping harness to the swarming air!
Silvery the rushing wake, surpassing call,
Beams yelling Aeolus! splintered in the straits!

From gulfs unfolding, terrible of drums,
Tall Vision-of-the-Voyage, tensely spare—
Bridge, lifting night to cycloramic crest
Of deepest day—O Choir, translating time
Into what multitudinous Verb the suns
And synergy of waters ever fuse, recast
In myriad syllables,—Psalm of Cathay!
O Love, thy white, pervasive Paradigm . . . !

We left the haven hanging in the night—
Sheened harbor lanterns backward fled the keel.
Pacific here at time's end, bearing corn,—
Eyes stammer through the pangs of dust and steel.
And still the circular, indubitable frieze
Of heaven's meditation, yoking wave
To kneeling wave, one song devoutly binds—
The vernal strophe chimes from deathless strings!

O Thou steeled Cognizance whose leap commits
The agile precincts of the lark's return;
Within whose lariat sweep encinctured sing
In single chrysalis the many twain,—

Of stars Thou art the stitch and stallion glow
And like an organ, Thou, with sound of doom—
Sight, sound and flesh Thou leadest from time's realm
As love strikes clear direction for the helm.

Swift peal of secular light, intrinsic Myth
Whose fell unshadow is death's utter wound,—
O River-throated—iridescently unborne
Through the bright drench and fabric of our veins;
With white escarpments swinging into light,
Sustained in tears the cities are endowed
And justified conclamant with ripe fields
Revolving through their harvests in sweet torment.

Forever Deity's glittering Pledge, O Thou
Whose canticle fresh chemistry assigns
To wrapt inception and beatitude,—
Always through blinding cables, to our joy,
Of thy white seizure springs the prophecy:
Always through spiring cordage, pyramids
Of silver sequel, Deity's young name
Kinetic of white choiring wings . . . ascends.

Migrations that must needs void memory,
Inventions that cobblestone the heart,—
Unspeakable Thou Bridge to Thee, O Love.
Thy pardon for this history, whitest Flower,
O Answerer of all,—Anemone,—
Now while thy petals spend the suns about us, hold—
(O Thou whose radiance doth inherit me)
Atlantis,—hold thy floating singer late!

So to thine Everpresence, beyond time,
Like spears ensanguined of one tolling star
That bleeds infinity—the orphic strings,
Sidereal phalanxes, leap and converge:
—One Song, one Bridge of Fire! Is it Cathay,
Now pity steeps the grass and rainbows ring
The serpent with the eagle in the leaves . . . ?
Whispers antiphonal in azure swing.

O Carib Isle!

The tarantula rattling at the lily's foot
Across the feet of the dead, laid in white sand
Near the coral beach—nor zigzag fiddle crabs
Side-stilting from the path (that shift, subvert
And anagrammatize your name)—No, nothing here
Below the palsy that one eucalyptus lifts
In wrinkled shadows—mourns.

And yet suppose
I count these nacreous frames of tropic death,
Brutal necklaces of shells around each grave
Squared off so carefully. Then

To the white sand I may speak a name, fertile
Albeit in a stranger tongue. Tree names, flower names
Deliberate, gainsay death's brittle crypt. Meanwhile
The wind that knots itself in one great death—
Coils and withdraws. So syllables want breath.

But where is the Captain of this doubloon isle
Without a turnstile? Who but catchword crabs
Patrols the dry groins of the underbrush?
What man, or What
Is Commissioner of mildew throughout the ambushed senses?
His Carib mathematics web the eyes' baked lenses!

Under the poinciana, of a noon or afternoon
Let fiery blossoms clot the light, render my ghost
Sieved upward, white and black along the air
Until it meets the blue's comedian host.

Let not the pilgrim see himself again
For slow evisceration bound like those huge terrapin
Each daybreak on the wharf, their brine caked eyes;
—Spiked, overturned; such thunder in their strain!
And clenched beaks coughing for the surge again!

Slagged of the hurricane—I, cast within its flow,
Congeal by afternoons here, satin and vacant.
You have given me the shell, Satan,—carbonic amulet
Sere of the sun exploded in the sea.

The Broken Tower

The bell-rope that gathers God at dawn
Dispatches me as though I dropped down the knell
Of a spent day—to wander the cathedral lawn
From pit to crucifix, feet chill on steps from hell.

Have you not heard, have you not seen that corps
Of shadows in the tower, whose shoulders sway
Antiphonal carillons launched before
The stars are caught and hived in the sun's ray?

The bells, I say, the bells break down their tower;
And swing I know not where. Their tongues engrave
Membrane through marrow, my long-scattered score
Of broken intervals . . . And I, their sexton slave!

Oval encyclicals in canyons heaping
The impasse high with choir. Banked voices slain!
Pagodas, campaniles with reveilles outleaping—
O terraced echoes prostrate on the plain! . . .

And so it was I entered the broken world
To trace the visionary company of love, its voice
An instant in the wind (I know not whither hurled)
But not for long to hold each desperate choice.

My word I poured. But was it cognate, scored
Of that tribunal monarch of the air
Whose thigh embronzes earth, strikes crystal Word
In wounds pledged once to hope,—cleft to despair?

The steep encroachments of my blood left me
No answer (could blood hold such a lofty tower
As flings the question true?)—or is it she
Whose sweet mortality stirs latent power?—

And through whose pulse I hear, counting the strokes
My veins recall and add, revived and sure
The angelus of wars my chest evokes:
What I hold healed, original now, and pure . . .

And builds, within, a tower that is not stone
(Not stone can jacket heaven)—but slip
Of pebbles,—visible wings of silence sown
In azure circles, widening as they dip

The matrix of the heart, lift down the eye
That shrines the quiet lake and swells a tower . . .
The commodious, tall decorum of that sky
Unseals her earth, and lifts love in its shower.

Thomas A. Dorsey

1899–1993

Take My Hand, Precious Lord

Precious Lord, take my hand,
Lead me on, let me stand,
I am tired, I am weak, I am worn.
Through the storm, through the night
Lead me on to the light,
Take my hand, precious Lord,
Lead me home.

When my way grows drear,
Precious Lord, linger near.
When my life is almost gone,
Hear my cry, hear my call,

Hold my hand lest I fall.
Take my hand, precious Lord,
Lead me home.

When the darkness appears
And the night draws near,
And the day is past and gone,
At the river I stand,
Guide my feet, hold my hand.
Take my hand, precious Lord,
Lead me home.

Allen Tate

1899–1979

The Cross

There is a place that some men know,
I cannot see the whole of it
Nor how I came there. Long ago
Flame burst out of a secret pit
Crushing the world with such a light
The day-sky fell to moonless black,
The kingly sun to hateful night
For those, once seeing, turning back:
For love so hates mortality
Which is the providence of life
She will not let it blessèd be
But curses it with mortal strife,
Until beside the blinding rood
Within that world-destroying pit
—Like young wolves that have tasted blood—
Of death, men taste no more of it.
So blind, in so severe a place
(All life before in the black grave)
The last alternatives they face
Of life, without the life to save,

Being from all salvation weaned—
A stag charged both at heel and head:
Who would come back is turned a fiend
Instructed by the fiery dead.

The Twelve

There by some wrinkled stones round a leafless tree
With beards askew, their eyes dull and wild
Twelve ragged men, the council of charity
Wandering the face of the earth a fatherless child,
Kneel, at their infidelity aghast,
For where was it, somewhere in Syria
Or Palestine when the streams went red,
The victor of Rome, his arms outspread,
His eyes cold with his inhuman ecstasy,
Cried the last word, the accursed last
Of the forsaken that seared the western heart
With the fire of the wind, the thick and the fast
Whirl of the damned in the heavenly storm:
Now the wind's empty and the twelve living dead
Look round them for that promontory Form
Whose mercy flashed from the sheet lightning's head;
But the twelve lie in the sand by the dry rock
Seeing nothing—the sand, the tree, rocks
Without number—and turn away the face
To the mind's briefer and more desert place.

Sonnets at Christmas

I

This is the day His hour of life draws near,
Let me get ready from head to foot for it
Most handily with eyes to pick the year
For small feed to reward a feathered wit.
Some men would see it an epiphany

At ease, at food and drink, others at chase;
Yet I, stung lassitude, with ecstasy
Unspent argue the season's difficult case
So: Man, dull creature of enormous head,
What would he look at in the coiling sky?
But I must kneel again unto the Dead
While Christmas bells of paper white and red,
Figured with boys and girls spilt from a sled,
Ring out the silence I am nourished by.

II

Ah, Christ, I love you rings to the wild sky
And I must think a little of the past:
When I was ten I told a stinking lie
That got a black boy whipped; but now at last
The going years, caught in an after-glow,
Reverse like balls englished upon green baize—
Let them return, let the round trumpets blow
The ancient crackle of the Christ's deep gaze.
Deafened and blind, with senses yet unfound,
Am I, untutored to the after-wit
Of knowledge, knowing a nightmare has no sound;
Therefore with idle hands and head I sit
In late December before the fire's daze
Punished by crimes of which I would be quit.

Sterling A. Brown

1901–1989

Sister Lou

Honey
When de man
Calls out de las' train
You're gonna ride,
Tell him howdy.

Gather up yo' basket
An' yo' knittin' an' yo' things,
An' go on up an' visit
Wid frien' Jesus fo' a spell.

Show Marfa
How to make yo' greengrape jellies,
An' give po' Lazarus
A passel of them Golden Biscuits.

Scald some meal
Fo' some rightdown good spoonbread
Fo' li'l box-punkin' David.

An' sit aroun'
An' tell them Hebrew Chillen
All yo' stories. . . .

Honey
Don't be feared of them pearly gates,
Don't go 'round to de back,
No mo' dataway
Not evah no mo'.

Let Michael tote yo' burden
An' yo' pocketbook an' evahthing
'Cept yo' Bible,
While Gabriel blows somp'n
Solemn but loudsome
On dat horn of his'n.

Honey
Go straight on to de Big House,
An' speak to yo' God
Widout no fear an' tremblin'.

Then sit down
An' pass de time of day awhile.

Give a good talkin' to
To yo' favorite 'postle Peter,
An' rub the po' head
Of mixed-up Judas,
An' joke awhile wid Jonah.

Then, when you gits de chance,
Always rememberin' yo' raisin',
Let 'em know youse tired
Jest a mite tired.

Jesus will find yo' bed fo' you
Won't no servant evah bother wid yo' room.
Jesus will lead you
To a room wid windows
Openin' on cherry trees an' plum trees
Bloomin' everlastin'.

An' dat will be yours
Fo' keeps.

Den take yo' time. . . .
Honey, take yo' bressed time.

Laura Riding

1901–1991

There Is No Land Yet

The long sea, how short-lasting,
From water-thought to water-thought
So quick to feel surprise and shame.
Where moments are not time
But time is moments.
Such neither yes nor no,
Such only love, to have to-morrow
By certain failure of now and now.

On water lying strong ships and men
In weakness skilled reach elsewhere:
No prouder places from home in bed
The mightiest sleeper can know.
So faith took ship upon the sailor's earth
To seek absurdities in heaven's name—
Discovery but a fountain without source,
Legend of mist and lost patience.

The body swimming in itself
Is dissolution's darling.
With dripping mouth it speaks a truth
That cannot lie, in words not born yet
Out of first immortality,
All-wise impermanence.

And the dusty eye whose accuracies
Turn watery in the mind
Where waves of probability
Write vision in a tidal hand
That time alone can read.

And the dry land not yet,
Lonely and absolute salvation—
Boasting of constancy
Like an island with no water round
In water where no land is.

Faith Upon the Waters

A ghost rose when the waves rose,
When the waves sank stood columnwise
And broken: archaic is
The spirituality of sea,
Water haunted by an imagination
Like fire previously.

More ghost when no ghost,
When the waves explain
Eye to the eye

And dolphins tease,
And the ventriloquist gulls
Their angular three-element cries.

Fancy ages.
A death-bed restlessness inflames the mind
And a warm mist attacks the face
With mortal premonition.

Langston Hughes

1902–1967

The Negro Speaks of Rivers

I've known rivers:
I've known rivers ancient as the world and older than the flow of
 human blood in human veins.

My soul has grown deep like the rivers.

I bathed in the Euphrates when dawns were young.
I built my hut near the Congo and it lulled me to sleep.
I looked upon the Nile and raised the pyramids above it.
I heard the singing of the Mississippi when Abe Lincoln went
 down to New Orleans, and I've seen its muddy bosom turn
 all golden in the sunset.

I've known rivers:
Ancient, dusky rivers.

My soul has grown deep like the rivers.

Prayer

I ask you this:
Which way to go?
I ask you this:
Which sin to bear?
Which crown to put
Upon my hair?
I do not know,
Lord God,
I do not know.

Heaven

Heaven is
The place where
Happiness is
Everywhere.

Animals
And birds sing—
As does
Everything.

To each stone,
"How-do-you-do?"
Stone answers back,
"Well! And you?"

Countee Cullen

1903–1946

Simon the Cyrenian Speaks

He never spoke a word to me,
  And yet He called my name;
He never gave a sign to me,
  And yet I knew and came.

At first I said, "I will not bear
His cross upon my back;
He only seeks to place it there
Because my skin is black."

But He was dying for a dream,
And He was very meek,
And in His eyes there shone a gleam
Men journey far to seek.

It was Himself my pity bought;
I did for Christ alone
What all of Rome could not have wrought
With bruise of lash or stone.

The Litany of the Dark People

Our flesh that was a battle-ground
Shows now the morning-break;
The ancient deities are downed
For Thy eternal sake.
Now that the past is left behind,
Fling wide Thy garment's hem
To keep us one with Thee in mind,
Thou Christ of Bethlehem.

The thorny wreath may ridge our brow,
The spear may mar our side,
And on white wood from a scented bough
We may be crucified;
Yet no assault the old gods make
Upon our agony
Shall swerve our footsteps from the wake
Of Thine toward Calvary.

And if we hunger now and thirst,
Grant our withholders may,
When heaven's constellations burst

Upon Thy crowning day,
Be fed by us, and given to see
Thy mercy in our eyes,
When Bethlehem and Calvary
Are merged in Paradise.

Carl Rakosi

1903–2004

Meditation

After Solomon Ibn Gabirol

Three things remind me of You,
the heavens
                    who are a witness to Your name
the earth
               which expands my thought
               and is the thing on which I stand
and the musing of my heart
                              when I look within.

Meditation

After Jehudah Halevi

How long will you remain a boy?
Dawns must end.
Behold the angels of old age.

Shake off temporal things then
the way a bird shakes off the night dew.
Dart like a swallow
                              from the raging ocean
of daily events
and pursue the Lord
in the intimate company
of souls flowing
                         into His virtue.

Richard Eberhart

1904–2005

The Groundhog

In June, amid the golden fields,
I saw a groundhog lying dead.
Dead lay he; my senses shook,
And mind outshot our naked frailty.
There lowly in the vigorous summer
His form began its senseless change,
And made my senses waver dim
Seeing nature ferocious in him.
Inspecting close his maggots' might
And seething cauldron of his being,
Half with loathing, half with a strange love,
I poked him with an angry stick.
The fever arose, became a flame
And Vigour circumscribed the skies,
Immense energy in the sun,
And through my frame a sunless trembling.
My stick had done nor good nor harm.
Then stood I silent in the day
Watching the object, as before;
And kept my reverence for knowledge
Trying for control, to be still,
To quell the passion of the blood;
Until I had bent down on my knees
Praying for joy in the sight of decay.
And so I left; and I returned
In Autumn strict of eye, to see
The sap gone out of the groundhog,
But the bony sodden hulk remained.
But the year had lost its meaning,
And in intellectual chains
I lost both love and loathing,
Mured up in the wail of wisdom.

Another summer took the fields again
Massive and burning, full of life,
But when I chanced upon the spot
There was only a little hair left,
And bones bleaching in the sunlight
Beautiful as architecture;
I watched them like a geometer,
And cut a walking stick from a birch.
It has been three years, now.
There is no sign of the groundhog.
I stood there in the whirling summer,
My hand capped a withered heart,
And thought of China and of Greece,
Of Alexander in his tent;
Of Montaigne in his tower,
Of Saint Theresa in her wild lament.

The Soul Longs to Return Whence It Came

I drove up to the graveyard, which
Used to frighten me as a boy,
When I walked down the river past it,
And evening was coming on. I'd make sure
I came home from the woods early enough.
I drove in, I found to the place, I
Left the motor running. My eyes hurried,
To recognize the great oak tree
On the little slope, among the stones.
It was a high day, a crisp day,
The cleanest kind of Autumn day,
With brisk intoxicating air, a
Little wind that frisked, yet there was
Old age in the atmosphere, nostalgia,
The subtle heaviness of the Fall.
I stilled the motor. I walked a few paces;
It was good, the tree; the friendliness of it.
I touched it, I thought of the roots;
They would have pierced her seven years.
O all peoples! O mighty shadows!

My eyes opened along the avenue
Of tombstones, the common land of death.
Humiliation of all loves lost,
That might have had full meaning in any
Plot of ground, come, hear the silence,
See the quivering light. My mind worked
Almost imperceptibly, I
In the command, I the wilful ponderer.
I must have stood silent and thoughtful
There. A host of dry leaves
Danced on the ground in the wind.
They startled, they curved up from the ground,
There was a dry rustling, rattling.
The sun was motionless and brittle.
I felt the blood darken in my checks
And burn. Like running. My eyes
Telescoped on decay, I out of command.
Fear, tenderness, they seized me.
My eyes were hot, I dared not look
At the leaves. A pagan urge swept me.
Multitudes, O multitudes in one.
The urge of the earth, the titan
Wild and primitive lust, fused
On the ground of her grave.
I was a being of feeling alone.
I flung myself down on the earth
Full length on the great earth, full length,
I wept out the dark load of human love.
In pagan adoration I adored her.
I felt the actual earth of her.
Victor and victim of humility,
I closed in the wordless ecstasy
Of mystery: where there is no thought
But feeling lost in itself forever,
Profound, remote, immediate, and calm.
Frightened, I stood up, I looked about
Suspiciously, hurriedly (a rustling),
As if the sun, the air, the trees
Were human, might not understand.

I drew breath, it made a sound,
I stepped gingerly away. Then
The mind came like a fire, it
Tortured man, I thought of madness.
The mind will not accept the blood.
The sun and sky, the trees and grasses,
And the whispering leaves, took on
Their usual characters. I went away,
Slowly, tingling, elated, saying, saying
 Mother, Great Being, O Source of Life
To whom in wisdom we return,
Accept this humble servant evermore.

Louis Zukofsky

1904–1978

FROM *"A"–12*

He saw Rabbi
Yizchok Elchonon
Walking
On the wharf
In Kovno.
The miracle of his first job
On the lower East Side:
Six years night watchman
In a men's shop
Where by day he pressed pants
Every crease a blade
The irons weighed
At least twenty pounds
But moved both of them
Six days a week
From six in the morning
To nine, sometimes eleven at night,
Or midnight;
Except Fridays

When he left, enough time before sunset
Margolis begrudged.
His own business
My father told Margolis
Is to keep Sabbath.

"Sleep," he prayed
For his dead.
Sabbath.

Moses released the horse
For one day from his harness
So that a man might keep pace.

A shop bench his bed,
He rose rested at four.
Half the free night
Befriended the mice:
Singing Psalms
As they listened.
A day's meal
A slice of bread
And an apple,
The evenings
What matter?
His boots shone.
Gone and out of fashion
His beard you stroked, Paul,
With the Sabbath Prince Albert.
I never saw more beautiful fingers
Used to lift bootstraps.
A beard that won over
A jeering Italian
Who wanted to pluck it—
With the love
His dark brown eyes
Always found in others.
Everybody loves Reb Pinchos
Because he loves everybody,

How many strangers—
He knew so many—
Said that to me
Every Sabbath
He took me—
I was a small boy—
To the birdstore-window to see
The blue-and-yellow Polly
The cardinal, the
Orchard oriole.

Everybody loved Reb Pinchos
Because he loved everybody.
Simple.
You must, myself,
As father of Nicomachus
Say very little
Except: such were his actions.

My life for yours.
Goodness dies—
The humming bird flies forward.
Buried beneath blue sky, bright sunlight.
You'll remember:
The eleventh of April
        1950.
The twelfth—
Snow flurries—
Tasting all unseasonable weather early
Alongside his "little fish"
There 23 years before him.
John Donne in his death-shroud
A saintly face in praying shawl—
He died happy
If you want to know
What he looked like,
Scop,
What are you asking?
He retired on old age pension—

$26 a month—
At 81—not too late,
He did not covet charity—
Or what has become of it—
And supported his children
Not sure now whether to
Put 91 or 95
On his tombstone.
He had forgotten birthright and birthday,
Who can remember
When every new day
May be turned into account.
What do you await?
If occasion warranted
He could tender his hand to a Polish countess
Playing the glass harmonica
And she wouldn't take offense.
His clasp pocketbook is in a lower drawer
Of his old chiffonier no one wanted.
$3 and some pennies
Saved for the synagogue—
He had hoped for more
But gave away
What he could not spare
To his bungling children—
Praising and showing their photos
They gave him.
The street never wide enough for him,
Taking a diagonal to cross it,
To open and close the synagogue
For over six times ten years
Until three days before he died—
A longer journey than Odysseus'.
Now his namesake says:
"If it's not my kind of words
    I don't want to hear them."
He died certain—
With such the angel of death does not wrestle—
And alone,

Not to let me see death:
"Isn't visiting over?
Go home,
Celia must be anxious,
Kiss Paul."

Measure, tacit is.
Listen to the birds—
And what do the birds sing.
He never saw a movie.
A rich sitter, a broad wake.
Not a sign that he is not here,
Yet a sign, to what side of the window
He sat by, creaks outside.
A speech tapped off music.
Draw off—
Still in the eye of—
                    an acacia.
Division: wits so undivided.
A source knows a tree
                still not in the earth
In no hurry to shadow the living
He opens the gates of the synagogue
As time never heard
Lifting up the voice.
Actions things; themselves; doing.

Stanley Kunitz

1905–2006

Benediction

God banish from your house
The fly, the roach, the mouse

That riots in the walls
Until the plaster falls;

Admonish from your door
The hypocrite and liar;

No shy, soft, tigrish fear
Permit upon your stair,

Nor agents of your doubt.
God drive them whistling out.

Let nothing touched with evil,
Let nothing that can shrivel

Heart's tenderest frond, intrude
Upon your still, deep blood.

Against the drip of night
God keep all windows tight,

Protect your mirrors from
Surprise, delirium,

Admit no trailing wind
Into your shuttered mind

To plume the lake of sleep
With dreams. If you must weep

God give you tears, but leave
You secrecy to grieve,

And islands for your pride,
And love to nest in your side.

Kenneth Rexroth

1905–1982

The Signature of All Things

I

My head and shoulders, and my book
In the cool shade, and my body
Stretched bathing in the sun, I lie
Reading beside the waterfall—
Boehme's 'Signature of all Things.'
Through the deep July day the leaves
Of the laurel, all the colors
Of gold, spin down through the moving
Deep laurel shade all day. They float
On the mirrored sky and forest
For a while, and then, still slowly
Spinning, sink through the crystal deep
Of the pool to its leaf gold floor.
The saint saw the world as streaming
In the electrolysis of love.
I put him by and gaze through shade
Folded into shade of slender
Laurel trunks and leaves filled with sun.
The wren broods in her moss domed nest.
A newt struggles with a white moth
Drowning in the pool. The hawks scream,
Playing together on the ceiling
Of heaven. The long hours go by.
I think of those who have loved me,
Of all the mountains I have climbed,
Of all the seas I have swum in.
The evil of the world sinks.
My own sin and trouble fall away
Like Christian's bundle, and I watch

My forty summers fall like falling
Leaves and falling water held
Eternally in summer air.

2

Deer are stamping in the glades,
Under the full July moon.
There is a smell of dry grass
In the air, and more faintly,
The scent of a far off skunk.
As I stand at the wood's edge,
Watching the darkness, listening
To the stillness, a small owl
Comes to the branch above me,
On wings more still than my breath.
When I turn my light on him,
His eyes glow like drops of iron,
And he perks his head at me,
Like a curious kitten.
The meadow is bright as snow.
My dog prowls the grass, a dark
Blur in the blur of brightness.
I walk to the oak grove where
The Indian village was once.
There, in blotched and cobwebbed light
And dark, dim in the blue haze,
Are twenty Holstein heifers,
Black and white, all lying down,
Quietly together, under
The huge trees rooted in the graves.

3

When I dragged the rotten log
From the bottom of the pool,
It seemed heavy as stone.
I let it lie in the sun
For a month; and then chopped it

Into sections, and split them
For kindling, and spread them out
To dry some more. Late that night;
After reading for hours,
While moths rattled at the lamp,
The saints and the philosophers
On the destiny of man;
I went out on my cabin porch,
And looked up through the black forest
At the swaying islands of stars.
Suddenly I saw at my feet,
Spread on the floor of night, ingots
Of quivering phosphorescence,
And all about were scattered chips
Of pale cold light that was alive.

Robert Penn Warren

1905–1989

Evening Hawk

From plane of light to plane, wings dipping through
Geometries and orchids that the sunset builds,
Out of the peak's black angularity of shadow, riding
The last tumultuous avalanche of
Light above pines and the guttural gorge,
The hawk comes.

His wing
Scythes down another day, his motion
Is that of the honed steel-edge, we hear
The crashless fall of stalks of Time.

The head of each stalk is heavy with the gold of our error.

Look! look! he is climbing the last light
Who knows neither Time nor error, and under

Whose eye, unforgiving, the world, unforgiven, swings
Into shadow.

Long now,
The last thrush is still, the last bat
Now cruises in his sharp hieroglyphics. His wisdom
Is ancient, too, and immense. The star
Is steady, like Plato, over the mountain.

If there were no wind we might, we think, hear
The earth grind on its axis, or history
Drip in darkness like a leaking pipe in the cellar.

Heart of Autumn

Wind finds the northwest gap, fall comes.
Today, under gray cloud-scud and over gray
Wind-flicker of forest, in perfect formation, wild geese
Head for a land of warm water, the *boom*, the lead pellet.

Some crumple in air, fall. Some stagger, recover control,
Then take the last glide for a far glint of water. None
Knows what has happened. Now, today, watching
How tirelessly *V* upon *V* arrows the season's logic,

Do I know my own story? At least, they know
When the hour comes for the great wing-beat. Sky strider,
Star-strider—they rise, and the imperial utterance,
Which cries out for distance, quivers in the wheeling sky.

That much they know, and in their nature know
The path of pathlessness, with all the joy
Of destiny fulfilling its own name.
I have known time and distance, but not why I am here.

Path of logic, path of folly, all
The same—and I stand, my face lifted now skyward,
Hearing the high beat, my arms outstretched in the tingling
Process of transformation, and soon tough legs,

With folded feet, trail in the sounding vacuum of passage,
And my heart is impacted with a fierce impulse
To unwordable utterance—
Toward sunset, at a great height.

W. H. Auden

1907–1973

FROM *Horae Canonicae*

"Immolatus vicerit"

I. PRIME

Simultaneously, as soundlessly,
   Spontaneously, suddenly
As, at the vaunt of the dawn, the kind
   Gates of the body fly open
To its world beyond, the gates of the mind,
   The horn gate and the ivory gate
Swing to, swing shut, instantaneously
   Quell the nocturnal rummage
Of its rebellious fronde, ill-favored,
   Ill-natured and second-rate,
Disenfranchised, widowed and orphaned
   By an historical mistake:
Recalled from the shades to be a seeing being,
   From absence to be on display,
Without a name or history I wake
   Between my body and the day.

Holy this moment, wholly in the right,
   As, in complete obedience
To the light's laconic outcry, next
   As a sheet, near as a wall,
Out there as a mountain's poise of stone,
   The world is present, about,

And I know that I am, here, not alone
  But with a world and rejoice
Unvexed, for the will has still to claim
  This adjacent arm as my own,
The memory to name me, resume
  Its routine of praise and blame,
And smiling to me is this instant while
  Still the day is intact, and I
The Adam sinless in our beginning,
  Adam still previous to any act.

I draw breath; that is of course to wish
  No matter what, to be wise,
To be different, to die and the cost,
  No matter how, is Paradise
Lost of course and myself owing a death:
  The eager ridge, the steady sea,
The flat roofs of the fishing village
  Still asleep in its bunny,
Though as fresh and sunny still, are not friends
  But things to hand, this ready flesh
No honest equal, but my accomplice now,
  My assassin to be, and my name
Stands for my historical share of care
  For a lying self-made city,
Afraid of our living task, the dying
  Which the coming day will ask.

5. VESPERS

If the hill overlooking our city has always been known as Adam's Grave, only at dusk can you see the recumbent giant, his head turned to the west, his right arm resting for ever on Eve's haunch,

can you learn, from the way he looks up at the scandalous pair, what a citizen really thinks of his citizenship, just as now you can hear in a drunkard's caterwaul his rebel sorrows crying for a parental discipline, in lustful eyes perceive a disconsolate soul,

scanning with desperation all passing limbs for some vestige of her faceless angel who in that long ago when wishing was a help mounted her once and vanished:

For Sun and Moon supply their conforming masks, but in this hour of civil twilight all must wear their own faces.

And it is now that our two paths cross.

Both simultaneously recognize his Anti-type: that I am an Arcadian, that he is a Utopian.

He notes, with contempt, my Aquarian belly: I note, with alarm, his Scorpion's mouth.

He would like to see me cleaning latrines: I would like to see him removed to some other planet.

Neither speaks. What experience could we possibly share?

Glancing at a lampshade in a store window, I observe it is too hideous for anyone in their senses to buy: He observes it is too expensive for a peasant to buy.

Passing a slum child with rickets, I look the other way: He looks the other way if he passes a chubby one.

I hope our senators will behave like saints, provided they don't reform me: He hopes they will behave like *baritoni cattivi*, and, when lights burn late in the Citadel,

I (who have never seen the inside of a police station) am shocked and think, "Were the city as free as they say, after sundown all her bureaus would be huge black stones.":

He (who has been beaten up several times) is not shocked at all but thinks, "One fine night our boys will be working up there."

You can see, then, why, between my Eden and his New Jerusalem, no treaty is negotiable.

In my Eden a person who dislikes Bellini has the good manners not to get born: In his New Jerusalem a person who dislikes work will be very sorry he was born.

In my Eden we have a few beam-engines, saddle-tank locomotives, overshot waterwheels and other beautiful pieces of obsolete machinery to play with: In his New Jerusalem even chefs will be cucumber-cool machine minders.

In my Eden our only source of political news is gossip: In his New Jerusalem there will be a special daily in simplified spelling for non-verbal types.

In my Eden each observes his compulsive rituals and superstitious tabus but we have no morals: In his New Jerusalem the temples will be empty but all will practise the rational virtues.

One reason for his contempt is that I have only to close my eyes, cross the iron footbridge to the tow-path, take the barge through the short brick tunnel and

there I stand in Eden again, welcomed back by the krum-horns, doppions, sordumes of jolly miners and a bob major from the Cathedral (romanesque) of St. Sophie (*Die Kalte*):

One reason for my alarm is that, when he closes his eyes, he arrives, not in New Jerusalem, but on some august day of outrage when hellikins cavort through ruined drawing-rooms and fishwives intervene in the Chamber or

some autumn night of delations and noyades, when the unrepentant thieves (including me) are sequestered and those he hates shall hate themselves instead.

So with a passing glance we take the other's posture. Already our steps recede, heading, incorrigible each, towards his kind of meal and evening.

Was it (as it must look to any god of cross-roads) simply a fortuitous intersection of life-paths, loyal to different fibs?

Or also a rendezvous between two accomplices who, in spite of themselves, cannot resist meeting

to remind the other (do both, at bottom, desire truth?) of that half of their secret which he would most like to forget,

forcing us both, for a fraction of a second, to remember our victim (but for him I could forget the blood, but for me he could forget the innocence),

on whose immolation (call him Abel, Remus, whom you will, it is one Sin Offering) arcadias, utopias, our dear old bag of a democracy are alike founded:

For without a cement of blood (it must be human, it must be innocent) no secular wall will safely stand.

7. LAUDS

Among the leaves the small birds sing;
The crow of the cock commands awaking:
In solitude, for company.

Bright shines the sun on creatures mortal;
Men of their neighbors become sensible:
In solitude, for company.

The crow of the cock commands awaking;
Already the mass-bell goes dong-ding:
In solitude, for company.

Men of their neighbors become sensible;
God bless the Realm, God bless the People:
In solitude, for company.

Already the mass-bell goes dong-ding;
The dripping mill-wheel is again turning:
In solitude, for company.

God bless the Realm, God bless the People;
God bless this green world temporal:
In solitude, for company.

The dripping mill-wheel is again turning;
Among the leaves the small birds sing:
In solitude, for company.

George Oppen

1908–1984

Psalm

Veritas sequitur . . .

In the small beauty of the forest
The wild deer bedding down—
That they are there!

Their eyes
Effortless, the soft lips
Nuzzle and the alien small teeth
Tear at the grass

The roots of it
Dangle from their mouths
Scattering earth in the strange woods.
They who are there.

Their paths
Nibbled thru the fields, the leaves that shade them
Hang in the distances
Of sun

The small nouns
Crying faith
In this in which the wild deer
Startle, and stare out.

Theodore Roethke

1908–1963

The Waking

I wake to sleep, and take my waking slow.
I feel my fate in what I cannot fear.
I learn by going where I have to go.

We think by feeling. What is there to know?
I hear my being dance from ear to ear.
I wake to sleep, and take my waking slow.

Of those so close beside me, which are you?
God bless the Ground! I shall walk softly there,
And learn by going where I have to go.

Light takes the Tree; but who can tell us how?
The lowly worm climbs up a winding stair;
I wake to sleep, and take my waking slow.

Great Nature has another thing to do
To you and me; so take the lively air,
And, lovely, learn by going where to go.

This shaking keeps me steady. I should know.
What falls away is always. And is near.
I wake to sleep, and take my waking slow.
I learn by going where I have to go.

In a Dark Time

In a dark time, the eye begins to see,
I meet my shadow in the deepening shade;
I hear my echo in the echoing wood—
A lord of nature weeping to a tree.
I live between the heron and the wren,
Beasts of the hill and serpents of the den.

What's madness but nobility of soul
At odds with circumstance? The day's on fire!
I know the purity of pure despair,
My shadow pinned against a sweating wall.
That place among the rocks—is it a cave,
Or winding path? The edge is what I have.

A steady storm of correspondences!
A night flowing with birds, a ragged moon,
And in broad day the midnight come again!
A man goes far to find out what he is—
Death of the self in a long, tearless night,
All natural shapes blazing unnatural light.

Dark, dark my light, and darker my desire.
My soul, like some heat-maddened summer fly,
Keeps buzzing at the sill. Which I is *I*?
A fallen man, I climb out of my fear.
The mind enters itself, and God the mind,
And one is One, free in the tearing wind.

James Agee

1909–1955

This little time the breath and bulk of being
Are met in me: who from the eldest shade
Of all undreamt am raised forth into seeing
As I may see, the state of all things made:
In sense and dream and death to make my heart
Wise in the loveliness and natural health
Of all, and God, upon the void a part:
Likewise to celebrate this commonwealth:
Believing nothing, and believing all,
In love, in detestation, but most
In naught to sing of all: to recall
What wisdom was before I was this ghost:
Such songs I shall not make nor truths shall know:
And once more mindless into truth shall go.

Elizabeth Bishop

1911–1979

The Unbeliever

He sleeps on the top of a mast.—Bunyan

He sleeps on the top of a mast
with his eyes fast closed.
The sails fall away below him
like the sheets of his bed,
leaving out in the air of the night the sleeper's head.

Asleep he was transported there,
asleep he curled
in a gilded ball on the mast's top,
or climbed inside
a gilded bird, or blindly seated himself astride.

"I am founded on marble pillars,"
said a cloud. "I never move.
See the pillars there in the sea?"
Secure in introspection
he peers at the watery pillars of his reflection.

A gull had wings under his
and remarked that the air
was "like marble." He said: "Up here
I tower through the sky
for the marble wings on my tower-top fly."

But he sleeps on the top of his mast
with his eyes closed tight.
The gull inquired into his dream,
which was, "I must not fall.
The spangled sea below wants me to fall.
It is hard as diamonds; it wants to destroy us all."

Over 2000 Illustrations and a Complete Concordance

Thus should have been our travels:
serious, engravable.
The Seven Wonders of the World are tired
and a touch familiar, but the other scenes,
innumerable, though equally sad and still,
are foreign. Often the squatting Arab,
or group of Arabs, plotting, probably,
against our Christian Empire,
while one apart, with outstretched arm and hand
points to the Tomb, the Pit, the Sepulcher.
The branches of the date-palms look like files.
The cobbled courtyard, where the Well is dry,
is like a diagram, the brickwork conduits
are vast and obvious, the human figure
far gone in history or theology,
gone with its camel or its faithful horse.
Always the silence, the gesture, the specks of birds
suspended on invisible threads above the Site,

or the smoke rising solemnly, pulled by threads.
Granted a page alone or a page made up
of several scenes arranged in cattycornered rectangles
or circles set on stippled gray,
granted a grim lunette,
caught in the toils of an initial letter,
when dwelt upon, they all resolve themselves.
The eye drops, weighted, through the lines
the burin made, the lines that move apart
like ripples above sand,
dispersing storms, God's spreading fingerprint,
and painfully, finally, that ignite
in watery prismatic white-and-blue.

Entering the Narrows at St. Johns
the touching bleat of goats reached to the ship.
We glimpsed them, reddish, leaping up the cliffs
among the fog-soaked weeds and butter-and-eggs.
And at St. Peter's the wind blew and the sun shone madly.
Rapidly, purposefully, the Collegians marched in lines,
crisscrossing the great square with black, like ants.
In Mexico the dead man lay
in a blue arcade; the dead volcanoes
glistened like Easter lilies.
The juke-box went on playing "Ay, Jalisco!"
And at Volubilis there were beautiful poppies
splitting the mosaics; the fat old guide made eyes.
In Dingle harbor a golden length of evening
the rotting hulks held up their dripping plush.
The Englishwoman poured tea, informing us
that the Duchess was going to have a baby.
And in the brothels of Marrakesh
the little pockmarked prostitutes
balanced their tea-trays on their heads
and did their belly-dances; flung themselves
naked and giggling against our knees,
asking for cigarettes. It was somewhere near there
I saw what frightened me most of all:
A holy grave, not looking particularly holy,

one of a group under a keyhole-arched stone baldaquin
open to every wind from the pink desert.
An open, gritty, marble trough, carved solid
with exhortation, yellowed
as scattered cattle-teeth;
half-filled with dust, not even the dust
of the poor prophet paynim who once lay there.
In a smart burnoose Khadour looked on amused.

Everything only connected by "and," and "and."
Open the book. (The gilt rubs off the edges
of the pages and pollinates the fingertips.)
Open the heavy book. Why couldn't we have seen
this old Nativity while we were at it?
—the dark ajar, the rocks breaking with light,
an undisturbed, unbreathing flame,
colorless, sparkless, freely fed on straw,
and, lulled within, a family with pets,
—and looked and looked our infant sight away.

At the Fishhouses

Although it is a cold evening,
down by one of the fishhouses
an old man sits netting,
his net, in the gloaming almost invisible
a dark purple-brown, and his shuttle worn and polished.
The air smells so strong of codfish
it makes one's nose run and one's eyes water.
The five fishhouses have steeply peaked roofs
and narrow, cleated gangplanks slant up
to storerooms in the gables
for the wheelbarrows to be pushed up and down on.
All is silver: the heavy surface of the sea,
swelling slowly as if considering spilling over,
is opaque, but the silver of the benches,
the lobster pots, and masts, scattered
among the wild jagged rocks,
is of an apparent translucence

like the small old buildings with an emerald moss
growing on their shoreward walls.
The big fish tubs are completely lined
with layers of beautiful herring scales
and the wheelbarrows are similarly plastered
with creamy iridescent coats of mail,
with small iridescent flies crawling on them.
Up on the little slope behind the houses,
set in the sparse bright sprinkle of grass,
is an ancient wooden capstan,
cracked, with two long bleached handles
and some melancholy stains, like dried blood,
where the ironwork has rusted.
The old man accepts a Lucky Strike.
He was a friend of my grandfather.
We talk of the decline in the population
and of codfish and herring
while he waits for a herring boat to come in.
There are sequins on his vest and on his thumb.
He has scraped the scales, the principal beauty,
from unnumbered fish with that black old knife,
the blade of which is almost worn away.

Down at the water's edge, at the place
where they haul up the boats, up the long ramp
descending into the water, thin silver
tree trunks are laid horizontally
across the gray stones, down and down
at intervals of four or five feet.

Cold dark deep and absolutely clear,
element bearable to no mortal,
to fish and to seals . . . One seal particularly
I have seen here evening after evening.
He was curious about me. He was interested in music;
like me a believer in total immersion,
so I used to sing him Baptist hymns.
I also sang "A Mighty Fortress Is Our God."
He stood up in the water and regarded me
steadily, moving his head a little.

Then he would disappear, then suddenly emerge
almost in the same spot, with a sort of shrug
as if it were against his better judgment.
Cold dark deep and absolutely clear,
the clear gray icy water . . . Back, behind us,
the dignified tall firs begin.
Bluish, associating with their shadows,
a million Christmas trees stand
waiting for Christmas. The water seems suspended
above the rounded gray and blue-gray stones.
I have seen it over and over, the same sea, the same,
slightly, indifferently swinging above the stones,
icily free above the stones,
above the stones and then the world.
If you should dip your hand in,
your wrist would ache immediately,
your bones would begin to ache and your hand would burn
as if the water were a transmutation of fire
that feeds on stones and burns with a dark gray flame.
If you tasted it, it would first taste bitter,
then briny, then surely burn your tongue.
It is like what we imagine knowledge to be:
dark, salt, clear, moving, utterly free,
drawn from the cold hard mouth
of the world, derived from the rocky breasts
forever, flowing and drawn, and since
our knowledge is historical, flowing, and flown.

William Everson

1912–1994

A Canticle to the Waterbirds

Written for the Feast of Saint Francis of Assisi, 1950

Clack your beaks you cormorants and kittiwakes,
North on those rock-croppings finger-jutted into the rough
    Pacific surge;

You migratory terns and pipers who leave but the temporal
clawtrack written on sandbars there of your presence;
Grebes and pelicans; you comber-picking scoters and you
shorelong gulls;
All you keepers of the coastline north of here to the Mendocino
beaches;
All you beyond upon the cliff-face thwarting the surf at Hecate
Head;
Hovering the under-surge where the cold Columbia grapples at
the bar;
North yet to the Sound, whose islands float like a sown flurry of
chips upon the sea:
Break wide your harsh and salt-encrusted beaks unmade for song
And say a praise up to the Lord.

And you freshwater egrets east in the flooded marshlands skirting
the sea-level rivers, white one-legged watchers of shallows;
Broad-headed kingfishers minnow-hunting from willow stems
on meandering valley sloughs;
You too, you herons, blue and supple-throated, stately, taking the
air majestical in the sunflooded San Joaquin,
Grading down on your belted wings from the upper lights of
sunset,
Mating over the willow clumps or where the flatwater rice fields
shimmer;
You killdeer, high night-criers, far in the moon-suffusion sky;
Bitterns, sand-waders, all shore-walkers, all roost-keepers,
Populates of the 'dobe cliffs of the Sacramento:
Open your water-dartling beaks,
And make a praise up to the Lord.

For you hold the heart of His mighty fastnesses,
And shape the life of His indeterminate realms.
You are everywhere on the lonesome shores of His wide
creation.
You keep seclusion where no man may go, giving Him praise;
Nor may a woman come to lift like your cleaving flight her clear
contralto song
To honor the spindrift gifts of His soft abundance.

You sanctify His hermitage rocks where no holy priest may kneel
to adore, nor holy nun assist;
And where his true communion-keepers are not enabled to
enter.

And well may you say His praises, birds, for your ways
Are verved with the secret skills of His inclinations,
And your habits plaited and rare with the subdued elaboration of
his intricate craft;
Your days intent with the direct astuteness needful for His
outworking,
And your nights alive with the dense repose of His infinite sleep.
You are His secretive charges and you serve His secretive ends,
In His clouded mist-conditioned stations, in His murk,
Obscure in your matted nestings, immured in His limitless
ranges.
He makes you penetrate through dark interstitial joinings of His
thicketed kingdoms,
And keep your concourse in the deeps of His shadowed world.

Your ways are wild but earnest, your manners grave,
Your customs carefully schooled to the note of His serious mien.
You hold the prime condition of His clean creating,
And the swift compliance with which you serve His minor means
Speaks of the constancy with which you hold Him.
For what is your high flight forever going home to your first
beginnings,
But such a testament to your devotion?
You hold His outstretched world beneath your wings, and mount
upon His storms,
And keep your sheer wind-lidded sight upon the vast perspectives
of His mazy latitudes.

But mostly it is your way you bear existence wholly within the
context of His utter will and are untroubled.
Day upon day you do not reckon, nor scrutinize tomorrow, nor
multiply the nightfalls with a rash concern,
But rather assume each instant as warrant sufficient of His final
seal.

Wholly in Providence you spring, and when you die you look on
death in clarity unflinched,
Go down, a clutch of feather ragged upon the brush;
Or drop on water where you briefly lived, found food,
And now yourselves made food for His deep current-keeping
fish, and then are gone:
Is left but the pinion-feather spinning a bit on the uproil
Where lately the dorsal cut clear air.

You leave a silence. And this for you suffices, who are not of the
ceremonials of man,
And hence are not made sad to now forgo them.
Yours is of another order of being, and wholly it compels.
But may you, birds, utterly seized in God's supremacy,
Austerely living under his austere eye—
Yet may you teach a man a necessary thing to know,
Which has to do of the strict conformity that creaturehood
entails,
And constitutes the prime commitment all things share.
For God has given you the imponderable grace to *be* His
verification,
Outside the mulled incertitude of our forensic choices;
That you, our lessers in the rich hegemony of Being,
May serve as testament to what a creature is,
And what creation owes.

Curlews, stilts and scissortails, beachcomber gulls,
Wave-haunters, shore-keepers, rockhead-holders, all cape-top
vigilantes,
Now give God praise.
Send up the strict articulation of your throats,
And say His name.

Jean Garrigue

1912–1972

A Demon Came to Me

A demon came to me in love's disguise,
One of the lower order of hell's guard,
The devil's angel, as it once was coined,
Cool as marble, with a heart like iron.
I could not see it then, the demon smiled
And past experience warned but would not prove.
Besides, the fellow was so very proud,
Immaculate in blackness like a god,
And rife with Adam's ruddy vainglory.
This angel, arrogant of life, swore love.
I, casting off the weight of my short past,
Swore truth was half in novelty's red chance,
And thus in his squat cage I basked.
Foul was fair and fair was foul, confess!
To such confusion have I paid betimes.
Who loves his demon fears his life,
Who loves his pain denies his god.

Robert Hayden

1913–1980

From the corpse woodpiles, from the ashes
and staring pits of Dachau,
Buchenwald they come—

O David, Hirschel, Eva,
cops and robbers with me once,
their faces are like yours—

From Johannesburg, from Seoul.
Their struggles are all horizons.
Their deaths encircle me.

Through target streets I run,
in light part nightmare
and part vision fleeing

What I cannot flee, and reach
that cold cloacal cell
where He, who is man beatified

And Godly mystery,
lies chained, His pain
our anguish and our anodyne.

Bahá'u'lláh in the Garden of Ridwan

Agonies confirm His hour,
        and swords like compass-needles turn
                toward His heart.

The midnight air is forested
        with presences that shelter Him
                and sheltering praise

The auroral darkness which is God
        and sing the word made flesh again
                in Him,

Eternal exile whose return
        epiphanies repeatedly
                foretell.

He watches in a borrowed garden,
        prays. And sleepers toss upon
                their armored beds,

Half-roused by golden knocking at
        the doors of consciousness. Energies
                like angels dance

Glorias of recognition.
        Within the rock the undiscovered suns
                release their light.

The Broken Dark

Sleepless, I stare
from the dark hospital room
at shadows of a flower and its leaves
the nightlight fixes like a blotto
on the corridor wall. Shadow-plays
of Bali—demons move to the left,
gods, in their frangipani crowns
and gold, to the right.
Ah and my life
in the shadow of God's laser light—
shadow of deformed homunculus?
A fool's errand given by fools.
Son, go fetch a pint of pigeon's milk
from the drugstore and be quick.
Demons on the left. Death on either side,
the Rabbi said, the way of life between.
That groaning. Man with his belly slashed,
two-timing lover. Dying?
The nightnurse rustles by.
Struggles in the pit. I have come back
to tell thee of struggles in the pit.
Perhaps is dying.
Free of pain, my own death still
a theorem to be proved.
Alláh'u'Abhá. O Healing Spirit,
Thy nearness our forgiving cure.

Ice Storm

Unable to sleep, or pray, I stand
by the window looking out
at moonstruck trees a December storm
has bowed with ice.

Maple and mountain ash bend
under its glassy weight,
their cracked branches falling upon
the frozen snow.

The trees themselves, as in winters past,
will survive their burdening,
broken thrive. And am I less to You,
my God, than they?

As my blood was drawn,
as my bones were scanned,
the People of Bahá
were savaged were slain;

skeletons were gleaning
famine fields,
horrors multiplying
like cancer cells.

World I have loved,
so lovingly hated,
is it your evil
that has invaded
my body's world?

As surgeons put
me to the knife,
innocents
were sacrificed.

I woke from a death
as exiles drowned.
I called on the veiled
irradiant One.

As spreading oilslicks
burned the seas,
the doctors confirmed
metastasis.

World I have loved
and loving hated,
is it your sickness
luxuriating
in my body's world?

In dreams of death
I call upon
the irradiant veiled
terrible One.

John Frederick Nims

1913–1999

Prayer

We who are nothingness can never be filled:
Never by orchards on the blowing sea,
Nor the rich foam of wheat all summer sunned.

Our hollow is deeper far than treasure can fill:
Helmets of gold swim ringing in the wells
Of our desire as thimbles in the sea.

Love cannot fill us either: children's love,
Nor the white care of mothers, nor the sweet
Concern of sister nor the effort of friends;

No dream-caress nor actual: the mixed breath,
Lips that fumble in dark and dizzily drink
Till all nerves tighten to the key of love.

The feasted man turns empty eyes about;
The king builds higher on a crumbling base,
His human mouth a weapon; his brain, maps.

The lover wakes in horror: he gropes out
For the known form, and even enfolding, fears
A bed by war or failing blood undone.

For we who are nothingness can nothing hold.

Only solution: come to us, conceiver,
You who are all things, held and holder, come to us;
Come like an army marching the long day
And the next day and week and all that year;

Come like an ocean thundering to the moon,
Drowning the sunken reef, mounting the shore.
Come, infinite answer to our infinite want.

Her ancient crater only the sea can fill.

The Dark Night

(trans. from St. John of the Cross)

Once in the dark of night
when love burned bright with yearning, I arose
(O windfall of delight!)
and how I left none knows—
dead to the world my house in deep repose;

in the dark, where all goes right,
thanks to a secret ladder, other clothes,
(O windfall of delight!)
in the dark, enwrapped in those—
dead to the world my house in deep repose.

There in the lucky dark,
none to observe me, darkness far and wide;
no sign for me to mark,
no other light, no guide
except for my heart—the fire, the fire inside!

That led me on
true as the very noon is—truer too!—
to where there waited one
I knew—how well I knew!—
in a place where no one was in view.

O dark of night, my guide!
night dearer than anything all your dawns discover!
O night drawing side to side
the loved and lover—
she that the lover loves, lost in the lover!

Upon my flowering breast,
kept for his pleasure garden, his alone,
the lover was sunk in rest;
I cherished him—my own!—
there in air from plumes of the cedar blown.

In air from the castle wall
as my hand in his hair moved lovingly at play,
he let cool fingers fall
—and the fire there where they lay!—
all senses in oblivion drift away.

I stayed, not minding me;
my forehead on the lover I reclined.
Earth ending, I went free,
left all my care behind
among the lilies falling and out of mind.

Knowledge of God

Nothing first-hand. I'm not your Saul. No burst
Of the Unendurable Dazzlement. Never durst
Claim more than a thrilling hunch: swirled autumn air,
Moon's stealth, or ado in the leaves—
shhh!
Someone there?

Muriel Rukeyser

1913–1980

Are You Born? / I

A man riding on the meaning of rivers
Sang to me from the cloud of the world:
Are you born? Are you born?
My name is gone into the burning heart
That knows the change deep in the form of things.
—I saw from the treeline all our cities shine.
A woman riding on the moon of ocean
Sang to me through the cloud of the world:
Are you born? Are you born?
The form of growing in leaf and crystal flows,
And in the eyes and rivers of the land.
—From the rock of our sky, I came to recognize.

A voice riding on the morning of air
Sang to me from the cloud of the world:
Are you born? Are you born?
Bring all the singing home;
There is a word of lightning in the grass.
—I stood alive in the young cloud.

Are You Born? / II

A child riding the stormy mane of noon
Sang to me past the cloud of the world:
Are you born? Are you born?
The form of this hope is the law of all things,
Our foaming sun is the toy of that force.
Touch us alive, developing light! Today,
Revealed over the mountains, every living eyes.

Child of the possible, who rides the hour
Of dream and process, lit by every fire.
Glittering blood of song, a man who changed
And hardly changed, only flickered, letting pass
A glint of time, showers of human meanings
Flashing upon us all : his story and his song.
The song of a child; the song of the cloud of the world,
Born, born, born. Cloud became real,
and change,
The starry form of love.

Delmore Schwartz

1913–1966

At a Solemn Musick

Let the musicians begin,
Let every instrument awaken and instruct us
In love's willing river and love's dear discipline:
We wait, silent, in consent and in the penance
Of patience, awaiting the serene exaltation
Which is the liberation and conclusion of expiation.

Now may the chief musician say:
"Lust and emulation have dwelt among us
Like barbarous kings: have conquered us:
Have inhabited our hearts: devoured and ravished

—With the savage greed and avarice of fire—
The substance of pity and compassion."

Now may all the players play:
"The river of the morning, the morning of the river
Flow out of the splendor of the tenderness of surrender."

Now may the chief musician say:
"Nothing is more important than summer."

And now the entire choir shall chant:
"How often the astonished heart,
Beholding the laurel,
Remembers the dead,
And the enchanted absolute,
Snow's kingdom, sleep's dominion."

Then shall the chief musician declare:
"The phoenix is the meaning of the fruit,
Until the dream is knowledge and knowledge is a dream."

And then, once again, the entire choir shall cry, in passionate unity,
Singing and celebrating love and love's victory,
Ascending and descending the heights of assent, climbing and chanting triumphantly:
Before the morning was, you were:
Before the snow shone,
And the light sang, and the stone,
Abiding, rode the fullness or endured the emptiness,
You were: you were alone.

Karl Shapiro

1913–2000

The Alphabet

The letters of the Jews as strict as flames
Or little terrible flowers lean
Stubbornly upwards through the perfect ages,
Singing through solid stone the sacred names.
The letters of the Jews are black and clean
And lie in chain-line over Christian pages.
The chosen letters bristle like barbed wire
That hedge the flesh of man,
Twisting and tightening the book that warns.
These words, this burning bush, this flickering pyre
Unsacrifices the bled son of man
Yet plaits his crown of thorns.

Where go the tipsy idols of the Roman
Past synagogues of patient time,
Where go the sisters of the Gothic rose,
Where go the blue eyes of the Polish women
Past the almost natural crime,
Past the still speaking embers of ghettos,
There rise the tinder flowers of the Jews.
The letters of the Jews are dancing knives
That carve the heart of darkness seven ways.
These are the letters that all men refuse
And will refuse until the king arrives
And will refuse until the death of time
And all is rolled back in the book of days.

May Swenson

1913–1989

Question

Body my house
my horse my hound
what will I do
when you are fallen

Where will I sleep
How will I ride
What will I hunt

Where can I go
without my mount
all eager and quick
How will I know
in thicket ahead
is danger or treasure
when Body my good
bright dog is dead

How will it be
to lie in the sky
without roof or door
and wind for an eye

With cloud for shift
how will I hide?

The Lightning

The lightning waked me. It slid unde r
my eyelid. A black book flipped ope n
to an illuminated page. Then insta ntly
shut. Words of destiny were being ut-
tered in the distance. If only I could
make them out! . . . Next day, as I lay
in the sun, a symbol for concei ving the
universe was scratched on my e yeball.
But quickly its point eclipse d, and
softened, in the scabbard of my brain.

My cat speaks one word: Fo ur vowels
and a consonant. He rece ives with the
hairs of his body the wh ispers of the
stars. The kinglet spe aks by flashing
into view a ruby feath er on his head.
He is held by a threa d to the eye of
the sun and cannot fall into error.
Any flower is a per fect ear, or else it
is a thousand lips . . . When will I grope
clear of the entr ails of intellect?

Big-Hipped Nature

Big-hipped nature bursts forth the head of god
from jungle clots of green
from pelvic heave of mountains
On swollen-breasted clouds he fattens and feeds
He is rocked in the crib of the sea

Stairways of the inner earth he crawls
and coos to us from the caves
The secret worms miracle his veins
Myriads of fish embellish his iridescent bowels
In multiple syllables the birds
inscribe on air his fledgling words

Swift and winding beasts with coats of flame
serpents in their languor black and blind
in the night of his dark mind express
his awe and anger his terror and magicness

Wherever we look his eye lies bottomless
fringed by fields and woods
and tragic moons
magnify his pupils with their tears

In fire he strides
Within the waterfall
he twines his limbs of light
Clothed in the wind and tall
he walks the roofs and towers
Rocks are all his faces
flowers the flesh of his flanks
His hair is tossed with the grasses everywhere
Stained by the rainbow every shell
roars his whispered spell

When sleep the enormous shadow of his hand descends
our tongues uncoil a prayer
to hush our ticking hearts our sparrow-like fear
and we lie naked within his lair
His cabalistic lightnings play upon us there

Each Like a Leaf

Each like a leaf
like a wave
To be replaced repeated

What do we crave
heated by cerebral
fire?

Transitive as flames
that turn
in a furnace

Or sleet falling
separately settling
to one sheet

Forms faced alike
we dance in some
frame

We are a sea its waves
cannot name
only be

We are a thick wood
by its leaves made
not understood

As flames
their flight and snow
its white

do not perceive
We weave asleep
a body

We awake unravel
the same veins
we travel

John Berryman

1914–1972

Eleven Addresses to the Lord

I

Master of beauty, craftsman of the snowflake,
inimitable contriver,
endower of Earth so gorgeous & different from the boring
    Moon,
thank you for such as it is my gift.

I have made up a morning prayer to you
containing with precision everything that most matters.
'According to Thy will' the thing begins.
It took me off & on two days. It does not aim at eloquence.

You have come to my rescue again & again
in my impassable, sometimes despairing years.
You have allowed my brilliant friends to destroy themselves
and I am still here, severely damaged, but functioning.

Unknowable, as I am unknown to my guinea pigs:
how can I 'love' you?
I only as far as gratitude & awe
confidently & absolutely go.

I have no idea whether we live again.
It doesn't seem likely
from either the scientific or the philosophical point of view
but certainly all things are possible to you,

and I believe as fixedly in the Resurrection-appearances to Peter
    and to Paul
  as I believe I sit in this blue chair.

Only that may have been a special case
to establish their initiatory faith.

Whatever your end may be, accept my amazement.
May I stand until death forever at attention
for any your least instruction or enlightenment.
I even feel sure you will assist me again, Master of insight &
beauty.

2

Holy, as I suppose I dare to call you
without pretending to know anything about you
but infinite capacity everywhere & always
& in particular certain goodness to me.

Yours is the crumpling, to my sister-in-law terrifying thunder,
yours the candelabra buds sticky in Spring,
Christ's mercy,
the gloomy wisdom of godless Freud:

yours the lost souls in ill-attended wards,
those agonized thro' the world
at this instant of time, all evil men,
Belsen, Omaha Beach,—

incomprehensible to man your ways.
May be the Devil after all exists.
'I don't try to reconcile anything' said the poet at eighty,
'This is a damned strange world.'

Man is ruining the pleasant earth & man.
What at last, my Lord, will you allow?
Postpone till after my children's deaths your doom
if it be thy ineffable, inevitable will.

I say 'Thy kingdom come,' it means nothing to me.
Hast Thou prepared astonishments for man?
One sudden Coming? Many so believe.
So not, without knowing anything, do I.

3

Sole watchman of the flying stars, guard me
against my flicker of impulse lust: teach me
to see them as sisters & daughters. Sustain
my grand endeavours: husbandship & crafting.

Forsake me not when my wild hours come;
grant me sleep nightly, grace soften my dreams;
achieve in me patience till the thing be done,
a careful view of my achievement come.

Make me from time to time the gift of the shoulder.
When all hurt nerves whine shut away the whiskey.
Empty my heart toward Thee.
Let me pace without fear the common path of death.

Cross am I sometimes with my little daughter:
fill her eyes with tears. Forgive me, Lord.
Unite my various soul,
sole watchman of the wide & single stars.

4

If I say Thy name, art Thou there? It may be so.
Thou art not absent-minded, as I am.
I am so much so I had to give up driving.
You attend, I feel, to the matters of man.

Across the ages certain blessings swarm,
horrors accumulate, the best men fail:
Socrates, Lincoln, Christ mysterious.
Who can search Thee out?

except Isaiah & Pascal, who saw.
I dare not ask that vision, though a piece of it
at last in crisis was vouchsafèd me.
I altered then for good, to become yours.

Caretaker! take care, for we run in straits.
Daily, by night, we walk naked to storm,
some threat of wholesale loss, to ruinous fear.
Gift us with long cloaks & adrenaline.

Who haunt the avenues of Angkor Wat
recalling all that prayer, that glory dispersed,
haunt me at the corner of Fifth & Hennepin.
Shield & fresh fountain! Manifester! Even mine.

5

Holy, & holy. The damned are said to say
'We never thought we would come into this place.'
I'm fairly clear, my Friend, there's no such place
ordained for inappropriate & evil man.

Surely they fall dull, & forget. We too,
the more or less just, I feel fall asleep
dreamless forever while the worlds hurl out.
Rest may be your ultimate gift.

Rest or transfiguration! come & come
whenever Thou wilt. My daughter & my son
fend will without me, when my work is done
in Your opinion.

Strengthen my widow, let her dream on me
thro' tranquil hours less & down to less.
Abrupt elsewhere her heart, I sharply hope.
I leave her in wise Hands.

6

Under new management, Your Majesty:
Thine. I have solo'd mine since childhood, since
my father's blow-it all when I was twelve
blew out my most bright candle faith, and look at me.

I served at Mass six dawns a week from five,
adoring Father Boniface & you,
memorizing the Latin he explained.
Mostly we worked alone. One or two women.

Then my poor father frantic. Confusions & afflictions
followed my days. Wives left me.
Bankrupt I closed my doors. You pierced the roof
twice & again. Finally you opened my eyes.

My double nature fused in that point of time
three weeks ago day before yesterday.
Now, brooding thro' a history of the early Church,
I identify with everybody, even the heresiarchs.

7

After a Stoic, a Peripatetic, a Pythagorean,
Justin Martyr studied the words of the Saviour,
finding them short, precise, terrible, & full of refreshment.
I am tickled to learn this.

Let one day desolate Sherry, fair, thin, tall,
at 29 today her life the Sahara Desert,
who never has once enjoyed a significant relation,
so find His lightning words.

8 A PRAYER FOR THE SELF

Who am I worthless that You spent such pains
and take may pains again?
I do not understand; but I believe.
Jonquils respond with wit to the teasing breeze.

Induct me down my secrets. Stiffen this heart
to stand their horrifying cries, O cushion
the first the second shocks, will to a halt
in mid-air there demons who would be at me.

May fade before, sweet morning on sweet morning,
I wake my dreams, my fan-mail go astray,
and do me little goods I have not thought of,
ingenious & beneficial Father.

Ease in their passing my beloved friends,
all others too I have cared for in a travelling life,
anyone anywhere indeed. Lift up
sober toward truth a scared self-estimate.

9

Surprise me on some ordinary day
with a blessing gratuitous. Even I've done good
beyond their expectations. What count we then
upon Your bounty?

Interminable: an old theologian
asserts that even to say You exist is misleading.
Uh-huh. I buy that Second-century fellow.
I press his withered glorifying hand.

You certainly do not as I exist,
impersonating as well the meteorite
& flaring in your sun your waterfall
or blind in caves pallid fishes.

Bear in mind me, Who have forgotten nothing,
& Who continues. I may not foreknow
& fail much to remember. You sustain
imperial desuetudes, at the kerb a widow.

10

Fearful I peer upon the mountain path
where once Your shadow passed, Limner of the clouds
up their phantastic guesses. I am afraid,
I never until now confessed.

I fell back in love with you, Father, for two reasons:
You were good to me, & a delicious author,
rational & passionate. Come on me again,
as twice you came to Azarias & Misael.

President of the brethren, our mild assemblies
inspire, & bother the priest not to be dull;
keep us week-long in order; love my children,
my mother far & ill, far brother, my spouse.

Oil all my turbulence as at Thy dictation
I sweat out my wayward works.
Father Hopkins said the only true literary critic is Christ.
Let me lie down exhausted, content with that.

II

Germanicus leapt upon the wild lion in Smyrna,
wishing to pass quickly from a lawless life.
The crowd shook the stadium.
The proconsul marvelled.

'Eighty & six years have I been his servant,
and he has done me no harm.
How can I blaspheme my King who saved me?'
Polycarp, John's pupil, facing the fire.

Make too me acceptable at the end of time
in my degree, which then Thou wilt award.
Cancer, senility, mania,
I pray I may be ready with my witness.

David Ignatow

1914–1997

Kaddish

Mother of my birth, for how long were we together
in your love and my adoration of your self?
For the shadow of a moment, as I breathed your pain
and you breathed my suffering. As we knew
of shadows in lit rooms that would swallow the light.

Your face beneath the oxygen tent was alive
but your eyes closed, your breathing hoarse.
Your sleep was with death. I was alone
with you as when I was young
but now only alone, not with you,
to become alone forever, as I was learning
watching you become alone.

Earth now is your mother, as you were mine, my earth,
my sustenance and my strength,
and now without you I turn to your mother
and seek from her that I may meet you again
in rock and stone. Whisper to the stone,
I love you. Whisper to the rock, I found you.
Whisper to the earth, Mother, I have found her,
and I am safe and always have been.

Randall Jarrell

1914–1965

Jonah

As I lie here in the sun
And gaze out, a day's journey, over Nineveh,
The sailors in the dark hold cry to me:
"What meanest thou, O sleeper? Arise and call upon
Thy God; pray with us, that we perish not."

All thy billows and thy waves passed over me.
The waters compassed me, the weeds were wrapped about my
    head;
The earth with her bars was about me forever.
A naked worm, a man no longer,
I writhed beneath the dead:

But thou art merciful.
When my soul was dead within me I remembered thee,
From the depths I cried to thee. For thou art merciful:
Thou hast brought my life up from corruption,
O Lord my God. . . . When the king said, "Who can tell

But God may yet repent, and turn away
From his fierce anger, that we perish not?"
My heart fell; for I knew thy grace of old—
In my own country, Lord, did I not say
That thou art merciful?

Now take, Lord, I beseech thee,
My life from me; it is better that I die . . .
But I hear, "Doest thou well, then, to be angry?"
And I say nothing, and look bitterly
Across the city; a young gourd grows over me

And shades me—and I slumber, clean of grief.
I was glad of the gourd. But God prepared
A worm that gnawed the gourd; but God prepared
The east wind, the sun beat upon my head
Till I cried, "Let me die!" And God said, "Doest thou well

To be angry for the gourd?"
And I said in my anger, "I do well
To be angry, even unto death." But the Lord God
Said to me, "Thou hast had pity on the gourd"—
And I wept, to hear its dead leaves rattle—

"Which came up in a night, and perished in a night.
And should I not spare Nineveh, that city
Wherein are more than six-score thousand persons
Who cannot tell their left hand from their right;
And also much cattle?"

William Stafford

1914–1993

With My Crowbar Key

I do tricks in order to know:
careless I dance,
then turn to see
the mark to turn God left for me.

Making my home in vertigo
I pray with my screams
and think with my hair
prehensile in the dark with fear.

When I hear the well bucket strike something soft
far down at noon,
then there's no place
far enough away to hide my face.

When I see my town over sights of a rifle,
and carved by light
from the lowering sun,
then my old friends darken one by one.

By step and step like a cat toward God
I dedicated walk,
but under the house
I realize the kitten's crouch.

And by night like this I turn and come
to this possible house
which I open, and see
myself at work with this crowbar key.

Thomas Merton

1915–1968

St. Paul

When I was Saul, and sat among the cloaks,
My eyes were stones, I saw no sight of heaven,
Open to take the spirit of the twisting Stephen.
When I was Saul, and sat among the rocks,
I locked my eyes, and made my brain my tomb,
Sealed with what boulders rolled across my reason!

When I was Saul and walked upon the blazing desert
My road was quiet as a trap.
I feared what word would split high noon with light
And lock my life, and try to drive me mad:
And thus I saw the Voice that struck me dead.

Tie up my breath, and wind me in white sheets of anguish,
And lay me in my three days' sepulchre
Until I find my Easter in a vision.

Oh Christ! Give back my life, go, cross Damascus,
Find out my Ananias in that other room:
Command him, as you do, in this my dream;
He knows my locks, and owns my ransom,
Waits for Your word to take his keys and come.

In Silence

Be still
Listen to the stones of the wall.
Be silent, they try
To speak your

Name.
Listen
To the living walls.
Who are you?
Who
Are you? Whose
Silence are you?

Who (be quiet)
Are you (as these stones
Are quiet). Do not
Think of what you are
Still less of
What you may one day be.
Rather
Be what you are (but who?) be
The unthinkable one
You do not know.

O be still, while
You are still alive,
And all things live around you
Speaking (I do not hear)
To your own being,
Speaking by the Unknown
That is in you and in themselves.

"I will try, like them
To be my own silence:
And this is difficult. The whole
World is secretly on fire. The stones
Burn, even the stones
They burn me. How can a man be still or
Listen to all things burning? How can he dare
To sit with them when
All their silence
Is on fire?"

Elegy for the Monastery Barn

As though an aged person were to wear
Too gay a dress
And walk about the neighborhood
Announcing the hour of her death,

So now, one summer day's end,
At suppertime, when wheels are still,
The long barn suddenly puts on the traitor, beauty,
And hails us with a dangerous cry,
For: "Look!" she calls to the country,
"Look how fast I dress myself in fire!"

Had we half guessed how long her spacious shadows
Harbored a woman's vanity
We would be less surprised to see her now
So loved, and so attended, and so feared.

She, in whose airless heart
We burst our veins to fill her full of hay,
Now stands apart.
She will not have us near her. Terribly,
Sweet Christ, how terribly her beauty burns us now!

And yet she has another legacy,
More delicate, to leave us, and more rare.

Who knew her solitude?
Who heard the peace downstairs
While flames ran whispering among the rafters?
Who felt the silence, there,
The long, hushed gallery
Clean and resigned and waiting for the fire?

Look! They have all come back to speak their summary:
Fifty invisible cattle, the past years
Assume their solemn places one by one.
This is the little minute of their destiny.
Here is their meaning found. Here is their end.

Laved in the flame as in a Sacrament
The brilliant walls are holy
In their first-last hour of joy.

Fly from within the barn! Fly from the silence
Of this creature sanctified by fire!
Let no man stay inside to look upon the Lord!
Let no man wait within and see the Holy
One sitting in the presence of disaster
Thinking upon this barn His gentle doom!

Robert Lowell

1917–1977

Where the Rainbow Ends

I saw the sky descending, black and white,
Not blue, on Boston where the winters wore
The skulls to jack-o'-lanterns on the slates,
And Hunger's skin-and-bone retrievers tore
The chickadee and shrike. The thorn tree waits
Its victim and tonight

The worms will eat the deadwood to the foot
Of Ararat: the scythers, Time and Death,
Helmed locusts, move upon the tree of breath;
The wild ingrafted olive and the root

Are withered, and a winter drifts to where
The Pepperpot, ironic rainbow, spans
Charles River and its scales of scorched-earth miles.
I saw my city in the Scales, the pans
Of judgment rising and descending. Piles
Of dead leaves char the air—
And I am a red arrow on this graph
Of Revelations. Every dove is sold
The Chapel's sharp-shinned eagle shifts its hold
On serpent-Time, the rainbow's epitaph.

In Boston serpents whistle at the cold.
The victim climbs the altar steps and sings:
"Hosannah to the lion, lamb, and beast
Who fans the furnace-face of IS with wings:
I breathe the ether of my marriage feast."
At the high altar, gold
And a fair cloth. I kneel and the wings beat
My cheek. What can the dove of Jesus give
You now but wisdom, exile? Stand and live,
The dove has brought an olive branch to eat.

William Bronk

1918–1999

Virgin and Child with Music and Numbers

Who knows better than you know,
Lady, the circumstances of this event
—meanness, the overhanging terror, and the need
for flight soon—hardly reflect the pledge

the angel gave you, the songs you exchanged in joy
with Elizabeth, your cousin? That was then
or that was for later, another time. Now—.

Still, the singing was and is. Song
whether or not we sing. The song is sung.
Are we cozened? The song we hear is like
those numbers we cannot factor whose overplus,
an indeterminate fraction, seems more than the part
we factor out. Lady, if our despair
is to be unable to factor ourselves in song
or factor the world there, what should our joy
be other than this same integer that sings
and mocks at satisfaction? We are not
fulfilled. We cannot hope to be. No,
we are held somewhere in the void of whole despair,
enraptured, and only there does the world endure.

Lady, sing to this Baby, even so.

The Mind's Limitations Are Its Freedom

The mind has a power which is unusable
and this is its real power. What else but the mind
senses the final uselessness of the mind?

How foolish we were, how smaller than what we are,
were we to believe what the mind makes of what
it meets. Whatever the mind makes is not.

You know there are always messages we find
—in bed, on the street or anywhere, and the mind
invents a translation almost plausible;
but it hasn't any knowledge of the language at all.

Sometimes the translations are cryptic in themselves.
I read them in wonderment. It is a wonderment
not usable. What could it all mean?
The mind does this. I stand in awe of the mind.

Robert Duncan

1919–1988

Often I Am Permitted to Return to a Meadow

as if it were a scene made-up by the mind,
that is not mine, but is a made place,

that is mine, it is so near to the heart,
an eternal pasture folded in all thought
so that there is a hall therein

that is a made place, created by light
wherefrom the shadows that are forms fall.

Wherefrom fall all architectures I am
I say are likenesses of the First Beloved
whose flowers are flames lit to the Lady.

She it is Queen Under The Hill
whose hosts are a disturbance of words within words
that is a field folded.

It is only a dream of the grass blowing
east against the source of the sun
in an hour before the sun's going down

whose secret we see in a children's game
of ring a round of roses told.

Often I am permitted to return to a meadow
as if it were a given property of the mind
that certain bounds hold against chaos,

that is a place of first permission,
everlasting omen of what is.

The Natural Doctrine

As I came needing wonder as the new shoots need water
to the letter A that sounds its mystery in wave and in wain,
trembling I bent as if there were a weight in words
like that old man bends under his age towards Death—

But it is the sun that sounds Day from the first brink,
it is the sea that in its dazzling holds my eye.
How under the low roof of desolate gray
a language not of words lies waiting!
There's depth, weight, force at the horizon
that levels all images.

Rabbi Aaron of Bagdad meditating upon the Word and the
    letters Yod and Hé
came upon the Name of God and achieved a pure rapture
in which a creature of his ecstasy that was once dumb clay, the
    Golem,
danced and sang and had being.

Reading of this devout jew I thought
there may be such power in a certain passage of a poem
that eternal joy may leap therefrom.

But it was for a clearing of the sky,
for a blue radiance, my thought cried.
Sublime Turner who dying said to Ruskin, *The Sun is God, my
    dear,* knew
the actual language is written in rainbows.

God-Spell

We have lost.   No,
we have not lost   our way

but we have found the way

dark, hard to make out,   and yet
joyous.

What we hold to is no more than
words.   Yes, it is hard to assay

the worth we hold to.

We said it was gold.   The soul

weighd against Maat's feather.

Our treasure, the light in the dandylion head shining,
they wld blow out.   "See, your heart holds to
a lost cause."

The light all but invisible

seeds   scatterd abroad,   rise

fall   upon the breath of the air

everywhere   and in heavy ground

find refuge.   This

the song of the *dent de lion* or of the thistledown

seeds of a rumor   from hearts long ago

defeated faiths   blown out

the ayre of the music   carries.

Amy Clampitt

1920–1994

A Procession at Candlemas

I

Moving on or going back to where you came from,
bad news is what you mainly travel with:
a breakup or a breakdown, someone running off

or walking out, called up or called home:
death in the family. Nudged from their stanchions
outside the terminal, anonymous of purpose

as a flock of birds, the bison of the highway
funnel westward onto Route 80, mirroring
an entity that cannot look into itself and know

what makes it what it is. Sooner or later
every trek becomes a funeral procession.
The mother curtained in Intensive Care

a scene the mind leaves blank, fleeing instead
toward scenes of transhumance, the belled sheep
moving up the Pyrenees, red-tasseled pack llamas

footing velvet-green precipices, the Kurdish
women, jingling with bangles, gorgeous
on their rug-piled mounts—already lying dead,

bereavement altering the moving lights
to a processional, a feast of Candlemas.
Change as child-bearing, birth as a kind

of shucking off: out of what began
as a Mosaic insult—such a loathing
of the common origin, even a virgin,

having given birth, needs purifying—
to carry fire as though it were a flower,
the terror and the loveliness entrusted

into naked hands, supposing God might have,
might actually need a mother: people have
at times found this a way of being happy.

A Candlemas of moving lights along Route 80;
lighted candles in a corridor from Arlington
over the Potomac, for every carried flame

the name of a dead soldier: an element
fragile as ego, frightening as parturition,
necessary and intractable as dreaming.

The lapped, wheelborne integument, layer
within layer, at the core a dream of
something precious, ripped: Where are we?

The sleepers groan, stir, rewrap themselves
about the self's imponderable substance,
or clamber down, numb-footed, half in a drowse

of freezing dark, through a Stonehenge
of fuel pumps, the bison hulks slantwise
beside them, drinking. What is real except

what's fabricated? The jellies glitter
cream-capped in the cafeteria showcase;
gumball globes, Life Savers cinctured

in parcel gilt, plop from their housings
perfect, like miracles. Comb, nail clipper,
lip rouge, mirrors and emollients embody,

niched into the washroom wall case,
the pristine seductiveness of money.
Absently, without inhabitants, this

nowhere oasis wears the place name
of Indian Meadows. The westward-trekking
transhumance, once only, of a people who,

in losing everything they had, lost even
the names they went by, stumbling past
like caribou, perhaps camped here. Who

can assign a trade-in value to that sorrow?
The monk in sheepskin over tucked-up saffron
intoning to a drum becomes the metronome

of one more straggle up Pennsylvania Avenue
in falling snow, a whirl of tenderly
remorseless corpuscles, street gangs

amok among magnolias' pregnant wands,
a stillness at the heart of so much whirling:
beyond the torn integument of childbirth,

sometimes, wrapped like a papoose into a grief
not merely of the ego, you rediscover almost
the rest-in-peace of the placental coracle.

II

Of what the dead were, living, one knows
so little as barely to recognize
the fabric of the backward-ramifying

antecedents, half-noted presences
in darkened rooms: the old, the feared,
the hallowed. Never the same river

drowns the unalterable doorsill. An effigy
in olive wood or pear wood, dank
with the sweat of age, walled in the dark

at Brauron, Argos, Samos: even the unwed
Athene, who had no mother, born—it's declared—
of some man's brain like every other pure idea,

had her own wizened cult object, kept
out of sight like the incontinent whimperer
in the backstairs bedroom, where no child

ever goes—to whom, year after year,
the fair linen of the sacred peplos
was brought in ceremonial procession—

flutes and stringed instruments, wildflower-
hung cattle, nubile Athenian girls, young men
praised for the beauty of their bodies. Who

can unpeel the layers of that seasonal
returning to the dark where memory fails,
as birds re-enter the ancestral flyway?

Daylight, snow falling, knotting of gears:
Chicago. Soot, the rotting backsides
of tenements, grimed trollshapes of ice

underneath the bridges, the tunnel heaving
like a birth canal. Disgorged, the infant
howling in the restroom; steam-table cereal,

pale coffee; wall-eyed TV receivers, armchairs
of molded plastic: the squalor of the day
resumed, the orphaned litter taken up again

unloved, the spawn of botched intentions,
grief a mere hardening of the gut,
a set piece of what can't be avoided:

parents by the tens of thousands living
unthanked, unpaid but in the sour coin
of resentment. Midmorning gray as zinc

along Route 80, corn-stubble quilting
the underside of snowdrifts, the cadaverous
belvedere of windmills, the sullen stare

of feedlot cattle; black creeks puncturing
white terrain, the frozen bottomland
a mush of willow tops; dragnetted in ice,

the Mississippi. Westward toward the dark,
the undertow of scenes come back to, fright
riddling the structures of interior history:

Where is it? Where, in the shucked-off
bundle, the hampered obscurity that has been
for centuries the mumbling lot of women,

did the thread of fire, too frail
ever to discover what it meant, to risk
even the taking of a shape, relinquish

the seed of possibility, unguessed-at
as a dream of something precious? Memory,
that exquisite blunderer, stumbling

like a migrant bird that finds the flyway
it hardly knew it knew except by instinct,
down the long-unentered nave of childhood,

late on a midwinter afternoon, alone
among the snow-hung hollows of the windbreak
on the far side of the orchard, encounters

sheltering among the evergreens, a small
stilled bird, its cap of clear yellow
slit by a thread of scarlet—the untouched

nucleus of fire, the lost connection
hallowing the wizened effigy, the mother
curtained in Intensive Care: a Candlemas

of moving lights along Route 80, at nightfall,
in falling snow, the stillness and the sorrow
of things moving back to where they came from.

Easter Morning

a stone at dawn
cold water in the basin
these walls' rough plaster
imageless
after the hammering
of so much insistence
on the need for naming
after the travesties
that passed as faces,
grace: the unction
of sheer nonexistence
upwelling in this
hyacinthine freshet
of the unnamed
the faceless

Brought From Beyond

The magpie and the bowerbird, its odd
predilection unheard of by Marco Polo
when he came upon, high in Badakhshan,
        that blue stone's

embedded glint of pyrites, like the dance
of light on water, or of angels
(the surface tension of the Absolute)
        on nothing,

turned, by processes already ancient,
into pigment: ultramarine, brought from
beyond the water it's the seeming
        color of,

and of the berries, blooms and pebbles
finickingly garnishing an avian
shrine or bower with the rarest hue
        in nature,

whatever nature is: the magpie's eye for
glitter from the clenched fist of
the Mesozoic folding: the creek sands,
        the mine shaft,

the siftings and burnishings, the ingot,
the pagan artifact: to propagate
the faith, to find the metal, unearth it,
        hoard it up,

to, by the gilding of basilicas,
transmute it: O magpie, O bowerbird,
O Marco Polo and Coronado, where do
        these things, these

fabrications, come from—the holy places,
ark and altarpiece, the aureoles,
the seraphim—and underneath it all
        the howling?

A Silence

past parentage or gender
beyond sung vocables
the slipped-between
the so infinitesimal
fault line
a limitless
interiority

beyond the woven
unicorn   the maiden
(man-carved   worm-eaten)
God at her hip
incipient
the untransfigured
cottontail
bluebell and primrose
growing wild   a strawberry
chagrin   night terrors
past the earthlit
unearthly masquerade

(we shall be changed)

a silence opens

§

the larval feeder
naked   hairy   ravenous
inventing from within
itself its own
raw stuffs'
hooked silk-hung
relinquishment

behind the mask
the milkfat   shivering
sinew   isinglass
uncrumpling   transient
greed to reinvest

§

names have been
given   (revelation
kif   nirvana
syncope)   for
whatever gift
unasked
gives birth to

torrents
fixities
reincarnations of
the angels
Joseph Smith
enduring
martyrdom

a cavernous
compunction driving
founder-charlatans
who saw in it
the infinite
love of God
and had
(George Fox
was one)
great openings

Howard Nemerov

1920–1991

The Loon's Cry

On a cold evening, summer almost gone,
I walked alone down where the railroad bridge
Divides the river from the estuary.
There was a silence over both the waters,
The river's concentrated reach, the wide
Diffusion of the delta, marsh and sea,
Which in the distance misted out of sight.

As on the seaward side the sun went down,
The river answered with the rising moon,
Full moon, its craters, mountains and still seas
Shining like snow and shadows on the snow.
The balanced silence centered where I stood,

The fulcrum of two poised immensities,
Which offered to be weighed at either hand.

But I could think only, Red sun, white moon,
This is a natural beauty, it is not
Theology. For I had fallen from
The symboled world, where I in earlier days
Found mysteries of meaning, form, and fate
Signed on the sky, and now stood but between
A swamp of fire and a reflecting rock.

I envied those past ages of the world
When, as I thought, the energy in things
Shone through their shapes, when sun and moon no less
Than tree or stone or star or human face
Were seen but as fantastic Japanese
Lanterns are seen, sullen or gay colors
And lines revealing the light that they conceal.

The world a stage, its people maskers all
In actions largely framed to imitate
God and His Lucifer's long debate, a trunk
From which, complex and clear, the episodes
Spread out their branches. Each life played a part,
And every part consumed a life, nor dreams
After remained to mock accomplishment.

Under the austere power of the scene,
The moon standing balanced against the sun,
I simplified still more, and thought that now
We'd traded all those mysteries in for things,
For essences in things, not understood—
Reality in things! and now we saw
Reality exhausted all their truth.

As answering my thought a loon cried out
Laughter of desolation on the river,
A savage cry, now that the moon went up
And the sun down—yet when I heard him cry

Again, his voice seemed emptied of that sense
Or any other, and Adam I became,
Hearing the first loon cry in paradise.

For sometimes, when the world is not our home
Nor have we any home elsewhere, but all
Things look to leave us naked, hungry, cold,
We suddenly may seem in paradise
Again, in ignorance and emptiness
Blessed beyond all that we thought to know:
Then on sweet waters echoes the loon's cry.

I thought I understood what that cry meant,
That its contempt was for the forms of things,
Their doctrines, which decayed—the nouns of stone
And adjectives of glass—not for the verb
Which surged in power properly eternal
Against the seawall of the solid world,
Battering and undermining what it built,

And whose respeaking was the poet's act,
Only and always, in whatever time
Stripped by uncertainty, despair, and ruin,
Time readying to die, unable to die
But damned to life again, and the loon's cry.
And now the sun was sunken in the sea,
The full moon high, and stars began to shine.

The moon, I thought, might have been such a world
As this one is, till it went cold inside,
Nor any strength of sun could keep its people
Warm in their palaces of glass and stone.
Now all its craters, mountains and still seas,
Shining like snow and shadows on the snow,
Orbit this world in envy and late love.

And the stars too? Worlds, as the scholars taught
So long ago? Chaos of beauty, void,
O burning cold, against which we define

Both wretchedness and love. For signatures
In all things are, which leave us not alone
Even in the thought of death, and may by arts
Contemplative be found and named again.

The loon again? Or else a whistling train,
Whose far thunders began to shake the bridge.
And it came on, a loud bulk under smoke,
Changing the signals on the bridge, the bright
Rubies and emeralds, rubies and emeralds
Signing the cold night as I turned for home,
Hearing the train cry once more, like a loon.

Richard Wilbur

b. 1921

"A World Without Objects Is a Sensible Emptiness"

The tall camels of the spirit
Steer for their deserts, passing the last groves loud
With the sawmill shrill of the locust, to the whole honey of the arid
Sun. They are slow, proud,

And move with a stilted stride
To the land of sheer horizon, hunting Traherne's
Sensible emptiness, there where the brain's lantern-slide
Revels in vast returns.

O connoisseurs of thirst,
Beasts of my soul who long to learn to drink
Of pure mirage, those prosperous islands are accurst
That shimmer on the brink

Of absence; auras, lustres,
And all shinings need to be shaped and borne.
Think of those painted saints, capped by the early masters
With bright, jauntily-worn

Aureate plates, or even
Merry-go-round rings. Turn, O turn
From the fine sleights of the sand, from the long empty oven
Where flames in flamings burn

Back to the trees arrayed
In bursts of glare, to the halo-dialing run
Of the country creeks, and the hills' bracken tiaras made
Gold in the sunken sun,

Wisely watch for the sight
Of the supernova burgeoning over the barn,
Lampshine blurred in the steam of beasts, the spirit's right
Oasis, light incarnate.

Advice to a Prophet

When you come, as you soon must, to the streets of our city,
Mad-eyed from stating the obvious,
Not proclaiming our fall but begging us
In God's name to have self-pity,

Spare us all word of the weapons, their force and range,
The long numbers that rocket the mind;
Our slow, unreckoning hearts will be left behind,
Unable to fear what is too strange.

Nor shall you scare us with talk of the death of the race.
How should we dream of this place without us?—
The sun mere fire, the leaves untroubled about us,
A stone look on the stone's face?

Speak of the world's own change. Though we cannot conceive
Of an undreamt thing, we know to our cost
How the dreamt cloud crumbles, the vines are blackened by
frost,
How the view alters. We could believe,

If you told us so, that the white-tailed deer will slip
Into perfect shade, grown perfectly shy,
The lark avoid the reaches of our eye,
The jack-pine lose its knuckled grip

On the cold ledge, and every torrent burn
As Xanthus once, its gliding trout
Stunned in a twinkling. What should we be without
The dolphin's arc, the dove's return,

These things in which we have seen ourselves and spoken?
Ask us, prophet, how we shall call
Our natures forth when that live tongue is all
Dispelled, that glass obscured or broken

In which we have said the rose of our love and the clean
Horse of our courage, in which beheld
The singing locust of the soul unshelled,
And all we mean or wish to mean.

Ask us, ask us whether with the worldless rose
Our hearts shall fail us; come demanding
Whether there shall be lofty or long standing
When the bronze annals of the oak-tree close.

A Christmas Hymn

And some of the Pharisees from among the multitude said unto him, Master, rebuke thy disciples.

And he answered and said unto them, I tell you that, if these should hold their peace, the stones would immediately cry out.

—St. Luke XIX, 39–40

A stable-lamp is lighted
Whose glow shall wake the sky;
The stars shall bend their voices,
And every stone shall cry.
And every stone shall cry,
And straw like gold shall shine;

A barn shall harbor heaven,
A stall become a shrine.

This child through David's city
Shall ride in triumph by;
The palm shall strew its branches,
And every stone shall cry.
And every stone shall cry,
Though heavy, dull, and dumb,
And lie within the roadway
To pave his kingdom come.

Yet he shall be forsaken,
And yielded up to die;
The sky shall groan and darken,
And every stone shall cry.
And every stone shall cry
For stony hearts of men:
God's blood upon the spearhead,
God's love refused again.

But now, as at the ending,
The low is lifted high;
The stars shall bend their voices,
And every stone shall cry.
And every stone shall cry
In praises of the child
By whose descent among us
The worlds are reconciled.

In a Churchyard

That flower unseen, that gem of purest ray,
Bright thoughts uncut by men:
Strange that you need but speak them, Thomas Gray,
And the mind skips and dives beyond its ken,

Finding at once the wild supposèd bloom,
Or in the imagined cave
Some pulse of crystal staving off the gloom
As covertly as phosphorus in a grave.

Void notions proper to a buried head!
Beneath these tombstones here
Unseenness fills the sockets of the dead,
Whatever to their souls may now appear;

And who but those unfathomably deaf
Who quiet all this ground
Could catch, within the ear's diminished clef,
A music innocent of time and sound?

What do the living hear, then, when the bell
Hangs plumb within the tower
Of the still church, and still their thoughts compel
Pure tollings that intend no mortal hour?

As when a ferry for the shore of death
Glides looming toward the dock,
Her engines cut, her spirits bating breath
As the ranked pilings narrow toward the shock,

So memory and expectation set
Some pulseless clangor free
Of circumstance, and charm us to forget
This twilight crumbling in the churchyard tree,

Those swifts or swallows which do not pertain,
Scuffed voices in the drive,
That light flicked on behind the vestry pane,
Till, unperplexed from all that is alive,

It shadows all our thought, balked imminence
Of uncommitted sound,
And still would tower at the sill of sense
Were not, as now, its honed abeyance crowned

With a mauled boom of summons far more strange
Than any stroke unheard,
Which breaks again with unimagined range
Through all reverberations of the word,

Pooling the mystery of things that are,
The buzz of prayer said,
The scent of grass, the earliest-blooming star,
These unseen gravestones, and the darker dead.

The Proof

Shall I love God for causing me to be?
I was mere utterance; shall these words love me?

Yet when I caused his work to jar and stammer,
And one free subject loosened all his grammar,

I love him that he did not in a rage
Once and forever rule me off the page,

But, thinking I might come to please him yet,
Crossed out *delete* and wrote his patient *stet*.

James Dickey

1923–1997

Adam in Winter

This road is a river, white
Of its slow-frozen light.
Not treading on earth, I walk
The turnpike of a dream,
Pursuing the buried stream
The fell beneath the snow.
I feel its waters grow
Thick ice to bear me up,
But now I have knelt down.

But now I have knelt down
As if I swam out of the sky,
Or fell with tremendous force
Of gentleness, like snow,
Toward a thing I know.
Last night I turned and found
I lay with a rifled wound.
That bone completes me; I
Must kneel with the gentle snow.

Some hand has entered the snow
To rummage me where I lay.
My rib has been plucked away
And taken to Heaven, or
Flung down on the icy floor.
A voice said, "Follow the river."
I have followed; now I hover
Near something the flakes half-hide
That has come from my sleeping side.

It has come from my sleeping side,
Some being that could not be
Made of anything other than me:
Whose curve my heart fits in.
I lift the light bone in my palm
And feel my whole body grow warm.
Exhaling my soul out, bare,
My lungs take shape in the air.
My rib moves in my hand.

My rib moves in my hand,
And all my other ribs move.
I whisper the warning of love.
A great image stirs in my breath,
Denying the body of death.
She stands in the shape of my lungs.
My heart beats like her wings,
Yet breath fades from my sight.
My mouth no longer sheds light.

My mouth no longer sheds light,
Though I laugh with a magical sound
That heals my amazing wound.
All things grow warm in this place.
The green river trembles its ice.
She comes to me weeping, as if
She came to return my life,
Though purity dies, and I feel
The ice turn sick at my heel.

Walking on Water

Feeling it with me
On it, barely float, the narrow plank on the water,
I stepped from the clam-shell beach,
Breaking in nearly down through the sun
Where it lay on the sea,
And poled off, gliding upright
Onto the shining topsoil of the bay.

Later, it came to be said
That I was seen walking on water,
Not moving my legs
Except for the wrong step of sliding:
A child who leaned on a staff,
A curious pilgrim hiking
Between two open blue worlds,

My motion a miracle,
Leaving behind me no footprint,
But only the shimmering place
Of an infinite step upon water
In which sat still and were shining
Many marsh-birds and pelicans.
Alongside my feet, the shark

Lay buried and followed,
His eyes on my childish heels.
Thus, taking all morning to stalk

From one littered beach to another,
I came out on land, and dismounted,
Making marks in the sand with my toes
Which truly had walked there, on water,

With the pelicans beating their shadows
Through the mirror carpet
Down, and the shark pursuing
The boy on the burning deck
Of a bare single ship-wrecked board.
Shoving the plank out to sea, I walked
Inland, on numb sparkling feet,

With the sun on the sea unbroken,
Nor the long quiet step of the miracle
Doing anything behind me but blazing,
With the birds in it nodding their heads,
That must ponder that footstep forever,
Rocking, or until I return
In my ghost, which shall have become, then,

A boy with a staff,
To loose them, beak and feather, from the spell
Laid down by a balancing child,
Unstable, tight-lipped, and amazed,
And, under their place of enthrallment,
A huge, hammer-headed spirit
Shall pass, as if led by the nose into Heaven.

Alan Dugan

1923–2003

Love Song: I and Thou

Nothing is plumb, level, or square:
  the studs are bowed, the joists
are shaky by nature, no piece fits

any other piece without a gap
or pinch, and bent nails
dance all over the surfacing
like maggots. By Christ
I am no carpenter. I built
the roof for myself, the walls
for myself, the floors
for myself, and got
hung up in it myself. I
danced with a purple thumb
at this house-warming, drunk
with my prime whiskey: rage.
Oh I spat rage's nails
into the frame-up of my work:
it held. It settled plumb,
level, solid, square and true
for that great moment. Then
it screamed and went on through,
skewing as wrong the other way.
God damned it. This is hell,
but I planned it, I sawed it,
I nailed it, and I
will live in it until it kills me.
I can nail my left palm
to the left-hand crosspiece but
I can't do everything myself.
I need a hand to nail the right,
a help, a love, a you, a wife.

Anthony Hecht

1923–2004

A Hill

In Italy, where this sort of thing can occur,
I had a vision once—though you understand
It was nothing at all like Dante's, or the visions of saints,

And perhaps not a vision at all. I was with some friends,
Picking my way through a warm sunlit piazza
In the early morning. A clear fretwork of shadows
From huge umbrellas littered the pavement and made
A sort of lucent shallows in which was moored
A small navy of carts. Books, coins, old maps,
Cheap landscapes and ugly religious prints
Were all on sale. The colors and noise
Like the flying hands were gestures of exultation,
So that even the bargaining
Rose to the ear like a voluble godliness.
And then, when it happened, the noises suddenly stopped,
And it got darker; pushcarts and people dissolved
And even the great Farnese Palace itself
Was gone, for all its marble; in its place
Was a hill, mole-colored and bare. It was very cold,
Close to freezing, with a promise of snow.
The trees were like old ironwork gathered for scrap
Outside a factory wall. There was no wind,
And the only sound for a while was the little click
Of ice as it broke in the mud under my feet.
I saw a piece of ribbon snagged on a hedge,
But no other sign of life. And then I heard
What seemed the crack of a rifle. A hunter, I guessed;
At least I was not alone. But just after that
Came the soft and papery crash
Of a great branch somewhere unseen falling to earth.

And that was all, except for the cold and silence
That promised to last forever, like the hill.

Then prices came through, and fingers, and I was restored
To the sunlight and my friends. But for more than a week
I was scared by the plain bitterness of what I had seen.
All this happened about ten years ago,
And it hasn't troubled me since, but at last, today,
I remembered that hill; it lies just to the left
Of the road north of Poughkeepsie; and as a boy
I stood before it for hours in wintertime.

Adam

Hath the rain a father? or who hath begotten the drops of dew?

"Adam, my child, my son,
These very words you hear
Compose the fish and starlight
Of your untroubled dream.
When you awake, my child,
It shall all come true.
Know that it was for you
That all things were begun."

Adam, my child, my son,
Thus spoke Our Father in heaven
To his first, fabled child,
The father of us all.
And I, your father, tell
The words over again
As innumerable men
From ancient times have done.

Tell them again in pain,
And to the empty air.
Where you are men speak
A different mother tongue.
Will you forget our games,
Our hide-and-seek and song?
Child, it will be long
Before I see you again.

Adam, there will be
Many hard hours,
As an old poem says,
Hours of loneliness.
I cannot ease them for you;
They are our common lot.
During them, like as not,
You will dream of me.

When you are crouched away
In a strange clothes closet
Hiding from one who's "It"
And the dark crowds in,
Do not be afraid—
O, if you can, believe
In a father's love
That you shall know some day.

Think of the summer rain
Or seedpearls of the mist;
Seeing the beaded leaf,
Try to remember me.
From far away
I send my blessing out
To circle the great globe.
It shall reach you yet.

Saul and David

It was a villainous spirit, snub-nosed, foul
Of breath, thick-taloned and malevolent,
That squatted within him wheresoever he went
    And possessed the soul of Saul.

There was no peace on pillow or on throne,
In dreams the toothless, dwarfed, and squinny-eyed
Started a joyful rumor that he had died
    Unfriended and alone.

The doctors were confounded. In his distress, he
Put aside arrogant ways and condescended
To seek among the flocks where they were tended
    By the youngest son of Jesse,

A shepherd boy, but goodly to look upon,
Unnoticed but God-favored, sturdy of limb
As Michelangelo later imagined him,
    Comely even in his frown.

Shall a mere shepherd provide the cure of kings?
Heaven itself delights in ironies such
As this, in which a boy's fingers would touch
        Pythagorean strings

And by a modal artistry assemble
The very Sons of Morning, the ranked and choired
Heavens in sweet laudation of the Lord,
        And make Saul cease to tremble.

Richard Hugo

1923–1982

St. Clement's: Harris

Lord, I'd rehearsed and rehearsed your loss.
You died and my rehearsed face, the words
I'd planned to say over your stone were ready.
I set my face. I said my words. The sea I worship
did nothing to relieve the grief in Rodel.
This day, December 28, 1977,
the church locked, I bang the door and no one comes.
Happy New Year, Lord. Almost that time.

We were something else that age of reptiles.
The triwinged dragonfly drove us to caves.
There we huddled and shook. Those days, all
huge creatures, dinosaur and those that end in -saurus,
no matter how imposing meant less than land.
For one example: white cliffs climbed
so straight they seemed geometry
and high high when we looked gave off
gratuitous white light that formed, fragmented,
floated and was cloud. I'm afraid
the introverted palm leaves even then
threatened to open and smile. The world would bloom
with or without us. Every dawn, the sky

turned pink like special places on girls.
No Lord then, we were something else. O.K.?

Three days and this year ends. Nothing's touched
after five hundred years. Brochures with photos
taken in some rare good weather
don't mention dead reptiles. Here it started
with man, woman and with what they believed
and couldn't understand. Christ came on so northern
he wore skins. Believe and fish will come.
If I was terminal and had six weeks and knew it
I'd fish every lake on Harris. That's a lot
of water. And I'd fake faith long enough
to leave room on my stone for favorable words.
I'd fish the ocean hard my last day on this page.

To get down to earth, if buried here
with faith—even in death we love beauty—
I'd be buried redeemed. Look,
the ocean below and forever, the wide void void
of eternity's nightmare, the lovely way
graves are spaced to leave room for grass.
The date of my death would endure
given good stone and some artisan's fine tools.
May he carve "decent" despite what came out at the inquest.
Please understand, that was just a bad time.
If I can't enter the church, at least
I can go on peeking. Inside, shadows
fall like jail from leaded windows wrong onto stone.

Lord, you're dead. Imagine five centuries gone
and me far as sky from ruin. Imagine
this locked church and my pounding, my hope
to study six hundred year old carvings inside.
Like anyone
I come from a monstrous age, white cliffs
climbing and climbing out of whatever painting
I saw once, climbing out of the frame
and somewhere above
issuing light that released became
some aimless immediate plural.

Denise Levertov

1923–1997

The Jacob's Ladder

The stairway is not
a thing of gleaming strands
a radiant evanescence
for angels' feet that only glance in their tread, and need not
touch the stone.

It is of stone.
A rosy stone that takes
a glowing tone of softness
only because behind it the sky is a doubtful, a doubting
night gray.

A stairway of sharp
angles, solidly built.
One sees that the angels must spring
down from one step to the next, giving a little
lift of the wings:

and a man climbing
must scrape his knees, and bring
the grip of his hands into play. The cut stone
consoles his groping feet. Wings brush past him.
The poem ascends.

Flickering Mind

Lord, not you,
it is I who am absent.
At first
belief was a joy I kept in secret,
stealing alone

into sacred places:
a quick glance, and away—and back,
circling.
I have long since uttered your name
but now
I elude your presence.
I stop
to think about you, and my mind
at once
like a minnow darts away,
darts
into the shadows, into gleams that fret
unceasing over
the river's purling and passing.
Not for one second
will my self hold still, but wanders
anywhere,
everywhere it can turn. Not you,
it is I am absent.
You are the stream, the fish, the light,
the pulsing shadow,
you the unchanging presence, in whom all
moves and changes.
How can I focus my flickering, perceive
at the fountain's heart
the sapphire I know is there?

Suspended

I had grasped God's garment in the void
but my hand slipped
on the rich silk of it.
The 'everlasting arms' my sister loved to remember
must have upheld my leaden weight
from falling, even so,
for though I claw at empty air and feel
nothing, no embrace,
I have not plummetted.

James Schuyler

1923–1991

Our Father

This morning view
is very plain: thou art
in Heaven: modern
brick, plate glass, unhallowéd,
as yct, by time,
yet Thy Name
blesses all: silver tanks
of propane gas, the sky,
Thy will,
is lucent blue, French
gray and cream,
is done: the night
on earth
no longer needs
the one white street globe light
as the light, it is
in heaven.
Give us this day
—and a Friday
13th. August '71,
at that:
our daily bread
and breakfast
(Product 19,
an egg, perchance: the hen-fruit,
food and symbol)
and forgive us our
trespasses
too numerous
to name—as we
forgive our debtors: "pay
me when you can:

I don't take
interest"
how green
the grass! so many
flowering weeds
Your free
will has freely
let us name: dandy-
lion (*pisse-en-lit*)
and, clover
(O Trinity)
it is
a temptation
to list them all,
all I know, that is:
the temptation
to show off—to
make a show
of knowing more,
than, in fact, I
know, is very real:
as real as a twelve
pane window sash
one pane slivered
by a crack, a flash,
a mountain line
that stays
to praise
Thee,
Your Name and Your
  Creation
let me surrender
ever—
poets do: it
is their way
and deliver me
from evil
and the Three
Illusions

of the Will—
for the power
that flows electrically
in me is thine
O glorious central,
O plant,
O dynamo!
and the glory
of this cool a.m.
now
all
silver, blue
and white.

James Baldwin

1924–1987

Amen

No, I don't feel death coming.
I feel death going:
having thrown up his hands,
for the moment.

I feel like I know him
better than I did.
Those arms held me,
for a while,
and, when we meet again,
there will be that secret knowledge
between us.

Edgar Bowers

1924–2000

*From William Tyndale to John Frith**

The letters I, your lone friend, write in sorrow
Will not contain my sorrow: it is mine,
Not yours who stand for burning in my place.
Be certain of your fate. Though some, benign,
Will urge by their sweet threats malicious love
And counsel dangerous fear of violence,
Theirs is illusion's goodness proving fair—
Against your wisdom—worldly innocence
And just persuasions' old hypocrisy.
Making their choice, reflect what you become:
Horror and misery bringing ruin where
The saintly mind has treacherously gone numb;
Despair in the deceit of your remorse
As, doubly heretic, you waste your past
Recanting, by all pitied, honorless,
Until you choose more easy death at last.
Think too of me. Sometimes in morning dark
I let my candle gutter and sit here
Brooding, as shadows fill my cell and sky
Breaks pale outside my window; then the dear
Companionship we spent working for love
Compels me to achieve a double portion.
In spite of age, insanity, despair,
Grief, or declining powers, we have done
What passes to the living of all men
Beyond our weariness. The fire shall find
Me hidden here, although its pain be less
If you have gone to it with half my mind,
Leaving me still enough to fasten flesh

*John Frith, Tyndale's most loyal disciple, returned to England from the continent in 1533, when he was thirty years old. He was arrested and burned at the stake. This letter would have been written to Frith, in prison from Tyndale in Holland, where, not long after, he too was imprisoned and burned at the stake for heresy.

Against the stake, flesh absolute with will.
And should your human powers and my need
Tremble at last and grow faint, worn, and ill,
Pain be too much to think of, fear destroy,
And animal reluctance from the womb,
Endurance of your end's integrity,
Be strong in this: heaven shall be your tomb.

Adam

The shadowtail, the cottontail, the jay,
The spider on her trembling web, the mote
Swimming my blood—all innocent, all true,
All unsuspecting! But someone was there.
The burden of the past and future, father
And child of choice, he offers count and name.
It is as though, beneath a foreign tree,
Gifted with tongues, familiar of the brute,
I made a garden, kissed a face, and died.
Children I might have had, remember me,
That, in your quiet house, your word emerge.

Jacob

In tangled vine and branch, high weed and scrub,
I found a tree my father planted once,
A thread-leaf maple, green and old, not tall
As I am tall, but ten-foot at the base—
Ten thousand leaves contained as of one leaf.
As though I lay wrapped in the ancestral root,
Head on the stone, awake in sleep, I knew
The unity in which earth walks the earth,
Struggles with speech until a name is said,
Is lamed and blessed. A cloudless summer day.
Years up the ladder of the sky, beyond
Air, fire, and water, a jet plane barely moved,
Marked on the blue as on the final stone—
Feather, leaf, shell, fish-print, or whitened bone.

Jack Gilbert

b. 1925

The White Heart of God

The snow falling around the man in the naked woods
is like the ash of heaven, ash from the cool fire
of God's mother-of-pearl, moon-stately heart.
Sympathetic but not merciful. His strictness
parses us. The discomfort of living this way
without birds, among maples without leaves, makes
death and the world visible. Not the harshness,
but the way this world can be known by pushing
against it. And feeling something pushing back.
The whiteness of the winter married to this river
makes the water look black. The water actually
is the color of giant mirrors set along the marble
corridors of the spirit, the mirrors empty
of everything. The man is doing the year's accounts.
Finding the balance, trying to estimate how much
he has been translated. For it does translate him,
well or poorly. As the woods are translated
by the seasons. He is searching for a base line
of the Lord. He searches like the blind man
going forward with a hand stretched out in front.
As the truck driver ice-fishing on the big pond
tries to learn from his line what is down there.
The man attends to any signal that might announce
Jesus. He hopes for even the faintest evidence,
the presence of the Lord's least abundance. He measures
with tenderness, afraid to find a heart more classical
than ripe. Hoping for honey, for love's alembic.

Carolyn Kizer

b. 1925

Shalimar Gardens

In the garden of earth a square of water;
In the garden of waters a spirit stone.

Here music rises: Barbelo! Barbelo!
Marble pavilions border the water.

Marble petals of lotus bevel
The edge of the pool.

All about us a green benediction!
God's breath a germination, a viridescence.

From you the heavens move, the clouds rain,
The stones sweat dew, the earth gives greenness.

We shiver like peacocks' tails
In the mist of a thousand colored fountains,

Miraculous water; God's emissary,
Lighting our spring once more!

Here spirit is married to matter.
We are the holy hunger of matter for form.

Kizer, you enter into the dark world forever
To die again, into the living stone.

Kenneth Koch

1925–2002

Alive for an Instant

I have a bird in my head and a pig in my stomach
And a flower in my genitals and a tiger in my genitals
And a lion in my genitals and I am after you but I have a song in
    my heart
And my song is a dove
I have a man in my hands I have a woman in my shoes
I have a landmark decision in my reason
I have a death rattle I have summer in my brain water
This is the matter with me and the hammer of my mother and
    father
Who created me with everything
But I lack calm I lack rose
Though I do not lack extreme delicacy of rose petal
Who is it that I wish to astonish?
In the birdcall I found a reminder of you
But it was thin and brittle and gone in an instant
Has nature set out to be a great entertainer?
Obviously not A great reproducer? A great Nothing?
Well I will leave that up to you
I have a knocking woodpecker in my heart and I think I have
    three souls
One for love one for poetry and one for acting out my insane self
Not insane but boring but perpendicular but untrue but true
The three rarely sing together take my hand it's active
The active ingredient in it is a touch
I am Lord Byron I am Percy Shelley I am Ariosto
I eat the bacon I went down the slide I have a thunderstorm in
    my inside I will never hate you
But how can this maelstrom be appealing? do you like
    menageries? my god
Most people want a man! So here I am
I have a pheasant in my reminders I have a goshawk in my clouds

Whatever is it which has led all these animals to you?
A resurrection? or maybe an insurrection? an inspiration?
I have a baby in my landscape and I have a wild rat in my secrets
from you.

Samuel Menashe

b. 1925

Paradise—After Giovanni di Paolo

Paradise is a grove
Where flower and fruit tree
Form oval petals and pears
And apples only fair . . .
Among these saunter saints
Who uphold one another
In sacred conversations
Shaping hands that come close
As the lilies at their knees
While seraphim burn
With the moment's breeze

Gerald Stern

b. 1925

Lord, Forgive a Spirit

So what shall we do about this angel,
growing dizzy every time he climbs a ladder,
crying over his old poems.
I walk out into the garden and there he is,
watering the lilies and studying the digitalis.
He is talking to his own invisible heart;
he is leaking blood.

The sun shines on him all day long
as he wanders from bush to bush.
His eyes flash with fire, his eyelashes blaze and
his skin shines like brass,
but he trips in the dirt just like any gardener, or grieving poet.
I watch him walk beside the cactus;
I watch him kneel in front of the wet horsetails;
I touch his lips.
I write all day. I sit beside him all
day long and write the garbled words.
I sit in the sun and fill a whole new book
with scrawls and symbols.
I watch the sky as he talks about the gold leaf
and the half-forgotten ruins; I watch the words
drift from his mouth like clouds.
I watch the colors change from orange to red
to pink as he tries to remember his old words—
his old songs, his first human songs—
lost somewhere in the broken glass and the cinders,
a foot below the soft nails and the hinges.

A. R. Ammons

1926–2001

Prodigal

After the shifts and dis-
continuities, after the congregations of orders,
black masses floating through
mind's boreal clarity, icebergs in fog,
flotillas of wintering ducks weathering the night,
chains of orders, multifilamentous chains
knobbed with possibility, disoriented
chains, winding back on themselves, unwinding,
intervolving, spinning, breaking off

(nomads clustering at dusk into tents of sleep,
disorganizing, widening out again with morning)
after the mental

blaze and gleam,
the mind in both motions building and tearing down,
running to link effective chains,
establish molecules of meaning,
frameworks, to
perfect modes of structuring
(so days can bend to trellising
and pruned take shape,
bloom into necessary event)

after these motions, these vectors,
orders moving in and out of orders, collisions
of orders, dispersions, the grasp weakens,

the mind whirls, short of the unifying
reach, short of the heat
to carry that forging:
after the visions of these losses, the spent
seer, delivered to wastage, risen
into ribs, consigns knowledge to
approximation, order to the vehicle
of change, and fumbles blind in blunt innocence
toward divine, terrible love.

Terrain

The soul is a region without definite boundaries:
it is not certain a prairie
can exhaust it
or a range enclose it:
it floats (self-adjusting) like the continental mass,
where it towers most
extending its deepest mantling base
(exactly proportional):
does not flow all one way: there is a divide:

   river systems thrown like winter tree-shadows
against the hills: branches, runs, high lakes:
         stagnant lily-marshes:

is variable, has weather: floods unbalancing
   gut it, silt altering the
distribution of weight, the nature of content:
         whirlwinds move through it
or stand spinning like separate orders: the moon comes:
   there are barren spots: bogs, rising
by self-accretion from themselves, a growth into
         destruction of growth,
change of character,
   invasion of peat by poplar and oak: semi-precious
stones and precious metals drop from muddy water into mud:

it is an area of poise, really, held from tipping,
   dark wild water, fierce eels, countercurrents:
a habitat, precise ecology of forms
         mutually to some extent
tolerable, not entirely self-destroying: a crust afloat:
   a scum, foam to the deep and other-natured:
but deeper than depth, too: a vacancy and swirl:

it may be spherical, light and knowledge merely
   the iris and opening
to the dark methods of its sight: how it comes and
         goes, ruptures and heals,
whirls and stands still: the moon comes: terrain.

The City Limits

When you consider the radiance, that it does not withhold
itself but pours its abundance without selection into every
nook and cranny not overhung or hidden; when you consider

that birds' bones make no awful noise against the light but
lie low in the light as in a high testimony; when you consider
the radiance, that it will look into the guiltiest

swervings of the weaving heart and bear itself upon them,
not flinching into disguise or darkening; when you consider
the abundance of such resource as illuminates the glow-blue

bodies and gold-skeined wings of flies swarming the dumped
guts of a natural slaughter or the coil of shit and in no
way winces from its storms of generosity; when you consider

that air or vacuum, snow or shale, squid or wolf, rose or lichen,
each is accepted into as much light as it will take, then
the heart moves roomier, the man stands and looks about, the

leaf does not increase itself above the grass, and the dark
work of the deepest cells is of a tune with May bushes
and fear lit by the breadth of such calmly turns to praise.

The Arc Inside and Out

for Harold Bloom

If, whittler and dumper, gross carver
into the shadiest curvings, I took branch
and meat from the stalk of life, threw

away the monies of the treasured,
treasurable mind, cleaved memory free
of the instant, if I got right down

shucking off periphery after periphery
to the glassy vague gray parabolas
and swoops of unnailable perception,

would I begin to improve the purity,
would I essentialize out the distilled
form, the glitter-stone that whether

the world comes or goes clicks gleams
and chinks of truth self-making, never
to be shuttered, the face-brilliant core

stone: or if I, amasser, heap shoveler,
depth pumper, took in all springs and
oceans, paramoecia and moons, massive

buttes and summit slants, rooted trunks
and leafages, anthologies of wise words,
schemata, all grasses (including the

tidal *Spartinas*, marginal, salty
broadsweeps) would I finally come on a
suasion, large, fully-informed, restful

scape, turning back in on itself, its
periphery enclosing our system with
its bright dot and allowing in nonparlant

quantities at the edge void, void, and
void, would I then feel plenitude
brought to center and extent, a sweet

easing away of all edge, evil, and surprise:
these two ways to dream! dreaming them's
the bumfuzzlement—the impoverished

diamond, the heterogeneous abundance
starved into oneness: ultimately, either
way, which is our peace, the little

arc-line appears, inside which is nothing,
outside which is nothing—however big,
nothing beyond: however small, nothing

within: neither way to go's to stay, stay
here, the apple an apple with its own hue
or streak, the drink of water, the drink,

the falling into sleep, restfully ever the
falling into sleep, dream, dream, and
every morning the sun comes, the sun.

For Harold Bloom

I went to the summit and stood in the high nakedness:
the wind tore about this
way and that in confusion and its speech could not
get through to me nor could I address it:
still I said as if to the alien in myself
        I do not speak to the wind now:
for having been brought this far by nature I have been
brought out of nature
and nothing here shows me the image of myself:
for the word *tree* I have been shown a tree
and for the word *rock* I have been shown a rock,
for stream, for cloud, for star
this place has provided firm implication and answering
        but where here is the image for *longing*:
so I touched the rocks, their interesting crusts:
I flaked the bark of stunt-fir:
I looked into space and into the sun
and nothing answered my word *longing*:
        goodbye, I said, goodbye, nature so grand and
reticent, your tongues are healed up into their own
element
and as you have shut up you have shut me out: I am
as foreign here as if I had landed, a visitor:
so I went back down and gathered mud
and with my hands made an image for *longing*:
        I took the image to the summit: first
I set it here, on the top rock, but it completed
nothing: then I set it there among the tiny firs
but it would not fit:
so I returned to the city and built a house to set
the image in
and men came into my house and said
        that is an image for *longing*
and nothing will ever be the same again

Easter Morning

I have a life that did not become,
that turned aside and stopped,
astonished:
I hold it in me like a pregnancy or
as on my lap a child
not to grow or grow old but dwell on

it is to his grave I most
frequently return and return
to ask what is wrong, what was
wrong, to see it all by
the light of a different necessity
but the grave will not heal
and the child,
stirring, must share my grave
with me, an old man having
gotten by on what was left

when I go back to my home country in these
fresh far-away days, it's convenient to visit
everybody, aunts and uncles, those who used to say,
look how he's shooting up, and the
trinket aunts who always had a little
something in their pocketbooks, cinnamon bark
or a penny or nickel, and uncles who
were the rumored fathers of cousins
who whispered of them as of great, if
troubled, presences, and school
teachers, just about everybody older
(and some younger) collected in one place
waiting, particularly, but not for
me, mother and father there, too, and others
close, close as burrowing
under skin, all in the graveyard
assembled, done for, the world they
used to wield, have trouble and joy
in, gone

the child in me that could not become
was not ready for others to go,
to go on into change, blessings and
horrors, but stands there by the road
where the mishap occurred, crying out for
help, come and fix this or we
can't get by, but the great ones who
were to return, they could not or did
not hear and went on in a flurry and
now, I say in the graveyard, here
lies the flurry, now it can't come
back with help or helpful asides, now
we all buy the bitter
incompletions, pick up the knots of
horror, silently raving, and go on
crashing into empty ends not
completions, not rondures the fullness
has come into and spent itself from
I stand on the stump
of a child, whether myself
or my little brother who died, and
yell as far as I can, I cannot leave this place, for
for me it is the dearest and the worst,
it is life nearest to life which is
life lost: it is my place where
I must stand and fail,
calling attention with tears
to the branches not lofting
boughs into space, to the barren
air that holds the world that was my world

though the incompletions
(& completions) burn out
standing in the flash high-burn
momentary structure of ash, still it
is a picture-book, letter-perfect
Easter morning: I have been for a
walk: the wind is tranquil: the brook
works without flashing in an abundant

tranquility: the birds are lively with
voice: I saw something I had
never seen before: two great birds,
maybe eagles, blackwinged, whitenecked
and -headed, came from the south oaring
the great wings steadily; they went
directly over me, high up, and kept on
due north: but then one bird,
the one behind, veered a little to the
left and the other bird kept on seeming
not to notice for a minute: the first
began to circle as if looking for
something, coasting, resting its wings
on the down side of some of the circles:
the other bird came back and they both
circled, looking perhaps for a draft;
they turned a few more times, possibly
rising—at least, clearly resting—
then flew on falling into distance till
they broke across the local bush and
trees: it was a sight of bountiful
majesty and integrity: the having
patterns and routes, breaking
from them to explore other patterns or
better ways to routes, and then the
return: a dance sacred as the sap in
the trees, permanent in its descriptions
as the ripples round the brook's
ripplestone: fresh as this particular
flood of burn breaking across us now
from the sun.

Robert Bly

b. 1926

The Night Abraham Called to the Stars

Do you remember the night Abraham first called
To the stars? He cried to Saturn: "You are my Lord!"
How happy he was! When he saw the Dawn Star,

He cried, "You are my Lord!" How destroyed he was
When he watched them set. Friends, he is like us:
We take as our Lord the stars that go down.

We are faithful companions to the unfaithful stars.
We are diggers, like badgers; we love to feel
The dirt flying out from behind our hind claws.

And no one can convince us that mud is not
Beautiful. It is our badger soul that thinks so.
We are ready to spend the rest of our life

Walking with muddy shoes in the wet fields.
We resemble exiles in the kingdom of the serpent.
We stand in the onion fields looking up at the night.

My heart is a calm potato by day, and a weeping,
Abandoned woman by night. Friend, tell me what to do,
Since I am a man in love with the setting stars.

Allen Ginsberg

1926–1997

Sunflower Sutra

I walked on the banks of the tincan banana dock and sat down under the huge shade of a Southern Pacific locomotive to look at the sunset over the box house hills and cry.
Jack Kerouac sat beside me on a busted rusty iron pole, companion, we thought the same thoughts of the soul, bleak and blue and sad-eyed, surrounded by the gnarled steel roots of trees of machinery.
The oily water on the river mirrored the red sky, sun sank on top of final Frisco peaks, no fish in that stream, no hermit in those mounts, just ourselves rheumy-eyed and hung-over like old bums on the riverbank, tired and wily.
Look at the Sunflower, he said, there was a dead gray shadow against the sky, big as a man, sitting dry on top of a pile of ancient sawdust—
—I rushed up enchanted—it was my first sunflower, memories of Blake—my visions—Harlem
and Hells of the Eastern rivers, bridges clanking Joes Greasy Sandwiches, dead baby carriages, black treadless tires forgotten and unretreaded, the poem of the riverbank, condoms & pots, steel knives, nothing stainless, only the dank muck and the razor-sharp artifacts passing into the past—
and the gray Sunflower poised against the sunset, crackly bleak and dusty with the smut and smog and smoke of olden locomotives in its eye—
corolla of bleary spikes pushed down and broken like a battered crown, seeds fallen out of its face, soon-to-be-toothless mouth of sunny air, sunrays obliterated on its hairy head like a dried wire spiderweb,
leaves stuck out like arms out of the stem, gestures from the sawdust root, broke pieces of plaster fallen out of the black twigs, a dead fly in its ear,
Unholy battered old thing you were, my sunflower O my soul, I loved you then!

The grime was no man's grime but death and human locomotives,
all that dress of dust, that veil of darkened railroad skin, that smog of cheek, that eyelid of black mis'ry, that sooty hand or phallus or protuberance of artificial worse-than-dirt—industrial—modern—all that civilization spotting your crazy golden crown—
and those blear thoughts of death and dusty loveless eyes and ends and withered roots below, in the home-pile of sand and sawdust, rubber dollar bills, skin of machinery, the guts and innards of the weeping coughing car, the empty lonely tincans with their rusty tongues alack, what more could I name, the smoked ashes of some cock cigar, the cunts of wheelbarrows and the milky breasts of cars, wornout asses out of chairs & sphincters of dynamos—all these
entangled in your mummied roots—and you there standing before me in the sunset, all your glory in your form!
A perfect beauty of a sunflower! a perfect excellent lovely sunflower existence! a sweet natural eye to the new hip moon, woke up alive and excited grasping in the sunset shadow sunrise golden monthly breeze!
How many flies buzzed round you innocent of your grime, while you cursed the heavens of the railroad and your flower soul?
Poor dead flower? when did you forget you were a flower? when did you look at your skin and decide you were an impotent dirty old locomotive? the ghost of a locomotive? the specter and shade of a once powerful mad American locomotive?
You were never no locomotive, Sunflower, you were a sunflower!
And you Locomotive, you are a locomotive, forget me not!
So I grabbed up the skeleton thick sunflower and stuck it at my side like a scepter,
and deliver my sermon to my soul, and Jack's soul too, and anyone who'll listen,
—We're not our skin of grime, we're not our dread bleak dusty imageless locomotive, we're all golden sunflowers inside, blessed by our own seed & hairy naked accomplishment-bodies growing into mad black formal sunflowers in the sunset, spied on by our eyes under the shadow of the mad locomotive riverbank sunset Frisco hilly tincan evening sitdown vision.

Berkeley, 1955

Psalm III

To God: to illuminate all men. Beginning with Skid Road.

Let Occidental and Washington be transformed into a higher place, the plaza of eternity.

Illuminate the welders in shipyards with the brilliance of their torches.

Let the crane operator lift up his arm for joy.

Let elevators creak and speak, ascending and descending in awe.

Let the mercy of the flower's direction beckon in the eye.

Let the straight flower bespeak its purpose in straightness—to seek the light.

Let the crooked flower bespeak its purpose in crookedness—to seek the light.

Let the crookedness and straightness bespeak the light.

Let Puget Sound be a blast of light.

I feed on your Name like a cockroach on a crumb—this cockroach is holy.

Seattle, June, 1956

Wales Visitation

White fog lifting & falling on mountain-brow
    Trees moving in rivers of wind
                        The clouds arise
  as on a wave, gigantic eddy lifting mist
    above teeming ferns exquisitely swayed
                              along a green crag
    glimpsed thru mullioned glass in valley raine—

Bardic, O Self, Visitacione, tell naught
  but what seen by one man in a vale in Albion,
    of the folk, whose physical sciences end in Ecology,
              the wisdom of earthly relations,
    of mouths & eyes interknit ten centuries visible
          orchards of mind language manifest human,
  of the satanic thistle that raises its horned symmetry

flowering above sister grass-daisies' pink tiny
bloomlets angelic as lightbulbs—

Remember 160 miles from London's symmetrical thorned tower
& network of TV pictures flashing bearded your Self
the lambs on the tree-nooked hillside this day bleating
heard in Blake's old ear, & the silent thought of Wordsworth
in eld Stillness
clouds passing through skeleton arches of Tintern Abbey—
Bard Nameless as the Vast, babble to Vastness!

All the Valley quivered, one extended motion, wind
undulating on mossy hills
a giant wash that sank white fog delicately down red runnels
on the mountainside
whose leaf-branch tendrils moved asway
in granitic undertow down—
and lifted the floating Nebulous upward, and lifted the arms of
the trees
and lifted the grasses an instant in balance
and lifted the lambs to hold still
and lifted the green of the hill, in one solemn wave

A solid mass of Heaven, mist-infused, ebbs thru the vale,
a wavelet of Immensity, lapping gigantic through Llanthony
Valley,
the length of all England, valley upon valley under Heaven's
ocean tonned with cloud-hang,
—Heaven balanced on a grassblade.
Roar of the mountain wind slow, sigh of the body,
One Being on the mountainside stirring gently
Exquisite scales trembling everywhere in balance,
one motion thru the cloudy sky-floor shifting on the million feet
of daisies,
one Majesty the motion that stirred wet grass quivering
to the farthest tendril of white fog poured down
through shivering flowers on the mountain's
head—

No imperfection in the budded mountain,
Valleys breathe, heaven and earth move together,
daisies push inches of yellow air, vegetables tremble,
grass shimmers green
sheep speckle the mountainside, revolving their jaws with
empty eyes,
horses dance in the warm rain,
tree-lined canals network live farmland,
blueberries fringe stone walls on hawthorn'd
hills,
pheasants croak on meadows haired with fern—

Out, out on the hillside, into the ocean sound, into delicate gusts
of wet air,
Fall on the ground, O great Wetness, O Mother, No harm on
your body!
Stare close, no imperfection in the grass,
each flower Buddha-eye, repeating the story, myriad-
formed—
Kneel before the foxglove raising green buds, mauve bells
drooped
doubled down the stem trembling antennae,
& look in the eyes of the branded lambs that stare
breathing stockstill under dripping hawthorn—
I lay down mixing my beard with the wet hair of the
mountainside,
smelling the brown vagina-moist ground, harmless,
tasting the violet thistle-hair, sweetness—
One being so balanced, so vast, that its softest breath
moves every floweret in the stillness on the valley floor,
trembles lamb-hair hung gossamer rain-beaded in the grass,
lifts trees on their roots, birds in the great draught
hiding their strength in the rain, bearing same weight,

Groan thru breast and neck, a great Oh! to earth heart
Calling our Presence together
The great secret is no secret
Senses fit the winds,
Visible is visible,
rain-mist curtains wave through the bearded vale,

gray atoms wet the wind's kabbala
Crosslegged on a rock in dusk rain,
rubber booted in soft grass, mind moveless,
breath trembles in white daisies by the roadside,
Heaven breath and my own symmetric
Airs wavering thru antlered green fern
drawn in my navel, same breath as breathes thru Capel-Y-Ffn,
Sounds of Aleph and Aum
through forests of gristle,
my skull and Lord Hereford's Knob equal,
All Albion one.

What did I notice? Particulars! The
vision of the great One is myriad—
smoke curls upward from ashtray,
house fire burned low,
The night, still wet & moody black heaven
starless
upward in motion with wet wind.

July 29, 1967 (LSD)–August 3, 1967 (London)

James Merrill

1926–1995

An Upward Look

O heart green acre sown with salt
by the departing occupier

lay down your gallant spears of wheat
Salt of the earth each stellar pinch

flung in blind defiance backwards
now takes its toll Up from his quieted

quarry the lover colder and wiser
hauling himself finds the world turning

toys triumphs   toxins into
this vast facility   the living come
dearest to die in   How did it happen

In bright alternation   minutely mirrored
within the thinking   of each and every

mortal creature   halves of a clue
approach the earthlights   Morning star

evening star   salt of the sky
First the grave   dissolving into dawn

then the crucial   recrystallizing
from inmost depths   of clear dark blue

John Ashbery

b. 1927

The Recital

All right. The problem is that there is no new problem. It must awaken from the sleep of being part of some other, old problem, and by that time its new problematical existence will have already begun, carrying it forward into situations with which it cannot cope, since no one recognizes it and it does not even recognize itself yet, or know what it is. It is like the beginning of a beautiful day, with all the birds singing in the trees, reading their joy and excitement into its record as it progresses, and yet the progress of any day, good or bad, brings with it all kinds of difficulties that should have been foreseen but never are, so that it finally seems as though they are what stifles it, in the majesty of a sunset or merely in gradual dullness that gets dimmer and dimmer until it finally sinks into flat, sour darkness. Why is this? Because not one-tenth or even one one-hundredth of the ravishing possibilities the birds sing about at dawn could ever be realized in the course of a single day, no matter how crammed with fortunate events it might turn out to be. And this brings on inevitable reproaches, unmerited of course, for we are all like children sulking because they cannot have the moon; and very soon the unreasonableness of these demands is forgotten and overwhelmed in a wave of melancholy of which it is the sole cause. Finally we know only that we are unhappy but we cannot tell why. We forget that it is our own childishness that is to blame.

That this is true is of course beyond argument. But we ought to look into the nature of that childishness a little more, try to figure out where it came from and how, if at all, we can uproot it. And when we first start to examine it, biased as we are, it seems as though we are not entirely to blame. We have all or most of us had unhappy childhoods; later on we tried to patch things up and as we entered the years of adulthood it was a relief, for a while, that everything was succeeding: we had finally left that long suffocating tunnel and emerged into an open place. We could not yet see very well due to the abrupt change from darkness to daylight, but we were beginning to make out things. We embarked on a series of adult relationships from which the sting and malignancy of childhood were absent, or so it seemed: no more hiding behind bushes to get a secret glimpse of the others; no more unspeakable rages of jealousy or the suffocation of unrequited and unrealizable love. Or at least these things retreated into their proper perspective as new things advanced into the foreground: new feelings as yet too complex to be named or closely inspected, but in which the breathless urgency of those black-and-white situations of childhood happily played no part. It became a delight to enumerate all the things in the new world our maturity had opened up for us, as inexhaustible in pleasures and fertile pursuits as some more down-to-earth Eden, from which the utopian joys as well as the torments of that older fantasy-world had been banished by a more reasonable deity.

But as the days and years sped by it became apparent that the naming of all the new things we now possessed had become our chief occupation; that very little time for the mere tasting and having of them was left over, and that even these simple, tangible experiences were themselves subject to description and enumeration, or else they too became fleeting and transient as the song of a bird that is uttered only once and disappears into the backlog of vague memories where it becomes as a dried, pressed flower, a wistful parody of itself. Meanwhile all our energies are being absorbed by the task of trying to revive those memories, make them real, as if to live again were the only reality; and the overwhelming variety of the situations we have to deal with begins to submerge our efforts. It becomes plain that we cannot interpret everything, we must be selective, and so the tale we are telling begins little by little to leave reality behind. It is no longer so much our description of the way things happen to us as our private song, sung in the wilderness, nor can we leave off singing, for that would be to retreat to the death of childhood, to the mere acceptance and dull living of all that is thrust upon us, a living death in a word; we must register our appraisal of the moving world that is around us, but our song is leading us on now, farther and farther into that wilderness and away from the shrouded but familiar forms that were its first inspiration. On and on into the gathering darkness—is there no remedy for this? It is as though a day which had begun brilliantly in the blaze of a new sunrise had become transfixed as a certain subtle change in the light can cast a chill over your heart, or the sight of a distant thin ribbon of cirrus ebbing into space can alter everything you have been feeling, dropping you back years and years into another world in which its fragile reminder of inexorable change was also the law, as it is here today. You know now the sorrow of continually doing something that you cannot name, of producing automatically as an apple tree produces apples this thing there is no name for. And you continue to hum as you move forward, but your heart is pounding.

All right. Then this new problem is the same one, and that is the problem: that our apathy can always renew itself, drawing energy from the circumstances that fill our lives, but emotional happiness blooms only once, like an annual, leaving not even roots or foliage behind when its flower withers and dies. We are forced to recognize that we are still living in the same old state of affairs and that it never really went away even when it seemed to. Well, but what can we do about it? Because even though the hydra-headed monster of apathy can grow a new head each day to slash back at us with, more fearsome than the one we just succeeded in cutting off, so too nothing says that we aren't to fight back at it, using the sword that our condition of reasoning beings has placed in our hands. Although the task seems hopeless and there is no end to the heads in sight, we are within our rights in fighting back, the weapon is ours to wield, and it is possible that by dint of continually doing so we might at length gain a slight foothold or edge, for the enemy's powers though superhuman are not inexhaustible: we are basically certain that nothing is except the capacity for struggle that unites us, foe to foe, on the vast plain of life. We are like sparrows fluttering and jabbering around a seemingly indifferent prowling cat; we know that the cat is stronger and therefore we forget that we have wings, and too often we fall in with the cat's plans for us, afraid and therefore unable to use the wings that could have saved us by bearing us aloft if only for a little distance, not the boundless leagues we had been hoping for and insisting on, but enough to make a crucial difference, the difference between life and death.

"It almost seems—" How often this locution has been forced on us when we were merely trying to find words for a more human expression of our difficulty, something closer to home. And with this formula our effort flies off again, having found no place to land. As though there were something criminal in trying to understand a little this uneasiness that is undermining our health, causing us to think crazy thoughts and behave erratically. We can no longer live our lives properly. Every good impulse is distorted into something like its opposite; the people we see are like parodies of reasonable human beings. There is no spiritual model for our aspirations; no *vademecum* beckons in the light around us. There is only the urge to get on with it all. It is like the difference between someone who is in love and someone who is merely "good in bed": there is no vital remnant which would transform one's entire effort into an image somewhat resembling oneself. Meanwhile everything conspires to protect the business-as-usual attitude of the diurnal scenery—no leaf or brick must be found out of place, no timbre ring false lest the sickening fakery of the whole wormy apparatus, the dry rot behind the correct façade suddenly become glaringly and universally apparent, its shame at last real for all to see. Appearances must be kept up at whatever cost until the Day of Judgment and afterward if possible.

We are trying with mortal hands to paint a landscape which would be a faithful reproduction of the exquisite and terrible scene that stretches around us. No longer is there any question of adjusting a better light on things, to show them ideally as they may never have existed, of taking them out from under the sun to place them in the clean light that meditation surrounds them with. Youth and happiness, the glory of first love—all are viewed naturally now, with all their blemishes and imperfections. Even the wonderful poetry of growing a little older and realizing the important role fantasy played in the *Sturm und Drang* of our earlier maturity is placed in its proper perspective, so as not to exaggerate the importance in the general pattern of living of the disabused intellect, whose nature it is to travel from illusion to reality and on to some seemingly superior vision, it being the quality of this ebbing and flowing motion rather than the relevance of any of its isolated component moments that infuses a life with its special character. Until, accustomed to disappointments, it seemed as though we had triumphed over the limitations of logic and blindfold passion alike; the masterpiece we were on the point of achieving was classic in the sense of the Greeks and simultaneously informed by a Romantic ardor minus the eccentricity, and this all-but-terminated work was the reflection of the ideal shape of ourselves, as we might have lived had we been gifted with foreknowledge and also the ability to go back and retrace our steps. And so, pleased with it and with ourselves, we stepped back a few paces to get the proper focus.

Any reckoning of the sum total of the things we are is of course doomed to failure from the start, that is if it intends to present a true, wholly objective picture from which both artifice and artfulness are banished: no art can exist without at least traces of these, and there was never any question but that this rendering was to be made in strict conformity with the rules of art—only in this way could it approximate most closely the thing it was intended to reflect and illuminate and which was its inspiration, by achieving the rounded feeling almost of the forms of flesh and the light of nature, and being thus equipped for the maximum number of contingencies which, in its capacity as an aid and tool for understanding, it must know how to deal with. Perhaps this was where we made our mistake. Perhaps no art, however gifted and well-intentioned, can supply what we were demanding of it: not only the figured representation of our days but the justification of them, the reckoning and its application, so close to the reality being lived that it vanishes suddenly in a thunderclap, with a loud cry.

The days fly by; they do not cease. By night rain pelted the dark planet; in the morning all was wreathed in false smiles and admiration, but the daylight had gone out of the day and it knew it. All the pine trees seemed to be dying of a mysterious blight. There was no one to care. The sky was still that nauseatingly cloying shade of blue, with the thin ribbon of cirrus about to disappear and materialize over other, alien lands, far from here. If only, one thought, one had begun by having the courage of one's convictions instead of finishing this way, but "once burned, twice shy"; one proceeds along one's path murmuring idiotic formulas like this to give oneself courage, noticing too late that the landscape isn't making sense any more; it is not merely that you have misapplied certain precepts not meant for the situation in which you find yourself, which is always a new one that cannot be decoded with reference to an existing corpus of moral principles, but there is even a doubt as to our own existence. Why, after all, were we not destroyed in the conflagration of the moment our real and imaginary lives coincided, unless it was because we never had a separate existence beyond that of those two static and highly artificial concepts whose fusion was nevertheless the cause of death and destruction not only for ourselves but in the world around us? But perhaps the explanation lies precisely here: what we were witnessing was merely the reverse side of an event of cosmic beatitude for all except us, who were blind to it because it took place inside us. Meanwhile the shape of life has changed definitively for the better for everyone on the outside. They are bathed in the light of this tremendous surprise as in the light of a new sun from which only healing and not corrosive rays emanate; they comment on the miraculous change as people comment on the dazzling beauty of a day in early autumn, forgetting that for the blind man in their midst it is a day like any other, so that its beauty cannot be said to have universal validity but must remain fundamentally in doubt.

This single source of so much pleasure and pain is therefore a thing that one can never cease wondering upon. On the one hand, such boundless happiness for so many; on the other so much pain concentrated in the heart of one. And it is true that each of us is this multitude as well as that isolated individual; we experience the energy and beauty of the others as a miraculous manna from heaven; at the same time our eyes are turned inward to the darkness and emptiness within. All records of how we came here have been effaced, so there is no chance of working backward to some more primitive human level: the spiritual dichotomy exists once and for all time, like the mind of creation, which has neither beginning nor end. And the proof of this is that we cannot even imagine another way of being. We are stuck here for eternity and we are not even aware that we are stuck, so natural and even normal does our quandary seem. The situation of Prometheus, bound to the crags for endless ages and visited daily by an eagle, must have seemed so to him. We were surprised once, long ago; and now we can never be surprised again.

What is it for you then, the insistent now that baffles and surrounds you in its loose-knit embrace that always seems to be falling away and yet remains behind, stubbornly drawing you, the unwilling spectator who had thought to stop only just for a moment, into the sphere of its solemn and suddenly utterly vast activities, on a new scale as it were, that you have neither the time nor the wish to unravel? It always presents itself as the turning point, the bridge leading from prudence to "a timorous capacity," in Wordsworth's phrase, but the bridge is a Bridge of Sighs the next moment, leading back into the tired regions from whence it sprang. It seems as though every day is arranged this way. The movement is the majestic plodding one of a boat crossing a harbor, certain of its goal and upheld by its own dignity on the waves, a symbol of patient, fruitful activity, but the voyage always ends in a new key, although at the appointed place; a note has been added that destroys the whole fabric and the sense of the old as it was intended. The day ends in the darkness of sleep.

Therefore since today, a day that is really quite cool despite the deceptive appearance of the sunlight on things, is to really be the point when everything changes for better or for worse, it might be good to examine it, see how far it goes, since the far reaches of sleep are to be delayed indefinitely. It is not even a question of them any more. What matters is how you are going to figure your way out of this new problem which has again come home to roost. Will the answer be another delay, prolonged beyond the end of time, and disguised once again as an active life intelligently pursued? Or is it to be a definite break with the past—either the no of death shutting you up in a small cell-like space or a yes whose vibrations you cannot even begin to qualify or imagine?

As I thought about these things dusk began to invade my room. Soon the outlines of things began to grow blurred and I continued to think along well-rehearsed lines like something out of the past. Was there really nothing new under the sun? Or was this novelty—the ability to take up these tattered enigmas again and play with them until something like a solution emerged from them, only to grow dim at once and fade like an ignis fatuus, a specter mocking the very reality it had so convincingly assumed? No, but this time something real did seem to be left over—some more solid remnant of the light as the shadows continued to pile up. At first it seemed to be made merely of bits and pieces of the old, haggard situations, rearranged perhaps to give a wan impersonation of modernity and fecundity. Then it became apparent that certain new elements had been incorporated, though perhaps not enough of them to change matters very much. Finally—these proportions remaining the same—something like a different light began to dawn, to make itself felt: just as the first glimmers of day are often mistaken for a "false dawn," and one waits a long time to see whether they will go away before gradually becoming convinced of their authority, even after it has been obvious for some time, so these tremors slowly took on the solidity, the robustness of an object. And by that time everything else had gone away, or retreated so far into the sidelines that one was no longer conscious of those ephemera that had once seemed the very structure, the beams and girders defining the limits of the ambiguous situation one had come to know and even to tolerate, if not to love.

The point was the synthesis of very simple elements in a new and strong, as opposed to old and weak, relation to one another. Why hadn't this been possible in the earlier days of experimentation, of bleak, barren living that didn't seem to be leading anywhere and it couldn't have mattered less? Probably because not enough of what made it up had taken on that look of worn familiarity, like pebbles polished over and over again by the sea, that made it possible for the old to blend inconspicuously with the new in a union too subtle to cause any comment that would have shattered its purpose forever. But already it was hard to distinguish the new elements from the old, so calculated and easygoing was the fusion, the partnership that was the only element now, and which was even now fading rapidly from memory, so perfect was its assimilation by the by-standers and décor that in other times would have filled up the view, and that now were becoming as transparent as the substance that was giving them back to life.

A vast wetness as of sea and air combined, a single smooth, anonymous matrix without surface or depth was the product of these new changes. It no longer mattered very much whether prayers were answered with concrete events or the oracle gave a convincing reply, for there was no longer anyone to care in the old sense of caring. There were new people watching and waiting, conjugating in this way the distance and emptiness, transforming the scarcely noticeable bleakness into something both intimate and noble. The performance had ended, the audience streamed out; the applause still echoed in the empty hall. But the idea of the spectacle as something to be acted out and absorbed still hung in the air long after the last spectator had gone home to sleep.

Syringa

Orpheus liked the glad personal quality
Of the things beneath the sky. Of course, Eurydice was a part
Of this. Then one day, everything changed. He rends
Rocks into fissures with lament. Gullies, hummocks
Can't withstand it. The sky shudders from one horizon
To the other, almost ready to give up wholeness.
Then Apollo quietly told him: "Leave it all on earth.
Your lute, what point? Why pick at a dull pavan few care to
Follow, except a few birds of dusty feather,
Not vivid performances of the past." But why not?
All other things must change too.
The seasons are no longer what they once were,
But it is the nature of things to be seen only once,
As they happen along, bumping into other things, getting along
Somehow. That's where Orpheus made his mistake.

Of course Eurydice vanished into the shade;
She would have even if he hadn't turned around.
No use standing there like a gray stone toga as the whole wheel
Of recorded history flashes past, struck dumb, unable to utter an
    intelligent
Comment on the most thought-provoking element in its train.
Only love stays on the brain, and something these people,
These other ones, call life. Singing accurately
So that the notes mount straight up out of the well of
Dim noon and rival the tiny, sparkling yellow flowers
Growing around the brink of the quarry, encapsulates
The different weights of the things.
                                    But it isn't enough
To just go on singing. Orpheus realized this
And didn't mind so much about his reward being in heaven
After the Bacchantes had torn him apart, driven
Half out of their minds by his music, what it was doing to them.
Some say it was for his treatment of Eurydice.
But probably the music had more to do with it, and
The way music passes, emblematic
Of life and how you cannot isolate a note of it
And say it is good or bad. You must
Wait till it's over. "The end crowns all,"
Meaning also that the "tableau"
Is wrong. For although memories, of a season, for example,
Melt into a single snapshot, one cannot guard, treasure
That stalled moment. It too is flowing, fleeting;
It is a picture of flowing, scenery, though living, mortal,
Over which an abstract action is laid out in blunt,
Harsh strokes. And to ask more than this
Is to become the tossing reeds of that slow,
Powerful stream, the trailing grasses
Playfully tugged at, but to participate in the action
No more than this. Then in the lowering gentian sky
Electric twitches are faintly apparent first, then burst forth
Into a shower of fixed, cream-colored flares. The horses
Have each seen a share of the truth, though each thinks,
"I'm a maverick. Nothing of this is happening to me,

Though I can understand the language of birds, and
The itinerary of the lights caught in the storm is fully apparent
to me.
Their jousting ends in music much
As trees move more easily in the wind after a summer storm
And is happening in lacy shadows of shore-trees, now, day after
day."

But how late to be regretting all this, even
Bearing in mind that regrets are always late, too late!
To which Orpheus, a bluish cloud with white contours,
Replies that these are of course not regrets at all,
Merely a careful, scholarly setting down of
Unquestioned facts, a record of pebbles along the way.
And no matter how all this disappeared,
Or got where it was going, it is no longer
Material for a poem. Its subject
Matters too much, and not enough, standing there helplessly
While the poem streaked by, its tail afire, a bad
Comet screaming hate and disaster, but so turned inward
That the meaning, good or other, can never
Become known. The singer thinks
Constructively, builds up his chant in progressive stages
Like a skyscraper, but at the last minute turns away.
The song is engulfed in an instant in blackness
Which must in turn flood the whole continent
With blackness, for it cannot see. The singer
Must then pass out of sight, not even relieved
Of the evil burthen of the words. Stellification
Is for the few, and comes about much later
When all record of these people and their lives
Has disappeared into libraries, onto microfilm.
A few are still interested in them. "But what about
So-and-so?" is still asked on occasion. But they lie
Frozen and out of touch until an arbitrary chorus
Speaks of a totally different incident with a similar name
In whose tale are hidden syllables
Of what happened so long before that
In some small town, one indifferent summer.

By Forced Marches

the prodigal returns—to what mechanical
consternation, din of slaughtered cattle.
It was better in the wilderness—there at least
the mind wanders daintily as a stream meanders
through a meadow, for no apparent reason.
And one can catch snatches of the old cries
that were good before this place began
on a day some seventeen centuries ago.

We have reached the tip of a long breakwater
dividing the lake from the deeper and silenter ship channel.
A still-functioning beacon flashes there, proud
of its purpose and its reflection in the night.
There is nothing to do except observe the horizon,
the only one, that seems to want to sever itself
from the passing sky.

Now the links we had left behind
must be reassembled, since this is the land we came from.
It is no place for the squeamish. But as a finger triggers
a catapult, so is the task of the day discharged.

There were many of us at the stream's tip.
I squatted nearby trying to eavesdrop on the sailors'
conversations, to learn where they were going. Finally
one comes to me and says I can have the job if I want it.
Want it! and so in this prismatic whirlpool I am renewed
for a space of time that means nothing to me.

And there is dancing under the porches—so be it.
I am all I have. I am afraid. I am left alone.
Yet it is the way to a certain kind of satisfaction.
I kiss myself in the mirror. And children are kind,
the boardwalk serves as a colorful backdrop
to the caprices acted out, the pavanes and chaconnes
that greet the ear in fragments, melodious
ones it must be said. And the old sense of a fullness
is here, though only lightly sketched in.

Galway Kinnell

b. 1927

To Christ Our Lord

The legs of the elk punctured the snow's crust
And wolves floated lightfooted on the land
Hunting Christmas elk living and frozen;
Inside snow melted in a basin, and a woman basted
A bird spread over coals by its wings and head.

Snow had sealed the windows; candles lit
The Christmas meal. The Christmas grace chilled
The cooked bird, being long-winded and the room cold.
During the words a boy thought, is it fitting
To eat this creature killed on the wing?

He had killed it himself, climbing out
Alone on snowshoes in the Christmas dawn,
The fallen snow swirling and the snowfall gone,
Heard its throat scream as the gunshot scattered,
Watched it drop, and fished from the snow the dead.

He had not wanted to shoot. The sound
Of wings beating into the hushed air
Had stirred his love, and his fingers
Froze in his gloves, and he wondered,
Famishing, could he fire? Then he fired.

Now the grace praised his wicked act. At its end
The bird on the plate
Stared at his stricken appetite.
There had been nothing to do but surrender,
To kill and to eat; he ate as he had killed, with wonder.

At night on snowshoes on the drifting field
He wondered again, for whom had love stirred?
The stars glittered on the snow and nothing answered.
Then the Swan spread her wings, cross of the cold north,
The pattern and mirror of the acts of earth.

W. S. Merwin

b. 1927

Lemuel's Blessing

Let Lemuel bless with the wolf, which is a
dog without a master, but the Lord hears his
cries and feeds him in the desert.
CHRISTOPHER SMART: *Jubilate Agno*

You that know the way,
Spirit,
I bless your ears which are like cypresses on a mountain
With their roots in wisdom. Let me approach.
I bless your paws and their twenty nails which tell their own
prayer
And are like dice in command of their own combinations.
Let me not be lost.
I bless your eyes for which I know no comparison.
Run with me like the horizon, for without you
I am nothing but a dog lost and hungry,
Ill-natured, untrustworthy, useless.

My bones together bless you like an orchestra of flutes.
Divert the weapons of the settlements and lead their dogs a
dance.
Where a dog is shameless and wears servility
In his tail like a banner,
Let me wear the opprobrium of possessed and possessors
As a thick tail properly used
To warm my worst and my best parts. My tail and my laugh
bless you.

Lead me past the error at the fork of hesitation.
Deliver me

From the ruth of the lair, which clings to me in the morning,
Painful when I move, like a trap;
Even debris has its favorite positions but they are not yours;
From the ruth of kindness, with its licked hands;
I have sniffed baited fingers and followed
Toward necessities which were not my own: it would make me
An habitué of back steps, faithful custodian of fat sheep;

From the ruth of prepared comforts, with its
Habitual dishes sporting my name and its collars and leashes of
vanity;

From the ruth of approval, with its nets, kennels, and
taxidermists;
It would use my guts for its own rackets and instruments, to play
its own games and music;
Teach me to recognize its platforms, which are constructed like
scaffolds;

From the ruth of known paths, which would use my feet, tail,
and ears as curios,
My head as a nest for tame ants,
My fate as a warning.

I have hidden at wrong times for wrong reasons.
I have been brought to bay. More than once.
Another time, if I need it,
Create a little wind like a cold finger between my shoulders, then
Let my nails pour out a torrent of aces like grain from a
threshing machine;
Let fatigue, weather, habitation, the old bones, finally,
Be nothing to me,
Let all lights but yours be nothing to me.
Let the memory of tongues not unnerve me so that I stumble or
quake.

But lead me at times beside the still waters;
There when I crouch to drink let me catch a glimpse of your
image
Before it is obscured with my own.

Preserve my eyes, which are irreplaceable.
Preserve my heart, veins, bones,
Against the slow death building in them like hornets until the
place is entirely theirs.
Preserve my tongue and I will bless you again and again.

Let my ignorance and my failings
Remain far behind me like tracks made in a wet season,
At the end of which I have vanished,
So that those who track me for their own twisted ends
May be rewarded only with ignorance and failings.
But let me leave my cry stretched out behind me like a road
On which I have followed you.
And sustain me for my time in the desert
On what is essential to me.

Noah's Raven

Why should I have returned?
My knowledge would not fit into theirs.
I found untouched the desert of the unknown,
Big enough for my feet. It is my home.
It is always beyond them. The future
Splits the present with the echo of my voice.
Hoarse with fulfilment, I never made promises.

Fourth Psalm: The Cerements

She made him a roof with her hands
from his own voice she wove
the walls to stop the wind
with his own dreams she painted the windows
each with its kingdom

and the doors were mirrors she fashioned
of his eyes

but when she opened it he was gone

gone the vision
gone
the witness

She made him a cage of wishes
he helped when he could
helped long
and indeed with all the heavy parts

but when she opened it

She made him a net of consents
where he might turn in his own place
like all eye in its veins
a globe in its hours
she hung it with tears
with both of theirs

but when she opened it he was gone

gone
the asking

She made him a box of some sweet wood
she knew he remembered from his childhood
in corners rose columns she had painted like smoke
she drew a star inside the lid

but when she opened it

She made him a bed such as the fates have
in the palms of the newly born
but there they do not lay them down
they have risen

and when she opened it
he was gone

gone the cry the laughter

They made him a fence of names
each with its story
like his own teeth
they laid claim
to his ears
but he had others

when they opened the echoes even the echoes
he had gone

They made him an ark of the one tree
and places for him builded in
two of every kind

but before the rain came
he was gone

laws of the hands gone
night of the veins gone
gone the beating in the temples

and every face in the sky

The Blind Seer of Ambon

I always knew that I came from
another language

and now even when I can no longer see
I continue to arrive at words

but the leaves
and the shells were already here

and my fingers finding them echo
the untold light and depth

I was betrayed into my true calling
and denied in my advancement
I may have seemed somewhat strange
caring in my own time for living things
with no value that we know
languages wash over them one wave at a time

when the houses fell
in the earthquake
I lost my wife
and my daughter
it all roared and stood still
falling
where they were in the daylight

I named for my wife a flower
as though I could name a flower
my wife dark and luminous
and not there

I lost the drawings of the flowers
in fire
I lost the studies
of the flowers
my first six books in the sea

then I saw that the flowers themselves
were gone
they were indeed gone
I saw
that my wife was gone
then I saw that my daughter was gone
afterward my eyes themselves were gone

one day I was looking
at infinite small creatures

on the bright sand
and the next day is this
hearing after music
so this is the way I see now

I take a shell in my hand
new to itself and to me
I feel the thinness the warmth and the cold
I listen to the water
which is the story welling up
I remember the colors and their lives
everything takes me by surprise
it is all awake in the darkness

James Wright

1927–1980

The Refusal

When we get back, the wagon will be gone,
The porchlight empty in the wind, no doubt;
        And everybody here,
Who damned us for the conscience of a stone,
        Will tell us to get out
And do our sniffling in the dark somewhere.

It may not be delight to hear that word,
The pride of mourners mocking in our faces.
        I offer no delight,
Neither a soft life, nor a grave deferred.
        I have known other places
Ugly as this, and shut them from my sight.

Inside the house, somebody we could love,
Who labored for us till the taut string gave,
        Stares from a half-closed eye.

Why should we gaze back in that pit of love?
    All the beloved lie
In the perpetual savagery of graves.

Come here to me; I will not let you go
To suffer on some relative's hard shoulder—
    Weeping woman or man.
God, I have died so many days ago,
    The funeral began
When I was born, and will go on forever:—

Unless I shut the door myself, and take
Your elbow, drag you bodily, out of breath
    And let the house grow dark.
Inside, that lamentation for the sake
    Of numbers on a rock
Starves me and freezes you, and kills us both.

Must we reel with the wine of mourning like a drunk?
Look there, the doors are latched, the windows close,
    And we are told to go.
When we come back, the granite will be sunk
    An inch or more below
The careful fingers of the healing snows.

Preacher and undertaker follow the cars;
They claimed the comfort of the earth, and lied.
    Better to trust the moon
Blown in the soft bewilderment of stars;
    The living lean on pain,
The hard stones of the earth are on our side.

A Blessing

Just off the highway to Rochester, Minnesota,
Twilight bounds softly forth on the grass.
And the eyes of those two Indian ponies
Darken with kindness.

They have come gladly out of the willows
To welcome my friend and me.
We step over the barbed wire into the pasture
Where they have been grazing all day, alone.
They ripple tensely, they can hardly contain their happiness
That we have come.
They bow shyly as wet swans. They love each other.
There is no loneliness like theirs.
At home once more,
They begin munching the young tufts of spring in the darkness.
I would like to hold the slenderer one in my arms,
For she has walked over to me
And nuzzled my left hand.
She is black and white,
Her mane falls wild on her forehead,
And the light breeze moves me to caress her long ear
That is delicate as the skin over a girl's wrist.
Suddenly I realize
That if I stepped out of my body I would break
Into blossom.

Saint Judas

When I went out to kill myself, I caught
A pack of hoodlums beating up a man.
Running to spare his suffering, I forgot
My name, my number, how my day began,
How soldiers milled around the garden stone
And sang amusing songs; how all that day
Their javelins measured crowds; how I alone
Bargained the proper coins, and slipped away.

Banished from heaven, I found this victim beaten,
Stripped, kneed, and left to cry. Dropping my rope
Aside, I ran, ignored the uniforms:
Then I remembered bread my flesh had eaten,
The kiss that ate my flesh. Flayed without hope,
I held the man for nothing in my arms.

Donald Hall

b. 1928

A Small Fig Tree

I am dead, to be sure,
for thwarting Christ's pleasure,
Jesus Christ called Saviour.

I was a small fig tree.
Unjust it seems to me
that I should withered be.

If justice sits with God,
Christ is cruel Herod
and I by magic dead.

If there is no justice
where great Jehovah is,
I will the devil kiss.

A Grace

God, I know nothing, my sense is all nonsense,
And fear of You begins intelligence:
Does it end there? For sexual love, for food,
For books and birch trees I claim gratitude,
But when I grieve over the unripe dead
My grief festers, corrupted into dread,
And I know nothing. Give us our daily bread.

Samuel Hazo

b. 1928

The Holy Surprise of Right Now

If you can see your path laid out ahead of you
step by step, then you know it's not your path.
—JOSEPH CAMPBELL

Inside Brooks Brothers' windows
it's July.
Sportshirts on sleek
dummies speak in turquoise,
polo, Bermuda, and golf.
Outside, it's very much the first
of March.
The sportshirts say
today's tomorrow and the present
tense be damned.
They tell me
to forget that *here's* the only place
we have.
They claim what matters
most is never now but next.
I've heard this argument before.
It leaves me sentenced to the future,
and that's much worse than being
sentenced to the past.
The past
at least was real just once . . .
What's
called religion offers me the same.
Life's never what I have
but what's to come.
But where
did Christ give heaven its address
except within each one of us?
So, anyone who claims it's not

within but still ahead is contradicting God.
          But why go on?
I'm sick of learning to anticipate.
I never want to live a second
   or a season or a heaven in advance
   of when I am and where.
I need the salt and spices
   of uncertainty to know I'm still
   alive.
          It makes me hunger
   for the feast I call today.
It lets desire keep what
   satisfaction ends.
                              Lovers
   remember that the way that smoke
   remembers fire.
                              Between anticipation
   and the aggravation of suspense, I choose
   suspense.
               I choose desire.

Philip Levine

b. 1928

A Late Answer

Beyond that stand of firs
was a small clearing
where the woods ran out
of breath or the winds
beat them back. No one
was born there and no one
would be, but you could
bury a lonely man there
or an animal you didn't
want out for flies to eat.
As we passed under the trees

you were cold and took
my hand and felt a shiver
pass through me, but you
didn't let go. When you
spoke at last it was to ask
after my thoughts, but
just then we broke into light
so unexpected I had to close
my eyes and saw the fire
swimming there and had
such a vision of the end
of my life, the trees
turning to great flowers
of flame and the field ringed
with sword bearing angels.
I could say nothing,
but held on to your hand
and you to mine
both in the dream and in
that bare place where
the North Sea winds lashed
our faces with sudden spurts
of rain. Now, on the other side
of the world, years later,
I know the ant came here
believing he would rule
and he waits for the wren
to fall, the grass waits
blowing its breath
into this morning that rises
darkly on wet winds. Somewhere
the sea saves its tears
for the rising tide, somewhere
we'll leave the world weighing
no more than when we came,
and the answer will be
the same, your hand in mine,
mine in yours, in that clearing
where the angels come toward us
without laughter, without tears.

To My God in His Sickness

I

A boy is as old as the stars
that will not answer
as old as the last snows
that blacken his hands
though he wakes at 3
and goes to the window
where the crooked fence is blessed
and the long Packard
and the bicycle wheel
though he walk the streets
warm in the halo of his breath
and is blessed over and over
he will waken in the slow dawn
he will call his uncles out
from the sad bars of Irish statesmen
all the old secret reds
who pledge in the park
and raise drinks
and remember Spain

Though he honor the tree
the sierra of snow
the stream that died years ago
though he honor his breakfast
the water in his glass
the bear in his belly
though he honor all crawling
and winged things
the man in his glory
the woman in her salt
though he savor the cup of filth
though he savor Lake Erie
savor the rain burning down
on Gary, Detroit, Wheeling
though my grandmother argues

the first cause of night
and the kitchen cantor mumbles his names
still the grave will sleep

I came this way before
my road ran by your house
crowded with elbows of mist
and pots banging to be filled
my coat was the colors of rain
and six gray sparrows sang
on the branches of my grave

2

A rabbit snared in a fence of pain
screams and screams
I waken, a child again
and answer
I answer my father
hauling his stone up the last few breaths
I answer Moses bumbling before you
the cat circling three times
before she stretches out and yawns
the mole gagged on fresh leaves

In Folsom, Jaroubi, alone before dawn
remembers the long legs of a boy
his own once and now his son's
Billy Ray holds my hand to his heart
in the black and white still photograph
of the exercise yard
in the long shadows of the rifle towers
we say goodbye forever
Later, at dusk the hills
across the dry riverbed
hold the last light
long after it's gone
and glow like breath

I wake
and it's not a dream
I see the long coast of the continent
writhing in sleep
this America we thought we dreamed
falling away flake by flake
into the sea
and the sea blackening and burning

I see a man curled up, the size of an egg
I see a woman hidden in a carburetor
a child reduced to one word
crushed under an airmail stamp
or a cigarette

Can the hands rebuild the rocks
can the tongue make air or water
can the blood flow back
into the twigs of the child
can the clouds take back their deaths

3

First light of morning
it is the world again
the domed hills across the gorge
take the air slowly
the day will be hot and long
Jimmy Ray, Gordon, Jaroubi
all the prisoners have been awake
for hours remembering
I walk through the dense brush
down to the river
that descended all night from snow
small stones worn away
old words, lost truths
ground to their essential nonsense
I lift you in my hand
and inhale, the odor of light

out of darkness, substance out of air
of blood before it reddens and runs

When I first knew you
I was a friend to the ox and walked
with Absalom and raised my hand
against my hand
and died for want of you
and turned to stone and air and water
the answer to my father's tears

Cynthia Ozick

b. 1928

When that with tragic rapture Moses stood on the edge and ledge,
the edge of the Land overlooked from the mountain's ledge,
the ledge of life which death, like all the others law
and being of the Law, might not overlook,

bound on that double threshold to cross the ledge but not the edge,
to see the plain of the valley and the palm and the wave-scaly
boundary of the sea fretting near, Judah's shining lip,
but not to go over,
to see the commanded boundary of sheol and death its
commander and
captain, likewise a leader of men according to the law and a
lawgiver, that promised country's single-minded king,
and sworn to go over,
loving limits because loving law, but liking not these to Land
and life;

when that he, the plucker of the Law from the thorny desert who
pricked the brows of idolators obeisant,
who cracked Sinai's pillar for the holy stones its
marrow-ore,
those grains and pebbles chipped from Rock more than
rock of
mountain, being mountain-maker,

and early wept for the oppressors whom the silt sucked in, and for
the mares whose eye-whites reddened with the splattered
yolk
of the broken wave, and for the chariot's axles hewn of
straight young trees, all being God's and though oppressors
all divine, men and steeds and wondrous wheels,
when that he ascended: ascended Nebo, he whose head history
had
hammered holy, hoary, heavy, bending down from Pisgah
toward the
rabble's luring ground rich with seed,
himself allured, him whom history brought to the edge and
ledge of
denial
lest history fever with more history that history-howling heart;

when that he ascended, and with proud lieutenant's measure the
given
territory scanned, given not for him but for the fickle mob,
in that moment it was enough: history dropped him from her
beak,
too fastidious for carrion,
and led in the gilded mob. Not that he was less than
they,
he who unbewildered the mazy riddle of the way through forty
years
of nomadry,
and laid his head upon the rock to be a chamber for the thunder's
voice,
not that he was less!—but was, being man, not more,
going squired, though the mob's ex-squire, to the territory
given him.

Its situation no man knows.

And since the border-crossing was jubilant, flag-wild and roaring
triumph, the pageant already winking sidewise at some
Canaanitish lady-baal with breasts of sanded wood and
smelling piney,

and he from Pisgah saw how we, the mob, noses barely over the
border and feet still prickled with the wilderness, raced
crying after abominations, again and after all,
no wonder he praised history for halting him at humanity, and
bringing him unhallowed to an unknown grave.

We would raise a sepulchre if we guessed the place, and over that
a palace,
and on every edge and ledge would lift his sacred likeness,
commissioned and called art,
in tapestry and marble, in majesty and crimson, hiding God in
Moses' pleats,
we adoring till God departed in disgust, and left us to the idol
we deserved;
or failing this, forgetting Sinai we'd suppose it all a symbol
and a dream, deafening ourselves with that technique
until once more we stood, a babbling rabble in the desert,
waiting for another Moses to give us back our ears,
more driven than desirous.

Anne Sexton

1928–1974

Rowing

A story, a story!
(Let it go. Let it come.)
I was stamped out like a Plymouth fender
into this world.
First came the crib
with its glacial bars.
Then dolls
and the devotion to their plastic mouths.
Then there was school,
the little straight rows of chairs,
blotting my name over and over,
but undersea all the time,

a stranger whose elbows wouldn't work.
Then there was life
with its cruel houses
and people who seldom touched—
though touch is all—
but I grew,
like a pig in a trenchcoat I grew,
and then there were many strange apparitions,
the nagging rain, the sun turning into poison
and all of that, saws working through my heart,
but I grew, I grew,
and God was there like an island I had not rowed to,
still ignorant of Him, my arms and my legs worked,
and I grew, I grew,
I wore rubies and bought tomatoes
and now, in my middle age,
about nineteen in the head I'd say,
I am rowing, I am rowing
though the oarlocks stick and are rusty
and the sea blinks and rolls
like a worried eyeball,
but I am rowing, I am rowing,
though the wind pushes me back
and I know that that island will not be perfect,
it will have the flaws of life,
the absurdities of the dinner table,
but there will be a door
and I will open it
and I will get rid of the rat inside of me,
the gnawing pestilential rat.
God will take it with his two hands
and embrace it.

As the African says:
This is my tale which I have told,
if it be sweet, if it be not sweet,
take somewhere else and let some return to me.
This story ends with me still rowing.

Joseph Awad

b. 1929

For Jude's Lebanon

It is said he was a relative of Jesus,
That his apostolate
Was to the land we know as Lebanon,
That he gave his blood for Christ.
What wonders did he perform
To win the Barnum & Bailey blurb,
"Patron saint of the impossible."

I'm beginning a novena to St. Jude.

His lone epistle opens lovingly:
"Jude, the servant of Jesus Christ
And brother of James, to the called
Who have been loved in God the Father
And preserved for Christ Jesus,
Mercy and peace and love
Be yours in abundance."

I'm beginning a novena to St. Jude.

He had a poet's way with words.
Evil, sensual men he called
"Wild waves of the sea,
Foaming up their shame,
Wandering stars for whom
The storm of darkness
Has been reserved forever."

I'm beginning a novena to St. Jude.

In Lebanon there is loud lamentation.
Beirut, once beautiful Beirut,

Bloodied by Christian, Jew and Druze,
Weeps like a wound just under the world's heart.
Pontius Pilates in world capitals
Wash their hands, pronouncing solemnly,
"The situation is impossible."

I'm beginning a novena to St. Jude.

Alvin Feinman

b. 1929

Pilgrim Heights

Something, something, the heart here
Misses, something it knows it needs
Unable to bless—the wind passes;
A swifter shadow sweeps the reeds,
The heart a colder contrast brushes.

So this fool, face-forward, belly
Pressed among the rushes, plays out
His pulse to the dune's long slant
Down from blue to bluer element,
The bold encompassing drink of air

And namelessness, a length compound
Of want and oneness the shore's mumbling
Distantly tells—something a wing's
Dry pivot stresses, carved
Through barrens of stillness and glare:

The naked close of light in light,
Light's spare embrace of blade and tremor
Stealing the generous eye's plunder
Like a breathing banished from the lung's
Fever, lost in parenthetic air.

Raiding these nude recesses, the hawk
Resumes his yielding balance, his shadow
Swims the field, the sands beyond,
The narrow edges fed out to light,
To the sea's eternal licking monochrome.

The foolish hip, the elbow bruise
Upright from the dampening mat,
The twisted grasses turn, unthatch,
Light-headed blood renews its stammer—
Apart, below, the dazed eye catches

A darkened figure abruptly measured
Where folding breakers lay their whites;
The heart from its height starts downward,
Swum in that perfect pleasure
It knows it needs, unable to bless.

November Sunday Morning

And the light, a wakened heyday of air
Tuned low and clear and wide,
A radiance now that would emblaze
And veil the most golden horn
Or any entering of a sudden clearing
To a standing, astonished, revealed . . .

That the actual streets I loitered in
Lay lit like fields, or narrow channels
About to open to a burning river;
All brick and window vivid and calm
As though composed in a rigid water
No random traffic would dispel . . .

As now through the park, and across
The chill nailed colors of the roofs,
And on near trees stripped bare,
Corrected in the scant remaining leaf

To their severe essential elegance,
Light is the all-exacting good,

That dry, forever verile stream
That wipes each thing to what it is,
The whole, collage and stone, cleansed
To its proper pastoral . . .
                                        I sit
And smoke, and linger out desire

And know if I closed my eyes I'd hear
Again what held me awake all night
Beside her breathing: a rain falling
It seemed into a distant stillness,
On broad low leaves beside a pond
And drop upon drop into black waters.

John Hollander

b. 1929

At the New Year

Every single instant begins another new year;
   Sunlight flashing on water, or plunging into a clearing
In quiet woods announces; the hovering gull proclaims
   Even in wide midsummer a point of turning: and fading
Late winter daylight close behind the huddled backs
   Of houses close to the edge of town flares up and shatters
As well as any screeching ram's horn can, wheel
   Unbroken, uncomprehended continuity,
Making a starting point of a moment along the way,
   Spinning the year about one day's pivot of change.
But if there is to be a high moment of turning
   When a great, autumnal page, say, takes up its curved
Flight in memory's spaces, and with a final sigh,
   As of every door in the world shutting at once, subsides
Into the bed of its fellows; if there is to be

A time of tallying, recounting and rereading
Illuminated annals, crowded with black and white
And here and there a capital flaring with silver and bright
Blue, then let it come at a time like this, not at winter's
Night, when a few dead leaves crusted with frost lie shivering
On our doorsteps to be counted, or when our moments of coldness
Rise up to chill us again. But let us say at a golden
Moment just on the edge of harvesting, "Yes. Now."
Times of counting are times of remembering; here amidst showers
Of shiny fruits, both the sweet and the bitter-tasting results,
The honey of promises gleams on apples that turn to mud
In our innermost of mouths, we can sit facing westward
Toward imminent rich tents, telling and remembering.
Not like merchants with pursed hearts, counting in dearth and darkness,
But as when from a shining eminence, someone walking starts
At the sudden view of imperturbable blue on one hand
And wide green fields on the other. Not at the reddening sands
Behind, nor yet at the blind gleam, ahead, of something
Golden, looking at such a distance and in such sunlight,
Like something given—so, at this time, our counting begins,
Whirling all its syllables into the circling wind
That plays about our faces with a force between a blow's
And a caress', like the strength of a blessing, as we go
Quietly on with what we shall be doing, and sing
Thanks for being enabled, again, to begin this instant.

Adam's Task

And Adam gave names to all cattle, and
to the fowl of the air, and to every
beast of the field . . . GEN. 2:20

Thou, paw-paw-paw; thou, glurd; thou, spotted
Glurd; thou, whitestap, lurching through
The high-grown brush; thou, pliant-footed,
Implex; thou, awagabu.

Every burrower, each flier
  Came for the name he had to give:
Gay, first work, ever to be prior,
  Not yet sunk to primitive.

Thou, verdle; thou, McFleery's pomma;
  Thou; thou; thou—three types of grawl;
Thou, flisket; thou, kabasch; thou, comma-
  Eared mashawk; thou, all; thou, all.

Were, in a fire of becoming,
  Laboring to be burned away,
Then work, half-measuring, half-humming,
  Would be as serious as play.

Thou, pambler; thou, rivarn; thou, greater
  Wherret, and thou, lesser one;
Thou, sproal; thou, zant; thou, lily-eater.
  Naming's over. Day is done.

A Shadow of a Great Rock in a Weary Land

Isaiah 32.2

Let him who is without light
Among you cast the first
Shadow, and let the worst
Among us here at our late

Hour now speak for the best:
There is nothing higher above
Our heads, and we whimper of
What once had been our boast.

When among all possessions
Knowledge, alone, is un-
Acknowledged to be one
Of our treasures or our passions.

Failing of wont and of will,
All we construct or construe
In neither sense holds true:
What can we still do well?

Bewail with an outraged heart
Infringements upon what
Is our Divine Right Not
To Have Our Feelings Hurt?

Not even that—the airs
And choruses of complaint
Are poorly intoned, and faint:
They fall on our own deaf ears.

Tell over the old tales
Of the hope from which we grew,
And our fading claims to be new
Now as some curfew tolls?

Not even that—in fear
Of singularity
Blockhead and airhead flee
Transports of metaphor.

Remember what we once were,
Even if too late to learn
How our fattening unconcern
Fed in the troughs of war?

Not even that—our boughs
Broke too soon, too soon
While an affable buffoon
Sang us his lullabies.

Sing in dumb unison—scared
Or ignorant of the joint
Divergence of counterpoint
In which true tunes are scored?

Not even that—our air
Amplifies voicelessness;
The silence of unsuccess
Sighs for all that we are

Still to contrive to succeed
In failing at; we play
At work and labor all day
At play, sad to be said.

That idiot, Paradox, laughed,
For the steps we had to take
To save ourselves would break
The best that we had left—

Those principles we still
Assure ourselves that we
Keep though imperfectly—
The air of assent grows stale,

And harsh the voice of each claim.
Hope and distrust of hope
Are braided together in rope
—To hang ourselves with, or climb

Out of acedia's pit?
There is no sign for us
In the ambiguous
Text of this bubbling pot

In which we seethe as a tame
Curl of smoke ascends
From the burning of candle-ends
That is the fire this time.

The fire that brings to a boil
A terror beyond all fears,
A broth of soured tears
Fills the horizon's bowl,

Loud in such darkness, whether
Soon to be burnt or drowned,
Our dimmed noise and unsound
Light will come together.

Gary Snyder

b. 1930

Milton by Firelight

Piute Creek, August 1955

"O hell, what do mine eyes
with grief behold?"
Working with an old
Singlejack miner, who can sense
The vein and cleavage
In the very guts of rock, can
Blast granite, build
Switchbacks that last for years
Under the beat of snow, thaw, mule-hooves.
What use, Milton, a silly story
Of our lost general parents,
eaters of fruit?

The Indian, the chainsaw boy,
And a string of six mules
Came riding down to camp
Hungry for tomatoes and green apples.
Sleeping in saddle-blankets
Under a bright night-sky
Han River slantwise by morning
Jays squall
Coffee boils

In ten thousand years the Sierras
Will be dry and dead, home of the scorpion.
Ice-scratched slabs and bent trees.
No paradise, no fall,
Only the weathering land

The wheeling sky,
Man, with his Satan
Scouring the chaos of the mind.
Oh Hell!

Fire down
Too dark to read, miles from a road
The bell-mare clangs in the meadow
That packed dirt for a fill-in
Scrambling through loose rocks
On an old trail
All of a summer's day.

Burning Island

O Wave God   who broke through me today
    Sea Bream
    massive pink and silver
    cool swimming down with me watching
                staying away from the spear

Volcano belly Keeper who lifted this island
    for our own beaded bodies adornment
    and sprinkles us all with his laugh—
                ash in the eye
    mist, or smoke,
    on the bare high limits—
        underwater lava flows easing to coral
                holes filled with striped feeding swimmers

O Sky Gods   cartwheeling
    out of   Pacific
    turning rainsqualls over like lids on us
    then shine on our sodden—
        (scanned out a rainbow today at the
                cow drinking trough
                    sluicing off
        LAKHS of crystal Buddha Fields
        right on the hair of the arm!)

Who wavers right now in the bamboo:
a half-gone waning moon.
drank down a bowlful of shochu
in praise of Antares
gazing far up the lanes of Sagittarius
richest stream of our sky—
a cup to the center of the galaxy!
and let the eyes stray
right-angling the pitch of the Milky Way:
horse-heads rings
clouds too distant to *be*
slide free.
on the crest of the wave.

Each night
O Earth Mother
I have wrappt my hand
over the jut of your cobra-hood
sleeping;
left my ear
All night long by your mouth.

O All
Gods tides capes currents
Flows and spirals of
pool and powers—

As we hoe the field
let sweet potato grow.
And as sit us all down when we may
To consider the Dharma
bring with a flower and a glimmer.
Let us all sleep in peace together.

Bless Masa and me as we marry
at new moon on the crater
This summer.

VIII 40067

Ripples on the Surface

"Ripples on the surface of the water—
were silver salmon passing under—different
from the ripples caused by breezes"

A scudding plume on the wave—
a humpback whale is
breaking out in air up
gulping herring
    —Nature not a book, but a *performance,* a
high old culture

Ever-fresh events
scraped out, rubbed out, and used, used, again—
the braided channels of the rivers
hidden under fields of grass—

The vast wild
    the house, alone.
The little house in the wild,
    the wild in the house.
Both forgotten.

        No nature

    Both together, one big empty house.

Allen Grossman

b. 1932

The Song of the Lord

There is a table bountifully spread.

In the full sunlight when there is no cloud
And under cloudy skies,
And when there are no stars and when the stars
Distill the time,

the table stands in a field.
It is late morning and the service shines.
The guests have wandered from the company.
The Lord is alone.

It is good to hear
The voice of the Lord at rest in his solitude.

The guests have wandered from the table set,

But they hear the voice of the Lord at rest:

The song of the Lord in solitude goes up,
Ten times enfolded, blue, and saturate
With law to the heavens at noon of gaze,
And down among the graves and the darker animals.
The song of the Lord indicates the dust
Of the roadway, the random hammer of the sea,
The riddled vase of mind and mind's dependencies

And pain lost otherwise and lost in this.

The voice of the Lord opens the gates of day.
Air streams through our eyes and brushes the pupils

Streams through our eyes and this is how we see.

Sylvia Plath

1932–1963

Black Rook in Rainy Weather

On the stiff twig up there
Hunches a wet black rook
Arranging and rearranging its feathers in the rain.
I do not expect a miracle
Or an accident

To set the sight on fire
In my eye, nor seek
Any more in the desultory weather some design,
But let spotted leaves fall as they fall,
Without ceremony, or portent.

Although, I admit, I desire,
Occasionally, some backtalk
From the mute sky, I can't honestly complain:
A certain minor light may still
Leap incandescent

Out of kitchen table or chair
As if a celestial burning took
Possession of the most obtuse objects now and then—
Thus hallowing an interval
Otherwise inconsequent

By bestowing largesse, honor,
One might say love. At any rate, I now walk
Wary (for it could happen
Even in this dull, ruinous landscape); sceptical,
Yet politic; ignorant

Of whatever angel may choose to flare
Suddenly at my elbow. I only know that a rook
Ordering its black feathers can so shine
As to seize my senses, haul
My eyelids up, and grant

A brief respite from fear
Of total neutrality. With luck,
Trekking stubborn through this season
Of fatigue, I shall
Patch together a content

Of sorts. Miracles occur,
If you care to call those spasmodic

Tricks of radiance miracles. The wait's begun again,
The long wait for the angel,
For that rare, random descent.

N. Scott Momaday

b. 1934

The Delight Song of Tsoai-talee

I am a feather on the bright sky
I am the blue horse that runs in the plain
I am the fish that rolls, shining, in the water
I am the shadow that follows a child
I am the evening light, the lustre of meadows
I am an eagle playing with the wind
I am a cluster of bright beads
I am the farthest star
I am the cold of the dawn
I am the roaring of the rain
I am the glitter on the crust of the snow
I am the long track of the moon in a lake
I am a flame of four colors
I am a deer standing away in the dusk
I am a field of sumac and the pomme blanche
I am an angle of geese in the winter sky
I am the hunger of a young wolf
I am the whole dream of these things

You see, I am alive, I am alive
I stand in good relation to the earth
I stand in good relation to the gods
I stand in good relation to all that is beautiful
I stand in good relation to the daughter of Tsen-tainte
You see, I am alive, I am alive

Carriers of the Dream Wheel

This is the Wheel of Dreams
Which is carried on their voices,
By means of which their voices turn
And center upon being.
It encircles the First World,
This powerful wheel.
They shape their songs upon the wheel
And spin the names of the earth and sky,
The aboriginal names.
They are old men, or men
Who are old in their voices,
And they carry the wheel among the camps,
Saying: Come, come,
Let us tell the old stories,
Let us sing the sacred songs.

Mark Strand

b. 1934

White

for Harold Bloom

Now in the middle of my life
all things are white.
I walk under the trees,
the frayed leaves,
the wide net of noon,
and the day is white.
And my breath is white,
drifting over the patches
of grass and fields of ice
into the high circles of light.
As I walk, the darkness of
my steps is also white,
and my shadow blazes

under me. In all seasons
the silence where I find myself
and what I make of nothing are white,
the white of sorrow,
the white of death.
Even the night that calls
like a dark wish is white;
and in my sleep as I turn
in the weather of dreams
it is the white of my sheets
and the white shades of the moon
drawn over my floor
that save me for morning.
And out of my waking
the circle of light widens,
it fills with trees, houses,
stretches of ice.
It reaches out. It rings
the eye with white.
All things are one.
All things are joined
even beyond the edge of sight.

Orpheus Alone

It was an adventure much could be made of: a walk
On the shores of the darkest known river,
Among the hooded, shoving crowds, by steaming rocks
And rows of ruined huts half-buried in the muck;
Then to the great court with its marble yard
Whose emptiness gave him the creeps, and to sit there
In the sunken silence of the place and speak
Of what he had lost, what he still possessed of his loss,
And, then, pulling out all the stops, describing her eyes,
Her forehead where the golden light of evening spread,
The curve of her neck, the slope of her shoulders, everything
Down to her thighs and calves, letting the words come,
As if lifted from sleep, to drift upstream,

Against the water's will, where all the condemned
And pointless labor, stunned by his voice's cadence,
Would come to a halt, and even the crazed, dishevelled
Furies, for the first time, would weep, and the soot-filled
Air would clear just enough for her, the lost bride,
To step through the image of herself and be seen in the light.
As everyone know's, this was the first great poem,
Which was followed by days of sitting around
In the houses of friends, with his head back, his eyes
Closed, trying to will her return, but finding
Only himself, again and again, trapped
In the chill of his loss, and, finally,
Without a word, taking off to wander the hills
Outside of town, where he stayed until he had shaken
The image of love and put in its place the world
As he wished it would be, urging its shape and measure
Into speech of such newness that the world was swayed,
And trees suddenly appeared in the bare place
Where he spoke and lifted their limbs and swept
The tender grass with the gowns of their shade,
And stones, weightless for once, came and set themselves there,
And small animals lay in the miraculous fields of grain
And aisles of corn, and slept. The voice of light
Had come forth from the body of fire, and each thing
Rose from its depths and shone as it never had.
And that was the second great poem,
Which no one recalls anymore. The third and greatest
Came into the world as the world, out of the unsayable,
Invisible source of all longing to be; it came
As things come that will perish, to be seen or heard
A while, like the coating of frost or the movement
Of wind, and then no more; it came in the middle of sleep
Like a door to the infinite, and, circled by flame,
Came again at the moment of waking, and, sometimes,
Remote and small, it came as a vision with trees
By a weaving stream, brushing the bank
With their violet shade, with somebody's limbs
Scattered among the matted, mildewed leaves nearby,
With his severed head rolling under the waves,

Breaking the shifting columns of light into a swirl
Of slivers and flecks; it came in a language
Untouched by pity, in lines, lavish and dark,
Where death is reborn and sent into the world as a gift,
So the future, with no voice of its own, nor hope
Of ever becoming more than it will be, might mourn.

FROM *Dark Harbor*

I am sure you would find it misty here,
With lots of stone cottages badly needing repair,
Groups of souls, wrapped in cloaks, sit in the fields

Or stroll the winding unpaved roads. They are polite,
And oblivious to their bodies, which the wind passes through,
Making a shushing sound. Not long ago,

I stopped to rest in a place where an especially
Thick mist swirled up from the river. Someone,
Who claimed to have known me years before,

Approached, saying there were many poets
Wandering around who wished to be alive again.
They were ready to say the words they had been unable to say—

Words whose absence had been the silence of love,
Of pain, and even of pleasure. Then he joined a small group,
Gathered beside a fire. I believe I recognized

Some of the faces, but as I approached they tucked
Their heads under their wings. I looked away to the hills
Above the river, where the golden lights of sunset

And sunrise are one and the same, and saw something flying
Back and forth, fluttering its wings. Then it stopped in mid-air.
It was an angel, one of the good ones, about to sing.

James Applewhite

b. 1935

The Sex of Divinity

The blooms have mostly gone
But rains have come. The river runs
Bright tan. June is almost
Upon us. I feel weak at first on
The trail in this third week after
My respiratory virus. The foliage has
Massed so as to make one imagine
Some fossil forest compacted to a coal
Of green. Leaves screen the sun
So I can endure its hard shine,
Its bead-bright splintering rattle.
The far bank yields a wild astilbe.
I see the sun whole, a transparent orb.
This androgyne is round as mind,
To illumine within and without.
I break spider webs as I run.
High on Buzzard's Roost, I look down
As on my shirt the hundreds
Of strands my chest has collected
Stretch and glisten, shirt of Nessus
Or Lilliput cables I break as
I breathe, giant in thought.
My small circumference has caught
Fire from the fierce eye shining
Its sexual round through leaves.

Ronald Johnson

1935–1998

FROM *Ark*

BEAM 30, THE GARDEN

for Patricia Anderson

"To do as Adam did"
through the twilight's fluoride glare Mercury in perihelion
(rotating exactly three times
while circling the sun twice)
to Pluto foot tilt up the slide at either plane
and build a Garden of the brain.

Internetted eternities, interspersed
with cypresses
ply ringed air about the many spectacled apples there.
Flamestitch niches orb in swivel orb, The Muses thrush at center
turning. *Phospheros arborescens* they sing
sense's

struck crystal clarities
to knock the knees
(or scarlet hollyhock, against a near blue sky).
No end of fountains lost among the shrubberies full eye may bare.
Fixed stars
with fireflies jam the lilac.

The Lord is a delicate hammerer.
Gold hive upon gray matter
He taps synapse ("carrying to") ("carrying away")
an immense bronze pinecone moon-knit at the end of a vista
of sunny *jets d'eau*, silver poplars. All
shivered in a pool.

Literally, a flowing: form-take-hand
-with-form
(That Which Fasteneth Us)
pillar to pillar the great dance arch itself through all that
is or was or will be, 3/4 time. This will be a glade
at the head of one stream

and a resonant gnomon before it will stretch regions of signaling
gnat-like resiliencies in the atmosphere
of where we are —
or were.
Or will be, when the mingled frame of mind
of man is celebration.

Mary Oliver

b. 1935

When Death Comes

When death comes
like the hungry bear in autumn;
when death comes and takes all the bright coins from his purse

to buy me, and snaps the purse shut;
when death comes
like the measle-pox;

when death comes
like an iceberg between the shoulder blades,

I want to step through the door full of curiosity, wondering:
what is it going to be like, that cottage of darkness?

And therefore I look upon everything
as a brotherhood and a sisterhood,
and I look upon time as no more than an idea,
and I consider eternity as another possibility,

and I think of each life as a flower, as common
as a field daisy, and as singular,

and each name a comfortable music in the mouth,
tending, as all music does, toward silence,

and each body a lion of courage, and something
precious to the earth.

When it's over, I want to say: all my life
I was a bride married to amazement.
I was the bridegroom, taking the world into my arms.

When it's over, I don't want to wonder
if I have made of my life something particular, and real.
I don't want to find myself sighing and frightened,
or full of argument.

I don't want to end up simply having visited this world.

Grace Schulman

b. 1935

Blessed Is the Light

Blessed is the light that turns to fire, and blessed the flames fire
makes of what it burns.
Blessed the inexhaustible sun, for it feeds the moon that shines
but does not burn.
Praised be hot vapors in earth's crust, for they force up
mountains that explode as molten rock and cool, like love
remembered.
Holy is the sun that strikes the sea, for surely as water burns, life
and death are one. Holy the sun, maker of change, as it
melts ice into water that lessens mountains, hones peaks,
and carves gullies.
Sacred is the mountain that crumbles over time. Jagged peaks
promise permanence but change, planed by rock slides, cut
by avalanche, crushed, eroded, leached of minerals.

Behold the arcs your eyes make when you speak. Behold the
hands, white fire. Branches of pine, holding votive candles,
they command, disturbed by wind, the fire that sings in me.
Blessed is whatever alters, turns, revolves, just as the gods move
when the mind moves them.
Praised be the body, our bodies, that lie down and open and rise,
falling in flame.

Prayer

For Agha Shahid Ali

Yom Kippur: wearing a bride's dress bought in Jerusalem,
I peer through swamp reeds, my thought in Jerusalem.

Velvet on grass. Odd, but I learned young to keep this day
just as I can, if not as I ought, in Jerusalem.

Like sleep or love, prayer may surprise the woman
who laughs by a stream, or the child distraught in Jerusalem.

My Arab dress has blue-green-yellow threads
the shades of mosaics hand-wrought in Jerusalem

that both peoples prize, like the blue-yellow Dome of the Rock,
like strung beads-and-cloves, said to ward off the drought in
Jerusalem.

Both savor things that grow wild—coreopsis in April,
the rose that buds late, like an afterthought, in Jerusalem.

While car bombs flared, an Arab poet translated
Hebrew verses whose flame caught in Jerusalem.

And you, Shahid, sail Judah Halevi's sea as I,
on Ghalib's, course like an Argonaut in Jerusalem.

Stone lions pace thc sultan's gate while almonds bloom
into images, Hebrew and Arabic, wrought in Jerusalem.

No words, no metaphors, for knives that gore flesh
on streets where the people have fought in Jerusalem.

As this spider weaves a web in silence,
may Hebrew and Arabic be woven taut in Jerusalem.

Here at the bay, I see my face in the shallows
and plumb for the true self our Abraham sought in Jerusalem.

Open the gates to rainbow-colored words
of outlanders, their sounds untaught in Jerusalem.

My name is Grace, Chana in Hebrew—and in Arabic.
May its meaning, "God's love," at last be taught in Jerusalem.

Charles Wright

b. 1935

Apologia Pro Vita Sua

I

How soon we come to road's end—
Failure, our two-dimensional side-kick, flat dream-light,
Won't jump-start or burn us in,

Dogwood insidious in its constellations of part-charred cross
        points,
Spring's via Dolorosa
                                        flashed out in a dread profusion,
Nowhere to go but up, nowhere to turn, dead world-weight,

They've gone and done it again,
                                                        dogwood,
Spring's sap-crippled, arthritic, winter-weathered, myth limb,
Whose roots are my mother's hair.

—

Landscape's a lever of transcendence—
                                        jack-wedge it here,
Or here, and step back,
Heave, and a light, a little light, will nimbus your going forth:

The dew bead, terminal bead, opens out
                                        onto a great radiance,
Sun's square on magnolia leaf
Offers us, entrance—
                        who among us will step forward,
Camellia brown boutonnieres
Under his feet, plum branches under his feet, white sky, white
    noon,
Church bells like monk's mouths tonguing the hymn?

—

Journal and landscape
—Discredited form, discredited subject matter—
I tried to resuscitate both, breath and blood,
                                        making them whole again

Through language, strict attention—
Verona mi fe', disfecemi Verona, the song goes.
I've hummed it, I've bridged the break

To no avail.
            April. The year begins beyond words,
Beyond myself and the image of myself, beyond
Moon's ice and summer's thunder. All that.

—

The meat of the sacrament is invisible meat and a ghostly
    substance.
I'll say.
        Like any visible thing,
I'm always attracted downward, and soon to be killed and
    assimilated.

Vessel of life, it's said, vessel of life, brought to naught,
Then gathered back to what's visible.
That's it, fragrance of spring like lust in the blossom-starred
    orchard,

The shapeless shape of darkness starting to seep through and
    emerge,
The seen world starting to tilt,
Where I sit the still, unwavering point
                                        under that world's waves.

—

How like the past the clouds are,
Building and disappearing along the horizon,
Inflecting the mountains,
                            laying their shadows under our feet

For us to cross over on.
Out of their insides fire falls, ice falls,
What we remember that still remembers us, earth and air fall.

Neither, however, can resurrect or redeem us,
Moving, as both must, ever away toward opposite corners.
Neither has been where we're going,
                                        bereft of an attitude.

—

Amethyst, crystal transparency,
                                    Maya and Pharaoh ring,
Malocchio, set against witchcraft,
Lightning and hailstorm, birthstone, savior from drunkenness.

Purple, color of insight, clear sight,
Color of memory—
                        violet, that's for remembering,
Star-crystals scattered across the penumbra, hard stars.

Who can distinguish darkness from the dark, light from light,
Subject matter from story line,
                                    the part from the whole
When whole is part of the part and part is all of it?

—

Lonesomeness. Morandi, Cézanne, it's all about lonesomeness.
And Rothko. Especially Rothko.
Separation from what heals us
                                    beyond painting, beyond art.

Words and paint, black notes, white notes.
Music and landscape; music, landscape and sentences.
Gestures for which there is no balm, no intercession.

Two tone fields, horizon a line between abysses,
Generally white, always speechless.
Rothko could choose either one to disappear into. And did.

—

Perch'io no spero di tornar giammai, ballatetta, in Toscana,
Not as we were the first time,
                                        not as we'll ever be again.
Such snowflakes of memory, they fall nowhere but there.

Absorbed in remembering, we cannot remember—
Exile's anthem, O stiff heart,
Thingless we came into the world and thingless we leave.

Every important act is wordless—
                                        to slip from the right way,
To fail, still accomplishes something.
Even a good thing remembered, however, is not as good as not
    remembering at all.

—

Time is the source of all good,
                                        time the engenderer
Of entropy and decay,
Time the destroyer, our only-begetter and advocate.

For instance, my fingenail,
                                    so pink, so amplified,
In the half-dark, for instance,
These force-fed dogwood blossoms, green-leafed, defused,
                                                limp on their long branches.

St. Stone, say a little prayer for me,
                                        grackles and jay in the black gum,
Drowse of the peony head,
Dandelion globes luminous in the last light, more work to be
    done . . .

II

Something will get you, the doctor said,
don't worry about that.
Melancholia's got me,
Pains in the abdomen, pains down the left leg and crotch.

Slurry of coal dust behind the eyes,
Massive weight in the musculature, dark blood, dark blood.
I'm sick and tired of my own complaints,

This quick flick like a compass foot through the testicle,
Deep drag and hurt through the groin—
Melancholia, black dog,
everyone's had enough.

—

Dew-dangled, fresh-cut lawn grass will always smell like a golf course
Fairway to me, Saturday morning, Chuck Ross and I
Already fudging our scores down,
happy as mockingbirds in deep weeds,

The South Fork of the Holston River
Slick as a nickel before its confluence behind our backs
At Rotherwood with the North Fork's distant, blurred thunder,

Our rounds in the seventies always including mulligans,
Nudged lies, "found" lost balls, some extraordinary shots
And that never-again-to-be-repeated
teen-age false sense of attainment.

—

One summer, aged 16, I watched—each night, it seemed—my roommate,
A college guy, gather his blanket up, and flashlight,
And leave for his rendezvous with the camp cook—
he never came back before dawn.

Some 40 years later I saw him again for the first time
Since then, in a grocery store, in the checkout line,
A cleric from Lexington, shrunken and small. Bearded even.

And all these years I'd thought of him, if at all, as huge
And encompassing,
Not rabbit-eyed, not fumbling a half-filled brown sack,
dry-lipped, apologetic.

—

In 1990 we dragged Paris
—back on the gut again after 25 years—
The Boulevard Montparnasse,
La Coupole, the Select, you know, the Dôme, the Closerie de
Lilas,

Up and down and back and forth.
Each night a Japanese girl would take a bath at 4 a.m.
In the room above ours,
each night someone beat his wife

In a room above the garage outside our window.
It rained all day for ten days.
Sleeplessness, hallucination, O City of Light . . .

—

What sane, impossible reason could Percy Heath have made up
To talk to me, drunk, white and awe-struck,
—And tone-deaf to boot—
that night at the Carmel Mission?

But talk he did, uncondescending, feigning interest,
As Milt Jackson walked by and John Lewis walked by,
Gerry Mulligan
Slouched in one corner, Paul Desmond cool in an opposite one.

October, 1958, Monterey Jazz Festival,
First advisors starting to leave the Army Language School for
South Vietnam,
The Pacific's dark eyelid
beginning to stir, ready to rise and roll back . . .

—

During World War II, we lived in Oak Ridge, Tennessee,
Badges and gates, checkpoints, government housing,
government rules.
One house we lived in was next door to a two-star admiral.

I learned a couple of things in the three-plus years we lived in
  Oak Ridge,
One from my first (and only) paper route, the second
After my first (and only) breaking-and-entering.

One thing I learned, however, I didn't know what to do with:
Death is into the water, life is the coming out.
I still don't, though nothing else matters but that, it seems,
                                        nothing even comes close.

—

Elm Grove, Pine Valley and Cedar Hill,
                                        what detritus one remembers—
The one-armed soldier we spied on making out in the sedge
  grass
With his red-haired girl friend behind the Elm Grove playground,

For instance, in 1944 . . . I was nine, the fourth grade . . .
I remember telling Brooklyn, my best friend,
                                        my dick was stiff all night.
Nine years old! My dick! All night!

We talked about it for days,
                                        Oak Ridge abstracted and elsewhere,
—D-Day and Normandy come and gone—
All eyes on the new world's sun king,
                                        its rising up and its going down.

—

It's Wednesday afternoon, and Carter and I are on the road
For the Sullivan County National Bank Loan Department,
1957, Gate City and Southwest Virginia.

We're after deadbeats, delinquent note payers, in Carter's words.
Cemetery plots—ten dollars a month until you die or pay up.
In four months I'll enter the Army, right now I'm Dr. Death,

Riding shotgun for Carter, bringing more misery to the
  miserable.
Up-hollow and down-creek, shack after unelectrified shack—
The worst job in the world, and we're the two worst people in it.

—

Overcast afternoon, then weak sun, then overcast again.
A little wind
                    whiffles across the back yard like a squall line
In miniature, thumping the clover heads, startling the grass.

My parents' 60th wedding anniversary
Were they still alive,
                    5th of June, 1994.
It's hard to imagine, I think, your own children grown older than
    you ever were, I can't.

I sit in one of the knock-off Brown-Jordan deck chairs we
    brought from California,
Next to the bearded grandson my mother never saw.
Some afternoon, or noon, it will all be over. Not this one.

III

June is a migraine above the eyes,
Strict auras and yellow blots,
                    green screen and tunnel vision,
Slow ripples of otherworldliness,

Humidity's painfall drop by drop.
Next door, high whine of the pest exterminator's blunt machine.
Down the street, tide-slap of hammer-and-nail,
                    hammer-and-nail from a neighbor's roof.

I've had these for forty years,
                    light-prints and shifting screed,
Feckless illuminations.
St. John of the Cross, Julian of Norwich, lead me home.

—

It's good to know certain things:
What's departed, in order to know what's left to come;
That water's immeasurable and incomprehensible

And blows in the air
Where all that's fallen and silent becomes invisible;
That fire's the light our names are carved in.

That shame is a garment of sorrow;
That time is the Adversary, and stays sleepless and wants for
nothing;
That clouds are unequal and words are.

—

I sense a certain uncertainty in the pine trees,
Seasonall discontent,
quotidian surliness,
Pre-solstice jitters, that threatens to rattle our equilibrium.

My friend has lost his larynx,
My friend who in the old days, with a sentence or two,
Would easily set things right,

His glasses light-blanks as he quoted a stanza from Stevens or Yeats
Behind his cigarette smoke.
Life's hard, our mutual third friend says . . . It is. It is.

—

Sundays define me.
Born on a back-lit Sunday, like today,
But later, in August,
And elsewhere, in Tennessee, Sundays dismantle me.

There is a solitude about Sunday afternoons
In small towns, surrounded by all that's familiar
And of necessity dear,

That chills us on hot days, like today, unto the grave,
When the sun is a tongued wafer behind the clouds, out of sight,
And wind chords work through the loose-roofed yard sheds,
a celestial music . . .

—

There is forgetfulness in me which makes me descend
Into a great ignorance,
And makes me to walk in mud, though what I remember remains.

Some of the things I have forgotten:
Who the Illuminator is, and what he illuminates;
Who will have pity on what needs have pity on it.

What I remember redeems me,
strips me and brings me to rest,
An end to what has begun,
A beginning to what is about to be ended.

—

What are the determining moments of our lives?
How do we know them?
Are they ends of things or beginnings?
Are we more or less of ourselves once they've come and gone?

I think this is one of mine tonight,
The Turkish moon and its one star
crisp as a new flag
Over my hometown street with its dark trash cans looming along the curb.

Surely this must be one. And what of me afterwards
When the moon and her sanguine consort
Have slipped the horizon? What will become of me then?

—

Some names are everywhere—they are above and they are below,
They are concealed and they are revealed.
We call them wise, for the wisdom of death is called the little wisdom.

And my name? And your name?
Where will we find them, in what pocket?
Wherever it is, better to keep them there not known—
Words speak for themselves, anonymity speaks for itself.

The Unknown Master of the Pure Poem walks nightly among his roses,
The very garden his son laid out.
Every so often he sits down. Every so often he stands back up . . .

—

Heavy, heavy, heavy hangs over our heads. June heat.
How many lives does it take to fabricate this one?
Aluminum pie pan bird frightener
dazzles and feints in a desultory breeze

Across the road, vegetable garden mojo, evil eye.
That's one life I know for sure.
Others, like insects in amber,
lie golden and lurking and hidden from us.

Ninety-four in the shade, humidity huge and inseparable,
Noon sun like a laser disk.
The grackle waddles forth in his suit of lights,
the crucifixion on his back.

—

Affection's the absolute
everything rises to,
Devotion's detail, the sum of all our scatterings,
Bright imprint our lives unshadow on.

Easy enough to say that now, the hush of late spring
Hung like an after-echo
Over the neighborhood,
devolving and disappearing.

Easy enough, perhaps, but still true,
Honeysuckle and poison ivy jumbling out of the hedge,
Magnolia beak and white tongue, landscape's off-load, love's lisp.

Jay Wright

b. 1935

The Origin of Mary in a Cathedral Choir

At the age of five Cecilia saw a meteor, and thereupon decided to be an astronomer. She remarked that she must begin quickly, in case there should be no research left when she grew up.

Beauty is splendor veritatis, a radiance of truth.
The fact of revelation the eye beholds can never lie.
Old harmonies dress themselves for eye and ear
with a blessedness all saints approve.

I shall now impose these buds the doctor universalis

has sent you, while he speaks of God,
the elegant architect, at work on a regal palace
with the "subtle chains" of musical consonance.
You have come from that different cave life,
out of the springs of distemper and possession.
Lying in a crypt, you gather your strangeness,
waiting to bejewel another city with your ecstasy.
Such rose leaves enfold your words that the king,
as he refuses, must bend to define the light
and hear the modulation in his voice that has gone.
True to the night and the cave's rejoicing,
you cover his eyes with flame.
                                                    I know
you have written this mystery of embodiment
in fire and a virgin birth; when the stone fell
from heaven, it flowered in an almond tree,
and a pine tree covered with violets became
                                            a token for your love.
All ways lead down to the politic mother
and the fear of celebration, the cleansing
in a new birth where the mother-bride rises.
Who rises first?
The memory of fire confuses me.
Your tunic rages blue with wrath.
You abandon me
in the ruin of an incomparable house.
Who rises first?
When now this clairvoyant rose rises over stone
in the choir, I can hear the burning,
clearing the path for a red sign and a figure
who will stand suspended
until a red mother claims him on a red shore.

Desire's Persistence

Yo ave del agua floreciente duro en fiesta.
—"Deseo de persistencia," *Poesía Náhuatl*

1

In the region of rain and cloud,
I live in shade,
under the moss mat of days bruised
purple with desire.
My dominion is a song in the wide ring of water.
There, I run to and fro,
braiding the logical act
in the birth of an Ear of Corn,
polychromatic story I will now tell
in the weaving, power's form in motion,
a devotion to the unstressed.
Once, I wreathed around a king,
became a fishing net, a maze
"a deadly wealth of robe."
Mothers who have heard me sing take heart;
I always prick them into power.

2

Y vengo alzando al viento la roja flor de invierno.
(I lift the red flower of winter into the wind.)
—*Poesía Náhuatl*

I

Out of the ninth circle,
a Phoenician boat rocks upward into light
and the warmth of a name—given to heaven—
that arises in the ninth realm.
Earth's realm discloses the Egyptian
on the point of invention,
deprived of life and death,
heart deep in the soul's hawk,
a thymos shadow knapping the tombed body.

Some one or thing is always heaven bound.
Some flowered log doubles my bones.
The spirit of Toltec turtledoves escapes.
A sharp, metaphorical cry sends me
into the adorned sepulchre,
and the thing that decays learns
how to speak its name.

LIFT

Down Hidalgo,
past Alvarado and Basurto,
I walk a straight line
to the snailed Paseo Los Berros.
Here, at noon, the sun,
a silver bead,
veils what the dawn has displayed.
Even so,
I have taken up the morning's bond again
—the lake with its pendulum leg
shining in the distance,
the boy in white
hauling his bottle of chalky milk home.
I know I sit in the deep of a city
with its brocade of hills,
where a thin rain is an evening's fire.
I have heard the women sing
near their gas lamps,
when the rose end of day lights a hunger
for the garlanded soups and meat they prepare.
Often, I have taken the high ground
by the pond, over a frog's voice
dampened by lilies,
and been exalted by the soothsayer
who knows I'm not at home.
I am the arcane body,
raised at the ninth hour,
to be welcomed by the moonlight
of such spirited air.

I am the Dane of degrees
who realizes how the spirit glows
                                        even as it descends.

Red

The heart, catalectic though it be, does glow,
responds to every midnight bell within you.
This is a discourse on reading heat,
the flushed char of burned moments one sees
after the sexton's lamp flows
over the body's dark book.

There is supicion
here that violet
traces of
sacrifice
stand
bare.

Flower

This marble dust recalls that sunset
with the best burgundy, and the way,
after the charm of it, the peacocks
escaped their cages on the green.
I would now embellish the flame
that ornaments you,
even as it once in that moment
                                                        did.
I carry you blossomed,
cream and salt of a high crown.
You *must* flare,
          stream forth,
blister and scale me,
even as you structure the enveloping kiss,
                                        sporophore of our highest loss.

Winter

Under the evergreens,
the grouse have gone under the snow.
Women who follow their fall flight
tell us that, if you listen, you can hear
their dove's voices ridge the air,
a singing that follows us to a bourne
                                        released from its heat sleep.
We have come to an imagined line,
                                                        celestial,
that binds us to the burr of a sheltered thing
and rings us with a fire that will not dance,
                              in a horn that will not sound.
We have learned, like these birds,
to publish our decline,
when over knotted apples and straw-crisp leaves,
the slanted sun welcomes us once again
to the arrested music in the earth's divided embrace.

Wind

Through winter,
harmattan blacks the air.
My body fat with oil,
I become another star at noon,
when the vatic insistence
of the dog star's breath clings to me.
Though I am a woman,
I turn south,
toward the fire,
and hear the spirits in the bush.
But this is my conceit:
water will come from the west,
and I will have my trance,
                                                                  be reborn,
perhaps in a Mediterranean air,
the Rhone delta's contention
with the eastern side of rain.

In all these disguises,
I follow the aroma of power.
So I am charged in my own field,
to give birth to the solar wind,
particles spiraling around the line
                                        of my body,
moving toward the disruption,
the moment when the oil of my star at noon
                is a new dawn.

3

I shall go away, I shall disappear,
I shall be stretched on a bed of yellow roses
and the old women will cry for me.
So the Toltecas wrote: their books are finished,
but your heart has become perfect.

Lucille Clifton

b. 1936

the astrologer predicts at mary's birth

this one lie down on grass.
this one old men will follow
calling mother   mother.
she womb will blossom then die.
this one she hide from evening.
at a certain time when she hear something
it will burn her ear.
at a certain place when she see something
it will break her eye.

anna speaks of the childhood of mary her daughter

we rise up early and
we work. work is the medicine
for dreams.
                    that dream
i am having again;
she washed in light,
whole world bowed to its knees,
she on a hill looking up,
face all long tears.
                         and shall i give her up
to dreaming then? i fight this thing.
all day we scrubbing   scrubbing.

mary's dream

winged women was saying
"full of grace" and like.
was light beyond sun and words
of a name and a blessing.
winged women to only i.
i joined them, whispering
yes.

how he is coming then

like a pot turned on the straw
nuzzled by cows and an old man
dressed like a father. like a loaf
a poor baker sets in the haystack to cool.
like a shepherd who hears in his herding
his mother whisper   my son   my son.

holy night

joseph, i afraid of stars,
their brilliant seeing.
so many eyes. such light.
joseph, i cannot still these limbs,
i hands keep moving toward i breasts,
so many stars. so bright.
joseph, is wind burning from east
joseph, i shine, oh joseph,   oh
illuminated night.

a song of mary

somewhere it being yesterday.
i a maiden in my mother's house.
the animals silent outside.
is morning.
princes sitting on thrones in the east
studying the incomprehensible heavens.
joseph carving a table somewhere
in another place.
i watching my mother.
i smiling an ordinary smile.

island mary

after the all been done and i
one old creature carried on
another creature's back, i wonder
could i have fought these thing?
surrounded by no son of mine save
old men calling mother like in the tale
the astrologer tell, i wonder
could i have walk away when voices
singing in my sleep? i one old woman.
always i seem to worrying now for
another young girl asleep

in the plain evening.
what song around her ear?
what star still choosing?

---

mary   mary astonished by God
on a straw bed circled by beasts
and an old husband. mary marinka
holy woman split by sanctified seed
into mother and mother for ever and ever
we pray for you sister woman shook by the
awe full affection of the saints.

C. K. Williams

b. 1936

The Vessel

I'm trying to pray; one of the voices of my mind says, "God,
please help me do this,"
but another voice intervenes: "How conceive God's interest
would be to help you believe?"

Is this prayer? Might this exercise be a sign, however impure, that
such an act's under way,
that I'd allowed myself, or that God had allowed me, to
surrender to this need in myself?

What makes me think, though, that the region of my soul in
which all this activity's occurring
is a site which God might consider an engaging or even an
acceptable spiritual location?

I thought I'd kept the lack of a sacred place in myself from
myself, therefore from God.

Is *this* prayer, recognizing that my isolation from myself is a
secret I no longer can keep?

Might prayer be an awareness that even our most belittling
secrets are absurd before God?
Might God's mercy be letting us think we haven't betrayed those
secrets to Him until now?

If I believe that there exists a thing I can call God's mercy, might I
be praying at last?
If I were, what would it mean: that my sad loneliness for God
might be nearing its end?

I imagine that were I in a real relation with God instead of just
being lonely for Him,
the way I'd apprehend Him would have nothing to do with
secrets I'd kept, from Him or myself.

I'd empty like a cup: that would be prayer, to empty, then fill
with a substance other than myself.
Empty myself of what, though? And what would God deign fill
me with except my own prayer?

Is this prayer now, believing that my offering to God would be
what He'd offered me?
I'm trying to pray, but I know that whatever I'm doing I'm not:
why aren't I, when will I?

Michael S. Harper

b. 1938

Peace on Earth

Tunes come to me at morning
prayer, after flax sunflower
seeds jammed in a coffee can;

when we went to Japan
I prayed at the shrine
for the war dead broken
at Nagasaki;

the tears on the lip of my soprano
glistened in the sun.

In interviews
I talked about my music's
voice of praise to our oneness,

them getting caught up in techniques
of the electronic school

lifting us into assault;

in live sessions, without an audience
I see faces on the flues of the piano,

cymbals driving me into ecstasies on my knees,

the demonic angel, Elvin,
answering my prayers on African drum,

on *Spiritual*

and on *Reverend King*

we chanted his words
on the mountain, where the golden chalice
came in our darkness.

I pursued the songless sound
of embouchures on Parisian thoroughfares,

the coins spilling across the arched
balustrade against my feet;

no high as intense as possessions
given up in practice

where the scales came to my fingers

without deliverance,
the light always coming at 4 A.M.

Syeeda's "Song Flute" charts
my playing for the ancestors;

how could I do otherwise,

passing so quickly in this galaxy

there is no time for being

to be paid in acknowledgment;
all praise to the phrase brought to me:
salaams of becoming:
A LOVE SUPREME:

Charles Simic

b. 1938

Mystic Life

lifetime's solitary thread
for CHARLES WRIGHT

It's like fishing in the dark,
If you ask me:
Our thoughts are the hooks,
Our hearts the raw bait.

We cast the line over our heads,
Past all believing,
Into the starless midnight sky,
Until it's lost to sight.

The line's long unravelling
Rising in our throats like a sigh
Of a long-day's weariness,
Soul-searching and revery

—

One little thought against
The supreme unthinkable.

How about that?

Mr. Looney Tunes fishing in the dark
Out of an empty sleeve
With a mourning band on it.

The fly and the spider on the ceiling
Looking on, brother.

—

In the highest school of hide-and-seek,

In its vast classroom
Of smoke and mirrors,
Where we are the twin dunces
Left standing in
The darkest corner.

Our fates in the silence of a mouth
Of the one
Who hath no image,
Glistening there
As if moistened by his tongue.

—

It takes a tiny nibble
From time to time.

Don't you believe it.

It sends a shiver clown our spines
In response.

Like hell it does.

There's a door you've never noticed before
Left ajar in your room.

Don't kid yourself.

—

The songs said: *Do nothing*
Till you hear from me.

Yes, of course.

In the meantime,

Wear mirror-tinted
Glasses to bed
Say in your prayers:
In that thou hast sought me,
Thou hast already found me.

That's what the leaves are
All upset about tonight.

—

Solitary fishermen
Lining up like zeros—

To infinity.

Lying in the shade
Chewing on the bitter verb
"To be."
The ripple of the abyss
Closing in on them.

Therein the mystery
And the pity.

—

The hook left dangling
In the Great "Nothing."

Surely snipped off
BY XXXXXX's own
Moustache-trimming scissors . . .

Nevertheless, aloft,

White shirttails and all—

I'll be damned!

Frank Bidart

b. 1939

The Sacrifice

When Judas writes the history of SOLITUDE,—
. . . let him celebrate

Miss Mary Kenwood; who, without
help, placed her head in a plastic bag,

then locked herself
in a refrigerator.

—

—Six months earlier, after thirty years
teaching piano, she had watched

her mother slowly die of throat cancer.
Watched her *want* to die . . .

What once had given Mary life
in the end didn't want it.

Awake, her mother screamed for help to die.
—She felt

GUILTY . . . She knew that *all* men in these situations felt
innocent—; helpless—; yet guilty.

—

Christ knew the Secret. Betrayal
is necessary; as is woe for the betrayer.

The solution, Mary realized at last,
must be brought out of my own body.

Wiping away our sins, Christ stained us with his blood—;
to offer yourself, yet need *betrayal*, by *Judas*, before
SHOULDERING

THE GUILT OF THE WORLD—;
. . . *Give me the courage not to need Judas.*

—

When Judas writes the history of solitude,
let him record

that to the friend who opened
the refrigerator, it seemed

death fought; before giving in.

Paul Mariani

b. 1940

Giottoesque

for Margaret and Jim Freeman

Hunched by the back door this frozen morning,
the sun a spangle-brilliant sluggish herniated giant
lifting itself over the low hills to the southeast,
I wave to my wife as she turns the iceblue Escort up
the glare-ice cinder-speckled ruts
on her way to teach her 40 four- & five-year-olds
(this is Bake-day for the letter B),

& thank the *bon Dieu* for the warmth & at moments
alabaster brilliant light he has seen fit
to pour my way in his good time, in this
the 46th year of my uncertain pilgrimage,
still confusing him at times with this other light
coming from outside & which makes the blameless birds
to sing & chitter even at this turning of the year,

where even now they congregate in nervous choirs
beneath the blue shadow of our majestic & denuded
late-June-perfume-blossoming catalpa: the brilliant blue
of jay & flick of yellow grosbeak & the Sienna-
mottled wooddove beige, all, all accented by the gift
this year of *two* pairs of spectral cardinals, a dash
of scarlet in the upper left quadrant of my window

as in the lower right, millet, sunflower, golden heart
of peanut flung high heavenward with abandon (& no stray tom
this year hiding in the lilac bush to scare them off, not yet
at least), & somewhere, over all, Halley's comet come again
as in Giotto's Christmas scene where it is meant—
tail and flash and all—to serve as star of David
come flaming over that other sleepy hilltown,

our three sons still hiberning in their beds,
their long semesters over or for the nonce on hold,
the still-fresh-painted memory of Margaret & Eileen
baking cookies in the kitchen for no other reason
than to give away, so startled by the beauty of the birds
that I rushed downstairs to see once more
what I have witnessed to these sixteen years, something

so resplendent that for centuries artists pinned their parti-
colored bare bright wings to choir on choir of angels
where they sang hosannas to a little baby sleeping
in a corncrib kept nestled from the cold as often the birds
themselves are not, and for a blessèd moment, in spite
of our collective losses at the Gander base when all that
youth in a phoenix flame of transcendent light went up,

in spite too of our local poor, huddled in shacks
& vacant rooms, who will be fed this season, thanks
to the largely hidden good of many decent people
whose deeds speak for the recurrent miracle of this turning
of the sun once more upon us, so that the heart is lifted
exactly as You promised by an unexpected brilliance
even in the midst of darkness, where it seems You bide & smile.

Robert Pinsky

b. 1940

The Knight's Prayer

He prayed in silence.

Even in his personal extreme
Of woe and dread, which was neither
Heroic nor intolerable but sufficiently
Woeful and dreadful, he would not waver
From that discipline.

In his vanity as severely
Logical as a clever adolescent, he found
All vocal terms of sanctity impertinent.

He also rejected gestures: the stagey pose
Of the figure in armor on one knee,
Hands and brow resting on the cruciform hilt
Of a still-scabbarded weapon.
The words and the pose contradicted
Themselves, their conventionality made them
Symbols of worldly attachment.

Therefore in his own prayers he strove
For intimacy, a near-absence of petition.
In his pride he began to abjure even
The request for the strength to ask nothing.

He prayed for steadfastness. In the exploits
He most envied, heroes of old
Endured hardship and ordeals. Worldly
Attachment was their assigned
Burden of imperfection:
Bearing it was their mission.

Lest these prayers be
For weariness of life, not love of Thee,
He had read: a standard he admired
Not in the name of love
But for its stringency: the gauntlet
Of chainmail not folded
On the breviary, but brandished,
Able for the task.

Then, that abrupt personal extreme
Of woe and dread, neither
Heroic nor intolerable: a cause
To fear the silence. The soul
Stammering to itself.

It was not "In fear of the Lord
Is the beginning of wisdom."

But in fear a new
Model for worldly attachment:

It was like the birth
Of an infant: the father, in sudden
Overthrow, turning from indifference
To absolute care, a ferocity
Of petition dwarfing desire,
All of life flowing at once
Toward the new, incompetent soul.

Simon J. Ortiz

b. 1941

The Creation, According to Coyote

"First of all, it's all true."
Coyote, he says this, this way,
humble yourself, motioning and meaning
what he says.

You were born when you came
from that body, the earth;
your black head burst from granite,
the ashes cooling,

until it began to rain.
It turned muddy then,
and then green and brown things
came without legs.

They looked strange.
Everything was strange.
There was nothing to know then,

until later, Coyote told me this,
and he was b.s.-ing probably,
two sons were born,
Uyuyayeh and Masaweh.
They were young then,
and then later on they were older.

And then the people were wondering
what was above.
They had heard rumors.

But, you know, Coyote,
he was mainly bragging
when he said (I think),

"My brothers, the Twins then said,
'Let's lead these poor creatures
and save them.'"

And later on, they came to light
after many exciting and colorful and tragic things of adventure;
and this is the life, all these, all these.

My uncle told me all this, that time,
Coyote told me too, but you know
how he is, always talking to the gods,
the mountains, the stone all around.

And you know, I believe him.

Alfred Corn

b. 1943

Jerusalem

Then keep thy heart. . . .
MELVILLE, *Clarel*

They will lift up their heads:
the Lion Gate, St. Stephen's, the New,
Jaffa, and, last, the Gate of Dung.
The gates will lift up their heads
that the King of Glory may come in.

As Judah means "Praised," its chief city will be
more highly praised, the ramparts and towers
of David's citadel praised and exalted.

—

Come this far, how close the door on what
not even they had stubbornness enough to bar?
The Rock where Isaac, his wrists bound tight,
saw above him a face clench in agony
moments before an angel dove down to stay

Abraham's hand is now perpetual,
preserved in the furnace of tradition
along with that ram whose horn became the shofar.

—Or is it rock as fact, one of the sights,
coated with dust and roofed with a golden dome
reverberant with a murmured sura
expanding on the Prophet's airborne nocturnal
journey, which fixed him like a star
on the cusp of the crescent moon?

—

Just as the present-day pilgrim goes from station
to station in a loud array of discount tours,
tenants have reconstrued the basilica
of the Holy Sepulchre as real estate
for hereditary zeal to balkanize
among several sects. Each has its sharply
defended square yardage of theology, but none
equals that stone niche off to one side where an oil lamp's
starred wick baffles the sway of archaic shadows.

—

The Temple abides in its myth
but also in limestone fact, at least the part
Roman demolition experts failed
to pound into undatable rubble.
Foundation Wall, you won't be alone again,
alive with the Shekhinah's quiet thunder,
bloodwarm dovecote of fissured building blocks
into which ten thousand handwritten
praises or lamentations have flown.

—

And Via Dolorosa toils south from Gabbatha's
courtyard, where a few detached centurions
gave their charge the prescribed flogging
before sending him on his forced march.
A path useless to retrace without spiriting away
two millennia or any obstacle
to contemplation of punished flesh at ground zero
staggering forward under a massive wooden T,

palm fronds still underfoot, but dry and broken,
whispering hosannas no one hears.

Because a Procurator exercised available
options, the name "Pilate" survives globally
on the lips of millions when the Credo's recited
tenets descend into history and make it faith.

—

What was truth? What will it be?
For the condemned whose breath comes shorter and shorter,
"Even death may prove unreal at the last"—unreal,
like the sound of a tree fallen to earth
far from any ear, or any human ear.
When the body atoned to its trunk and limbs toppled
out of time, did it finally become audible
to his listeners? To some. To Clarel, and for later
pilgrims who risked as much as one step beyond doubt.

No other dispatch could outdistance the silence
following on that farewell to his friend—
who, standing at the Place of the Skull,
heard him say, "Woman, behold thy son,"
as prelude to, "Behold thy mother."
Seeing where sons of earth were bound to go,
from that day forth he housed a second mother under his roof.

Lift up your heads.

Louise Glück

b. 1943

Lamentations

I THE LOGOS

They were both still,
the woman mournful, the man
branching into her body.

But god was watching.
They felt his gold eye
projecting flowers on the landscape.

Who knew what he wanted?
He was god, and a monster.
So they waited. And the world
filled with his radiance,
as though he wanted to he understood.

Far away, in the void that he had shaped,
he turned to his angels.

2 NOCTURNE

A forest rose from the earth.
O pitiful, so needing
God's furious love—

Together they were beasts.
They lay in the fixed
dusk of his negligence;
from the hills, wolves came, mechanically
drawn to their human warmth,
their panic.

Then the angels saw
how He divided them:
the man, the woman, and the woman's body.

Above the churned reeds, the leaves let go
a slow moan of silver.

3 THE COVENANT

Out of fear, they built a dwelling place.
But a child grew between them
as they slept, as they tried
to feed themselves.

They set it on a pile of leaves,
the small discarded body
wrapped in the clean skin
of an animal. Against the black sky
they saw the massive argument of light.

Sometimes it woke. As it reached its hands
they understood they were the mother and father,
there was no authority above them.

4 THE CLEARING

Gradually, over many years,
the fur disappeared from their bodies
until they stood in the bright light
strange to one another.
Nothing was as before.
Their hands trembled, seeking
the familiar.

Nor could they keep their eyes
from the white flesh
on which wounds would show clearly
like words on a page.

And from the meaningless browns and greens
at last God arose, His great shadow
darkening the sleeping bodies of His children,
and leapt into heaven.

How beautiful it must have been,
the earth, that first time
seen from the air.

Matins

What is my heart to you
that you must break it over and over
like a plantsman testing
his new species? Practice

on something else: how can I live
in colonies, as you prefer, if you impose
a quarantine of affliction, dividing me
from healthy members of
my own tribe: you do not do this
in the garden, segregate
the sick rose; you let it wave its sociable
infested leaves in
the faces of the other roses, and the tiny aphids
leap from plant to plant, proving yet again
I am the lowest of your creatures, following
the thriving aphid and the trailing rose— Father,
as agent of my solitude, alleviate
at least my guilt; lift
the stigma of isolation, unless
it is your plan to make me
sound forever again, as I was
sound and whole in my mistaken childhood,
or if not then, under the light weight
of my mother's heart, or if not then,
in dream, first
being that would never die.

Vespers

Even as you appeared to Moses, because
I need you, you appear to me, not
often, however. I live essentially
in darkness. You are perhaps training me to be
responsive to the slightest brightening. Or, like the poets,
are you stimulated by despair, does grief
move you to reveal your nature? This afternoon,
in the physical world to which you commonly
contribute your silence, I climbed
the small hill above the wild blueberries, metaphysically
descending, as on all my walks: did I go deep enough
for you to pity me, as you have sometimes pitied
others who suffer, favoring those

with theological gifts? As you anticipated,
I did not look up. So you came down to me:
at my feet, not the wax
leaves of the wild blueberry but your fiery self, a whole
pasture of fire, and beyond, the red sun neither falling nor
rising—
I was not a child; I could take advantage of illusions.

Michael Palmer

b. 1943

Untitled (September '92)

Or maybe this
is the sacred, the vaulted and arched, the
nameless, many-gated
zero where children

where invisible children
where the cries
of invisible children rise
between the Cimetière M

and the Peep Show Sex Paradise
Gate of Sound and Gate of Sand—
Choirs or Mirrors—
Choir like a bundle of tongues

Mirror like a ribbon of tongues
(such that images will remain
once the objects are gone)
Gate of the Body and Gate of the Law

Gate of Public Words, or Passages,
of Suddenness and Cells, Compelling Logic, Gate
of the Hat Filled with Honey
and Coins Bathed in Honey

As the light erases
As heat will etch a d, a design, a
descant of broken lines into glass
Exactly here

between thought and extended arm,
between the gate named for lies
and the double X of the empty sign,
a kind of serous field,

fluid scene or site
peopled with shadows
pissing blood in doorways
yet versed in the mathematics of curves,

theory of colors,
history of time
At Passages we peer out
over a tracery of bridges,

patchwork of sails
At Desire is it possible
we speak without tongues
or see only with tongues

And at Lateness we say
This will be the last
letter you'll receive,
final word you'll hear

from me for now
Is it that a fire
once thought long extinguished
continues to burn

deep within the ground,
a fire finally acknowledged
as impossible to put out,
and that plumes of flame and smoke

will surface at random
enlacing the perfect symmetries
of the Museum of the People
and the Palace of the Book

Or that a Gate of Hours speaks
in a language unfamiliar,
unlike any known,
yet one clear enough

clear as any other
and clear as the liquid
reflection of a gate,
gate whose burnt pages

are blowing through the street
past houses of blue paper
built over fault lines
as if by intent

J. D. McClatchy

b. 1945

Dervish

Everything revolves:
the dreams of the body,
the blood, the earth itself,
a man's coming from it
and his return.
In their tombstone caps
and flaring shroud skirts,
the dervishes spin
toward that moment
when monotony and ecstasy,
knowing and unknowing
are the same, planets

wheeled around some
spindle disguised
as the five-petalled rose
on a tile underfoot
in a weightless self-regard
meant to worship the power
that keeps them in motion.
From a corbelled balcony
the choir's melisma
twists on a lost soul:
oud and heartbeat,
the drummed air lifting.
This one—so close
he brushes against
the fanatic's prayer—
arms open to anything,
right hand pointing up,
eyes caught by his left hand,
which he's turned downward
as if toward the rapture
of, at last, submission . . .
here is our world.
It is time now to come back
to the work of creation.
High over the planets
a golden whiplash script
around the inmost rim
of today's great dome
calls down: God
is the light of the heavens,
a niche wherein is a lamp.
The lamp is in glass.
The glass is a high,
brightening, constant
star.

Carol Muske-Dukes

b. 1945

When He Fell

When he fell, strangers ran to him.
Strangers called for help, lifted
his body and carried it. Then strangers
cut him, emptied him. Their ideas

of death determined when I would
touch him again. Their ideas of death
closed door after door between us,
altered his face, altered his presence—

violated the contract, the marriage,
took away even his wounded heart.
When he was at last delivered to me,
I was no longer myself—just as he

no longer had a self. They
had taken everything from us. Authority—
everywhere I turned. Just as he and I
once thought we were authorities over

our own lives, our work, our sense of
mortality, imagination—oh, and that
"sense of loss" that predicated everything—
you know, what we called *our personal lives.*

Vicki Hearne

1946–2001

Good Friday: No Way Out but Straight Through, Jack

It's like chance, but chance knocks but
Won't open the door, and here's
A greater thing than we have
Ever done (before we learn
What we are doing). The god
Will become so resplendent
With wounds our eyes must dazzle,

But now our hands hold aloft
The spears that dance in the light
From the hillside. Ecstasy,
Even, should not distract us:
The flesh must be opened full
To the light and wait, bleeding
In welcome. And in welcome

The elegant wounds will close
With all of us safe inside.
But we are not now to know
With Whom we trifle, not yet
To ask forgiveness lest we
Not plunge the gleaming weapons
Heartily. Grief will give wings

And song reveal the purple
Gold, the burnished ground, the flame.

The Leisure of God

The Word was one thing, clear song,
Until language, day seven
That was, or so Nietzsche said,

Became amusement disguised
As something we must languish
Without—language as a noise

Of refusal, all song gone,
All agreement between Word
Work Beauty Praise. Diatribe

Became duty, tribal thrust,
Weapons of bright righteousness
And no good came of it, none,

Though our poems bear up under
Morality as only
They can, taking that black weight

From our astonished shoulders,
Bearing the leisure of God
As if they had chosen to

However careless of love
Truth might be, or however
Profligate in her revenge.

Linda Hogan

b. 1947

Me, Crow, Fish, and the Magi

Rooster,
the smaller he is,
the more he fills his chest with air
and crows.

He is not afraid of morning.
Nor is trout afraid, leaping into deadly air.
And I forget my own suspicions to follow some line
even with its hook:
Why don't you look me up sometime?

I'm going for the lure,
driving a highway,
wearing all my old lives,
scars on both knees
and crow's feet, a history
like broken fishline
carried by Old Whiskers
that Colorado fish, showing off
his escapes.

These are gods we follow,
sunlight or worm,
and we are trusting
as chickens walking to their death
along a hypnotic line of chalk
drawn by the good lord or Mesmer.

But the odds are good,
yes they are,
that sometimes we quit crowing
or chasing lunch. We forget running away
and stop in our tracks to listen
and hear the pull of our own voices
like the Magi with their star,
the wise ones with their camels,
perfumes and gold,
believing their inner songs,
a journey in the bones of their feet,
like migrating birds
or salmon swimming ladders of stars
to the beginning of life.

The Inside of Things

Such lovely voices, the angels
singing at night in the showers,
sitting among plants
talking about their pasts on earth.

They don't care
about the inside of daily things
the bones in an open palm
or feet that start tapping
to inner songs.

Angels have better things to think about
than houses sitting on the shabby planet
with night lights in dark halls,
or attics, filled
with records of war and birth.

Angels have no time
for horses in the barn
or the three white geese.
They are busy preening their own wings
or pecking at one another.

But the demons
come knocking right on the door
telling how angels have failed
to look at the inside of lies and history,
at ticks on horses in the barn,
at broken beams of houses.
They point out the cat's thin ribs
and sore teeth.

I am back and forth,
held in soft wings
then falling, then saved,
dancing through air
to earth made of bones,

to new green rising up,
descending,
like the bountiful rain
taken in by earth,
taken in by sky.

Jane Kenyon

1947–1995

Briefly It Enters, and Briefly Speaks

I am the blossom pressed in a book,
found again after two hundred years. . . .

I am the maker, the lover, and the keeper. . . .

When the young girl who starves
sits dawn to a table
she will sit beside me. . . .

I am food on the prisoner's plate. . . .

I am water rushing to the wellhead,
filling the pitcher until it spills. . . .

I am the patient gardener
of the dry and weedy garden. . . .

I am the stone step,
the latch, and the working hinge. . . .

I am the heart contracted by joy . . .
the longest hair, white
before the rest. . . .

I am there in the basket of fruit
presented to the widow. . . .

I am the musk rose opening
unattended, the fern on the boggy summit. . . .

I am the one whose love
overcomes you, already with you
when you think to call my name. . . .

Yusef Komunyakaa

b. 1947

Thanks

Thanks for the tree
between me & a sniper's bullet.
I don't know what made the grass
sway seconds before the Viet Cong
raised his soundless rifle.
Some voice always followed,
telling me which foot
to put down first.
Thanks for deflecting the ricochet
against that anarchy of dusk.
I was back in San Francisco
wrapped up in a woman's wild colors,
causing some dark bird's love call
to be shattered by daylight
when my hands reached up
& pulled a branch away
from my face. Thanks
for the vague white flower
that pointed to the gleaming metal
reflecting how it is to be broken
like mist over the grass,
as we played some deadly
game for blind gods.
What made me spot the monarch
writhing on a single thread

tied to a farmer's gate,
holding the day together
like an unfingered guitar string,
is beyond me. Maybe the hills
grew weary & leaned a little in the heat.
Again, thanks for the dud
hand grenade tossed at my feet
outside Chu Lai. I'm still
falling through its silence.
I don't know why the intrepid
sun touched the bayonet,
but I know that something
stood among those lost trees
& moved only when I moved.

Geoffrey O'Brien

b. 1948

The Prophet

You stepped out of a frame, or more properly
out of a framed image in a store specializing
in images from a variety of periods, early Egyptian,
late Rococo, the advent of the talkies. Wherever
people have an urge to stand framed in doorways,
to let strings of beads drape them, wherever they feel free
to choreograph a dance interpretive of a windstorm,
that's where I'll find you. Your bedroom is splashed
with mythological scenes, your radio hums with polka music.
In the lost history of the world, the one whose revolutions
were achieved without ceremonial burnings, you play the role
of the prophet who on second thought preferred to remain silent
or of the ambassador, at once grave and sparkling,
from a country whose policy is to remain as relaxed as possible.

Agha Shahid Ali

1949–2001

First Day of Spring

On this perfect day, perfect for forgetting God,
why are they—Hindu or Muslim, Gentile or Jew—
shouting again some godforsaken word of God?

The Angel, his wings flailing—no, burning—stood awed.
The Belovéd, dark with excessive bright, withdrew
and the day was not perfect for forgetting God.

On a face of stone it bends, the divining rod:
Not silver veins but tears: Niobe, whereunto
your slain children swaddled dark with the Names of God?

And now on earth, you and I, with longing so flawed
that: Angel forced to grow not wings but arms, why aren't you
holding me this day—perfect for forgetting God?

You spent these years on every street in Hell? How odd,
then, that I never saw you there, I who've loved you
against (*Hold me!*) against every word of God.

The rumor? It's again the reign of Nimrod.
Whoever you are, I depend on your message,
but you—
Angel I suspect no longer of God—
are still bringing me word from (*Could it be?*) from God.

God

Of all things He's the King Allah King God.
Then why this fear of idolizing God?

Outgunned Chechens hold off Russian tanks—
They have a prayer. Are you listening, God?

I begged for prayers to the Surgeon's answer,
my heart alone against terrorizing God.

Masked, I hold him enthralled who's harmed me most—
I will hurt him as he's been hurting God.

So what make you of cosmic background noise?
Well, there's the Yoni (*My!*) and the Ling (*God!*).

A butterfly's wings flutter in the rain.
In which storm looms the fabricating God?

I believe in prayer and the need to believe—
even the great Nothing signifying God.

Of Fidelity I've made such high style
that, jealous of my perfect devotion,
even the angels come down from Heaven
and beg—beg—me to stop worshipping God.

How come you simply do not age, Shahid?
Well, I wish everyone well, including God.

Tonight

Pale hands I loved beside the Shalimar
—Laurence Hope

Where are you now? Who lies beneath your spell tonight?
Whom else from rapture's road will you expel tonight?

Those "Fabrics of Cashmere—" "to make Me beautiful—"
"Trinket"—to gem—"Me to adorn—How tell"—tonight?

I beg for haven: Prisons, let open your gates—
A refugee from Belief seeks a cell tonight.

God's vintage loneliness has turned to vinegar—
All the archangels—their wings frozen—fell tonight.

Lord, cried out the idols, *Don't let us be broken;*
Only we can convert the infidel tonight.

Mughal ceilings, let your mirrored convexities
multiply me at once under your spell tonight.

He's freed some fire from ice in pity for Heaven.
He's left open—for God—the doors of Hell tonight.

In the heart's veined temple, all statues have been smashed.
No priest in saffron's left to toll its knell tonight.

God, limit these punishments, there's still Judgment Day—
I'm a mere sinner, I'm no infidel tonight.

Executioners near the woman at the window.
Damn you, Elijah, I'll bless Jezebel tonight.

The hunt is over, and I hear the Call to Prayer
fade into that of the wounded gazelle tonight.

My rivals for your love—you've invited them all?
This is mere insult, this is no farewell tonight.

And I, Shahid, only am escaped to tell thee—
God sobs in my arms. Call me Ishmael tonight.

Edward Hirsch

b. 1950

Away from Dogma

I was prevented by a sort of shame from going into churches . . . Nevertheless, I had three contacts with Catholicism that really counted.

SIMONE WEIL

1. IN PORTUGAL

One night in Portugal, alone in a forlorn
village at twilight, escaping her parents,
she saw a full moon baptized on the water
and the infallible heavens stained with clouds.

Vespers at eventide. A ragged procession
of fishermen's wives moving down to the sea,
carrying candles onto the boats, and singing
hymns of heartrending sadness. She thought:

this world is a smudged blue village
at sundown, the happenstance of stumbling
into the sixth canonical hour, discovering
the tawny sails of evening, the afflicted

religion of slaves. She thought: I am
one of those slaves, but I will not kneel
before Him, at least not now, not with
these tormented limbs that torment me still.

God is not manifest in this dusky light
and humiliated flesh: He is not among us.
But still the faith of the fishermen's wives
lifted her toward them, and she thought:

this life is a grave, mysterious moment
of hearing voices by the water and seeing
olive trees stretching out in the dirt,
of accepting the heavens cracked with rain.

2. IN ASSISI

To stand on the parcel of land where the saint
knelt down and married Lady Poverty, to walk
through the grasses of the Umbrian hills
where he scolded wolves and preached

to doves and jackdaws, where he chanted
canticles to the creatures who share our earth,
praising Brother Sun who rules the day,
Sister Moon who brightens the night.

Brother Fire sleeps in the arms of Sister Water.
Brother Wind kisses Sister Earth so tenderly.
To carry a picnic and eat whatever he ate—
bread and wine, the fare of tourists and saints.

She disliked the Miracles in the Gospels.
She never believed in the mystery of contact,
here below, between a human being and God.
She despised popular tales of apparitions.

But that afternoon in Assisi she wandered
through the abominable Santa Maria degli Angeli
and happened upon a little marvel of Romanesque
purity where St. Francis liked to pray.

She was there a short time when something absolute
and omnivorous, something she neither believed
nor disbelieved, something she understood—
but what was it?—forced her to her knees.

3. AT SOLESMES

From Palm Sunday to Easter Tuesday,
from Matins to Vespers and beyond, from
each earthly sound that hammered her skull
and entered her bloodstream, from the headaches

she sent into the universe and took back
into her flesh, from the suffering body
to the suffering mind, from the unholy breath
to the memories that never forgot her—

the factory whistle and the branding-iron
of the masters, the sixty-hour work week
and the machine that belched into her face,
the burns that blossomed on her arms—

from whatever weighs us down to whatever
lifts us up, from whatever mutilates us
to whatever spirits us away, from soul
descending to soul arising, moment by moment

she felt the body heaped up and abandoned
in the corner, the skin tasted and devoured;
she felt an invisible hand wavering
over the rags she was leaving behind.

Between the voices chanting and her own recitation,
between the heartbeats transfigured to prayer,
between the word *forsaken* and the word *joy*,
God came down a possessed her.

James Richardson

b. 1950

Evening Prayer

How can we blame you for what we have made of you,
war, panic rulings, desperate purity?
Who can blame us? Lord knows, we are afraid of time,
terrible, wonderful time, the only thing not yours.
Granted, we heard what we wanted to hear,
were sentenced, therefore, to our own strange systems
whose main belief was that we should believe.

You, of course, are not religious, don't need any rules
that can he disobeyed, have no special people,
and since a god, choosing (this the myths got right),
becomes human, avoided choices
in general, which is why there is Everything,
even imagination, which thinks it imagines
what isn't, an error you leave uncorrected.

The rumor you were dead, you, I think,
suggested, letting us go with only *Pray*
into what you had made. By which you meant,
I know, nothing the divine accountants
could tote up on their abaci *click click*,
but to widen like a pupil in the dark.
To be a lake, on which the overhanging pine,
the late-arriving stars, and all the news of men,
weigh as they will, are peacefully received,
to hear within the silence not quite silence
your prayer to us, *Live kindly, live.*

Arthur Sze

b. 1950

The Unnamable River

I

Is it in the anthracite face of a coal miner,
crystalized in the veins and lungs of a steel
worker, pulverized in the grimy hands of a railroad engineer?
Is it in a child naming a star, coconuts washing
ashore, dormant in a volcano along the Rio Grande?

You can travel the four thousand miles of the Nile
to its source and never find it.
You can climb the five highest peaks of the Himalayas
and never recognize it.
You can gaze through the largest telescope
and never see it.

But it's in the capillaries of your lungs.
It's in the space as you slice open a lemon.
It's in a corpse burning on the Ganges,
in rain splashing on banana leaves.

Perhaps you have to know you are about to die
to hunger for it. Perhaps you have to go
alone into the jungle armed with a spear
to truly see it. Perhaps you have to
have pneumonia to sense its crush.

But it's also in the scissor hands of a clock.
It's in the precessing motion of a top
when a torque makes the axis of rotation describe a cone:
and the cone spinning on a point gathers
past, present, future.

2

In a crude theory of perception, the apple you
see is supposed to be a copy of the actual apple,
but who can step out of his body to compare the two?
Who can step out of his life and feel
the Milky Way flow out of his hands?

An unpicked apple dies on a branch;
that is all we know of it.
It turns black and hard, a corpse on the Ganges.
Then go ahead and map out three thousand miles of the
Yangtze;
walk each inch, feel its surge and
flow as you feel the surge and flow in your own body.

And the spinning cone of a precessing top
is a form of existence that gathers and spins death and life into one.
It is in the duration of words, but beyond words–
river river river, river river.
The coal miner may not know he has it.
The steel worker may not know he has it.
The railroad engineer may not know he has it.
But it is there. It is in the smell
of an avocado blossom, and in the true passion of a kiss.

Chase Twichell

b. 1950

Cloud of Unknowing

In spring, the apple and cherry trees are clouds
in twenty shades of pink. Yet always,
behind them, a vaster radiance flares.
What I see, I see through drifts and veils—
there must be cloud in me too.

Snow is a cloud of distracting beauty,
its tiny sharp flowers aloft with weight
they can't bear. Each question must have a body.
I know my body, so what is my question?
Who speaks to me out of the blossoming cloud?

Bill Wadsworth

b. 1950

The Authority of Elsewhere

for Agha Shahid Ali

Smiling unconsciously under the Northern Lights,
the authority of elsewhere
sleeps in my bed.
I shamble in with my entire entourage of appetites
demanding to be fed,
but her authority lies unconscious in my bed.
I want the particulars of her appearance.
I beat my claws on the empty air
because I want to live in her lively head,
I want my incoherent prayer
to awaken her coherence.

The atmosphere is turning red
but she continues dreaming in my bed.
Wherever I go, she goes
one step ahead
into foreign languages
I have never understood.
She is Asia. She languishes
in some further wood
where no one knows
the meaning of what is said.
Her eyes are closed. She's in my bed.

Shall I take a photograph
to prove that she existed here,

that my bed was warm enough for her,
that the possibility of happiness
is never exhausted so long
as I can see it? That there is no abyss
between the astronomer and the star,
nor any universal grief
that whispers we are far, far
from what it is we want in life?
But the photograph is wrong—

she illustrates a law
that postulates the heart:
if the heart grows a body, the body grows a paw,
the paw begins to think what part
it wants to play. Whatever it might reach,
whatever we touch,
whatever is stolen, constructed, caressed, or bought
is the fateful destination of the heart.
So any thoughts that circle in my head
are only photographs pretending to be art—
the authority of elsewhere posing in my bed.

A woman in the marketplace
in Oaxaca is picturesque.
The history of sunlight has imprinted on her face
the stark topography of a mask.
I took her picture but I'm not there:
I stare into her eyes which are placed upon my desk
and I think her life continues, or has ended, elsewhere.
Thus Mexico and Africa and Asia rise into the mist
as pyramids and history and hieroglyphs which we at best
under northern lights are qualified to dream about.
In a dream I wander out

beyond these premises to prove
that extravagant darkness is what I love.
I am searching for the ground.
I am told there is a fabulous beast
which certain populations east

of here consider sacred,
or so they say or so I've read,
or so, according to some authority, is not an unfounded
fact. The authority of elsewhere sleeps in my bed,
she is undercover, she is naked,
she leaves every word unsaid.

Jorie Graham

b. 1951

Prayer

Am I still in the near distance
where all things are overlooked
if one just passes by. Do you pass
by?
I love the idea of consequence.
Is that itself consequence—(the idea)?
I have known you to be cheap
(as in not willing to pay out the extra
length of
blessing, weather, ignorance—all other
[you name them] forms of exodus).
What do I (call) you after all the necessary
ritual and protocol
is undertaken? Only-diminished?
Great-and steady-perishing? Unloosening
thirst,
or thirst unloosening ribbony storylines
with births
and history's ever-tightening
plot
attached? We're in too deep the bluebird
perched on
the seaweed-colored
limb (fringed with sky as with ever-lightening echoes of
those selfsame light-struck weeds, those seas)

seems to be chattering at me. Too deep?
Someplace that is all speech?
Someplace everything can be said to be
about?
Will we all know if it's blindness, this
way of seeing
when it becomes
apparent? Is there, in fact [who could
tell me
this?] a
we? Where? The distances have everything in their
grip of
in-betweenness.
For better [she said] or for worse [he said]
taking their place alongside the thirst
in line, something vaguely audible about
the silence
(a roar
actually)(your sea at night) but not as
fretful nor as monstrously tender
as the sea wind-driven was
earlier on
in "creation." Oh creation!
What a mood that was. Seeding then dragging-up life and
death in swatches
for us to forage in. Needle, story, knot, the
knot bit off,
the plunging-in of its silvery proposal,
stitch stitch still clicks
the bird still on
its limb, still in the mood, at the very edge
of the giddy
woods
through which even this sharpest noon must
bleed, ripped into
flickering bits.
But it is nothing compared to us
is it, that drip and strobe of the old-world's
gold

passaging-through,
nothing bending its forwardness, nothing
being bent
by it (though the wind, rattling the whole business,
would make one think
it so). Nothing
compared. And yet it is
there, truly there, in all sizes, that dry
creation—
woods, dappling melancholias of singled-out
limb-ends, lichened trunk-
flanks—shocked
transparencies as if a rumor's just passed
through
leaving this trail of inconclusive
trembling bits of some
momentous story.
Was it true, this time, the rumor?
The wherefore of our being here?
Does it *come* true in the retelling?
and truer in
the re-
presenting? It looks like laughter as the
wind picks up and the blazing is tossed
from branch to branch, dead bits, live
bits,
new growth taking the light less brightly than
the blown-out lightning-strikes. Look:
it is as if you are remembering
the day
you were born. The *you*. The newest witness. Bluish then
empurpling then
pink and ready to begin continuing.
Lord of objects. Lord of bleeding and self-
expression.
I keep speaking this to you, as if in pity
at the gradual filling of the vacancy
by my very own gaze etcetera. Also the
words—here and here—hoping

this thing—along with all else that
                                        wears-out—will
                                        do. I think
about you. Yet is only *thinking* omnipresent?
Omniscience, omnipotence: that is all drama.
But omnipresence: time all over the
                                                        place!
It's like a trance, this time unspooling in
                                                          this telling.
Like land one suspects must be there, but where?
The ocean kisses every inch of the seeable.
We live. We speak at the horizon. After a
                                                    while even the
                                                    timidity
wears off. One speaks. One is not mad.
One lives so long one feels the *noticing*
                                            in all one sees.
                                            Years. Chapters.
Someone is asking for your hand. One turns
                                                            to speak.
One wishes so one could be interrupted.

Joy Harjo

b. 1951

A Map to the Next World

for Desiray Kierra Chee

In the last days of the fourth world I wished to make a map for
    those who would climb through the hole in the sky.

My only tools were the desires of humans as they emerged from
    the killing fields, from the bedrooms and the kitchens.

For the soul is a wanderer with many hands and feet.

The map must be of sand and can't be read by ordinary light. It
must carry fire to the next tribal town, for renewal of spirit.

In the legend are instructions on the language of the land, how it
was we forgot to acknowledge the gift, as if we were not in it
or of it.

Take note of the proliferation of supermarkets and malls, the
altars of money. They best describe the detour from grace.

Keep track of the errors of our forgetfulness; the fog steals our
children while we sleep.

Flowers of rage spring up in the depression. Monsters are born
there of nuclear anger.

Trees of ashes wave good-bye to good-bye and the map appears
to disappear.

We no longer know the names of the birds here, how to speak to
them by their personal names.

Once we knew everything in this lush promise.

What I am telling you is real and is printed in a warning on the
map. Our forgetfulness stalks us, walks the earth behind us,
leaving a trail of paper diapers, needles, and wasted blood.

An imperfect map will have to do, little one.

The place of entry is the sea of your mother's blood, your
father's small death as he longs to know himself in another.

There is no exit.

The map can be interpreted through the wall of the intestine—a
spiral on the road of knowledge.

You will travel through the membrane of death, smell cooking
from the encampment where our relatives make a feast of
fresh deer meat and corn soup, in the Milky Way.

They have never left us; we abandoned them for science.

And when you take your next breath as we enter the fifth world
there will be no *X*, no guidebook with words you can carry.

You will have to navigate by your mother's voice, renew the song
she is singing.

Fresh courage glimmers from planets.

And lights the map printed with the blood of history, a map you
will have to know by your intention, by the language of suns.

When you emerge note the tracks of the monster slayers where
they entered the cities of artificial light and killed what was
killing us.

You will see red cliffs. They are the heart, contain the ladder.

A white deer will greet you when the last human climbs from the
destruction.

Remember the hole of shame marking the act of abandoning
our tribal grounds.

We were never perfect.

Yet, the journey we make together is perfect on this earth who
was once a star and made the same mistakes as humans.

We might make them again, she said.

Crucial to finding the way is this: there is no beginning or end.

You must make your own map.

Garrett Hongo

b. 1951

O-Bon: Dance for the Dead

I have no memories or photograph of my father
coming home from war, thin as a caneworker,
a splinter of flesh in his olive greens
and khakis and spit-shined G.I. shoes;

Or of my grandfather in his flower-print shirt,
humming his bar-tunes, tying the bandana
to his head to hold the sweat back from his face
as he bent to weed and hoe the garden that Sunday
while swarms of planes maneuvered overhead.

I have no memories of the radio that day
or the clatter of machetes in the Filipino camp,
the long wail of news from over the mountains,
or the glimmerings and sheaths of fear in the village.

I have no story to tell about lacquer shrines
or filial ashes, about a small brass bell,
and incense smoldering in jade bowls, about the silvered,
black face of Miroku gleaming with detachment,
anthurium crowns in the stoneware vase
the hearts and wheels of fire behind her:

And though I've mapped and studied the strike march
from the North Shore to town in 1921, though I've
sung psalms at festival and dipped the bamboo cup
in the stone bowl on the Day of the Dead,
though I've pitched coins and took my turn
at the *taiko* drum, and folded paper fortunes
and strung them on the graveyard's *hala* tree;

Though I've made a life and raised my house
oceans east of my birth, though I've craned
my neck and cocked my ear for the sound of flute
and *shamisen* jangling its tune of woe—

The music nonetheless echoes in its slotted box,
the cold sea chafes the land and swirls over gravestones,
and wind sighs its passionless song through ironwood trees.

More than memory or the image of the slant of grey rain
pounding the thatch coats and peaked hats
of townsmen racing across the blond arch of a bridge,
more than the past and its aches and brocade
of tales and ritual, its dry mouth of repetition,

I want the cold stone in my hand to pound the earth,
I want the splash of cool or steaming water to wash my feet,
I want the dead beside me when I dance, to help me
flesh the notes of my song, to tell me it's all right.

Volcano House

for Charles Wright

Mists in the lantern ferns,
                    green wings furled against the cold,
and a mountain wind
                    starts its low moan through *ohia* trees.
The lava land blazes in primrose and thimbleberry,
scented fires of pink and blue
                    racing through jungled underbrush.
I'm out feeding chickens,
                    slopping a garbage of melon seeds and rind
over the broken stones and woodrot of the forest path.
I'm humming a blues,
                    some old song about China Nights
and boarding a junk,
                    taking me from my village.

Miles in the distance,
Kilauea steams and vents
through its sulphurous roads,
and a yellow light spills through
a faultline in the clouds,
glazing the slick beaks of the feeding chickens,
shining in their eyes
like the phosphorous glow
from a cave tunneled miles through the earth.
What was my face before I was born?
the white mask and black teeth
at the bottom of the pond? What is the mind's insensible,
the gateless gate?
Through overgrowth and the leaning drizzle,
through the pile and dump of tree fern
and the indigoed snare of lasiandra
shedding its collars of sadness by the broken fence,
I make my way down a narrow path
to the absolute and the house of my last days,
a dazzle of light scripting in the leaves and on the weeds,
tremors in the shivering trees.

Andrew Hudgins

b. 1951

Christ as a Gardener

The boxwoods planted in the park spell LIVE.
I never noticed it until they died.
Before, the entwined green had smudged the word
unreadable. And when they take their own advice
again—come spring, come Easter—no one will know
a word is buried in the leaves. I love the way
that Mary thought her resurrected Lord
a gardener. It wasn't just the broad-brimmed hat
and muddy robe that fooled her: he was *that* changed.
He looks across the unturned field, the riot

of unscythed grass, the smattering of wildflowers.
Before he can stop himself, he's on his knees.
He roots up stubborn weeds, pinches the suckers,
deciding order here—what lives, what dies,
and how. But it goes deeper even than that.
His hands burn and his bare feet smolder. He longs
to lie down inside the long, dew-moist furrows
and press his pierced side and his broken forehead
into the dirt. But he's already done it—
passed through one death and out the other side.
He laughs. He kicks his bright spade in the earth
and turns it over. Spring flashes by, then harvest.
Beneath his feet, seeds dance into the air.
They rise, and he, not noticing, ascends
on midair steppingstones of dandelion,
of milkweed, thistle, cattail, and goldenrod.

Judith Ortiz Cofer

b. 1952

The Campesino's Lament

It is Ash Wednesday, and Christ is waiting
to die. I have left my fields dark and moist
from last night's rain, to take the sacrament.
My face is streaked with ashes. Come back,
Mujer. Without you,
  I am an empty place
where spiders crawl and nothing takes root.
Today, taking the Host, I remembered
your hands—incense and earth, fingertips
like white grapes I would take into my mouth
one by one.
  When I enter the house,
it resists me like an angry woman. Our room,
your things, the bed—a penance
I offer up for Lent. Waking with you,
I would fill myself with the morning,

in sweet mango breaths. Watching you sleep,
I willed my dreams into you.

But clouds cannot be harvested, nor children
wished into life.

In the wind that may travel
as far as you have gone, I send this message: Out here,
in a place you will not forget, a simple man
has been moved to curse the rising sun and to question
God's unfinished work.

Chard DeNiord

b. 1952

Transubstantiation

I said yes immediately when you asked if I believed
in it   and I didn't feel that foolish for saying so
although I did feel foolish afterwards in thinking
about it   for there was nothing I could say to prove it
I only knew that it was true in another way that made
religious sense   in *linking back* to a metaphor that kept
its word   that loved the body as well as mind and took
another form by which we came to call something else
the blood and body of Christ   fully conscious then
of the difference between the *substitute* and flesh itself
which was so mutable in his duress that vanity proposed
to death   and fruit transformed from words to flesh
or else His voice lacked the strength to bear a hazelnut
from nothingness   the taste of *it* quite moot as long
as we believe   lives in us in such a way that we could say
with confidence that this was that and that was this because
he said it was and what he said was not a metaphor in the way
we think   in curious ways that made us feel and see anew
and think again   but not believe in bleeding bread
I mean my love *was* the rose of Sharon but only because

she inspired this while staying herself and knowing
the difference   hearts were prone to such fallaciousness
yet when we said *we take this bread* our hearts were seized
by what was possible   which was *all things* but not everything
you see   which was absurd and mystical   which was
the Paraclete becoming a meal and entering *our* bodies
like an idea   but not an idea since the host was form
already   and fusing him with us in prayer   but only then
when we were ready and knew the presence of his body as real
if changed for a while   for the sake of becoming him

Rita Dove

b. 1952

Receiving the Stigmata

There is a way to enter a field
empty-handed, your shoulder
behind you and air tightening.

The kite comes by itself,
a spirit on a fluttering string.

Back when people died for
the smallest reasons, there was
always a field to walk into.
Simple men fell to their knees
below the radiant crucifix
and held out their palms

in relief. Go into the field
and it will reward. Grace

is a string growing straight
from the hand. Is
the hatchet's shadow on the
rippling green.

Mark Jarman

b. 1952

Transfiguration

And there appeared to them Elijah and Moses
and they were talking to Jesus.
Mark 9:2

I

They were talking to him about resurrection, about law, about
the suffering ahead.
They were talking as if to remind him who he was and who they
were. He was not
Like his three friends watching a little way off, not like the crowd
At the foot of the hill. A gray-green thunderhead massed from
the sea
And God spoke from it and said he was his. They were talking
About how the body, broken or burned, could live again,
remade.
Only the fiery text of the thunderhead could explain it. And they
were talking
About pain and the need for judgement and how he would make
himself
A law of pain, both its spirit and its letter in his own flesh, and
then break it,
That is, transcend it. His clothes flared like magnesium, as they
talked.

2

When we brought our mother to him, we said, "Lord, she falls
down the stairs.
She cannot hold her water. In the afternoon she forgets the
morning."

And he said, "All things are possible to those who believe. Shave her head,
Insert a silicone tube inside her skull, and run it under her scalp,
Down her neck, and over her collarbone, and lead it into her stomach."
And we did and saw that she no longer stumbled or wet herself.
She could remember the morning until the evening came. And we went our way,
Rejoicing as much as we could, for we had worried many years.

3

They were talking to him about heaven, how all forms there were luciform,
How the leather girdle and the matted hair, how the lice coursing the skin
And the skin skinned alive, blaze with perfection, the vibrance of light.
And they were talking about the complexities of blood and lymph,
Each component crowding the vessels, the body and the antibody,
And they were talking about the lamp burning in the skull's niche,
The eyes drinking light from within and light from without,
And how simple it is to see the future, if you looked at it like the past,
And how the present belonged to the flesh and its density and darkness
And was hard to talk about. Before and after were easier. They talked about light.

4

A man came to him who said he had been blind since his wedding day
And had never seen his wife under the veil or the children she had given him.

And the Lord said, "'Tell me about your parents." And the man talked
A long time, remembering how his mother cut his father's meat at dinner,
And how at night their voices crept along his bedroom ceiling, like—
But he could not say what they were like. And in the morning, everything began to tick
And ticked all day as if. . . . Now, he remembered!
And suddenly his sight came back and blinded him, like a flashbulb.

5

They were talking to him about law and how lawgiving should be
Like rainfall, a light rain falling all morning and mixing with dew—
A rain that passes through the spiderweb and penetrates the dirt clod
Without melting it, a persistent, suffusing shower, soaking clothes,
Making sweatshirts heavier, wool stink, and finding every hair's root on the scalp.
And that is when you hurled judgement into the crowd and watched them
Spook like cattle, reached in and stirred the turmoil faster, scarier.
And they were saying that; to save the best, many must be punished,
Including the best. And no one was exempt, as they explained it,
Not themselves, not him, or anyone he loved, anyone who loved him.

6

Take anyone and plant a change inside them that they feel
And send them to an authority to assess that feeling.
When they are told

That for them alone there waits a suffering in accordance with the laws
Of their condition, from which they may recover or may not,
Then they know the vortex on the mountaintop, the inside of the unspeakable,
The speechlessness before the voices begin talking to them,
Talking to prepare them, arm them and disarm them, until the end.
And if anybody's looking, they will seem transfigured.

7

I want to believe that he talked back to them, his radiant companions,
And I want to believe he said too much was being asked and too much promised.
I want to believe that that was why he shone in the eyes of his friends,
The witnesses looking on, because he spoke for them, because he loved them
And was embarrassed to learn how he and they were going to suffer.
I want to believe he resisted at that moment, when he appeared glorified,
Because he could not reconcile the contradictions and suspected
That love had a finite span and was merely the comfort of the lost.
I know he must have acceded to his duty, but I want to believe
He was transfigured by resistance, as he listened, and they talked.

Naomi Shihab Nye

b. 1952

My Uncle Mohammed at Mecca, 1981

This year the wheels of cars
are stronger than the wheels of prayer.
Where were you standing when it hit you,
what blue dome rose up in your heart?

I hold the birds you sent me,
olivewood clumsily carved.
The only thing I have
that you touched.

Why is it so many singulars
attend your name? You lived on one mountain,
sent one gift. You went on one journey
and didn't come home.

We search for the verb
that keeps a man complete.
To resign, to disappear, that's how
I've explained you.

Now I want to believe it was true.
Because you lived apart,
we hold you up. Because no word connected us,
we complete your sentence.

And your house with wind in the windows
instead of curtains
is the house we are building
in the cities of the world.

Uncle of sadness, this is the last pretense:
you understood the world was no pilgrim,
and were brave, and wise,
and wanted to die.

Alberto Ríos

b. 1952

The Death of Anselmo Luna

Since he was the priest,
No one could say for certain about Anselmo Luna.
What began as a lark
One slow afternoon of interminable chores
Regarding candles and residue on the walls,
Became his drawings:
First of the saints,
Then the twelve Stations of the Cross,
The sketches of simpler remembrances.
All of these chiaroscuros he made
In and from the soot on the walls of this church,
A work that moved into years
And which finally filled his life.
What began as a lark became the seed
Of his miracle, a simple
Moving of a finger along a pillar
Just to see, was there enough
To require cleansing,
This test also used on parked cars,
A line spelling *wash me* in the soil of a window.
He died while perched on a ladder
High behind the altar, underneath
The fine woodwork: that moment
As he fell, and as he made a mark
Not unlike a moustache
Where none should have been,
He died already partway

Toward heaven. It was said
His soul took the advantage,
Leaping out from his body
Right there, stepping from his ribs
As he had stepped
On the rungs of the ladder.
It was a strong soul, muscular,
On account of his years of devoted effort,
And it knew like an animal what to do
When the moment came.

Alan Shapiro

b. 1952

Prayer on the Temple Steps

Devious guide, strange parent,
what are you
but the movable ways
I lose you by?
Opulent honeycomb
of nowhere
where the bee-ghosts cluster,
hymning your each cell
with all the sweetness that you hold
from me,
so I might know
instead the fitful aspic
of this readiness—
what is it
you bring out of the veils
of air but this, these words—
gate opening on to you
and burning sword
above it turning
every way I turn.

Gjertrud Schnackenberg

b. 1953

Supernatural Love

My father at the dictionary-stand
Touches the page to fully understand
The lamplit answer, tilting in his hand

His slowly scanning magnifying lens,
A blurry, glistening circle he suspends
Above the word "Carnation." Then he bends

So near his eyes are magnified and blurred,
One finger on the miniature word,
As if he touched a single key and heard

A distant, plucked, infinitesimal string,
"The obligation due to every thing
That's smaller than the universe." I bring

My sewing needle close enough that I
Can watch my father through the needle's eye,
As through a lens ground for a butterfly

Who peers down flower-hallways toward a room
Shadowed and fathomed as this study's gloom
Where, as a scholar bends above a tomb

To read what's buried there, he bends to pore
Over the Latin blossom. I am four,
I spill my pins and needles on the floor

Trying to stitch "Beloved" X by X.
My dangerous, bright needle's point connects
Myself illiterate to this perfect text

I cannot read. My father puzzles why
It is my habit to identify
Carnations as "Christ's flowers," knowing I

Can give no explanation but "Because."
Word-roots blossom in speechless messages
The way the thread behind my sampler does

Where following each X I awkward move
My needle through the word whose root is love.
He reads, "A pink variety of Clove,

Carnatio, the Latin, meaning flesh."
As if the bud's essential oils brush
Christ's fragrance through the room, the iron-fresh

Odor carnations have floats up to me,
A drifted, secret, bitter ecstasy,
The stems squeak in my scissors, *Child, it's me*,

He turns the page to "Clove" and reads aloud:
"The clove, a spice, dried from a flower-bud."
Then twice, as if he hasn't understood,

He reads, "From French, for *clou*, meaning a nail."
He gazes, motionless. "Meaning a nail."
The incarnation blossoms, flesh and nail,

I twist my threads like stems into a knot
And smooth "Beloved," but my needle caught
Within the threads, *Thy blood so dearly bought*,

The needle strikes my finger to the bone.
I lift my hand, it is myself I've sewn,
The flesh laid bare, the threads of blood my own,

I lift my hand in startled agony
And call upon his name, "Daddy Daddy"—
My father's hand touches the injury

As lightly as he touched the page before,
Where incarnation bloomed from roots that bore
The flowers I called Christ's when I was four.

Rosanna Warren

b. 1953

Hagar

And the water was spent in the bottle, and
she cast the child under one of the shrubs.
Gen. 21:15

Was it a mountain wavering on the rim
of sky, or only air, shaken like a flame?
Dust stung my nostrils. Lizards fled
over the sharp track where my feet had bled.
My sandal thongs were broken. The water was gone.
I cracked the jar, it cracked like an old bone.
Lord of the desert, did you bless
that birth? Bonded to Abraham, did I guess
his wilderness? He thrust
us out from the squandering of his lust
after I'd framed its future. Hers as well,
griping mistress whose belly would not swell,
witch whose hair I brushed and wound in braids,
whose robe I stitched, whose veil I decked with beads
to snag his pleasure. What was left my own?
Not my bought body, surely. Not my son.
Only that core of shock from which he surged,
the spasm that unbonded me, and purged
me of Master and Mistress and the Lord.
I pressed my knees to the rock, and poured
my body out like sand across the sand.
Not to see him die, I pressed my hand
into my sockets, but his cry broke through
all bone and fiber, shattered the sealed blue
of heaven to wound your vast and hovering ear,

Lord of the desert, Lord who cannot hear
our prayers, but the deathwail of a child
startling from the rootclutch in the wild.
You are the God of stone and stony eyes
and water dripping through stone crevices
to the swollen tongue that cannot taste your name.
Lord of thistle and mica. Here I am.

Cyprian

Phi Beta Kappa Poem, Yale 2000

We could almost see her
where she is said to have risen in the bay
from sea foam and the blood of Ouranos' sliced genitals
tossed out of heaven.

We could almost see
how she must have sat on the long arm of rock
that half-cradled the bay
and how she combed seaweed out of her hair with a scallop shell

before rising in a commotion of salt light and doves' wings
to terrorize the earth.
Squinting, we could almost believe
as we could almost see

inland, at Paphos, her temple erect
on the ruined marble floor paving
amid column chunks and cringing olive trees
as the horizon trembled in haze

and distant mountains tried in their softness to resemble the
female body.
But it was inside
that shed of a museum across the spongy road, our eyes
maladjusted to dimness, that

she appeared, I think: if it is in
the sudden intake of breath, the fluttered pulse, that she
registers:
not as one would have imagined,
no body at all, no womanliness,

not Greek, not even human as a god should be,
but that uncarven black vertical basalt thrust
into consciousness
throbbed in the room alone,

just a rock
on a pedestal, a terrible rock
they worshipped epochs ago before the Greeks
gave her a name a story a shape:

a rock in the dark for which we had paid in Cypriot coins,
for which we still clutched
small paper tickets, damp in our palms.
When I have fought you

most, when we have lain
separate in the puzzle of sheets
until dawn flushed away clots of night, and still we lay apart:
she was there, she presided—

she of the many names:
sea-goddess; foam-goddess; heavenly
Ourania crowned, braceleted and beringed in gold and gems;
Melaina the black one; Skotia, dark one;

Killer of Men; Gravedigger; She-Upon-the-Graves;
Pasiphaessa the Far-Shining;
and she to whom we sacrificed,
Aphrodite Apostrophia,

She Who Turns Herself Away.

Antique

It doesn't happen these days, the retinal shock when
one of them slips by, shoots

a glance, is gone—We were singed but
kept breathing. They don't

appear, after childhood. But
if he were to shiver into view, that

other one—lowercase kouros, lithe—
if he were to slide into sunlight here,

it would be on such a day: silver flakes
brisking in the woods as wind

whisks off mist and rainspatter, bark
ignites, birches sway: he can only step

from deepest shade. Do we have
darks enough to afford him

light? Over the pond, it's bronze, a Mycenaean
blade, black light smelted, that cleaves

sky from water, cirrus from leaf: he'd rise
from the gash, the core

of arterial night. He knows
the weight and lightness of a sword, how one flesh falls

from another, and both are true as he stands
in his gleam of rain, godsweat, oil. We know it

differently. By clasping—which is all we know
how, in our heaviness, to do—clasping

subtraction, and hearing it cry aloud, nightly, in our arms.

Scott Cairns

b. 1954

Prospect of the Interior

A little daunting, these periodic
incursions into what is, after all,
merely suspected territory.

One can determine nothing from the low
and, I'm afraid, compromised perspective
of the ship, save that the greenery is thick,

and that the shoreline is, in the insufficient
light of morning and evening, frequently
obscured by an unsettling layer of mist.

If there are inhabitants, they've chosen
not to show themselves. Either they fear us,
or they prefer ambush to open threat.

We'd not approach the interior at all
except for recurrent, nagging doubts
about the seaworthiness of our craft.

So, as a matter of course, necessity
mothers us into taking stock of our
provisions, setting out in trembling parties

of one, trusting the current, the leaky
coracle, the allocated oar.

Louise Erdrich

b. 1954

New Vows

The night was clean as the bone of a rabbit blown hollow.
I cast my hood of dogskin
away, and my shirt of nettles.
Ten years had been enough. I left my darkened house.

The trick was in living that death to its source.
When it happened, I wandered toward more than I was.

Widowed by men, I married the dark firs,
as if I were walking in sleep toward their arms.
I drank, without fear or desire,
this odd fire.

Now shadows move freely within me as words.
These are eternal, these stunned, loosened verbs.
And I can't tell you yet
how truly I belong

to the hiss and shift of wind,
these slow, variable mouths
through which, at certain times, I speak in tongues.

Thylias Moss

b. 1954

The Warmth of Hot Chocolate

Somebody told me I didn't exist even though he was looking dead at me. He said that since I defied logic, I wasn't real for reality is one of logic's definitions. He said I was a contradiction in terms, that one side of me cancelled out the other side leaving nothing. His shaking knees were like polite maracas in the small clicking they made. His moustache seemed a misplaced smile. My compliments did not deter him from insisting he conversed with an empty space since there was no such thing as an angel who doesn't believe in God. I showed him where my wings had been recently trimmed. Everybody thinks they grow out of the back, some people even assume shoulder blades are all that man has left of past glory, but my wings actually grow from my scalp, a heavy hair that stiffens for flight by the release of chemical secretions activated whenever I jump off a bridge. Many angels are discovered when people trying to commit suicide ride and tame the air. I was just such an accident. We're simply a different species, not intrinsically holy, just intrinsically airborne. Demons have practical reasons for not flying; it's too hot in their home base to endure all the hair; besides, the heat makes the chemicals boil away so demons plummet when they jump and keep falling. Their home base isn't solid. Demons fall perpetually, deeper and deeper into evil until they reach a level where even to ascend is to fall.

I think God covets my wings. He forgot to create some for himself when he was forging himself out of pure thoughts rambling through the universe on the backs of neutrons. Pure thoughts were the original cowboys. I suggested to God that he jump off a bridge to activate the wings he was sure to have, you never forget yourself when you divvy up the booty, but he didn't have enough faith that his fall wouldn't be endless. I suggested that he did in fact create wings for himself but had forgotten; his first godly act had been performed a long time ago, afterall.

I don't believe in him; he's just a comfortable acquaintance, a close associate with whom I can be myself. To believe in him would place him in the center of the universe when he's more secure in the fringes, the farthest corner so that he doesn't have to look over his shoulder to nab the backstabbers who want promotions but are tired of waiting for him to die and set in motion the natural evolution. God doesn't want to evolve. Has been against evolution from its creation. He doesn't figure many

possibilities are open to him. I think he's wise to bide his time
although he pales in the moonlight to just a glow, just the
warmth of hot chocolate spreading through the body like
a subcutaneous halo. But to trust him implicitly would be a
mistake for he then would not have to maintain his worthiness
to be God. Even the thinnest, flyweight modicum of doubt gives
God the necessity to prove he's worthy of the implicit trust I can
never give because I protect him from corruption, from the
complacence that rises within him sometimes, a shadowy
ever-descending brother.

A Man

How handsome he was, that man who did not court
the girls fawning all over him as if he'd already saved them,
it's my leg, one said, raising her hem as she'd raised it in dreams
he knew of, for everything reached him as prayer, *my leg, Sir,*
is not perfect although as he looked, it glistened and the blood
became more productive. He did not date, nor rendezvous in tunnels and tents,
did not kiss except to heal, did not harass, malign nor mutilate;
threew no stones

and he was a man; never forget that he was a man,

that being a man improved him. Before the mothering, He was a solo act
ramming omnipotence down the throats of Ramses, Job, all the sinning nobodies
of Sodom. He was feared before he was born a triplet of flesh completing
the one vaporous, the other heavy and strict; now he's desirable, vulnerable;
in the mother he visited stages of: fig, fish, pig, chicken, chimp before settling irrevocably
on a form more able to strive. This was a more significant time in darkness,
gestation of forty weeks, than three days in a hillside morgue; he learned maternal heartbeat

and circulation of her blood so well they became dependency,
and so he learned that some radiance is not his, hers

came in large part just from being Mary—how content she was even before pregnancy,
betrothed, blushing to ripen the fields; content even before she knew of angels,
and now, with this mound of baby, she was parent of a world whose prospering
she encouraged, activity of fish, magma, sulfur, the earth striving just as she did.

He was a man
yet the usher of miracles, preaching on a mountain
where reverberation gave him the power of five thousand tongues, yet not
a big man, not athletic, ordinary looking except for that glow and doves circling
him in the desert, doves that had been vultures earning their transfiguration
by consuming decaying meat just as he ate all the sin; for that flattery, he bid them dip their
feathers in his eye, drawing into them that sweet milk around the iris.

He was a man
when he began to understand love, erasing the lines between
Gentile, Jew, and invited any who wanted to come to his father's house for bottomless milk,
honey, ripe fruit, baskets of warm bread and eggs, wine, live angels singing. Weary revelers
could lay their heads on his breast, he said, needing intimacy; he thinks
as a man, therefore
he is a man
and good times, memories can be
adequate heaven. He knows the distance a man
is from his father, how likely it increases till the deathbed; he knows

what a man knows

the now and here, and can be called by name,
and can be wounded, and must struggle, and must be proud
every now and then or could not continue, must be worth
something,
must be precious to himself and preferably to at least one other,
must be,
in these thousands of post-Neandertal years, improving, must
have
more potential, becoming not only more like God, but more like
what God needs to become, so moves also,
so God moves also

because a man moves.

John Burt

b. 1955

On the Will to Believe

Who is awake? The wind is awake.
But will you stir? Her wakefulness is part of yours.
Will you walk with her in the darkness?
Here is the star she stole for you alone.
She will show to you a tree of thorns,
Her empty hands, that broken bridge.
You will read in the book of faces
But you will not find your own.

And you will remember then to stop, to lie
Down still, to say that if there were a mark
It would be there, and there would demonstrate
The love, the will, the calm necessity.
The clouds will scud among the glaciers of the mountain.
The idiot moon will watch in the cold.

Sonnets for Mary of Nazareth

I

Our gods resemble us only in rage,
Where we are undissembled, undisclosed,
A cryptic self we'd never recognize,
Not what we are, not what we'd ever be,
But what escapes us, makes us real.
To find a god, we must break all things else,
Lest we be left with what he's like, not him.
In angry certitude, baffled gracefully,
We seek more cunning ways to disavow
What thrilled us once, when it could still be strange,
What stung us into truth with daring cruelty.
We want an idol made of restlessness.
That is the discontent the flesh would have
Hung over with a three days drunk of death.

II

Homer's gods, bored with endless life,
Loved mortals, whose fragile bodies puzzled them.
How suddenly they came apart! How little
One discovers after all from them.
There is some secret in them they don't know,
That shadows them in love, then intimates
Some deeper source, which sought for, vanishes.
One looks abashed into a glassy eye.

Achilles sought to kill his way to fame,
Immortal through excess, a man made god.
Wide-eyed, happy in the clash of shields,
It did not matter to him what he was.
Nor did he matter, till he saw in tears
Priam with his duty-smitten son.

III

Because he was so plain a god, so calm,
Riding at her heart like any child,
A stirring and attentive passenger
Wakeful in her wordless rush of breath,
She would have been amused, not terrified.
What did he have in mind? she thought at nights
While patient Joseph snored and shepherds woke.
It came to her at last: he didn't know;
He himself would catch it up from her.
What could he want, except to want like her?
To know what weakness is, and casualty,
How being done to teaches her to be,
How losing love enables her to learn
To make of fear her honor and of death her gift.

Robert Vasquez

b. 1955

Belief

for Jon and Ernesto

There are those—old aunts, far-off
godparents—whose houses seem ready
for ghosts: east of Madera, bricked
and scarred in the last century,
is the house my mother's aunt
lit candles in (though wired
for lights in '38; her parlor
nightly sent forth a dozen
"flamedrops"). A Stevens .22 pump
was found in the cellar, and a woman
in a black nightgown cried and walked
from shadows to the outhouse.
She was dead; she rose

some nights the way clouds
of insects lift from long grass—dark
breath of the earth, brief, wind-broken. . . .
Take care, they warn, these
death-long witnesses of grief
any hour can dole out, unresolved,
and flood the soul. Aunt Esther
gestured back with wick yarn alone.
"But don't worry," she said. "Most
never glimpse one; even more
think you're nuts if you do." But
belief can start anywhere, even here
in a plum orchard, wind-stirred
and radiating leaf-spurs, or out beyond
the old washroom where "someone
you can't touch, some stranger
doing eternal chores, touches you."

Susan Wheeler

b. 1955

That Been to Me My Lives Light and Saviour

Purse be full again, or else must I die. This is the wish
the trees in hell's seventh circle lacked, bark ripped by monstrous
dogs,
bleeding from each wound. We see them languid there,
the lightened purse a demon drug. *Less, less.*

At the canal, the dog loops trees in a figure eight—
a cacophony of insects under sun. A man against a tree nods off.

Let there be no sandwich for the empty purse.
Let there be no raiment for someone skint.
Let blood run out, let the currency remove.
Let that which troubles trouble not.

My father in the driveway. Legs splayed behind him. Pail beside
him.
Sorting handfuls of gravel by shade and size. One way to calm
a pecker, compensate for stash. *Dad!* I lied.

The man shifts by the tree and now grace is upon him.
The slant of sun picks up the coins dropped by travelers and—
lo!—
grace enables him to see. The demon dog fresh off an eight
barks, too,
standing, struck by the man, by the coins, barks at their glare;
the man reaches in scrim at the glint in the light and thinks
Another
malt. The flesh is willing, the spirit spent,
the cloud passes over—
relief is not what you think, not the light. Regard the barking
dog now tugging at the dead man's leg becoming bark.

You be my life, you be my heart's guide,
you be the provision providing more,
you be the blood—stanch the sore!—
you be failing
proportion (mete) . . .

Steward of gravel squints up at the girl who is me.
What? defensively. Out of the east woods, a foaming raccoon
spills.
Palmolive executive? Palmolive customer? Palm's stony olives
on the embankment of limestone or
soapstone or
shale. Leg of the man clamped in the dog's mouth. Mouth
of the man open and unmoved. Voice of the man:

Three dolls sat within a wood, and stared, and wet when it rained
into their kewpie mouths. They were mine to remonstrate to the
trees at large, the catalpas and the fir, the sugar maples in the
glade turning gold. To each is given, one doll began, so I had
to turn her off. Consider how it was for me—

Flash of the arrow and the foam falls down. Three balletists
ignoring pliés bound onto the long lawn and its canalward
slope. I am underwater and they haze in the light,
mouth
but do not sound. In the arrow's blink they start.

Decimal as piercing of the line—
Table as imposition of the grid—
Sum as heuristic apoplex—
Columns in honeysuckle cents—or not.

Just this transpired. Against a tree I swooned and fell, and
water seeped into my shoe, and a dream began to grow in me.
Or despair, and so I chose the dream. And while I slept,
I was being fed, and clothed, addressed—as though awake
with every faculty, and so it went. Then: blaze, blare of sun
after years uncounted, and synesthesia of it and sound,
the junco's chirp and then the jay's torn caw, arc
of trucks on the distant interstate, your *what the fuck*
and then her call. Beside me, pinned to a green leaf,
in plastic and neat hand, a full account. I had indeed still
lived, and been woke for more. So, weeping then, I rose.

April Bernard

b. 1956

Psalm of the Tree-Dweller

Do not reward those who walk at night with torches
threatening the feet of cobby oaks and birches silver with sorrow,
O God.

Do not smile upon those who spread the stink of kerosene
so that it thickens in the wren's wing
and scalds the throats of all your little ones,
O God.

Slay those who march with axe and adze,
who chop and pry for water.

Slay the tyrants:
the liontamer, fisherman, inquisitor, gossip, athlete, marksman,
O God.

Blot the sun on the forest floor
that they mine enemies drop dead into darkness.

Send your light to smile only in the feathered canopy
where I have with such difficulty climbed;
where I sway, drunk;
where it is yet rumored
I may look upon your face.

Lucie Brock-Broido

b. 1956

The One Theme of Which Everything Else Is a Variation

Innocence is a catarrh of the mind, distressed,
As finite as the grade school teacher in Sierra Leone

Whose arms were axed off only at the hand, first left
And then the right, and then his mouth as he was making noise

And should be shut. A man can learn to speak again,
But never pray.
Wisdom is experience bundled, with prosthetic
wrists.

I cannot master anymore the surgical or magical,
I do not know how the specific punishments or amputations are
so

Meted out. When you delete a wing or limb
From a creature's form, it will inevitably cry out against this

Taking, but in the end it will become grievously docile,
Shut; far gone old god, you have been plain.

Let me list here the things I wish to bring with me,
For the life after this or that. I will not go back the way I came,

Carrying my clay Picasso and my tin of ginger,
Flying toward home on my way away from home.

If I am lucky in this life, here, I will go on
Being whole, and speak again old god, I will be plain.

Henri Cole

b. 1956

Apollo

O let me clean my spirit of all doubt,
Give me the signature of what I am.
OVID, *The Metamorphoses,* II

I

With a shriek gulls fled across a black sky,
all of us under the pier were silent,
my blood ached from waiting, then we resumed.
"You're just like us," some bastard said;
and it was true: my hair was close-cropped,
my frame reposed against a piling, my teeth
glistened, my prick was stiff. Little by little
they had made me like them, raptly feeding
in silhouette, with exposed abdomen,
like a spider sating itself. For a moment,
I was the eye through which the universe

beheld itself, like God. And then I gagged,
stumbling through brute shadows to take a piss,
a fly investigating my wet face.

II

Stay married, God said. One marriage.
        Don't abortion. Ugly mortal sin.
Beautiful gorgeous Mary loves you
        so much. Heaven tremendous thrill
of ecstasy forever. What you are,
        they once was, God said, the beloved ones
before you; what they are, you will be.
        All the days. Don't fornicate. Pray be good.
Serpent belly thorn and dust. Serpent belly
        sing lullaby. Beautiful gorgeous Jesus
loves you so much. Only way to Heaven
        church on Sunday. You must pray rosary.
Toil in fields. Heaven tremendous thrill
        of ecstasy forever. Don't fornicate.

III

hefting me onto him
he let me cling on
like a little bear
my ardor my enemy
my cold legs clenching
the hard hairy chest
that was his body
middle-aged floating
under me until
a wall of salt
took us down
in a good clean break
I could feel like a stump
where love had been

IV

The search for a single dominant gene—
"the 'O-God' hypothesis" (one-gene,
one disorder)—which, like an oracle,
foreknows the sexual brain, is fruitless.

The human self is undeconstructable
montage, is poverty, learning, & war,
is DNA, words, is acts in a bucket,
is agony and love on a wheel that sparkles,

is a mother and father creating
and destroying, is mutable
and one with God, is man and wife speaking,
is innocence betrayed by justice,

is not sentimental but sentimentalized,
is a body contained by something bodiless.

V

"Knowledge enormous makes a God of me,"
Apollo cried, square-shouldered, naked, hair falling
down his back. Now that I am forty, nothing
I have learned proves this. Inside my chest
there is loose straw. Inside my brain there are
syllables and sound. Living inwardly,
how can I tell what is real and what is not?

Joy and grief pulse like water from a fountain
over me, a stone, but do not end as knowledge.
All my life, doing things in moderation,
I have wooed him, whose extremes are forgotten,
whose battered faceless torso fills me
with longing and shame. I lie in the grass
like a man whose being has miscarried.

VI

On the sand there were dead things from the deep.
Faint-lipped shells appeared and disappeared,
like language assembling out of gray.

Then a seal muscled through the surf,
like a fetus, and squatted on a sewage pipe.
I knelt in the tall grass and grinned at it.

Body and self were one, vaguely
coaxed onward by the monotonous waves,
recording like compound sentences.

The seal was on its way somewhere cold, far.
Nothing about it exceeded what it was
(unlike a soul reversing itself to be

something more or a pen scratching words
on vellum after inking out what came before).

VII

Dirt so fine it is like flour.
Dirt mixed with ice.
Huge expanses of it.
The ground frozen.
With deep exceptional holes.
This is what I see
spilling down a nave.
Then Daddy kissing
a cardinal's ring.
And the long black snake
of his belt yanked
around him. His legs
planted apart like a clergyman's.
My body
prostrate on the counterpane
where man and wife lay.

The inflamed buttocks.
The Roman letters,
TU ES PETRUS,
though I knew I was not.
Daddy's voice moving slowly,
like a cancer
toward the brain,
a sky-blue globe
it cannot penetrate.
Leather flying against flesh.
In the mouth
dirt so fine it is like flour.

VIII

Walking in woods, I found him bound to a tree,
moaning like a dove, a kerchief stopping his mouth;
a sweat-smell mixed with mulch and lotion,
a ten dollar bill at his dirty feet.
How easily in him I could see myself,
poor wannabe Sebastian, sucked and bitten
like a whore! I blushed for him, hurrying home.

Memory: the diplomats in white tie
stepping from a Mercedes at the Vatican.
The limousine door swung wide like a gate
to a realm I wanted, a way of being,
formal as Bernini's rigid colonnade.
Then purple-sashed bishops flooded the square,
smearing out the white surplices of acolytes.

IX

All I want is to trust a man with plain
unshaken faith. Because I was not loved,
I cannot love. Sometimes I think I am not alive
but frozen like debris in molten glass.
White hairs sprout from my ears like a donkey's.
I do not feel sorry so much as weak,
like a flower with a broken stem.

A little blood or forgiveness does not
improve things. My brain is staunch as a crow,
my tongue buoyant as a dolphin. Yet, I
do not grow. You, with your unfalse nature
and silver arrows, won't you take my wrist.
Speak to me. My words are sounds
and sounds are not what I feel. Make me a man.

X

To write what is human, not escapist:
that is the problem of the hand moving
apart from my body.
                    Yet, subject is
only pretext for assembling the words
whose real story is process is flow.
So the hand lurches forward, gliding back
serenely, radiant with tears, a million
beings and objects hypnotizing me
as I sit and stare.
                    Not stupefied. Not aching.
Today, I am one. The hand jauntily
at home with evil, with unexamined feelings,
with just the facts.
                    Mind and body, like spikes,
like love and hate, recede pleasantly.
Do not be anxious. The hand remembers them.

XI

When I was a boy our father cooked
to seek forgiveness for making our house
a theater of hysteria and despair.
How could I not eat gluttonously?

You, my Apollo, cannot see that your hands
moving over me, the plainer one,

make me doubt you, that a son's life is punishment
for a father's. Young and penniless,

you serve me lobster. Scalding in the pot,
how it shrieked as I would with nothing left!
Please forgive my little dramas of the self.
And you do . . . in an interruption of the night,

when one body falls against another—
in the endless dragging of chains that signifies love.

XII

Morning of Puritans. Ice on the pond.
Giblets boiling. Any sort of movement
makes the bluejays fly. Father's door is opening.
Why are the titmice so unafraid of him?
Wrapped in cellophane on a granite slab,
the iced heart of our turkey stops time.

I remember my life in still pictures
that fall, inflamed, as in the seventh circle
the burning rain prevents the sodomites
from standing still. But I am in motion,
stroking toward what I cannot see, like an oar
dipped into the blood that ravishes it,

until blood-sprays rouse the dissolute mind,
the ineffable tongue arouses itself.

XIII CYPARISSUS

"I am here. I will always succor you,"
he used to say, a little full of himself.
What did I know, I was just a boy
loved by Apollo. There had been others.
All I wanted was to ride my deer,
who made me feel some knowledge of myself,
letting me string his big antlers with violets.

One day, in a covert, not seeing the deer
stray to drink at a cool spring, I thrust
my spear inadvertently into him.
Not even Apollo could stop the grief,
which gave me a greenish tint, twisting my
forehead upward; I became a cypress.
Poor Apollo: nothing he loves can live.

XIV

This is not a poem of resurrection.
The body secretes its juices and then is gone.
This is a poem of insurrection
against the self. In the beginning was the child,
fixating on the mother, taking himself
as the sexual object. . . . You know the story.
In the mirror I see a man with a firm
masculine body. Mouth open like a fish,
I look at him, one of the lucky ones
above the surface where the real me
is bronzed in the Apollonian sun.
I stay a while, mesmerized by the glass
whose four corners frame the eyes of a man
I might have been, not liquid, not pent in.

Presepio

This is the world God didn't create,
but an artist copying the original,
or some nostalgic idea of the original,
with Mary and Joseph, or statues of Mary and Joseph,
bowing their lamp-lit faces to the baby Jesus.
Language is not the human medium here,
where every eight minutes the seasons repeat themselves,
a rainbow appears, bleeding like an iris,
and the illusion of unity is achieved,
before blowing snow buries everything again.

Looked at from above, the farmer's sheep
are as big as conifers. Something is wrong with his sons,
whose pale bony necks make them look feral.
And the rooster cries more like a miserable donkey.
A light goes off. Another comes on.
In a little window, with a lamp to be read by,
nobody is reading. If God is around,
he seems ineffectual.
In the alps, a little trolley grinds its gears,
floating into the valley, where heavy droplets fall,
as the farmer's wife hurries—like a moving target
or a mind thinking—to unpin her laundry
from the wet white clothesline, and the farmer,
in the granary, stifles the little cries
of the neighbor girl parting her lips.
If the meaning of life is love, no one seems to be aware,
not even Mary and Joseph, exhausted with puffy eyes,
fleeing their dim golden crib.

Blur

Little Lamb,
Here I am,
Come and lick
My white neck.
WILLIAM BLAKE

I

It was a Christian idea, sacrificing
oneself to attain the object of one's desire.
I was weak and he was like opium to me,
so present and forceful. I believed I saw myself
through him, as if in a bucket being drawn
up a well, cold and brown as tea.
My horse was wet all that summer.
I pushed him, he pushed me back—proud, lonely,
disappointed—until I rode him,
or he rode me, in tight embrace, and life went on.
I lay whole nights—listless, sighing, gleaming

like a tendril on a tree—withdrawn
into some desiccated realm of beauty.
The hand desired, but the heart refrained.

2

The strong sad ritual between us could not be broken:
the empathetic greeting; the apologies
and reproaches; the narrow bed of his flesh;
the fear of being shown whole in the mirror
of another's fragmentation; the climbing on;
the unambiguous freedom born of submission;
the head, like a rock, hefted on and off moist earth;
the rough language; the impermeable core
of one's being made permeable; the black hair
and shining eyes; and afterward, the marrowy
emissions, the gasping made liquid; the torso,
like pale clay or a plank, being dropped;
the small confessional remarks that inscribe
the soul; the indolence; the being alone.

3

Then everything decanted and modulated,
as it did in a horse's eye, and the self—
pure, classical, like a figure carved from stone—
was something broken off again.
Two ways of being: one, seamless
saturated color (not a bead of sweat),
pure virtuosity, bolts of it; the other,
raw and unsocialized, "an opera of impurity,"
like super-real sunlight on a bruise.
I didn't want to have to choose.
It didn't matter anymore what was true
and what was not. Experience was not facts,
but uncertainty. Experience was not events,
but feelings, which I would overcome.

4

Waking hungry for flesh, stalking flesh
no matter where—in the dunes, at the Pantheon,
in the Tuileries, at the White Party—
cursing and fumbling with flesh, smelling flesh,
clutching flesh, sucking violently on flesh,
cleaning up flesh, smiling at flesh, running away
from flesh, and later loathing flesh,
half of me was shattered, half was not,
like a mosaic shaken down by earthquake.
All the things I loved—a horse, a wristwatch,
a hall mirror—and all the things I endeavored to be—
truthful, empathetic, funny—presupposed
a sense of self locked up in a sphere,
which would never be known to anyone.

5

Running, lifting, skipping rope at the gym,
I was a man like a bronze man;
I was my body—with white stones
in my eye sockets, soldered veins in my wrists
and a delicately striated, crepelike scrotum.
Sighs, grunts, exhales, salt stains, dingy mats,
smeared mirrors and a faintly sour smell
filled the gulf between the mind and the world,
but the myth of love for another remained
bright and plausible, like an athlete painted
on the slope of a vase tying his sandal.
In the showers, tears fell from our hair,
as if from bent glistening sycamores.
It was as if Earth were taking us back.

6

In front of me, you are sleeping. I sleep also.
Probably you are right that I project
the ambiguities of my own desires.
I feel I only know you at the edges.

Sometimes in the night I jump up panting,
see my young gray head in the mirror
and fall back, as humans do, from the cold glass.
I don't have the time to invest in what
I purport to desire. But when you open
your eyes shyly and push me on the shoulder,
all I am is impulse and longing
pulled forward by the rope of your arm,
I, flesh-to-flesh, sating myself
on blurred odors of the soft black earth.

Dionisio D. Martinez

b. 1956

Standard Time: Novena for My Father

We're turning back the clocks tonight
to live an hour longer.
I suppose this is a useless ritual to you now.

Late October brings life to the wind chimes
with that perpetually nocturnal music
so reminiscent of you.

I memorize a small song, a seasonable dirge
for the night that lives outside my
window. I call each note by name:
All Hallows Eve; All Saints Day; all the souls
in my music pacing, talking to themselves.

All day I sit by a statue of Saint
Francis of Assisi, birds on his shoulders,
nothing but faith in his hands.

At dusk I return to the house you knew
and a life you would probably understand.
There are night birds waiting to

breathe music back into the wind chimes when
the forecast calls for stillness.

I still remember what you said about belief,
how you laughed when I said I thought
the world could carry the cross I'd carved
around my shoulder and through my fist.

The world is busy with its clocks and its
wind chimes and the night birds that never fly
home once they learn the secret of exile.

I let out one sigh that is almost musical.
I know you can hear this much.
I take a small step back and picture
you here before I light the last candle.

All the souls in hell couldn't set this world
on fire. Even if they prove that our lives
are mathematically impossible, we
will cling to the last flame in the equation.

Joseph Harrison

b. 1957

The Relic

From mishap in the King's baker's house
In Pudding Lane
It raced like plague or rumor,
Forking in waves the wakened failed to douse,
Finding on Thames Street oil and hemp and booze
To feed its humor
And roll its catastrophic train
Through side street, square and mews,

    And torch St. Magnus' Church to ash
            Before it came
        Scorching the length of the Bridge
And down to the steelyard in a murderous flash
Levelling strata, consuming poverty
            With privilege,
    A "horrid malicious bloody flame
        As far as we could see"

    (Saw Pepys) arcing "in a bow up the hill"
            Into the City
        As houses cracked and tumbled,
Streets jammed with panic, the chaotic spill
Of carts, goods, horses, people jostled and churned
            And fortunes were fumbled
    In flight from ruin without pity
        Or pause, and London burned.

    When calm and citizens returned
            To the charred scene,
        Little was left of St. Paul's
(Where Wycliffe was tried, and Tyndall's Bible burned).
Among all those memorialized, just one,
            Whose madrigals
    Gave way to sermons, the old Dean,
        Stone-shrouded Dr. Donne,

    Survived as monument and sign,
            Though singed, intact,
        As if a voice should say:
"Lord, prelate, deacon, burgher, concubine
Shall crumble utterly, with king and queen,
            And blow away,
    But not this word of my contract,
        The English Augustine."

Li-Young Lee

b. 1957

This Hour and What Is Dead

Tonight my brother, in heavy boots, is walking
through bare rooms over my head,
opening and closing doors.
What could he be looking for in an empty house?
What could he possibly need there in heaven?
Does he remember his earth, his birthplace set to torches?
His love for me feels like spilled water
running back to its vessel.

At this hour, what is dead is restless
and what is living is burning.

Someone tell him he should sleep now.

My father keeps a light on by our bed
and readies for our journey.
He mends ten holes in the knees
of five pairs of boy's pants.
His love for me is like his sewing:
various colors and too much thread,
the stitching uneven. But the needle pierces
clean through with each stroke of his hand.

At this hour, what is dead is worried
and what is living is fugitive.

Someone tell him he should sleep now.

God, that old furnace, keeps talking
with his mouth of teeth,
a beard stained at feasts, and his breath
of gasoline, airplane, human ash.

His love for me feels like fire,
feels like doves, feels like river-water.

At this hour, what is dead is helpless, kind
and helpless. While the Lord lives.

Someone tell the Lord to leave me alone.
I've had enough of his love
that feels like burning and flight and running away.

Night Mirror

Li-Young, don't feel lonely
when you look up
into great night and find
yourself the far face peering
hugely out from between
a star and a star. All that space
the nighthawk plunges through,
homing, all that distance beyond embrace,
what is it but your own infinity.

And don't be afraid
when, eyes closed, you look inside you
and find night is both
the silence tolling after stars
and the final word
that founds all beginning, find night,

abyss and shuttle,
a finished cloth
frayed by the years, then gathered
in the songs and games
mothers teach their children.

Look again
and find yourself changed
and changing, now the bewildered honey
fallen into your own hands,

now the immaculate fruit born of hunger.
Now the unequaled perfume of your dying.
And time? Time is the salty wake
of your stunned entrance upon
no name.

Esther Schor

b. 1957

Alef

For Robbe

Sunday, far north
  the broad air
leafless, farmstands
  hunch at the roadside
boarded, murmur
  a *brucha* for last fruits—
last pumpkin, last apple,
  last week;
the chill Sabbath
  kept at bay
returns to the schoolroom.
  A moment before learning
what do we remember?
  lamed, a lamp
mem, a mouth
  taf, a table, a tack
as though all letters
  bloomed into things
as though God were wandering
  the vineyard, blessing
the heavy vines. But God's become
  forgetful, we've all noticed
the change; frost cracks
  the folding husks
binds the soil

where we planted
marigolds; my daughter paints
in crimson streaks
alef, akimbo, unimaged:
it says nothing
because the sound it says
is invisible

Carl Phillips

b. 1959

Visitation

When it was over, they told me
that the creak of wings folding
was only the bed, that shutters

do not clap of themselves. Morning
was what it had always been, any woman
marooned in the air,
                                        the nicked
blooms of suggestion, in the lamp,
in the lemonwood stool, every seam
or pocket slowly retrieved,

were the usual ones, what
everyone knows. Father spat
into the unswept yard below,
as if it too were an unseemly desire,

and passed through the door.

I am no mystic. I know
nothing rises that doesn't
know how to already.
In my ears, only the clubbed
foot of routine, no voices, no
clatter of dreams: but I saw
what I saw.

A Great Noise

Then he died.
And they said: *Another soul free.*

Which was the wrong way to see it, I thought,
having been there,
having lain down beside him until

his body became rigid with what I believe
was not the stiffening of death
but of surprise, the initial
unbelief of the suddenly ex-slave hearing
Rest; let it fall now, this burden.

The proof most commonly put forth for the soul
as a thing that exists and weighs
something is that
the body weighs something less, after death—

a clean fact.

In *The Miraculous Translation of the Body*
of Saint Catherine of Alexandria to Sinai,
the number of angels required to bear the body
all that way through the air
comes to four,

which tells us nothing
about weight, or the lack of it, since
the angels depicted
are clearly those for whom

the only business is hard labor,
the work angels,
you can tell:
the musculature;
the resigned way they wear clothes.

Beyond them in rank,
in the actual presence of God,
the seraphim stand naked, ever-burning,

six-winged: two to fly with,
in back; two at the face to withstand
the impossible winds that
are God;

and a third pair—for modesty,
for the covering
of sex.

A great
noise is said to always
attend them:
less the humming of wings than
the grinding you'd expect

from the hitching of what is hot,
destructive,
and all devotion

to the highest, brightest star.

From the Devotions

1.

As if somewhere, away, a door had slammed shut.
—But not metal; not wood.

Or as when something is later remembered only
as something dark in the dream:

torn, bruised, dream-slow
descending, it could be anything—

tiling, clouds,
you again, beautifully consistent, in no

usual or masterable way *leaves, a woman's*
shaken-loose throat, shattered

eyes of the seer, palms, ashes, the flesh
instructing; you, silent.

A sky, a sea requires crossing and, like that,
there is a boat or, like that, a plane:

for whom is it this way now, when
as if still did I lie down beside, still

turn to, touch
I can't, I could not save you?

II.

Not, despite what you believed, that
all travel necessarily ends here, at the sea.

I am back, but only because.
As the sun only happens to meet the water

in such a way that the water becomes
a kind of cuirass: how each piece takes

and, for nothing, gives back whatever light—
sun's, moon's. A bird that is not a gull

passes over; I mark what you would: underneath,
at the tip of either wing, a fluorescent-white

moon, or round star. Does the bird itself
ever see this? According to you *many have*

had the ashes of lovers strewn here,
on this beach on this water that now beats at,

now seems to want just to rest alongside.
The dead can't know we miss them Presumably,

we were walking *that we are walking*
upon them.

III.

All night, again,
a wind that failed to bring storm—

instead, the Paradise dream: the abandoned
one nest at a bad angle—in danger,

and what it is to not know it;
the equally abandoned one tree that,

for the time being, holds it—alone,
and what it is to not know it.

All morning, it has been the fog
thinning at last,

as if that were the prayer,
the streets filling with men *as if they*

were divine answer and not just
what happens. Do I love less, if less is

all I remember? Your mouth, like a hole
to fly through. What you understood

of the flesh: how always first are we
struck down. *Then we rise; are astounded.*

Josephine Singer

b. 1959

Provision

I'm talking
but I'm wishing it was over.

Let's go back
to the bubble of the evening:
lamplight, homework,

the moment that enfolds itself

bends over itself
and smiles

dispelling
its complement.

It's good
though bare,

abbreviated,

a circle of ash,
and warm within.

I shall have it,
says the pilgrim,

where the light falls,

in place of utter nakedness.

David Woo

b. 1959

Eden

Yellow-oatmeal flowers of the windmill palms
like brains lashed to fans—
even they think of cool paradise,

not this sterile air-conditioned chill
or the Arizona hell in which they sway becomingly.
Every time I return to Phoenix I see these palms

as a child's height marks on a kitchen wall,
taller now than the yuccas they were planted with,
taller than the Texas sage trimmed

to a perfect gray-green globe with pointillist
lavender blooms, taller than I,
who stopped growing years ago and commenced instead

my slow, almost imperceptible slouch
to my parents' old age:
Father's painful bend—really a bending of a bend—

to pick up the paper at the end of the sidewalk;
Mother, just released from Good Samaritan,
curled sideways on a sofa watching the soaps,

an unwanted tear inching down
at the plight of some hapless Hilary or Tiffany.
How she'd rail against television as a waste of time!

Now, with one arthritis-mangled hand,
she aims the remote control at the set
and flicks it off in triumph, turning to me

as I turn to the trees framed in the Arcadia door.
Her smile of affection melts into the back of my head,
a throb that presses me forward,

hand pressed to glass. I feel the desert heat
and see the beautiful shudders of the palms in the yard
and wonder why I despised this place so,

why I moved from city to temperate city, anywhere
without palms and cactus trees.
I found no paradise, as my parents know,

but neither did they, with their eager sprinklers
and scrawny desert plants pumped up to artificial splendor,
and their lives sighing away, exhaling slowly,

the man and woman
who teach me now as they could not before
to prefer real hell to any imaginary paradise.

Ballad of Infinite Forgetfulness

(After Hugo von Hofmannsthal)

And strangers will arrive as they'll depart, shaking your hand,
And friends will say, "Sorry," and walk right through you,
And thought will slip through a sieve, honeyed with sadness.

And lovers will spin in the windows of a cinquefoil,
And minutes will stream like corpuscles through the streets
Until they're caught in a frontage road labeled, "No Outlet."

And dogs will listen for a master who'll never return,
For a garage door to rise at the touch of a remote control,
For the latch to unlock and the presence of a god to enter in.

And a god will throw down a fog that clarifies, not obscures,
And leaves will grow clear and have no need to fall,
And a root-sphere will pulse in the clear ground, like a mind.

And your father will grow senile and fretful, and your mother
Will lose the strength to lift the side of her hand,
And the grave-digger will send a bill marked "Past Due."

So why the outrage, why the dread, if the funeral is dark
As you willed it to be, and the stained glass luminous
With temporary light? Why not rest here, in the nave,

Where the living will pass by and murmur how rich
Your life was, after all, in the end? Say "I am poor,"
Show them the invisible patches in your black suit,

Ask them to praise your forgetfulness and make it last.

David Daniel

b. 1960

Seven-Star Bird

And god's anger called his rivers all and told them to let the river horses run wild as they ever would, and the leaping rivers flooded the great plains . . . —OVID

As breezes lap the shallow-tugged tide flow
And swallows twitter and skirt the dusk,
We lie within the wreckage of the stars—
The moon spill, our planet's pull—this sad machine.

With you sleeping against my chest,
Having drifted off as Venus began to blaze,
I feel my father's heavy breath bear
Down against my cheek, a finger toward the comet's tail:
Like a damn flashlight looking down, he said.
For three nights we watched it, then that light was out.
So we steered by the swirling mathematics
Of whiskey and revenge, the business of getting,
Then of letting go. Stars gather in the sky like rain—
Dizzy atoms that collapse, collide:

In our dream the dead of Friendship, Texas,
Stand on the shore of their once-town singing:
Let the river horses run
Let them run . . .

Once, in America, in full nakedness,
Our family rivered these lands with abandon—
From Moravia to Galveston to Friendship, Texas—
Their wild seeds sown, their hearts full of leaving,
They longed to stay: Abide, Abide, Reside—
But the tide comes to meet us and also to take us away:

When the dam was built to swell the rich towns south,
The flood spilled over . . .

Let the river horses run . . .

Valentinian speculation holds
That our souls, as light, are drawn to the waxing moon
Which then, upon the wane, delivers its freight
To the darker dark beyond—electrons
Finally freed into streams of gravity
Gone wild: while alone
In the dust of Palestine, sad Luria
Watches as God withdraws and so the world arises.

Let the river horses run
Let them run . . .

If, as has been said, it is our very love of God
That separates us from Him, can't we say
That the names we sketch on the churning atoms
Of this world's things, while keeping us apart,
Allow us also to love? Isn't this enough,
The shadow that we know a swallow by?

The tide flows in, the moon spill: let's
Hymn down the river, witness the wresting away:
If America drew us to a destiny of desire,

It was the outfall of a single star stunned,
Our sweet metals and machines: so
Return, exile, then return again:
Want no more than water does, low places
To dwell and the gravity to change.
And if you, too, are lost one day in loss itself,
May you trace a bird amid the mess of stars—
May you name it as you wish—
Seven-Star Bird, Lover, God—
And may its wandering guide your own.

Let the river horses run, Let them run,
Let them run wild as they ever would . . .

Martha Serpas

b. 1965

As If There Were Only One

In the morning God pulled me onto the porch,
a rain-washed gray and brilliant shore.

I sat in my orange pajamas and waited.
God said, "Look at the tree." And I did.

Its leaves were newly yellow and green,
slick and bright, and so alive it hurt

to take the colors in. My pupils grew
hungry and wide against my will.

God said, "Listen to the tree."
And I did. It said, "Live!"

And it opened itself wider, not with desire,
but the way I imagine a surgeon spreads

the ribs of a patient in distress and rubs
her paralyzed heart, only this tree parted

its own limbs toward the sky—I was the light in that sky.
I reached in to the thick, sweet core

and I lifted it to my mouth and held it there
for a long time until I tasted the word

tree (because I had forgotten its name).
Then I said my own name twice softly.

Augustine said, *God loves each of us as if
there were only one of us*, but I hadn't believed him.

And God put me down on the steps with my coffee
and my cigarettes. And, although I still

could not eat nor sleep, that evening
and that morning were my first day back.

Witness Tree

To the right of the altar, Jeanne d'Arc, shorn and shielded,
And very much alive. How surprised I would have been,

As a child, to see her lashed to tree branches instead of
Wielding her blade over the front pews, over Mary's votive

Stand—Mary, determined and confident, her cloak parted
To shelter the roses and beads of the vulnerable.

Now when the priest's lips press against the marble altar,
I see how we love blood spilled best—what moves in us

We mistrust—corrupted flesh confirms our
Deepest knowledge, our mouths aching

For the relics we become. In the forest's cathedral
The firs refuse to still, pulsing on the hillside,

Chanting even as the brush below them smolders
And the fields settle into a deep red-brown.

How small the bloodshed must look to the witness tree,
From its vantage on the ridge—its maroon

Stripes, only paint warning loggers away. Still it notes
Every gesture in its rings, tastes acrid smoke

From the fires below, recognizes the faces in the fields,
Dogs that chase elk, those that lie down in the dust

And are welcomed on some other hill it alone sees.
Vision without sacrifice, the tree that cannot be felled,

Stronger and greener, that breathes in death and joy
With disinterest and breathes out life and more life.

Psalm at High Tide

Rain on the river's vinyl surface:
water that glitters,
water that hardly moves,
its branches witness to trees,
to fronds, leaves, crab floats, pilings,
shopping carts, appliances—
the divine earth takes everything
in its wounded side and gives back
wholeness.
It bears the huddled profane
and endures the soaking
venerated in its wild swirls—
this river fixed with wooden weirs,
radiant in misshapen glory.

Poem Found

New Orleans, September 2005

. . . And God said, "Let there be a dome in the midst
of the waters" and into the dome God put

the poor, the addicts, the blind, and the oppressed.
God put the unsightly sick and the crying young

into the dome and the dry land did not appear.
And God allowed those who favored themselves

born in God's image to take dominion over
the dome and everything that creeped within it

and made them to walk to and fro above it
in their jumbo planes and in their copy rooms

and in their conference halls. And then
God brooded over the dome and its multitudes

and God saw God's own likeness in the shattered
tiles and the sweltering heat and the polluted rain.

God saw everything and chose to make it very good.
God held the dome up to the light

like an open locket and in every manner called
the others to look inside and those who saw

rested on that day and those who didn't
went to and fro and walked up and down

the marsh until the loosened silt gave way
to a void, and darkness covered the faces with deep sleep.

Khaled Mattawa

b. 1966

I Was Buried in Janzoor

is what I keep telling them, but they hook me
up to monitors, point to screens and show
flashes of my pulse. They draw blood from my arms,
smear my face with warm dabs. I say, listen:
June, two years after the war, a hundred
and four degrees in late afternoon, they prayed
for me without kneeling, arms lifted to the sky,
chanted "God is great." A plain cedar coffin,
unvarnished, used, the shroud made of Egyptian gauze.
Six cousins settled me on cool dirt,
and a man, the son of a slave, the one
who washed my body placing a rag on my waist,
the one who did not want to insult the dead,
he heaped the world over me, pressing dirt
with small feminine feet. I'd like to say that
my wives mourned my death for years, that my children
did not fight over my inheritance—forty hectares,
two houses, seven cows, a mule. I'd like to say
that when my name is mentioned in the village
teahouse, no one spits on the sidewalk, no one
curses the day of my birth. I'd like to say
that a grandson is named after me, my picture
on his desk as he eyes foreign words. He thinks of me
rarely, but always as an example of the decency
and apathy that made us prey to strangers from abroad,
that I'm remembered by a woman from Milan, who as a girl,
pressed me to her in her father's tobacco shed.
We stared at each other knowing no words
for the misery that bound us, the nuances
of skin that tore us apart. I'd like to say
I feared or betrayed no one, that I taught

my children all they deserved to know,
that I did not desire the neighbors'
daughters and sons. I'd like to say that you
made me happy, that I would love to return.
I looked at the sky on holy nights and saw
no palm fronds flaming copper gold, no pit for me
to shake Satan's hand. I visited a thousand weddings,
gave rice and pearls; I fed beggars from my table
and helped the blind find their way home;
I sacrificed she-goats and roosters
for local saints; I built a mosque. Stupid
were most of my thoughts, listless most my days.
I loved nothing more than my mother's coffee,
I loved a spoon of her lentil soup more than
I loved the truth. I'm still buried in Janzoor.

Suji Kwock Kim

b. 1968

The Tree of Unknowing

Uncertainty, take me into the forest
leaf by leaf—

where an immigrant sits in a Jersey slum,
a young mother rocking her child.

Where, along the endless road, are you going away from me like a cloud?
Like a cloud, like a cloud?

I lay in your arms, watching your lips.
I touched your chin with my tiny fingers.

Your loneliness sang to me,
each word a crumb of light, burning in the skull—

until a galaxy of sparks flashed among the branches,
lighting the way where?

I lifted my head. What was it I saw
in your gaze, the maze

of you: corridors of years, corridors of war, black wheat-hair
ripening—
the last shape sown in closing eyes.

The words have their own woods.
Where the words can't go further: where the woods begin

that make us mad, too real and not
real enough. Whose memory was it? Why did I feel such joy?

Look, the cloud-tree will never die—

I wonder who you were: I wonder
because you were.

Brett Foster

b. 1973

The First Request of Lazarus

1.

". . . so newly separated
From the old fire of Heaven."
—Ovid

Already weary
from second living, new
dying of renewed patience,

old Lazarus of Bethany
betrays the uplift, desperate
for a death pregnant

with meaning, reliable passing.
How does one return,
happily, to work the olive groves?

How to age now? Even feasts
felt nebulous, and villages—
he seemed beyond them. True,

nothing terrifies like that
desertion: fading one
swallowed in the cave mouth,

linen strips to bind
the limbs. Though loss like this,
however uniquely it strikes

the forsaken, is ordinary still,
more familiar than altars,
fruitful as peasant markets.

2.

". . . there is nothing
But howling wind and solitary birds."
—William Butler Yeats

This Lazarus, body rich
with sickness, deathbed-ridden,
spoke of spent candles,

tabernacles, frankincense.
Dogs licked his sores.
His suffering justified

the rage, his matted beard,
the pure fear. Ah, the tomb's
thick silence: its air balmed

his aches like lanolin. Those days
undenied, then the honor—
a *rabbi's* tears as he bid

the boulder gone. He staggered
toward the stone aperture,
face wrapped in canvas.

Sisters could not barter grief
so quickly. Younger ones were called,
their return more painful.

They also know desire:
daughter of the synagogue ruler,
the widow's son at Nain.

3.

"Changed from glory into glory,
Till in heaven we take our place . . ."
—Charles Wesley

As for him, he waits—
impatient, stone-jawed, face hanging
like spoiled fish. He gainsays

symbolism. He knows at last
we are destined for this,
we serve one purpose, fatally,

make good on this clay-made
existence only in keeping
our good, last word.

Ether, end breath. Mindless
derelictions near soliloquy, twice
uttered. Truth is less beautiful

in rehearsal. This vocation
serves an instant, laid for everyone.
Then, only then, would the earth

surrender its mortal turning,
open wide the oceans
to let its inhabitants pass,

carrying clumsy dynasties,
their destinations somewhere
otherwise, and not here.

AMERICAN INDIAN SONGS AND CHANTS

The Thanksgivings

(Iroquois)

We who are here present thank the Great Spirit that we are here
to praise Him.
We thank Him that He has created men and women, and
ordered that these beings shall always be living to multiply
the earth.
We thank Him for making the earth and giving these beings its
products to live on.
We thank Him for the water that comes out of the earth and
runs for our lands.
We thank Him for all the animals on the earth.
We thank Him for certain timbers that grow and have fluids
coming from them for us all.
We thank Him for the branches of the trees that grow shadows
for our shelter.
We thank Him for the beings that come from the west, the
thunder and lightning that water the earth.
We thank Him for the light which we call our oldest brother, the
sun that works for our good.
We thank Him for all the fruits that grow on the trees and vines.
We thank Him for his goodness in making the forests, and thank
all its trees.
We thank Him for the darkness that gives us rest, and for the
kind Being of the darkness that gives us light, the moon.
We thank Him for the bright spots in the skies that give us signs,
the stars.
We give Him thanks for our supporters, who have charge of our
harvests.
We give thanks that the voice of the Great Spirit can still be
heard through the words of Ga-ne-o-di-o.
We thank the Great Spirit that we have the privilege of this
pleasant occasion.

We give thanks for the persons who can sing the Great Spirit's music, and hope they will be privileged to continue in his faith.
We thank the Great Spirit for all the persons who perform the ceremonies on this occasion.

This Is to Frighten a Storm

(*Cherokee*)

Yuhahí, yuhahí, yuhahí, yuhahí, yuhahí,
Yuhahí, yuhahí, yuhahí, yuhahí, yuhahí—Yû!
Listen! O now you are coming in rut. Ha! I am exceedingly afraid of you. But yet you are only tracking your wife. Her footprints can be seen there, directed upward toward the heavens. I have pointed them out for you. Let your paths stretch out along the treetops on the lofty mountains. You shall have them—the paths—lying down without being disturbed. Let your path as you go along be where the waving branches meet. Listen!

To Go to the Water

(*Cherokee*)

Now
you have come to listen,
Long Person,
you are staying right here,
Helper of Humans,
you never relax your grip,
you never let go your grip on the soul.
You have taken a firm hold on the soul.
I originated at the cataract, not so far away.
I will stretch out my hand to where you are.
My soul has come to bathe in your body.
The white foam will cling to my head
as I go on with my life,
the white staff will come into my outstretched hand.
The fire in the hearth will be left burning for me.
The soul has been raised gradually to the seventh upper world.

Is This Real

(Pawnee)

Let us see, is this real,
Let us see, is this real,
This life I am living?
You, Gods, who dwell everywhere,
Let us see, is this real,
This life I am living?

Ghost-Dance Songs

(Kiowa)

The father will descend,
The father will descend.
The earth will tremble,
The earth will tremble.
Everybody will arise,
Everybody will arise.
Stretch out your hands,
Stretch out your hands.

The spirit army is approaching,
The spirit army is approaching,
The whole world is moving onward,
The whole world is moving onward.
See! Everybody is standing watching,
See! Everybody is standing watching.
Let us all pray,
Let us all pray.

My father has much pity for us,
My father has much pity for us.
I hold out my hands toward him and cry,
I hold out my hands toward him and cry.
In my poverty I hold out my hands toward him and cry,
In my poverty I hold out my hands toward him and cry.

That wind, that wind
Shakes my tipi, shakes my tipi,
And sings a song for me,
And sings a song for me.

God has had pity on us,
God has had pity on us.
Jesus has taken pity on us,
Jesus has taken pity on us.
He teaches me a song,
He teaches me a song.
My song is a good one,
My song is a good one.

Therefore I Must Tell the Truth

(Navajo)

I am ashamed before the earth:
I am ashamed before the heavens:
I am ashamed before the dawn:
I am ashamed before the evening twilight:
I am ashamed before the blue sky:
I am ashamed before the darkness:
I am ashamed before the sun.
I am ashamed before that standing within me which speaks with me.
Some of these things are always looking at me.
I am never out of sight.
Therefore I must tell the truth.
That is why I always tell the truth.
I hold my word tight to my breast.

by Torlino

FROM *The Night Chant*

(Navajo)

Prayer of First Dancers

In Tse'gíhi,
In the house made of the dawn,
In the house made of the evening twilight,
In the house made of the dark cloud,
In the house made of the he-rain,
In the house made of the dark mist,
In the house made of the she-rain,
In the house made of pollen,
In the house made of grasshoppers,
Where the dark mist curtains the doorway,
The path to which is on the rainbow,
Where the zigzag lightning stands high on top,
Where the he-rain stands high on top,
Oh, male divinity!
With your moccasins of dark cloud, come to us.
With your leggings of dark cloud, come to us.
With your shirt of dark cloud, come to us.
With your head-dress of dark cloud, come to us.
With your mind enveloped in dark cloud, come to us.
With the dark thunder above you, come to us soaring.
With the shapen cloud at your feet, come to us soaring.
With the far darkness made of the dark cloud over your head, come to us soaring.
With the far darkness made of the he-rain over your head, come to us soaring.
With the far darkness made of the dark mist over your head, come to us soaring.
With the far darkness made of the she-rain over your head, come to us soaring.
With the zigzag lightning flung out on high over your head, come to us soaring.
With the rainbow hanging high over your head, come to us soaring.
With the far darkness made of the dark cloud on the ends of your wings, come to us soaring.

With the far darkness made of the he-rain on the ends of your wings, come to us soaring.
With the far darkness made of the dark mist on the ends of your wings, come to us soaring.
With the far darkness made of the she-rain on the ends of your wings, come to us soaring.
With the zigzag lightning flung out on high on the ends of your wings, come to us soaring.
With the rainbow hanging high on the ends of your wings, come to us soaring.
With the near darkness made of the dark cloud, of the he-rain, of the dark mist and of the she-rain, come to us.
With the darkness on the earth, come to us.
With these I wish the foam floating on the flowing water over the roots of the great corn.
I have made your sacrifice.
I have prepared a smoke for you.
My feet restore for me.
My limbs restore for me.
My body restore for me.
My mind restore for me.
My voice restore for me.
To-day, take out your spell for me.
To-day, take away your spell for me.
Away from me you have taken it.
Far off from me it is taken.
Far off you have done it.
Happily I recover.
Happily my interior becomes cool.
Happily my eyes regain their power.
Happily my head becomes cool.
Happily my limbs regain their power.
Happily I hear again.
Happily for me the spell is taken off.
Happily I walk.
Impervious to pain, I walk.
Feeling light within, I walk.
With lively feelings, I walk.
Happily abundant dark clouds I desire.

Happily abundant dark mists I desire.
Happily abundant passing showers I desire.
Happily an abundance of vegetation I desire.
Happily an abundance of pollen I desire.
Happily abundant dew I desire.
Happily may fair white corn, to the ends of the earth, come with you.
Happily may fair yellow corn, to the ends of the earth, come with you.
Happily may fair blue corn, to the ends of the earth, come with you.
Happily may fair corn of all kinds, to the ends of the earth, come with you.
Happily may fair plants of all kinds, to the ends of the earth, come with you.
Happily may fair goods of all kinds, to the ends of the earth, come with you.
Happily may fair jewels of all kinds, to the ends of the earth, come with you.
With these before you, happily may they come with you.
With these behind you, happily may they come with you.
With these below you, happily may they come with you.
With these above you, happily may they come with you.
With these all around you, happily may they come with you.
Thus happily you accomplish your tasks.
Happily the old men will regard you.
Happily the old women will regard you.
Happily the young men will regard you.
Happily the young women will regard you.
Happily the boys will regard you.
Happily the girls will regard you.
Happily the children will regard you.
Happily the chiefs will regard you.
Happily, as they scatter in different directions, they will regard you.
Happily, as they approach their homes, they will regard you.
Happily may their roads home be on the trail of pollen.
Happily may they all get back.
In beauty I walk.

With beauty before me, I walk.
With beauty behind me, I walk.
With beauty below me, I walk.
With beauty above me, I walk.
With beauty all around me, I walk.
It is finished again in beauty,
It is finished in beauty,
It is finished in beauty,
It is finished in beauty.

Song of the Sky Loom

(*Tewa*)

Oh our Mother the Earth, oh our Father the Sky,
Your children are we, and with tired backs
We bring you the gifts that you love.
Then weave for us a garment of brightness;
May the warp be the white light of morning,
May the weft be the red light of evening,
May the fringes be the falling rain,
May the border be the standing rainbow.
Thus weave for us a garment of brightness
That we may walk fittingly where birds sing,
That we may walk fittingly where grass is green,
Oh our Mother the Earth, oh our Father the Sky!

Prayer to the Deceased

(*Tewa*)

We have muddied the waters for you,
We have cast shadows between us,
We have mad steep gullies between us,
Do not, therefore, reach for even a hair of our heads,
Rather, help us attain that which we are always seeking,
Long life, that our children may grow,
Abundant game, the raising of crops,
And in all the works of man
Ask for these things for all, and do no more,
And now you must go, for now you are free.

The Creation of the Earth

(Pima)

Earth Magician shapes this world.
   Behold what he can do!
Round and smooth he molds it.
   Behold what he can do!
Earth Magician makes the mountains.
   Heed what he has to say!
He it is that makes the mesas.
   Heed what he has to say.
Earth Magician shapes this world;
   Earth Magician makes its mountains;
Makes all larger, larger, larger.
   Into the earth the Magician glances;
Into its mountains he may see.

Special Request for the Children of Mother Corn

(Zuni)

Perhaps if we are lucky
Our earth mother
Will wrap herself in a fourfold robe
Of white meal,
Full of frost flowers;
A floor of ice will spread over the world,
The forests,
Because of the cold, will lean to one side,
Their arms will break beneath the weight of snow.
When the days are thus,
The flesh of our earth mother
Will crack with cold.
Then in the spring when she is replete with living waters,
Our mothers,
All different kinds of corn,
In their earth mother
We shall lay to rest.
With their earth mother's living waters
They will be made into new beings;

Into their sun father's daylight
They will come out standing;
Yonder to all directions
They will stretch out their hands calling for rain.
Then with their fresh waters
The rain makers will pass us on our roads.
Clasping their young ones in their arms,
They will rear their children.
Gathering them into our houses,
Following these toward whom our thoughts bend,
With our thoughts following them,
Thus we shall always live.

Deer Song

(*Yaqui*)

There he comes out,
    there from the enchanted house,
        I come out from there.
There he comes out,
    there from the enchanted house,
        I come out from there.

There he comes out,
    there from the enchanted house,
        I come out from there.
There he comes out,
    there from the enchanted house,
        I come out from there.

Over there, I, in Yevuku Yoleme's
    flower-covered, flower patio,
        I have sparsely flowered antlers.
There he comes out,
    there from the enchanted house,
        I come out from there.

Shaman's Song

(*Modoc*)

What do I remove from my mouth?
The disease I remove from my mouth.

What do I take out?
The disease I take out.

What do I suck out?
The disease I suck out.

What do I blow about?
The disease I blow about.

As a head only, I roll around.

I stand on the rim of my nest.

I am enveloped in flames.

What am I? what am I?

I, the song, I walk here.

I the dog stray.

In the north wind I stray.

An arrowpoint I am about to shoot.

A bad song I am.

The earth I sing of.

Shaman's Song

(Inuit)

The whale
the beluga
the hooded seal
the salmon
the caribou
the ground seal
the walrus
the polar bear
the fox
the bird
the wolf
the bone

SPIRITUALS AND ANONYMOUS HYMNS

Balm in Gilead

How lost was my condition
Till Jesus made me whole—
There's a balm in Gilead
To make the wounded whole;
There's pow'r enough in Jesus
To cure a sin-sick soul.

There is but one Physician
Can cure a sin-sick soul.
There's a balm in Gilead
To make the wounded whole;
There's pow'r enough in Jesus
To cure a sin-sick soul.

Didn't My Lord Deliver Daniel

Didn't my Lord deliver Daniel,
D'liver Daniel, d'liver Daniel,
Didn't my Lord deliver Daniel,
And why not a every man?

He deliver'd Daniel from the lion's den,
Jonah from the belly of the whale,
And the Hebrew children from the fiery furnace,
And why not every man?

The moon run down in a purple-stream,
The sun forbear to shine,
And every star disappear,
King Jesus shall be mine.

The wind blows East, and the wind blows West,
It blows like the judgment day,
And every poor soul that never did pray,
'll be glad to pray, that day.

I set my foot on the Gospel ship,
And the ship it begin to sail,
It landed me over on Canaan's shore,
And I'll never come back any more.

Ezekiel Saw de Wheel

Ezekiel saw de wheel,
'Way up in de middle ob de air,
Ezekiel saw de wheel,
'Way in de middle ob de air;
An' de little wheel run by faith,
An' de big wheel run by de grace ob God,
'Tis a wheel in a wheel,
'Way in de middle ob de air.

Some go to church fo' to sing an' shout,
'Way in de middle ob de air;
Befo' six months dey are all turned out,
'Way in de middle ob de air.

Let me tell you what a hypocrit'll do,
'Way in de middle ob de air;
He'll talk 'bout me an' he'll talk 'bout yo',
'Way in de middle ob de air.

One o' dese days, 'bout twelve o'clock,
'Way in de middle ob de air;
Dis ole worl' gwine reel an' rock,
'Way in de middle ob de air.

Free at Last

Free at last, free at last;
I thank God I'm free at last;
Free at last, free at last,
I thank God I'm free at last,
O free at last.

'Way down yonder in the grave-yard walk,
I thank God I'm free at last,
Me and my Jesus goin' to meet and talk,
I thank God I'm free at last,
O free at last.

On-a my knees when the light pass'd by,
I thank God I'm free at last,
Tho't my soul would rise and fly,
I thank God I'm free at last,
O free at last.

Some of these mornings, bright and fair,
I thank God I'm free at last,
Goin' meet King Jesus in the air,
I thank God I'm free at last,
O free at last.

Got a Home in That Rock

I've got a home in a-that Rock,
Don't you see? Don't you see?
I've got a home in a-that Rock,
Don't you see? Don't you see?
Between the earth and sky,
Thought I heard my Saviour cry,
I've got a home in a-that Rock,
Don't you see?

Poor old Laz'rus, poor as I,
Don't you see? Don't you see?

Poor old Laz'rus, poor as I,
Don't you see? Don't you see?
Poor old Laz'rus, poor as I
When he died had a home on high.
He had a home in a-that Rock,
Don't you see?

Rich man, Dives, lived so well,
Don't you see? Don't you see?
Rich man, Dives, lived so well,
Don't you see? Don't you see?
Rich man, Dives, lived so well,
When he died he found a home in hell,
Had no home in that Rock,
Don't you see?

God gave Noah the Rainbow sign,
Don't you see? Don't you see?
God gave Noah the Rainbow sign,
Don't you see? Don't you see?
God gave Noah the Rainbow sign,
No more water but fire next time,
Better get a home in that Rock,
Don't you see?

I Know Moon-Rise

I know moon-rise, I know star-rise,
   Lay dis body down.
I walk in de moonlight, I walk in de starlight,
   To lay dis body down.
I'll walk in de graveyard, I'll walk through de graveyard,
   To lay dis body down.
I'll lie in de grave and stretch out my arms;
   Lay dis body down.
I go to de judgment in de evenin' of de day,
   When I lay dis body down;
And my soul and your soul will meet in de day
   When I lay dis body down.

Let My People Go

A Song of the"Contrabands"

When Israel was in Egypt's land,
  O let my people go!
Oppressed so hard they could not stand,
  O let my people go!

    O go down, Moses
    Away down to Egypt's land,
    And tell King Pharaoh,
    To let my people go!

Thus saith the Lord, bold Moses said,
  O let my people go!
If not, I'll smite your first born dead,
  O let my people go!

No more shall they in bondage toil,
  O let my people go!
Let them come out with Egypt's spoil,
  O let my people go!

Then Israel out of Egypt came,
  O let my people go!
And left the proud oppressive land,
  O let my people go!

O 'twas a dark and dismal night,
  O let my people go!
When Moses led the Israelites,
  O let my people go!

'Twas good old Moses, and Aaron, too,
  O let my people go!
'Twas they that led the armies through,
  O let my people go!

The Lord told Moses what to do,
O let my people go!
To lead the children of Israel through,
O let my people go!

O come along Moses, you'll not get lost,
O let my people go!
Stretch out your rod and come across,
O let my people go!

As Israel stood by the water side,
O let my people go!
At the command of God it did divide,
O let my people go!

When they had reached the other shore,
O let my people go!
They sang a song of triumph o'er,
O let my people go!

Pharaoh said he would go across,
O let my people go!
But Pharaoh and his host were lost,
O let my people go!

O Moses, the cloud shall cleave the way,
O let my people go!
A fire by night, a shade by day,
O let my people go!

You'll not get lost in the wilderness,
O let my people go!
With a lighted candle in your breast,
O let my people go!

Jordan shall stand up like a wall,
O let my people go!
And the walls of Jericho shall fall,
O let my people go!

Your foe shall not before you stand,
O let my people go!
And you'll possess fair Canaan's land,
O let my people go!

'Twas just about in harvest time,
O let my people go!
When Joshua led his host Divine,
O let my people go!

O let us all from bondage flee,
O let my people go!
And let us all in Christ be free,
O let my people go!

We need not always weep and mourn,
O let my people go!
And wear these Slavery chains forlorn,
O let my people go!

This world's a wilderness of woe,
O let my people go!
O let us on to Canaan go,
O let my people go!

What a beautiful morning that will be!
O let my people go!
When time breaks up in eternity,
O let my people go!

Lonesome Valley

You got to walk that lonesome valley,
You got to go there by yourself,
Ain't nobody here can go there for you,
You got to go there by yourself.

If you cannot preach like Peter,
If you cannot pray like Paul,
You can tell the love of Jesus,
You can say he died for all.

Your mother's got to walk that lonesome valley,
She's got to go there by herself,
Ain't nobody else can go there for her,
She's got to go there by herself.

Your father's got to walk that lonesome valley,
He's got to go there by himself,
Ain't nobody else can go there for him,
He's got to go there by himself.

Your brother's got to walk that lonesome valley,
He's got to go there by himself,
Ain't nobody else can go there for him,
He's got to go there by himself.

Nobody Knows the Trouble I've Had

Nobody knows de trouble I've had,
Nobody knows but Jesus,
Nobody knows de trouble I've had,
Glory hallelu!

One morning I was a-walking down, O yes, Lord!
I saw some berries a-hanging down, O yes, Lord!

I pick de berry and I suck de juice, O yes, Lord!
Just as sweet as the honey in de comb, O yes, Lord!

Sometimes I'm up, sometimes I'm down, O yes, Lord!
Sometimes I'm almost on de groun', O yes, Lord!

What make ole Satan hate me so? O yes, Lord!
Because he got me once and he let me go, O yes, Lord!

Poor Wayfaring Stranger

I am a poor wayfaring stranger
While trav'ling through this world of woe,
Yet there's no sickness, toil nor danger
In that bright world to which I go.
I'm going there to see my father,
I'm going there no more to roam;
I'm only going over Jordan,
I'm only going over home.

I know dark clouds will gather round me,
I know my way is rough and steep;
Yet beauteous fields lie just before me
Where God's redeem'd their vigils keep.
I'm going there to see my mother,
She said she'd meet me when I come;
I'm only going over Jordan,
I'm only going over home.

I'll soon be freed from every trial,
My body sleep in the church-yard;
I'll drop the cross of self-denial
And enter on my great reward.
I'm going there to see my class-mates,
Who've gone before me one by one;
I'm only going over Jordan,
I'm only going over home.

I want to wear a crown of glory,
When I get home on that good land;
I want to shout salvation's story,
In concert with the blood-wash'd band;
I'm going there to see my Savior,
To sing his praise forever more;
I'm only going over Jordan,
I'm only going over home.

Simple Gifts

'Tis the gift to be simple, 'tis the gift to be free,
'Tis the gift to come down where we ought to be,
And when we find ourselves in the place just right,
'Twill be in the valley of love and delight.
When true simplicity is gain'd,
To bow and to bend we shan't be asham'd,
To turn, turn will be our delight
'Till by turning, turning we come round right.

Sometimes I Feel Like a Motherless Child

Sometimes I feel like a motherless child,
Sometimes I feel like a motherless child,
Sometimes I feel like a motherless child,
A long ways from home,
A long ways from home.
True believer.
A long ways from home,
A long ways from home.

Ef this was judgment day,
Ef this was judgment day,
Ef this was judgment day,
Eb'ry little soul would pray,
Eb'ry little soul would pray.
True believer.
Eb'ry little soul would pray,
Eb'ry little soul would pray.

Sometimes I feel like I'm almos' gone,
Sometimes I feel like I'm almos' gone,
Sometimes I feel like I'm almos' gone,
Way up in de Hebbenly lan',
Way up in de Hebbenly lan'.
True believer.
Way up in de Hebbenly lan',
Way up in de Hebbenly lan'.

Steal Away

Steal away, steal away, steal away to Jesus!
Steal away, steal away home,
I hain't got long to stay here.

My Lord calls me,
He calls me by the thunder;
The trumpet sounds it in my soul:
I hain't got long to stay here.

Green trees are bending,
Poor sinners stand trembling;
The trumpet sounds it in my soul:
I hain't got long to stay here.

My Lord calls me,
He calls me by the lightning;
The trumpet sounds it in my soul:
I hain't got long to stay here.

Tombstones are bursting,
Poor sinners stand trembling;
The trumpet sounds it in my soul:
I hain't got long to stay here.

Swing Low, Sweet Chariot

Swing low, sweet chariot,
Coming for to carry me home,
Swing low, sweet chariot,
Coming for to carry me home.

I looked over Jordan, and what did I see,
Coming for to carry me home?
A band of angels coming after me,
Coming for to carry me home.

If you get there before I do,
Coming for to carry me home,

Tell all my friends I'm coming too,
Coming for to carry me home.

The brightest day that ever I saw,
Coming for to carry me home,
When Jesus wash'd my sins away,
Coming for to carry me home.

I'm sometimes up and sometimes down,
Coming for to carry me home,
But still my soul feels heavenly bound,
Coming for to carry me home.

Reader's Guide

[*Note*: The guide presented here is not intended to serve as an exhaustive list of topics suggested by the poems in this anthology, nor does it seek to characterize poems as subsumed by a single topic or category. It is meant to facilitate reading, directing readers toward specific poems touching on certain areas of religious experience.]

Apocalypse

In "And, the last day being come, Man stood alone" (**p. 170**), Trumbull Stickney envisions the world's end in a tableau as sensuous as it is abstract: the generalized personification Man is beset by the tumultuous wailing of "every manner of beast innumerable" swept up in the apocalypse, which culminates in a sublime image, spectacular and terrifying, of "the last sea-serpent" extinguishing the sun. Robert Frost, in "Once by the Pacific" (**p. 176**), sees apocalyptic energies at work in an ominous coastal landscape, though the invocation of the world's end that closes the poem, with the word of God cast in the American vernacular, is as much playful as prophetic: "There would be more than ocean-water broken / Before God's last *Put out the Light* was spoken." For an ironic treatment of the theme, see John Crowe Ransom's "Armageddon" (**p. 236**).

Being

Attitudes of reverence and wonder at the mystery of being are at the core of spiritual experience, regardless of one's formal affiliation with a particular religion or belief system. In a mood of stately awe, one of Wallace Stevens' last poems, "Of Mere Being" (**p. 194**), explores the ineffable transcendence of existence itself, which surpasses human modes of feeling and understanding: "You know then that it is not the reason / That makes us happy or unhappy. / The bird sings. Its feathers shine." Where Stevens' meditation on being is rich in imaginative symbols and metaphors, other poets evoke being by focusing on actual things in the world. William Carlos Williams' dictum, "No ideas but in things," expresses a fusion of the particular and the transcendent, in which the simple act of naming has metaphysical import: as George Oppen writes in the first stanza of "Psalm" (**p. 307**): "In the small beauty of the forest / The wild deer bedding down— / That they are there!" In "God's World" (**p. 245**), Edna St. Vincent Millay finds herself smitten to the point of ecstasy with being's abundance; in a similarly lyric outpouring, E. E. Cummings, in "i thank You God for most this amazing" (**p. 246**), exults in "everything / which is natural which is infinite which is yes." The last stanza of N. Scott Momaday's "The Delight Song of Tsoai-talee" (**p. 453**) begins and ends with a joyous affirmation of life: "You see, I am alive, I am alive."

Covenant

In "The New Ezekiel" (**p. 154**), Emma Lazarus takes as her point of departure Ezekiel's plaintive cry, "Can these bones live?" (Ezekiel 37:3) to affirm God's covenant with the Jewish people. A precociously gifted poet who published her first book as a teenager, Lazarus began her career writing sonorous nature poetry under the sway of Romanticism but evolved into a poet whose treatment of Jewish themes complemented her work as a proto-Zionist activist, a commitment that intensified after widespread pogroms against Jews in Russia in 1880. "The New Ezekiel" is a rejoinder to Longfellow's wistful "The Jewish Cemetery at Newport" (**p. 80**), which regards Jewish history as a saga of persecution with religious and racial extinction as its inevitable end: "But ah! what once has been shall be no more! / The groaning earth in travail and in pain / Brings forth its races, but does not restore, / And the dead nations never rise again." Lazarus, envisioning a different future for the Jews after "twenty scorching centuries of wrong," figures God's covenant as a promise of transformation: "where lay dead bones, a host of armed men stand!"

Often expressed in legalistic imagery, convenant theology was a key building block of the Puritan sensibility shared by several of the early poets in this anthology. Edward Taylor's (**p. 18**) courtroom sketch of his soul in the dock and Christ his advocate before the Father vividly affirms this way of conceiving of redemption.

The Creation

James Weldon Johnson's "The Creation" (**p. 163**) is taken from his *God's Trombones: Seven Negro Sermons in Verse*, an exuberant homage to the power of the African-American sermonic tradition. In "The Creation, According to Coyote" (**p. 493**), the first poem of his collection *Going for the Rain* (1976), Simon J. Ortiz retells the creation myth of the Acoma Pueblo people. As in Johnson's poem, Ortiz domesticates, as it were, the story of the world's creation through his use of vernacular speech: "Coyote told me too, but you know / how he is, always talking to the gods, / the mountains, the stone all around." Ortiz also highlights the importance of the myth's transmission: the story comes down to him from both his uncle and the trickster-figure Coyote, a recurring character in *Going for the Rain*. Both Johnson and Ortiz translate the most fundamental traditional myths into a living language, and yet in making these traditions their own they also affirm links with the collective and communal past.

See also: "The Creation of the Earth" (Pima) (**p. 605**).

The Crucifixion and the Resurrection

In Sidney Lanier's haunting "A Ballad of Trees and the Master" (**p. 150**), the crucifixion story is pared down to a stark opposition between Christ's union with nature and his estrangement from the human community that puts him to death. His contemporary, the Catholic priest John Bannister Tabb, explores the apparent paradoxes in the crucifixion in "Nekros" (**p. 151**). Lizette Woodworth Reese, in "This Very Hour" (**p. 155**), brings the story to the setting of a humble American village, in which the personae of the ancient drama—Pilate, Peter, James—go about mundane tasks. A less orthodox treatment of the crucifixion is given by Walt Whitman in the fragment "In vain were nails driven through my hands" (**p. 115**). Speaking through the persona of Jesus, Whitman rejects the "cold mortar and brick" of established religion—"Not all the traditions can put vitality in churches"—to affirm the spirit of Christ as present in the world today.

In "The Litany of the Dark People" (**p. 287**), Countee Cullen regards the crucifixion as an allegory of racial persecution in the United States. The title of Conrad Aiken's "Tetélestai" (**p. 239**)—"It is finished" in Greek—is derived from Jesus' words on the Cross; Aiken's meditation on mortality takes shape against the backdrop of the Christian theology of death and resurrection. In sections 3 and 7 of her *The Flowering of the Rod* (**p. 202**), H.D. considers resurrection not as the ending of the crucifixion story but as a "sense of direction," the origin of a journey toward fulfillment: "we know ultimately we will find // happiness; *to-day shalt thou be / with me in Paradise*" (citing Christ's words, Luke 23:43).

See also: Allen Tate, "The Cross" (**p. 279**); Amy Clampitt, "Easter Morning" (**p. 358**); Vicki Hearne, "Good Friday: No Way Out but Straight Through, Jack" (**p. 505**); Mark Jarman, "Transfiguration" (**p. 535**).

Death and Mortality

Thomas Dudley, a governor of Massachusetts Bay Colony and the father of Anne Bradstreet, is represented here by the one extant poem attributed to him, "Dim Eyes, deaf Ears, cold stomack shew" (**p. 2**), which was found in his pocket just after his death. Dudley's valedictory poem, written in his mid-seventies, begins with a description of his ravaged body that is striking in its terseness. Refusing to dwell on his suffering, he casts himself as an example for posterity and, imagining himself already dead, closes the poem with the defiant assertion that he "dy'd no libertine" (referring not merely to licentious behavior but also heresy and blasphemy).

Other considerations of mortality include Melville's lapidary pronouncement of matter's "ancient brutal claim" in "Fragments of a Lost Gnostic Poem of the 12th Century" (**p. 112**), and his evocation of earthly transience in "Pontoosuce" (**p. 112**). James Baldwin's "Amen" (**p. 383**) alludes to a brush with death without revealing what actually happened to him. In "Thanks" (**p. 510**), Yusef Komunyakaa reflects on his luck surviving as a soldier in the Vietnam War. Mary Oliver's "When Death Comes" (**p. 460**) is a reckoning of death's inevitability that inspires a vow to seize the day: "I don't want to end up simply having visited the world."

See also: "Great GOD, how frail a thing is man" (**p. 38**); John Leland, "The day is past and gone"(**p. 47**); Jones Very, "The Cup" (**p. 95**); Louise Bogan, "Night" (**p. 250**); Richard Eberhart, "The Groundhog" (**p. 289**).

Divine Love

A grateful sense of God's beneficence and love informs the optimism of John Greenleaf Whittier's "The Eternal Goodness" (**p. 84**). Ralph

Waldo Emerson, optimistic but in a different fashion, regards divine love as residing within everyone; in his manuscript poem beginning "There is in all the sons of men" (**p. 73**), God's love is figured as a "Chord" that resonates as a moral power and a source of hope. For Whitman, whose spiritual vision owes a debt to Emerson but is ultimately larger and more comprehensive, love is a fundamental force, suffusing the self with transcendent, transformative energies; as he writes in the fifth section of "Song of Myself" (**p. 115**): "a kelson of the creation is love." Writing in quite a different register, one of plain yet striking lyricism, Lizette Woodworth Reese accepts God's love as a power that encompasses the sweetness of vitality and the certainty of death: "Love holds me here; Love cuts me down; / And it is well with me" ("Trust," **p. 155**). In our own time, Gjertrud Schnackenberg's consideration of "Supernatural Love" (**p. 542**) makes no overtly theological pronouncements but instead tells a story about early childhood.

See also: T. S. Eliot, "Little Gidding" (**p. 228**); Muriel Rukeyser, "Are You Born? / II" (**p. 327**).

The Divine Word

Poets, whose work of creation carries an aura of mystery and transcendence, have often written about the sacred and mystical nature of the divine Word as imparted to men and women and as manifested in the world. Emerson, in "Γνωθι Σεαυτον" [Know Thyself] (**p. 70**), declares that human speech expresses the "stifled voice" of the Godhead, but "if thou listen to his voice / If thou obey the royal thought / It will grow clearer to thine ear / More glorious to thine eye / The clouds will burst that veil him now / And thou shalt see the Lord." Characteristically for Emerson, such a revelation shines forth without the mediation of doctrines, books, or ritual, all of which he distrusted—the simple act of listening, if performed with the right spiritual orientation, yields a radiant encounter with God. (As it does, perhaps, for Thomas Merton: see his "In Silence," **p. 345**.) For Anna Hempstead Branch, however, in "In the Beginning Was the Word" (**p. 171**), God reveals himself through the medium of scripture—in this case, over the course of a ten-day reading of the Bible from start to finish. The reading Branch describes is a process of utter absorption in the Word, in which the body is incorporated into the very fabric of revelation—"And my flesh was in the Book, / And its blood was in me,"—and the ecstatic reading experience is best summed up in retrospect in a refrain of tautological certainty: "I saw what I saw, / And I knew what I knew."

See also: Henry David Thoreau, "Inspiration" (**p. 103**); Hart Crane, "The Broken Tower" (**p. 277**); Robert Duncan, "The Natural Doctrine" (**p. 351**); Louise Glück, "The Logos" from "Lamentations" (**p. 496**); Chase Twichell, "Cloud of Unknowing" (**p. 520**).

Doubt and Belief

Best known for his novels, William Dean Howells published the short poem "What Shall It Profit?" (**p. 150**) in *Harper's New Monthly Magazine* in 1891, addressing a crisis of faith that, though it has affected believers across the centuries, was experienced especially acutely by many in the nineteenth century in the wake of scientific advancements and the dissemination of Darwin's ideas. (As Melville wrote in the epilogue to *Clarel* [**p. 110**]: "If Luther's day expand to Darwin's year, / Shall that exclude the hope—foreclose the fear?") Howells' rejection of the corrosive effects of doubt resonate with the sentiment of Edwin Arlington Robinson's "The Children of the Night" (**p. 161**). In his own life a man with an austere and often depressive temperament, Robinson exhorts those mired in a "sullen" darkness in which there is "No God but in a prophet's lie" to cast off "the cloak that hides the scar" and become "Children of the Light." Written nearly a century later, John Burt's "On the Will to Believe" (**p. 553**) is a meditation on the concept elucidated by William James in an essay published, like Robinson's poem, in 1897.

See also: Wallace Stevens, "Sunday Morning" (**p. 187**); E. E. Cummings, "i thank You God for most this amazing" (**p. 246**), especially the third stanza; Elinor Wylie's, "Address to My Soul" (**p. 216**), especially the lines, "Fear not, pathetic flame; / Your sustenance is doubt"; Richard Hugo," St. Clement's Harris" (**p. 377**).

Evil

Two poems by Robert Hayden struggle with the problem of evil as manifested in the political persecutions of the twentieth century. "From the corpse woodpiles, from the ashes" (**p. 319**) shows the poet haunted by the unspeakable horror of the Holocaust, whereas in the unsettling "As my blood was drawn" (**p. 322**) he imagines a terrifying symmetry between his own illness and the world's evil, as if the failures of his body were an uncanny expression of global corruption: "World I have loved, / so lovingly hated, / is it your evil / that has invaded / my body's world?"

See also: Lucie Brock-Broido, "'The One Theme of Which Everything Else Is a Variation" (**p. 559**).

Grief and Consolation

The elegy was the predominant genre of poetry for American Puritans. Benjamin Tompson's "A Neighbour's Tears" (**p. 29**) commemorates the sudden passing of a five-year-old named Rebekah Sewell, who is remembered in a tender, poignant image—"I saw this little One but t'other day / With a small flock of Doves, just in my way: / What New-made Creature's this so bright? thought I"—before Tompson attempts to assuage the grief of the girl's mother with familiar, though certainly not trivial, religious commonplaces. Nicolas Noyes addresses to Cotton Mather an elegy (**p. 30**) that lauds Mather's late wife as daughter, mother, and woman whose "Maiden Vertues rendred her / A Meet-Help for a minister." The death of Anne Bradstreet, who described her bodily suffering in harrowing terms in "From Deliveʳᵉ from a feaver" (**p. 8**), is an occasion for John Norton to praise her poetry in his "A Funeral Elogy" (**p. 34**).

The conventions of the elegy are part of the comfort the genre provides; the standard sentiments and rhetoric of the form help to fill the void of grief, which often seems too great for words. For some, no matter what words are used to express sympathy, the pain of loss is still too raw. James Russell Lowell, in "After the Burial" (**p. 107**), insists on his grief and resists all attempts to comfort him: "Console if you will, I can bear it; / 'T is a well-meant alms of breath; / But not all the preaching since Adam / Has made Death other than Death."

See also: Donald Hall, "A Grace" (**p. 428**); David Ignatow, "Kaddish" (**p. 341**); Carol Muske-Dukes, "When He Fell" (**p. 504**).

The Miraculous

In "Visitation" (**p. 577**), Carl Phillips reflects on the aftermath of a mysterious nocturnal experience that, elliptically described, yields to the note of stubborn insistence that closes the poem: "I saw / what I saw," Phillips writes—regardless of the rational explanations offered to explain what happened. Phillips' poem is a vignette about how people respond to and frequently explain away the possibility of the miraculous, a category much easier to accept when it appears, as it does in William Carlos Williams' "The Gift" (**p. 198**), in a traditional story like that of the Magi. The power of Sylvia Plath's account of the miraculous ("those spasmodic / Tricks of radiance," as she writes in "Black Rook in Rainy Weather," **p. 451**) comes from her description of having a rare epiphany "Even in this dull, ruinous landscape" as she endures the "long wait for the angel."

See also: Anna Hempstead Branch, "In the Beginning Was the Word" (**p. 171**); Anthony Hecht, "A Hill" (**p. 373**).

Nature

So many poems are about nature in this anthology that it's fair to conclude that for many American poets, the worship of nature is indistinguishable from the worship of God. Although the Puritans wrote poems that consider natural phenomena in light of their doctrines and philosophies—see Edward Taylor's poems about insects, "Upon a Spider Catching a Fly" (**p. 24**) and "Upon a Wasp Child with Cold" (**p. 25**) —the dominant strain of American religious nature poetry emerges in the first half of the nineteenth century, epitomized by works by Bryant and transcendentalist poets such as Emerson, Thoreau, and, later, Whitman. As early as 1815, Philip Freneau articulated what would become a familiar equation of benevolent nature and an ideal spirituality: "Religion, such as nature taught, / With all divine perfection suits; / Had all mankind this system sought / Sophists would cease their vain disputes, / And from this source would nations know / All that can make their heaven below" ("On the Religion of Nature," **p. 44**). "The groves were God's first temples," asserts Bryant in "Forest Hymn" (**p. 57**), with the authority of a self-evident truth; Longfellow echoes Bryant's characterization in "My Cathedral" (**p. 83**), inviting the reader to silent communion with the serenity of the forest: "Enter! the pavement, carpeted with leaves, / Gives back a softened echo to thy tread! / Listen! the choir is singing; all the birds, / In leafy galleries beneath the eaves, / Are singing! listen, ere the sound be fled, / And learn there may be worship without words." Christopher Pearse Cranch writes that "Nature is but a scroll; God's handwriting thereon" (in "Correspondences," **p. 92**), and William Ellery Channing posits a perfect accord between the particulars of the natural world and the realm of the transcendent when he declares, "No leaf may fall, no pebble roll, / No drop of water lose the road, / The issues of the general Soul / Are mirrored in its round abode" ("Hymn of the Earth," **p. 100**).

In their sense of natural harmony and grandeur, the landscapes figured in these reverent poems are close kin to those depicted in the paintings of the Hudson River School. Other American locales elicit different sorts of poems. In "In Death Valley" (**p. 154**), Edwin Markham goes against the grain of much American poetry that sees nature suffused with a beneficent spirit. No less sublime than the mountains and groves of the transcendentalists, Death Valley in Markham's poem yields a revelation of a "Grief that began before the ancient flood" as the poet surveys the desolation of the landscape. The California settings of Robinson Jeffers' poems are places of harsh beauty throbbing with violent undercurrents that suggest a more primitive religion: "here the granite cliff the gaunt cypresses crown / Demands what victim? The dykes of red lava and black what Titan? The hills like pointed flames / Beyond Soberanes, the terrible peaks of the bare hills under the sun, what immolation?" ("Apology for Bad Dreams," **p. 208**).

Gary Snyder's Buddhist-inflected poems seek to move away from a sense of nature that is mediated by our ideas about it: "Nature not a book, but a *performance*," he writes in "Ripples on the Surface" (**p. 450**), a poem that ends by collapsing the opposition of human consciousness and the world outside: "The little house in the wild, / the wild in the house. / Both forgotten. // No nature. // Both together, one big empty house."

See also: Ralph Waldo Emerson, "The Rhodora" (**p. 64**); May Swenson, "The Lightning" (**p. 331**), "Big-Hipped Nature" (**p. 331**), and "Each Like a Leaf" (**p. 332**); Allen Ginsberg, "Wales Visitation" (**p. 402**); James Wright, "A Blessing" (**p. 426**); Donald Hall, "A Small Fig Tree" (**p. 428**); Philip Levine, "A Late Answer" (**p. 430**); Gary Snyder, "Burning Island" (**p. 448**).

The Next World

With simplicity and grace, two nineteenth-century hymns, Robert Lowry's "Beautiful River" (**p. 138**) and Sanford F. Bennett's "There's a land that is fairer than day" (**p. 149**), offer hopeful and consoling visions of heaven by opposing the toil and burden of this world with the peace and rest of the next. Langston Hughes imagines the happy harmony of the afterlife in "Heaven" (**p. 286**). In envisioning the apotheosis of Salvation Army leader William Booth, Vachel Lindsay captures some of the more brash and raucous registers of American religious celebration ("General William Booth Enters Heaven," **p. 184**); Sterling A. Brown's beguiling "Sister Lou" (**p. 281**) counsels the right way to take "de las' train / You're gonna ride."

Other poets write about the mysteries on the other side of death; see "Question" (**p. 330**), in which May Swenson wonders what will happen after "Body my good / bright dog is dead," and Emily Dickinson's "I felt a Funeral, in my Brain" (**p. 141**) and "I heard a Fly buzz – when I died" (**p. 144**). Joy Harjo evokes the next world as, among other things, a means to criticize contemporary America in "A Map to the Next World" (**p. 526**).

Organized Religion

In "First-Day Thoughts" (**p. 83**) John Greenleaf Whittier praises the Quaker meeting, a gathering where, "syllabled by silence," he listens for the "still small voice which reached the prophet's ear." Whittier's poem is fairly exceptional in this anthology in its enthusiasm for a religious service. Indeed, many American poets, not least Whitman, have regarded orthodox worship as much an impediment as a means to spiritual growth, or, at the very least, have accused established religion of hypocrisy and smug self-regard. One of this anthology's few satirical poems, the excerpt from Timothy Dwight's *The Triumph of Infidelity* (**p. 43**; a section sometimes referred to as "The Smooth Divine"), singles out the sort of clergyman who uses his position to secure bland comforts and degrades the institution he is supposed to serve. T. S. Eliot's ironic poem "The Hippopotamus" (**p. 217**) satirizes what he regards as the unctuous self-assurance of the church: "The hippo's feeble steps may err / In compassing material ends, / While the True Church need never stir / To gather in its dividends."

Dwight (himself a clergyman) and Eliot were devout believers, and the satiric import of these poems is rooted in passionate views about what religion should be but often isn't. For many of the other poets in this volume, formal religious belonging is largely irrelevant to their spiritual concerns and explorations. Still others are conflicted about the place of established religion in their spiritual lives; searchingly, "The Problem" (**p. 62**) dramatizes Ralph Waldo Emerson's complicated views about the clerical vocation, reflecting his own experience as a young Unitarian minister who, in 1832, felt compelled to leave the clergy and forge a career as poet, lecturer, essayist, and philosopher. "I like a church; I like a cowl;" Emerson writes. "I love a prophet of the soul; / And on my heart monastic aisles / Fall like sweet strains, or pensive smiles; / Yet not for all his faith can see / Would I that cowlèd churchman be."

Praise

"All men by their nature give praise," writes William Carlos Williams in "The Gift" (**p. 198**). "It is all / they can do." Many poems in this anthology eschew the exploration of spiritual questions for a more devotional stance of awe and gratitude before God. One of the more worshipful of these poems is William Everson's "A Canticle to the Waterbirds" (**p. 315**), written shortly before Everson entered the Dominican Order as a lay monk in 1951, taking the name Brother Antoninus (he left the order in 1969). As a poet, he was an acolyte of Robinson Jeffers, whose long bardic lines and sense of the rugged sublimity of nature are echoed in Everson's poems. But whereas Jeffers' beliefs led him to an uncompromising pessimism that at times tends toward wholesale misanthropy—"I'd sooner, except the penalties, kill a man than a hawk," Jeffers writes in "Hurt Hawks" (**p. 211**)—Everson embraced orthodoxy in poems that express a passionate, idiosyncratic striving to understand his relationship to God. His best-known poem "A Canticle to the Waterbirds" is a majestic praise-song to God as he manifests himself in the otherness of nature, in realms beyond human habitation and experience: "You leave a silence. And this for you suffices, who are not of the ceremonials of man, / And hence are not made sad to now forgo them. / Yours is of another order of being, and wholly it compels. / But may you, birds, utterly seized in God's supremacy, / Austerely living under his austere eye— / Yet may you teach a man a necessary thing to know . . ."

See also: The Bay Psalm Book, "Psalme 19" (**p. 1**); William Billings, "An Anthem, for Thanksgiving" (**p. 42**); Knowles Shaw, "Sowing in the Morning" (**p. 147**); Claude McKay, "Russian Cathedral" (**p. 244**); Delmore Schwartz, "At a Solemn Musick" (**p. 327**); Carolyn Kizer, "Shalimar Gardens" (**p. 387**); Grace Schulman, "Blessed Is the Light" (**p. 461**).

Prayer

Poetry and prayer are both forms of exalted speech, uses of language distinct from our common, utilitarian way of talking (even if sometimes composed of quite colloquial words and expressions). Prayer is at once a form and a subject for poetry, a means of addressing God and an occasion for reflection about how to properly speak to the divine (or, as in Thomas Merton's "In Silence," **p. 345**, how *not* to speak). Edward Taylor wrote his "Preparatory Meditations" (**pp. 17–22**), two series of poems composed over more than four decades, to ready himself for the sacrament of communion. Rhetorically dense, richly exploratory in terms of its tropes and metaphors, these poems are deeply personal attempts by Taylor to rightly orient himself before participating in holy ritual. The poems record the inner struggles of a man who confesses in supplication: "My case is bad. Lord, be my Advocate."

In the "Preparatory Meditations" Taylor luxuriates in his metaphors, leaping with impatience from one figure to the next. Other poets, particularly those of the twentieth century, express a wary distrust of their own speech. Consider John Berryman's "Eleven Addresses to the Lord" (**p. 334**): "I have made up a morning prayer to you / containing with precision everything that most matters. / 'According to Thy will' the thing begins. / It took me off & on two days. It does not aim at eloquence." The insomniac speaker of Robert Hayden's "Ice Storm" (**p. 322**) finds his desire to pray thwarted; reflecting on the "moonstruck trees" outside his window, he emerges from his sleepless night to address God with a simple, understated, celebratory question: "And am I less to You / my God, than they?" When C. K. Williams (in "The Vessel," **p. 482**) thinks about his efforts to pray, his detachment from the act yields a torrent of unanswerable questions, underscoring the difficulties of genuine prayer: "I'm trying to pray, but

I know that whatever I'm doing I'm not: why aren't I, when will I?" Denise Levertov explores similar concerns in "Flickering Mind" (**p. 379**): "How can I focus my flickering, perceive / at the fountain's heart / the sapphire I know is there?" A more assured and steadfast mode of prayer is imagined through the invention of a fictional character (evoking a less skeptical and self-conscious era) in Robert Pinsky's "The Knight's Prayer" (**p. 491**).

See also: Carl Sandburg, "Our Prayer of Thanks" (**p. 181**); W. H. Auden, "Horae Canonicae" (**p. 302**); James Schuyler, "Our Father" (**p. 381**), an ebullient adaptation of the Lord's Prayer; John Frederick Nims, "Prayer" (**p. 323**); Louise Glück, "Matins" (**p. 498**) and "Vespers" (**p. 499**); Jorie Graham, "Prayer" (**p. 523**); Alan Shapiro, "Prayer on the Temple Steps" (**p. 541**); April Bernard, "Psalm of the Tree-Dweller" (**p. 558**).

Providence

Faith in God's guidance has enabled believers to see the hand of God in events large and small. In "They see Gods wonders that are call'd" (**p. 4**), Roger Williams attributes his survival at sea to the will of the Almighty: "I have in *Europes* ships, oft been / In King of terrours hand; / When all have cri'd, *Now, now we sinck* / Yet God brought safe to land." John Quincy Adams, whose poems on religious and moral subjects were numerous enough to fill a posthumous volume of his verse, senses God's plan in everything he does, though he admits that God's ultimate purposes are obscure to him: "Before, behind, I meet thine eye, / And feel thy heavy hand: / Such knowledge is for me too high, / To reach or understand" ("O Lord, Thy All-Discerning Eyes," **p. 49**). Less affirming and more skeptical about the divine blueprint is Robert Frost's "Design" (**p. 176**), a vignette of nature's cruelty in miniature that concludes with Frost wondering "if design govern in a thing so small."

See also: William Cullen Bryant, "To a Waterfowl" (**p. 56**).

Social Struggles

Grounding the fight for independence in the fervent belief that "Newengland's God forever reigns," the rousing Revolutionary War song "Chester" (**p. 41**) was the most renowned of colonial hymnist William Billings' compositions. Emerson's "Boston Hymn" (**p. 67**), recited publicly on the day the Emancipation Proclamation was declared, connects the view that Providence guided the Pilgrims in the name of freedom with the abolitionist call to "unbind the captive / So only are ye unbound." Two of the most indelible pieces of writing to emerge from the Civil War and its aftermath, Julia Ward Howe's "Battle-Hymn of the Republic" (**p. 106**) and Walt Whitman's "When Lilacs Last in the Dooryard Bloom'd" (**p. 125**), glimpse the workings of the divine during America's greatest national trauma.

Religious denominations and institutions have often campaigned for social justice, and many poets have fused their calls to speak out against oppression and societal problems with ideas and rhetorical styles drawn from religion. W.E.B. Du Bois, for example, uses a liturgical call-and-response form to deliver an impassioned indictment of lynching in "A Litany at Atlanta" (**p. 158**). More generally, in "Religion" (**p. 169**), Paul Laurence Dunbar rejects any brand of Christianity that is not engaged with the here and now: "Take up your arms, come out with me, / Let Heav'n alone; humanity / Needs more and Heaven less from thee."

See also: Robinson Jeffers' poems, which give voice to his outraged pacifism and ecological consciousness. Anguish over recent conflicts informs poems written in the last few decades: the Lebanese civil war in Joseph Awad's "For Jude's Lebanon" (**p. 439**), the Arab-Israeli conflict in Grace Schulman's "Prayer" (**p. 462**), and violence in Sierra Leone in Lucie Brock-Broido's "The One Theme of Which Everything Else Is a Variation" (**p. 559**).

The Spiritual Quest

"We shall not cease from exploration," writes T. S. Eliot at the end of "Little Gidding" (**p. 228**), "And the end of all our exploring / Will be to arrive where we started / And know the place for the first time." Melvin B. Tolson expresses a similar sentiment in a pithier form when he writes, in "A Song for Myself" (**p. 256**): "I seek / Frontiers, / Not worlds / on biers." At the beginning of the twenty-first century, perhaps the most common metaphors Americans use to describe their spirituality are *quest*, *journey*, and *road*. Of course, such metaphors are not new or surprising in a country first settled, in part, by a religious sect known as Pilgrims. Some of the most poignant American expressions of life as spiritual road or journey are contained in hymns such as "Lonesome Valley" (**p. 615**), "Poor Wayfaring Stranger" (**p. 617**), and Thomas A. Dorsey's "Take My Hand, Precious Lord" (**p. 278**). In a different idiom, Whitman's expansive lines are propelled forward by a sense of continual movement. "I shall be good health to you," he writes in the closing stanzas of "Song of Myself" (**p. 115**), and enjoins the reader: "Failing to fetch me at first keep encouraged, / Missing me one place search another." A more anguished sense of journeying is given in Anne Sexton's poem "Rowing" (**p. 437**).

Some of the poets in this anthology have looked to the past and to myth for examples of spiritual quests. Edward Hirsch's "Away from Dogma" (**p. 515**) is based on the restless life of Simone Weil. Charles Reznikoff's short poem (**p. 247**) on the eighteenth-century kabbalist Moses Chaim Luzzato, who claimed at the age of twenty to be receiving mystical communications from an otherworldly being called the *maggid*, focuses on Luzzato's independence and subversive self-assurance in his own quest: "the law itself is nothing but the road; / I have become impatient of what the rabbis said, / and try to listen to what the angels say."

See also: Robert Frost, "Directive" (**p. 177**); H.D., *The Flowering of the Rod* (**p. 202**); William Stafford, "With My Crowbar Key" (**p. 343**); Jack Gilbert, "The White Heart of God" (**p. 386**); Scott Cairns, "Prospect of the Interior" (**p. 548**).

Spiritual Rebirth

American religion places great emphasis on the possibility of the self's renewal, and over the course of his anthology poets repeatedly express the desire to be made anew spiritually: the baroque conceit of Edward Taylor, when he implores God to "Wipe off my Rust, Lord, with thy wisp me scoure" (**p. 20**), resonates with John Berryman's declaration that he is "Under new management, Your Majesty: / Thine" (**p. 337**). Theodore Roethke's "In a Dark Time" (**p. 309**) charts the ego's dissolution as it renews itself in a state in which "The mind enters itself, and God the mind, / And one is One, free in the tearing wind." In Thomas Merton's poem about St. Paul (**p. 344**), the apostle beseeches God to help him "find my Easter in a vision." Louise Erdrich's "New Vows" (**p. 549**) is a parable of spiritual redemption that is also an affirmation of linguistic potency: "Ten years had been enough. I left my darkened house. / . . . Now shadows move freely within me as words. / These are eternal, these stunned, loosened verbs."

See also: Cotton Mather, "The Rain gasped for" (**p. 37**); Henry Wadsworth Longfellow, "The Bridge" (**p. 78**); Robert Frost, "Directive" (**p. 177**), particularly the final line; William Carlos Williams, "Burning the Christmas Greens" (**p. 195**); H.D., *The Flowering of the Rod* (**p. 202**), especially section 7.

Sources and Acknowledgments

Great care has been taken to locate and acknowledge all sources of copyrighted material included in this book. If any owner has inadvertently been omitted, acknowledgment will gladly be made in future printings.

John Quincy Adams. O Lord, Thy All-Discerning Eyes: *Poems of Religion and Society* (Auburn: Derby and Miller, 1850).

Léonie Adams. Bell Tower. *Poems: A Selection* (New York: Funk & Wagnalls, 1954). Copyright © 1954. Reprinted by permission of Judith Farr, Literary Executrix.

James Agee. "This little time the breath and bulk of being": *Permit Me Voyage* (New Haven, CT: Yale University Press, 1934). Copyright © 1968 The James Agee Trust. Reprinted with the permission of The Wylie Agency, Inc.

Conrad Aiken. Tetélestai: *Priapus and the Pool and Other Poems* (New York: Boni & Liveright, 1925). Copyright © 1925, 1953, 1970 by Conrad Aiken. Reprinted by permission of Oxford University Press.

Agha Shalid Ali. First Day of Spring: *Country Without a Post Office* (New York: Norton, 1997). Copyright © 1997 by Agha Shahid Ali. Used by permission of W. W. Norton & Company, Inc. God; Tonight: *Call Me Ishmail Tonight* (New York: Norton, 2003). Copyright © 2003 by Agha Shahid Ali Literary Trust. Used by permission of W. W. Norton & Company.

American Indian Songs and Chants: The Thanksgiving (Iroquois): Harriet Maxwell Converse, *Journal of American Folk-Lore*, 1891. This Is to Frighten a Storm (Cherokee); To Go to the Water (Cherokee): James Mooney, *The Swimmer Manuscript: Cherokee Sacred Formulas and Medicinal Prescriptions*, ed. Frans M. Olbrechts, Bureau of American Ethnology Bulletin 99, 1932. Is This Real (Pawnee): Daniel Garrison Brinton, *Essays of an Americanist* (Philadelphia: Porter & Coates, 1890). Ghost-Dance Songs (Kiowa): James Mooney, "The Ghost-Dance Religion and the Sioux Outbreak of 1890," *Fourteenth Annual Report of the Bureau of American Ethnology*, 1896. Therefore I Must Tell the Truth (Navajo); From The Night Chant (Navajo): Washington Matthews, "The Night Chant, a Navaho Ceremony," *Memoirs of the American Museum of Natural History*, 1902. Song of the Sky Loom (Tewa); Prayer to the Deceased (Tewa): Herbert J. Spinden, *Songs of the Tewa* (New York: Eposition of Indian Tribal Arts, 1933). The Creation of the Earth (Pima): Frank Russell, *The Pima Indians*, 26th Annual Report of the Bureau of American Ethnology, Washington, 1904. Special Request for the Children of Mother Corn (Zuni): Ruth Bunzel, *Zuni Texts*, Publications of the American Ethnological Society 15, 1933. Deer Song (Yaqui): *Yaqui Deer Songs*, ed. Larry Evers and Felipe S. Molina (Tucson: University of Arizona Press, 1987). Copyright © 1987 The Arizona Board of Regents. Reprinted by permission of the University of Arizona Press. Shaman's Song (Modoc): A. L. Kroeber, *Handbook of the Indians of California*, Bureau of American Ethnology Bulletin 78, 1925. Shaman's Song (Inuit): Franz Boas, "Eskimo Tales and Songs," *Journal of American Folk-Lore* 7, 1894.

A. R. Ammons. Prodigal; Terrain; The Arc Inside and Out; The City Limits: *Collected Poems 1951–1971* (New York: Norton, 1972). Copyright © 1972 by A. R. Ammons. Used by permission of W. W. Norton & Company, Inc. For Harold Bloom: *Sphere: The Form of a Motion*

(New York: Norton, 1974). Copyright © 1974 by A. R. Ammons. Used by permission of W. W. Norton & Company, Inc. Easter Morning: *A Coast of Trees* (New York: Norton, 1981). Copyright © 1981 by A. R. Ammons. Used by permission of W. W. Norton & Company, Inc.

James Applewhite. The Sex of Divinity: *Selected Poems* (Durham, NC: Duke University Press, 2005). Copyright © 2005 Duke University Press. All rights reserved. Used by permission of the publisher.

John Ashbery. The Recital: *Three Poems* (New York: Viking, 1972). Copyright © 1970, 1971, 1972 by John Ashbery. Reprinted by permission of Georges Borchardt, Inc., on the behalf of the author. Syringa: *Selected Poems* (New York: Viking, 1985). Copyright © 1975, 1977 by John Ashbery. Reprinted by permission of Georges Borchardt, Inc., on behalf of the author. By Forced Marches: *Hotel Lautreamont* (New York: Knopf, 1992). Copyright © 1992 by John Ashbery. Reprinted by permission of Georges Borchardt, Inc., on behalf of the author.

W. H. Auden. from Horae Canonicae: *Collected Poems*, ed. Edward Mendelson (New York: Vintage, 1991). Copyright © 1976 by Edward Mendelson, William Meredith and Monroe K. Pears, Executors of the Estate of W. H. Auden. Used by permission of Random House, Inc.

Joseph Awad. For Jude's Lebanon: *Grape Leaves: An Anthology of Arab-American Poetry*, ed. Gregory Orfalea and Sharif Elmusa (Salt Lake City: University of Utah Press, 1988). Copyright © 1988. Reprinted by permission of the University of Utah Press.

James Baldwin. Amen: *Jimmy's Blues: Selected Poems* (New York: St. Martin's Press, 1985). Copyright © 1985 by James Baldwin. Reprinted by arrangement with the James Baldwin Estate.

Joel Barlow. from The Columbiad: *The Columbiad: A Poem, with the Last Corrections of the Author* (Washington, DC: Joseph Milligan, 1825).

From The Bay Psalm Book: Psalme 19: *The Whole Booke of Psalmes Faithfully Translated into English Metre* (Cambridge, MA: Stephen Daye, 1640).

Sanford F. Bennett. There's a Land That Is Fairer Than Day: Albert Christ-Janer, Charles W. Hughes, and Carleton Sprague Smith, *American Hymns Old and New* (New York: Columbia University Press, 1980).

April Bernard. Psalm of the Tree-Dweller: *Psalms* (New York: Norton, 1995). Copyright © 1993 by April Bernard. Used by permission of W. W. Norton & Company, Inc.

John Berryman. Eleven Addresses to the Lord: *Collected Poems 1937–1971*, ed. Charles Thornbury (New York: Farrar, Straus and Giroux, 1989). Copyright © 1989 by Kate Donahue Berryman. Reprinted by permission of Farrar, Straus and Giroux, LLC.

Frank Bidart. The Sacrifice: *In the Western Night: Collected Poems 1965–1990* (New York: Farrar, Straus and Giroux, 1990). Copyright © 1990 by Frank Bidart. Reprinted by permission of Farrar, Straus and Giroux, LLC.

William Billings. Chester: *The Singing Master's Assistant* (Boston: Draper and Folsom, 1778). An Anthem for Thanksgiving: *The Continental Harmony* (Boston: Isaiah Thomas and Ebenezer T. Andrews, 1794).

Elizabeth Bishop. The Unbeliever: *The Complete Poems 1927–1979* (New York: Farrar, Straus and Giroux, 1990). Copyright © 1979, 1983 by Alice Helen Methfessel. Reprinted by permission of Farrar, Straus and Giroux, LLC. Over 2000 Illustrations and a Complete Concordance; At the Fishhouses: *Poems: North & South—A Cold Spring* (Boston: Houghton Mifflin, 1955). Copyright © 1979, 1983 by Alice Helen Methfessel. Reprinted by permission of Farrar, Straus and Giroux, LLC.

Robert Bly. The Night Abraham Called to the Stars: *The Night Abraham Called to the Stars* (New York: HarperCollins, 2001). Copyright © 2001 by Robert Bly. Reprinted by permission of HarperCollins Publishers.

Louise Bogan. Night: *The Blue Estuaries: Poems 1923–1968* (New York: Farrar, Straus and Giroux, 1968). Copyright © 1968 by Louise Bogan. Copyright renewed 1996 by Ruth Limmer. Reprinted by permission of Farrar, Straus and Giroux, LLC.

Edgar Bowers. From William Tyndale to John Frith; Adam; Jacob: *Collected Poems* (New York: Knopf, 1997). Copyright © 1997 by Edgar Bowers. Used by permission of Alfred A. Knopf, a division of Random House, Inc.

Anne Bradstreet. The Flesh and the Spirit; For Delive[re] from a feaver; "In silent night when rest I took"; "As weary pilgrim, now at rest": *Complete Works of Anne Bradstreet*, ed. Joseph R. McElrath, Jr., and Allan P. Robb. (Boston: Twayne Publishers, 1981). Reprinted by permission of the Gale Group.

William Stanley Braithwaite. The Eternal Self: *The House of Falling Leaves with Other Poems* (Boston: John W. Luce and Company, 1908).

Anna Hempstead Branch. In the Beginning Was the Word: *Sonnets from a Lockbox* (Boston: Houghton Mifflin, 1929).

Lucie Brock-Broido. The One Theme of Which Everything Else Is a Variation: *Trouble in Mind* (New York: Knopf, 2004). Copyright © 2004 by Lucie Brock-Broido. Used by permission of Alfred A. Knopf, a division of Random House, Inc.

William Bronk. Virgin and Child with Music and Numbers: *Life Supports* (San Francisco: North Point Press, 1982). Copyright © 1995 by William Bronk. Reprinted by permission of New Directions Publishing Corp. The Mind's Limitations Are Its Freedom: *Selected Poems* (New York: New Directions, 1995). Copyright © 1972 by Williams Bronk. Reprinted by permission of New Directions Publishing Corp.

Phillips Brooks. O Little Town of Bethlehem: *The Church Porch* (New York, 1874).

Sterling A. Brown. Sister Lou: *Southern Road* (New York: Harcourt, Brace, 1932). Copyright 1932, renewed © 1960 by Sterling A. Brown. Reprinted by permission of HarperCollins Publishers, Inc.

William Cullen Bryant. Thanatopsis; To a Waterfowl; Forest Hymn: *Poems* (New York: E. Bliss, 1936). Hymn of the Waldenses: *Poems* (Boston: Rusell, Odiorne, and Metcalf, 1834).

John Burt. On the Will to Believe; Sonnets for Mary of Nazareth: *The Way Down* (Princeton, NJ: Princeton University Press, 1988). Copyright © 1988 Princeton University Press. Reprinted by permission of Princeton University Press.

Mather Byles. "Great GOD, how frail a Thing Is Man!": *Poems* (Boston: S. Kneeland and T. Green, 1744).

Scott Cairns. Prospect of the Interior: *Figures for the Ghost* (Athens: University of Georgia Press, 1994). Copyright © 1994 by Scott Cairns. Reprinted by permission of the author.

William Ellery Channing. Hymn of the Earth: *Poems: Second Series* (Boston: James Munroe, 1847).

Amy Clampitt. A Procession at Candlemas; Easter Morning; Brought from Beyond; A Silence: *Collected Poems* (New York: Knopf, 1997). Copyright © 1983, 1994, 1997 by Amy Clampitt. Used by permission of Alfred A. Knopf, a division of Random House, Inc.

Lucille Clifton. the astrologer predicts at mary's birth; anna speaks of the childhood of mary her daughter; mary's dream; how he is coming then; holy night; a song of mary; island mary; "mary mary astonished by God": *Good Woman: Poems and a Memoir 1969–1980* (Rochester, NY: BOA Editions, 1987). Copyright © 1987 by Lucille Clifton. Reprinted by permission of Curtis Brown, Ltd.

Judith Ortiz Cofer. The Campesino's Lament: *The Latin Deli* (Athens: University of Georgia Press, 1993). Copyright © 1993. Reprinted by permission of the University of Georgia Press.

Henri Cole. Apollo: *The Visible Man* (New York: Knopf, 1998). Copyright © 1998 by Henri Cole. Reprinted by permission of Farrar, Straus and Giroux, LLC. Presepio; Blur: *Middle Earth* (New York: Farrar, Straus and Giroux, 2003). Copyright © 2003 by Henri Cole. Reprinted by permission of Farrar, Straus and Giroux, LLC.

Alfred Corn: Jerusalem: *Contradictions* (Port Townsend, WA: Copper Canyon Press, 2002). Copyright © 2002 by Alfred Corn. Reprinted with the permission of Copper Canyon Press, www.coppercanyonpress.org.

Christopher Pearse Cranch: Correspondences; Enosis: *Poems* (Philadelphia: Carey & Hart, 1844).

Hart Crane. Lachrymae Christi; from "Voyages"; from *The Bridge*; O Carib Isle!; The Broken Tower: *The Poems of Hart Crane*, ed. Marc Simon (New York: Liveright, 1986). Copyright © 1933, 1958, 1966 by Liveright Publishing Corporation. Copyright © 1986 by Marc Simon. Used by permission of Liveright Publishing Corporation.

Countee Cullen. Simon the Cyrenian Speaks; The Litany of the Dark People: *My Soul's High Song: The Collected Writings of Countee Cullen*, ed. Gerald Early (New York: Doubleday, 1990). Copyright © 1990. Reprinted by permission.

E. E. Cummings. "i thank You God for most this amazing": *Complete Poems 1904–1962*, rev. edition, ed. George Firmage (New York: Liveright, 1991). Copyright © 1950, 1978, 1991 by the Trustees for the E. E. Cummings Trust. Copyright © 1979 by George James Firmage. Used by permission of Liveright Publishing Corporation.

Richard Henry Dana, Sr. The Little Beach Bird: *Poems and Prose Writings* (New York: Baker and Scribner, 1850).

David Daniel. Seven-Star Bird: *Seven-Star Bird* (St. Paul: Graywolf Press, 2003). Copyright © 2003 by David Daniel. Reprinted with the permission of Graywolf Press, Saint Paul, Minnesota.

Chard DeNiord. Transubstantiation: *Sharp Golden Thorn* (East Rockaway, NY: Marsh Hawk Press, 2003). Copyright © 2003 Chard DeNiord. Used by permission of Marsh Hawk Press.

James Dickey. Adam in Winter; Walking on Water: The Whole Motion: *Collected Poems 1945–1992* (Middletown, CT: Wesleyan University Press, 1992). Copyright © 1992 by James Dickey. Reprinted by permission of Wesleyan University Press.

Emily Dickinson. "I got so I could take his name–"; "I felt a Funeral, in my Brain"; "I know that He exists"; "After great pain, a formal feeling comes–"; "Dare you see a Soul at the 'White Heat'?"; "Our journey had advanced–"; "It might be lonelier"; "I heard a Fly buzz–when I died"; "To pile like Thunder to it's close"; "'Heavenly Father'–take to thee"; "The Spirit lasts–but in what mode–"; "My life closed twice before it's close": *The Poems of Emily Dickinson*, ed. R. W. Franklin (Cambridge, MA: The Belknap Press of Harvard University Press, 1998). Copyright © 1998 by the President and Fellows of Harvard College. Copyright © 1951, 1955, 1979, 1983 by the President and Fellows of Harvard College. Reprinted by permission of the publishers and the Trustees of Amherst College.

George W. Doane. Evening: *Songs by the Way*, ed. William Croswell Doane (Albany: Joel Munsell, 1875.

Thomas A. Dorsey. Take My Hand, Precious Lord: Words and music by Thomas A. Dorsey. Copyright © 1938 (Renewed) by Unichappell Music Inc. Rights for the extended term in the U.S. assigned to Warner-Tamerlane Publishing Corp. Lyrics used by permission of Alfred Publishing Co. All rights reserved.

Rita Dove. Receiving the Stigmata: *Selected Poems* (New York: Vintage, 1993). Copyright © 1983 by Rita Dove. Reprinted by permission of the author.

W.E.B. Du Bois. A Litany at Atlanta: *Darkwater* (New York: Harcourt Brace, 1921).

Thomas Dudley. "Dim Eyes, deaf Ears, cold stomack shew": Nathaniel Morton, *New-Englands memoriall* (Boston: John Usher, 1669).

Alan Dugan. Love Song: I and Thou. *Poems Seven: New and Complete Poetry* (New York: Seven Stories Press, 2001). Copyright © 2001. Reprinted by permission.

Paul Laurence Dunbar. An Ante-Bellum Sermon; Religion: *Lyrics of Lowly Life* (New York: Dodd, Mead & Co., 1897). Faith: *The Complete Poems of Paul Laurence Dunbar* (New York: Dodd, Mead and Company, 1913).

Robert Duncan. Often I am Permitted to Return to a Meadow; The Natural Doctrine: *The Opening of the Field* (New York: Grove, 1960). Copyright © 1960 by Robert Duncan. Reprinted by permission of New Directions Publishing Corp. God-Spell: *Bending the Bow* (New York:

New Directions, 1968). Copyright © 1968 by Robert Duncan. Reprinted by permission of New Directions Publishing Corp.

Timothy Dwight. from *The Triumph of Infidelity*: Colin Wells, *The Devil and Doctor Dwight* (Durham: University of North Carolina Press, 2002). Copyright © 2002 by the University of North Carolina Press. Used by permission of the publisher.

Richard Eberhart. The Groundhog: *Reading the Spirit* (New York: Oxford University Press, 1937). The Soul Longs to Return Whence It Came: *Collected Poems 1930–1986* (Oxford: Oxford University Press, 1987). Copyright © 1960, 1976, 1987 by Richard Eberhart. Reprinted by permission of Oxford University Press.

T. S. Eliot. Ash-Wednesday: *Ash-Wednesday* (London: Faber & Faber, 1930). The Hippopotamus; Journey of the Magi; A Song for Simeon; Little Gidding: *Complete Poems and Plays* (New York: Harcourt, Brace & World, 1952). Copyright © 1936 by Harcourt, Inc., and renewed 1964 by T. S. Eliot. Reprinted by permission of the publisher.

Ralph Waldo Emerson. The Problem; The Rhodora; Dirge: *Poems* (Boston: James Munroe and Co., 1847). Brahma; Boston Hymn: *May-Day and Other Pieces* (Boston: Ticknor & Fields, 1867). Γνωθι Σεαυτον; "There is in all the sons of men . . .": *Journals and Miscellaneous Notebooks of Ralph Waldo Emerson*, vol. 3, ed. William H. Gilman and Alfred R. Ferguson (Cambridge, MA: The Belknap Press of Harvard University Press, 1963). "I will not live out of me . . .": *Journals and Miscellaneous Notebooks of Ralph Waldo Emerson*, vol. 4, ed. Alfred R. Ferguson (Cambridge, MA: The Belknap Press of Harvard University Press, 1964)." He walked the streets of great New York"; "Shun passion, fold the hands of thrift": *The Poetry Notebooks of Ralph Waldo Emerson*, ed. Ralph H. Orth, Albert J. von Frank, Linda Allardt, and David W. Hill (Columbia: University of Missouri Press, 1986). Reprinted by permission of the Ralph Waldo Emerson Memorial Association.

Louise Erdrich. New Vows: *Original Fire: Selected and New Poems* (New York: HarperCollins, 1993). Copyright © 2003 by Louise Erdrich. Reprinted by permission of HarperCollins Publishers.

William Everson. A Canticle to the Waterbirds: *The Crooked Lines of God: Poems 1949–1954* (Detroit: University of Detroit Press, 1959). Copyright © 1997, 1998, and 1999 by Jude Everson and the William Everson Literary Estate. Reprinted by permission of Black Sparrow Books, an imprint of David R. Godine, Publisher, Inc.

Alvin Feinman. Pilgrim Heights; November Sunday Morning: *Poems* (Princeton, NJ: Princeton University Press, 1990). Copyright © 1990 Princeton University Press. Reprinted by permission of Princeton University Press.

Brett Foster. The First Request of Lazarus: text courtesy of the author; originally published in *Image*. Copyright © 2006 by Brett Foster. Reprinted with permission of the author.

Philip Freneau. On the Religion of Nature: *A Collection of Poems, on American Affairs, and a Variety of Other Subjects, Chiefly Moral and Political* (New York: David Longworth, 1815).

Robert Frost. Once by the Pacific; A Prayer in Spring; Bereft; Design; Directive: *Complete Poems of Robert Frost 1949* (New York: Henry Holt and Company, 1950). Copyright © 1936, 1956, 1962 by Robert Frost, © 1964, 1975 by Lesley Frost Balantine, copyright © 1928, 1934, 1947, 1969 by Henry Holt and Company. Reprinted by permission of Henry Holt and Company, LLC.

Jean Garrigue. A Demon Came to Me: *Selected Poems* (Urbana: University of Illinois Press, 1992). Copyright © 1992 by the Estate of Jean Garrigue. Used with permission of the poet and the University of Illinois Press.

Kahlil Gibran. O Soul: *Visions of the Prophet*, trans. Margaret Crosland (Berkeley, CA: Frog Ltd, 1997). English translation copyright © 1995 by Souvenir Press and Margaret Crosland. First American edition published in 1997 by Frog Ltd. Reprinted by permission of Frog. Ltd.

Jack Gilbert. The White Heart of God: *The Great Fires: Poems 1982–1992* (New York: Knopf, 1995). Copyright © 1994 by Jack Gilbert. Used by permission of Alfred A. Knopf, a division of Random House, Inc.

Allen Ginsberg. Wales Visitation; Sunflower Sutra; Psalm III: *Collected Poems 1947–1980* (New York: Harper & Row, 1980). Copyright © 1984 by Allen Ginsberg. Reprinted by permission of HarperCollins Publishers.

Jacob Glatshteyn. Without Offerings: *American Yiddish Poetry*, ed. Benjamin and Barbara Harshav (Berkeley: University of California Press, 1986). Copyright © 1986. Reprinted by permission of University of California Press.

Louise Glück. Lamentations: *The Triumph of Achilles* (New York: The Ecco Press, 1985). Matins; Vespers: *The Wild Iris* (New York: The Ecco Press, 1992). Copyright © 1968, 1971, 1973, 1974, 1975, 1976, 1977, 1978, 1979, 1980, 1985, 1992, 1995 by Louise Glück. Reprinted by permission of HarperCollins Publishers.

Jorie Graham. Prayer: *Never* (New York: The Ecco Press, 2002). Copyright © 2002 by Jorie Graham. Reprinted by permission of HarperCollins Publishers.

Samuel Greenberg. *Poems by Samuel Greenberg*, ed. Harold Holden and Jack McManis (New York Henry Holt and Company, 1947). Copyright © 1947, 1975 by Harold Holden and Jack McManis. Reprinted by permission of Henry Holt and Company, LLC.

Allen Grossman. The Song of the Lord: *The Ether Dome: New and Selected Poems 1979–1991* (New York: New Directions, 1991). Copyright © 1991 by Allen Grossman. Reprinted by permission of New Directions Publishing Corp.

H.D. from The Walls Do Not Fall: *The Walls Do Not Fall* (London: Oxford University Press, 1944). Copyright © 1982 by The Estate of Hilda Doolittle. Reprinted by permission of New Directions Publishing Corp. from The Flowering of the Rod: *The Flowering of the Rod* (London: Oxford University Press, 1946). Copyright © 1944, 1945, 1946 Oxford University Press, renewed 1973 by Norman Holmes Pearson. Reprinted by permission of New Directions Publishing Corp.

Donald Hall. A Small Fig Tree; A Grace: *Old and New Poems* (New York: Mariner Books, 1990). Copyright © 1990 by Donald Hall. Reprinted by permission of Houghton Mifflin Company. All rights reserved.

Moyshe-Leyb Halpern. Memento Mori: *The Penguin Book of Modern Yiddish Verse*, ed. Irving Howe, Ruth R. Wisse, and Khone Shmeruk (New York: Viking, 1987). Copyright © 1987 by Irving Howe, Ruth Wise, and Chone Shmeruk. Used by permission of Viking Penguin, a division of Penguin Group (USA) Inc.The Will: John Hollander, *Selected Poetry* (New York: Knopf, 1993). Copyright © 1993 by John Hollander. Used by permission of Alfred A. Knopf, a division of Random House, Inc.

Joy Harjo. A Map to the Next World: *How We Became Human: New and Selected Poems* (New York: Norton, 2002). Copyright © 2002 by Joy Harjo. Used by permission of W. W. Norton & Company, Inc.

Michael S. Harper. Peace on Earth: *Songlines in Michaeltree: New and Collected Poems* (Urbana: University of Illinois Press, 2000). Copyright © 2000 by Michael S. Harper. Used with permission of the poet and the University of Illinois Press.

Joseph Harrison. The Relic: *Someone Else's Name* (Lincoln, NE: Zoo Press, 2004). Copyright © 2004 by Joseph Harrison. Reprinted by permission.

Robert Hayden. "From the corpse woodpiles, from the ashes"; Bahá'u'lláh in the Garden of Ridwan; The Broken Dark; Ice Storm; "As my blood was drawn": *Collected Poems*, ed. Frederick Glaysher (New York: Liveright, 1985). Copyright © 1985 by Emma Hayden. Used by permission of Liveright Publishing Corporation.

Samuel Hazo. The Holy Surprise of Right Now: *The Holy Surprise of Right Now: Selected and New Poems* (Fayetteville: University of Arkansas Press, 1996). Copyright © 1996 by Samuel Hazo. Reprinted with the permission of the University of Arkansas Press, www.uapress.com.

Vicki Hearne. Good Friday: No Way Out but Straight Through, Jack: *Nervous Horses* (Austin: University of Texas Press, 1980). Copyright © 1980 by Vicki Hearne. Reprinted by permission of the University of Texas Press. The Leisure of God: *The Parts of Light* (Baltimore: Johns Hopkins University Press, 1994). Copyright © 1994 by Vicki Hearne. Reprinted with permission of The Johns Hopkins University Press.

Anthony Hecht. A Hill; Adam: *Collected Early Poems* (New York: Knopf, 1990). Copyright © 1990 by Anthony E. Hecht. Used by permission of Alfred A. Knopf, a division of Random House, Inc. Saul and David: *Collected Later Poems* (New York: Knopf, 2003). Copyright © 2003 by Anthony E. Hecht. Used by permission of Alfred A. Knopf, a division of Random House, Inc.

Edward Hirsch. Away from Dogma: *Earthly Measures* (New York: Knopf, 1994). Copyright © 1994 by Edward Hirsch. Used by permission of Alfred A. Knopf, a division of Random House, Inc.

Linda Hogan. Me, Crow, Fish, and the Magi; The Inside of Things: *Savings* (Minneapolis: Coffee House Press, 1988). Copyright © 1988 by Linda Hogan. Reprinted with the permission of Coffee House Press, Minneapolis, Minnesota.

John Hollander. At the New Year; Adam's Task: *Selected Poetry* (New York: Knopf, 1993). Copyright © 1993 by John Hollander. Used by permission of Alfred A. Knopf, a division of Random House, Inc. A Shadow of a Great Rock in a Weary Land: *Figurehead, and Other Poems* (New York: Knopf, 1999). Copyright © 1999 by John Hollander. Used by permission of Alfred A. Knopf, a division of Random House, Inc.

Oliver Wendell Holmes. The Chambered Nautilus; The Living Temple: *The Autocrat of the Breakfast-Table* (Boston: Phillips, Samson & Co., 1858).

Garrett Hongo. O-Bon: Dance for the Dead; Volcano House: *River of Heaven* (New York: Knopf, 1988). Copyright © 1988 by Garrett Hongo. Used by permission of Alfred A. Knopf, a division of Random House, Inc.

Julia Ward Howe. Battle-Hymn of the Republic: *Later Lyrics* (Boston: J. E. Tilton & Company, 1866).

William Dean Howells. What Shall It Profit? *Harper's New Monthly Magazine*, February 1891.

Andrew Hudgins. Christ as a Gardener: *The Never-ending: New Poems* (Boston: Houghton Mifflin, 1991). Copyright © 1991 by Andrew Hudgins. Reprinted by permission of Houghton Mifflin Company. All rights reserved.

Langston Hughes. The Negro Speaks of Rivers; Prayer; Heaven: *Collected Poems*, ed. Arnold Rampersad (New York: Random House, 1994). Copyright © 1994 by The Estate of Langston Hughes. Used by permission of Alfred A. Knopf, a division of Random House, Inc.

Richard Hugo. St. Clement's: Harris: *Making Certain It Goes On: The Collected Poems of Richard Hugo* (New York: Norton, 1984). Copyright © 1984 by The Estate of Richard Hugo. Used by permission of W. W. Norton & Company, Inc.

David Ignatow. Kaddish: *Against the Evidence: Selected Poems 1934–1994* (Middletown, CT: Wesleyan University Press, 1994). Copyright © 1994 by David Ignatow. Reprinted by permission of Wesleyan University Press.

Helen Hunt Jackson. A Last Prayer: *Sonnets and Lyrics* (Boston: Roberts Brothers, 1886).

Mark Jarman. Transfiguration: *Questions for Ecclesiastes* (Ashland, OR: Story Line Press, 1998). Copyright © 1998. Reprinted by permission of the author and Story Line Press.

Randall Jarrell. Jonah: *The Complete Poems* (New York: Farrar, Straus and Giroux, 1969). Copyright © 1969, renewed 1997 by Mary von Schrader Jarrell. Reprinted by permission of Farrar, Straus and Giroux, LLC.

Robinson Jeffers. Apology for Bad Dreams; Hurt Hawks; Shine, Perishing Republic: *The Collected Poetry of Robinson Jeffers*, 3 vols., ed. Tim Hunt (Stanford, CA: Stanford University Press, 1987). Copyright © 1934 by Robinson Jeffers, renewed 1962 by Donnan Jeffers and Garth Jeffers. Copyright © 1925, 1928, renewed 1953, 1956 by Robinson Jeffers. Used by permission of Random House, Inc. The Treasure. Copyright © 1938, renewed 1966 by Donnan and Garth Jeffers; copyright by the Jeffers Literary Properties. All rights reserved. Used with the permission of Stanford University Press, www.sup.org.

James Weldon Johnson. The Creation: *God's Trombones: Seven Negro Sermons in Verse* (New York: Viking, 1927). Copyright © 1927 The Viking Press, Inc., renewed 1955 by Grace Nail Johnson. Used by permission of Viking Penguin, a division of Penguin Group (USA) Inc.

Ronald Johnson. Beam 30, The Garden: *To Do As Adam Did: The Selected Poems of Ronald Johnson*, ed. Peter O'Leary (Jersey City, NJ: Talisman House, 2000). Copyright © 1996 by Ronald Johnson. Reprinted by permission of the Literary Estate of Ronald Johnson.

Jane Kenyon. Briefly It Enters, and Briefly Speaks. *Otherwise: New and Selected Poems* (St. Paul: Graywolf Press, 1996). Copyright © 2005 by the Estate of Jane Kenyon. Reprinted with the permission of Graywolf Press, Saint Paul, Minnesota.

Suji Kwock Kim. Tree of Unknowing: *Notes from the Divided Country* (Baton Rouge: Louisiana State University Press, 2003). Copyright © 2003 by Suji Kwock Kim. Reprinted by permission of Louisiana State University Press.

Galway Kinnell. To Christ Our Lord: *The Avenue Bearing the Initial of Christ into the New World: Poems 1946–64* (Boston: Houghton Mifflin, 1974). Copyright © 1960, renewed 1988 by Galway Kinnell. Reprinted by permission of Houghton Mifflin Company. All rights reserved.

Caroline Kizer. Shalimar Gardens: *Cool, Calm, and Collected: Poems 1960–2000* (Port Townsend, WA: Copper Canyon Press, 2001). Copyright © 2001 by Carolyn Kizer. Reprinted with the permission of Copper Canyon Press, www.coppercanyonpress.org.

Kenneth Koch. Alive for an Instant: *The Collected Poems of Kenneth Koch* (New York: Knopf, 2005). Copyright © 2005 by The Kenneth Koch Literary Estate. Used by permission of Alfred A. Knopf, a division of Random House, Inc.

Yusef Komunyakaa. Thanks: *Dien Cai Dau* (Middletown, CT: Wesleyan University Press, 1998). Copyright © 1994 by Yusef Komunyakaa. Reprinted by permission of Wesleyan University Press.

Stanley Kunitz. Benediction: *The Poems of Stanley Kunitz 1928–1978* (Boston: Little Brown and Company, 1979). Copyright © 1979 by Stanley Kunitz. Reprinted courtesy of Darhansoff, Verrill, Feldman Literary Agents.

Sidney Lanier. A Ballad of Trees and the Master: *Poems of Sidney Lanier* (New York: Charles Scribners' Sons, 1916).

Emma Lazarus. In the Jewish Synagogue at Newport: *Admetus and Other Poems* (New York: Hurd and Houghton, 1871). The New Ezekiel: *Poems* (Boston: Houghton, Mifflin, 1889).

Li-Young Lee. This Hour and What Is Dead: *The City in Which I Love You* (Rochester, NY: BOA Editions, 1990). Copyright © 1990 by Li-Young Lee. Reprinted with the permission of BOA Editions, Ltd., www.BOAEditions.org. Night Mirror: *Book of My Nights* (Rochester, NY: BOA Editions, 2001). Copyright © 2001 by Li-Young Lee. Reprinted with the permission of BOA Editions, Ltd., www.BOAEditions.org.

H. Leivick. The Sturdy in Me: *American Yiddish Poetry*, ed. Benjamin and Barbara Harshav (Berkeley: University of California Press, 1986). Copyright © 1986. Reprinted by permission of University of California Press.

John Leland. The Day Is Past and Gone. *The Sacred Harp* (Philadelphia: S. C. Collins, 1860).

Denise Levertov. The Jacob's Ladder; Flickering Mind; Suspended: *Selected Poems* (New York: New Directions, 2002). Copyright © 1961, 1989, 1992 by Denise Levertov. Reprinted by permission of New Directions Publishing Corp.

Philip Levine. A Late Answer; To My God in His Sickness: *They Feed They Lion and The Names of The Lost* (New York: Knopf, 1999). Copyright © 1968, 1969, 1970, 1971, 1972, 1976 by Philip Levine. Used by permission of Alfred A. Knopf, a division of Random House, Inc.

Vachel Lindsay. General William Both Enters Heaven. The Unpardonable Sin: *The Congo and Other Poems* (New York: Macmillan, 1914).

Henry Wadsworth Longfellow. A Psalm of Life; The Bridge; The Jewish Cemetery at Newport;

Christmas Bells; My Cathedral: *Works*, ed. Horace E. Scudder (Boston: Houghton, Mifflin, 1886).

James Russell Lowell. After the Burial: *Under the Willows* (Boston: Fields, Osgood, 1869).

Robert Lowell. Where the Rainbow Ends: *Collected* Poems, ed. Frank Bidart and David Gewanter (New York : Farrar, Straus and Giroux, 2003). Copyright © 2003 by the Estate of Robert Lowell. Reprinted by permission of Harcourt, Inc.

Robert Lowry. Beautiful River: *Bright Jewels for the Sunday School*, ed. Robert Lowry (New York: Biglow & Main, 1869).

Paul Mariani. Giottoesque: *Salvage Operations: New and Selected Poems* (New York: Norton, 1990). Copyright © 1990 by Paul Mariani. Used by permission of W. W. Norton & Company, Inc.

Edwin Markham. In Death Valley: *The Man with the Hoe and Other Poems* (New York: Doubleday & McClure, 1899).

Dionisio D. Martinez. Standard Time: Novena for My Father: *History as a Second Language* (Columbus: Ohio State University Press, 1993). Copyright © 1993 by Dionisio D. Martinez. Reprinted by permission of the author.

Cotton Mather. The Rain gasped for: *Cotton Mather's Verse in English*, ed. Denise D. Knight (Newark: University of Delaware Press, 1989). Copyright © 1989. Reprinted by permission of the University of Delaware Press.

Khaled Mattawa. I Was Buried in Janzoor: *Ismaila Eclipse* (Riverdale-on-Hudson, NY: The Sheep Meadow Press, 1995). Copyright © 1995 by Khaled Mattawa. Reprinted with permission of the author.

J. D. McClatchy. Dervish: *Ten Commandments* (New York: Knopf, 1998). Copyright © 1998 by J. D. McClatchy. Used by permission of Alfred A. Knopf, a division of Random House, Inc.

Claude McKay. I Know My Soul: *Harlem Shadows* (New York: Harcourt, Brace, 1922). Russian Cathedral: *Complete Poems of Claude McKay*, ed. William J. Maxwell (Urbana: University of Illinois Press, 2004). Reprinted courtesy of the Literary Representative for the Works of Claude McKay, Schomburg Center for Research in Black Culture, The New York Public Library, Astor, Lenox and Tilden Foundations.

Herman Melville. from *Moby-Dick*: *The Writings of Herman Melville: Moby-Dick*, ed. Harrison Hayford et al (Chicago: Northwestern-Newberry, 1988). Copyright © 1988. Reprinted by permission of Northwestern University Press. Epilogue from Clarel: A Poem and Pilgrimage in the Holy Land: *The Writings of Herman Melville: Clarel*, ed. Harrison Hayford et al. (Chicago: Northwestern-Newberry, 1991). Copyright © 1991. Reprinted by permission of Northwestern University Press. The Enthusiast: *Collected Poems*, ed. Howard P. Vincent (New York: Hendricks House, 1947). Fragments of a Lost Gnostic Poem of the 12th Century. *The Writings of Herman Melville: Published Poems*, ed. Harrison Hayford et al. (Chicago: Northwestern-Newberry, not yet published). Reprinted by permission of Northwestern University Press. Pontoosuce: *The Writings of Herman Melville: Billy Budd and Other Late Manuscripts*, ed. Harrison Hayford et al. (Chicago: Northwestern-Newberry, not yet published). Reprinted by permission of Northwestern University Press.

Samuel Menashe. Paradise—After Giovanni di Paolo: *New and Selected Poems* (New York: Library of America, 2005). Copyright © 2005 by Samuel Menashe. Reprinted by permission of the author.

James Merrill. An Upward Look: *A Scattering of Salts* (New York: Knopf, 1995). Copyright © 1995 by James Merrill. Used by permission of Alfred A. Knopf, a division of Random House, Inc.

Thomas Merton. St. Paul: *Collected Poems* (New York: New Directions, 1977). Copyright © 1946 by New Directions Publishing Corporations, 1977 by The Trustees of the Merton Legacy Trust. Reprinted by permission of New Directions Publishing Corp. In Silence; Elegy for the Monastery Barn: *Collected Poems* (New York: New Directions, 1977): Copyright © 1957 by The Abbey of Gethsemani. Reprinted by permission of New Directions Publishing Corp.

W. S. Merwin. Lemuel's Blessing; Noah's Raven; The Cerements: *The Second Four Books of Poetry* (Port Townsend, WA: Copper Canyon Press, 1993). Copyright © 2005 by W.S. Merwin. Reprinted with the permission of The Wylie Agency, Inc. The Blind Seer of Ambon: *Travels* (New York: Knopf, 1992). Copyright © 1992 by W. S. Merwin. Used by permission of Alfred A. Knopf, a division of Random House, Inc.

Edna St. Vincent Millay. God's World: *Renascence* (New York: Mitchell Kennerley, 1917).

N. Scott Momaday. The Delight Song of Tsoai-talee; Carriers of the Dream Wheel: *In the Presence of the Sun: Stories and Poems 1961–1991* (New York: St. Martin's Press, 1992). Copyright © 1993 by N. Scott Mornaday. Reprinted by permission of St. Martin's Press, LLC.

Marianne Moore. The Steeple-Jack: *The Complete Poems of Marianne Moore* (New York: Viking, 1967). Copyright © 1951, 1970 by Marianne Moore, renewed 1979 by Lawrence E. Brinn and Louise Crane, Executors of the Estate of Marianne Moore. Used by permission of Viking Penguin, a division of Penguin Group (USA) Inc.

Thylias Moss. The Warmth of Hot Chocolate: *Rainbow Remnants in Rock Bottom Ghetto Sky* (New York: Persea Books, 1991). Copyright © 1993 by Thylias Moss. Reprinted by permission of Persea Books, Inc. (New York) A Man: *Last Chance for the Tarzan Holler* (New York: Persea Books, 1999). Copyright © 1999 by Thylias Moss. Reprinted by permission of Persea Books, Inc. (New York).

Carol Muske-Dukes. When He Fell: *Sparrow* (New York: Random House, 2003). Copyright © 2003 by Carol Muske-Dukes. Used by permission of Random House, Inc.

Mikhail Naimy. Autumn Leaves: *Grape Leaves: An Anthology of Arab-American Poetry*, ed. Gregory Orfalea and Sharif Elmusa (Salt Lake City: University of Utah Press, 1988). Copyright © 1988. Reprinted by permission of the University of Utah Press.

Howard Nemerov. The Loon's Cry: *The Selected Poems of Howard Nemerov*, ed. Daniel Anderson (Athens, OH: Swallow Press / Ohio University Press, 2003). Copyright © 1981 by Howard Nemerov. Reprinted with permission of Margaret Nemerov.

John Frederick Nims. Prayer: *The Powers of Heaven and Earth: New and Selected Poems* (Baton Rouge: Louisiana State University Press, 2002). Copyright © 2002 by Bonnie Larkin Nims, Frank McReynolds Nims, Susan Hoyt Nims Martin, Emily Anne Nims. Reprinted by permission of Louisiana State University Press. The Dark Night (trans. from St. John of the Cross): *The Poems of St. John of the Cross*, trans. John Frederick Nims (New York: Grove, 1959). Copyright © 1995. Reprinted by permission of the University of Chicago Press. Knowledge of God: *Invisible Light: Poems About God*, ed. Diana Culbertson (New York: Columbia University Press, 2000). Copyright © 2000. Reprinted by permission of Bonnie Larkin Nims.

John Norton, Jr. A Funeral Elogy: Anne Bradstreet, *Several Poems* (Boston: John Foster, 1678).

Nicholas Noyes. A Consolatory Poem: Cotton Mather, *Meat Out of the Eater; or, Funeral-Discourses Occasioned by the Death of Several Relatives* (Boston: Benjamin Eliot, 1703).

Naomi Shihab Nye. My Uncle Mohammed at Mecca, 1981: *Yellow Glove* (Portland, OR: Breitenbush Books, 1986). Copyright © 1986. Used by permission of the author.

Geoffrey O'Brien. The Prophet: *Floating City: Selected Poems 1978–1995* (Jersey City, NJ: Talisman House, 1996). Copyright © 1996. Reprinted by permission of the author.

Mary Oliver. When Death Comes: *New and Selected Poems* (Boston: Beacon Press, 1992). Copyright © 1992 by Mary Oliver. Reprinted by permission.

George Oppen. Psalm: *This In Which* (New York: New Directions, 1965). Copyright © 1975 by George Oppen. Reprinted by permission of New Directions Publishing Corp.

Simon J. Ortiz. The Creation, According to Coyote: *Woven Stone* (Tuscon: University of Arizona Press, 1992). Copyright © 1992 by Simon J. Oritz. Reprinted by permission of the author.

Vincent O'Sullivan. Out of the Cloud: *The Houses of Sin* (London: Leonard Smithers, 1897).

Cynthia Ozick. When That With Tragic Rapture Moses Stood—: *A Cynthia Ozick Reader* (Bloomington: Indiana University Press, 1992). Copyright © 1992 by Cynthia Ozick. Reprinted by permission of the author.

Michael Palmer. Untitled (September '92): *The Lion Bridge: Selected Poems 1972–1995* (New York: New Directions, 1998). Copyright © 1998 by Michael Palmer. Reprinted by permission of New Directions Publishing Corp.

Carl Phillips. Visitation: *In the Blood* (Boston: Northeastern University Press, 1992). Copyright © 1990 by Carl Phillips. Reprinted by permission of University Press of New England. From the Devotions; A Great Noise: *From the Devotions* (Saint Paul, MN: Graywolf Press, 1999). Copyright © 1998 by Carl Phillips. Reprinted with the permission of Graywolf Press, Saint Paul, Minnesota.

Robert Pinsky. The Knight's Prayer: *Jersey Rain* (New York: Farrar, Straus and Giroux, 2000). Copyright © 2000 by Robert Pinsky. Reprinted by permission of Farrar, Straus and Giroux, LLC.

Sylvia Plath. Black Rook in Rainy Weather: *Crossing the Water: Transitional Poems* (New York: Harper & Row, 1971). Copyright © 1960 by Ted Hughes. Reprinted by permission of HarperCollins Publishers.

Carl Rakosi. Meditation (after Solomon Ibn Gabirol); Meditation (after Jehuda Halevi): *The Collected Poems of Carl Rakosi* (Orono, Maine: National Poetry Foundation, 1986). Copyright © 1986 by Callman Rawley. Reprinted by permission of Marilyn J. Kane, Literary Executor.

John Crowe Ransom. Armageddon: *Selected Poems* (New York: Knopf, 1990). Copyright © 1924, 1927 by Alfred A. Knopf, Inc., renewed 1952, 1955 by John Crowe Ransom. Used by permission of Alfred A. Knopf, a division of Random House, Inc.

Lizette Woodworth Reese. Trust: *An American Anthology*, ed. Edmund Clarence Stedman (Boston: Houghton, Mifflin, 1900). This Very Day: *Wild Cherry* (Baltimore: Norman, Remington Co., 1923).

Kenneth Rexroth. The Signature of All Things: *The Signature of All Things* (New York: New Directions, 1949). Copyright © 1949 by Kenneth Rexroth. Reprinted by permission of New Directions Publishing Corp.

Charles Reznikoff. Luzzato; Spinoza; "There is nobody in the street": *Poems 1918–1975: The Complete Poems of Charles Reznikoff*, ed. Seamus Cooney (Santa Rosa, CA: Black Sparrow Press, 1989). Copyright © 2005 by the Estate of Charles Reznikoff. Reprinted by permission of Black Sparrow Books, an imprint of David R. Godine, Publisher, Inc.

James Richardson. Evening Prayer: *Interglacial: New and Selected Poems & Aphorisms* (Keene, NY: Ausable Press, 2004). Copyright © 2004 by James Richardson. Reprinted with permission of Ausable Press.

Laura Riding. There Is No Land Yet; Faith Upon the Waters: *Collected Poems* (New York: Random House, 1938). Copyright © 2001 by the Board of Literary Management of the late Laura (Riding) Jackson. Reprinted by permission of Persea Books, Inc. (New York). In conformity with the wishes of the late Laura (Riding) Jackson, her Board of Literary Management asks us to record that, in 1941, Laura (Riding) Jackson renounced, on the grounds of linguistic principle, the writing of poetry: she had come to hold that "poetry obstructs general attainment to something better in our linguistic way-of-life than we have."

Ameen Rihani. The Song of Siva; Renunciation; A Sufi Song: *A Chant of Mystics and Other Poems* (New York: James T. White & Co., 1921).

Alberto Rios. The Death of Anselmo Luna: *Teodoro Luna's Two Kisses* (New York: Norton, 1990). Copyright © 1990 by Alberto Rios. Used by permission of W. W. Norton & Company, Inc.

Edwin Arlington Robinson. The Children of the Night: *The Children of the Night*: (Boston: Richard G. Badger & Co., 1897). Karma: *Dionysus in Doubt* (New York: Macmillan, 1925).

Theodore Roethke. The Waking: *The Waking* (Garden City, NY: Doubleday and Co., 1953). Copyright © 1953 by Theodore Roethke. Used by permission of Doubleday, a division of Random House. In a Dark Time: *The Far Field* (Garden City, NY: Doubleday and Co., 1958). Copyright © 1960 by Beatrice Roethke, Administratrix of the Estate of Theodore Roethke. Used by permission of Doubleday, a division of Random House, Inc.

Muriel Rukeyser. Are You Born? / I; Are You Born? / II: *Collected Poems* (New York: McGraw-Hill, 1979). Copyright © 1978 by Muriel Rukeyser. Reprinted by permission of International Creative Management, Inc.

John Saffin. Consideratus Considerandus: *Seventeenth-Century American Poetry*, ed. Harrison T. Meserole (New York: New York University Press, 1968). Reprinted by permission of Harrison T. Meserole.

Carl Sandburg. Our Prayer of Thanks: *Chicago Poems* (New York: Holt, 1916). For You: *Smoke and Steel* (New York: Harcourt, Brace & Howe, 1920).

Gjertrud Schnackenberg. Supernatural Love: *Supernatural Love: Poems 1976–1992* (New York: Farrar, Straus and Giroux, 2000). Copyright © 2000 by Gjertrud Schnackenberg. Reprinted by permission of Farrar, Straus and Giroux, LLC.

Esther Schor. Alef: *The Hills of Holland* (Santa Maria, CA: Archer Books, 2002). Copyright © 2002. Reprinted by permission of Archer Books.

James Schuyler. Our Father: *Collected Poems* (New York: Farrar, Straus and Giroux, 1993). Copyright © 1993 by the Estate of James Schuyler. Reprinted by permission of Farrar, Straus and Giroux, LLC.

Delmore Schwartz. At a Solemn Musick: *Summer Knowledge: New and Selected Poems 1938–1958* (Garden City, NY: Doubleday & Co., 1959). Copyright © 1959 by Delmore Schwartz. Reprinted by permission of New Directions Publishing Corp.

Edward Hamilton Sears: It Came Upon the Midnight Clear: *Songs and Sermons of the Christian Life* (Boston: Noyes, Holmes, 1875).

Martha Serpas. As If There Were Only One: *Côte Blanche* (Kalamazoo, MI: New Issues / Western Michigan University Press, 2002). Copyright © 2002 by Martha Serpas. Reprinted by permission of New Issues Poetry and Prose. Psalm at High Tide: *The New Yorker*, September 12, 2005. Copyright © 2005. Reprinted by permission of the author. Witness Tree; Poem Found: texts provided courtesy of the author. Copyright © 2003, 2005. Reprinted by permission of the author.

Anne Sexton. Rowing: *Selected Poems of Anne Sexton*, ed. Diane Wood Middlebrook and Diana Hume George (Boston: Houghton Mifflin, 1988). Copyright © 1975 by Loring Conant, Jr., Executor of the Estate of Anne Sexton. Reprinted by permission of Houghton Mifflin Company. All rights reserved.

Alan Shapiro. Prayer on the Temple Steps: *Covenant* (Chicago: University of Chicago Press, 1991). Copyright © 1991. Reprinted by permission of the author.

Karl Shapiro. The Alphabet: *Poems of a Jew* (New York: Random House, 1958). Copyright © 1958 by the Estate of Karl Jay Shapiro by arrangement with Wieser & Elwell, New York, NY. Reprinted by permission.

Knowles Shaw. Sowing in the Morning: *Sing His Praise* (Springfield, MO: Gospel Publishing House, 1991).

Grace Shulman. Blessed Is the Light; Prayer: *Days of Wonder: New and Selected Poems* (Boston: Houghton Mifflin, 2002). Copyright © 2002 by Grace Schulman. Reproduced by permission of Houghton Mifflin Company. All rights reserved.

Lydia H. Sigourney. The Coral Insect: *Illustrated Poems* (Philadelphia: Carey and Hart, 1849).

Charles Simic. Mystic Life: *Jackstraws* (New York: Harcourt Brace, 1999). Copyright © 1999 by Charles Simic. Reprinted by permission of Harcourt, Inc.

Josephine Singer. Provision: text provided courtesy of the author. Copyright © Laura Qinney. Reprinted by permission.

Gary Snyder. Milton by Firelight: *No Nature: New and Selected Poems* (New York: Pantheon, 1992). Copyright © 2004 by Gary Snyder. Reprinted by permission of Shoemaker & Hoard Publishers. Burning Island: *No Nature: New and Selected Poems* (New York: Pantheon, 1992). Copyright © 1970 by Gary Snyder. Reprinted by permission of New Directions Publishing Corp. Ripples on the Surface: *No Nature: New and Selected Poems* (New York: Pantheon, 1992). Copyright © 1992 by Gary Snyder. Used by permission of Pantheon Books, a division of Random House, Inc.

Spirituals and Anonymous Hymns. Balm in Gilead; Poor Wayfaring Stranger: George Pullen Jackson, *Spiritual Folk-Songs of Early America* (New York: J. J. Augustin, 1964). Didn't My Lord Deliver Daniel; Steal Away; Swing Low, Sweet Chariot: *Jubilee Songs: As Sung by the Jubilee Singers of Fisk* University, ed. Theodore Frelinghuysen Seward (New York: Biglow, Main & Co., 1872). Ezekiel Saw de Wheel: *Religious Folk Songs of the Negro,* ed. Thomas P. Fenner (Hampton, VA: Hampton Institute, 1909). Free at Last; Got a Home in That Rock: *Folk Songs of the American Negro*, ed. John Wesley Work (Nashville, TN: Work Brothers, 1907). I Know Moon-Rise: Thomas Wentworth Higginson, "Negro Spirituals," *Atlantic Monthly*, June 1867. Let My People Go: *The National Anti-Slavery Standard*, December 21, 1861. Lonesome Valley: *Folk Song: U.S.A.*, ed. John A. Lomax and Alan Lomax (New York: Meredith Press, 1947). Nobody Knows the Trouble I've Had: *Slave Songs of the United States*, ed. William Francis Allen et. al (New York: A. Simpson & Co., 1867). Simple Gifts: Edward Demings Andrews, *The Gift To Be Simple* (New York: J. J. Augustin, 1940). Sometimes I Feel Like a Motherless Child: *Cabin and Plantation Songs*, ed. Thomas P. Fenner (Hampton, VA: Hampton Institute, 1901).

William Stafford. With My Crowbar Key: *The Way It Is: New and Selected Poems* (St. Paul, MN: Graywolf Press, 1998). Copyright © 1962, 1998 by the Estate of William Stafford. Reprinted with the permission of Graywolf Press, Saint Paul, Minnesota.

Gerald Stern. Lord, Forgive a Spirit: *Red Coal* (Boston: Houghton Mifflin, 1981). Copyright © 1981 by Gerald Stern. Reprinted by permission of the author.

Wallace Stevens. Tea at the Palaz of Hoon; Sunday Morning: *Harmonium* (New York: Knopf, 1923). God Is Good, It Is a Beautiful Night; Less and Less Human, O Savage Spirit: *Transport to Summer* (New York: Knopf, 1947). Angel Surrounded by Paysans: *The Auroras of Autumn* (New York: Knopf, 1950). Final Soliloquy of the Interior Paramour: *Collected Poems* (New York: Knopf, 1961). Copyright © 1954 by Wallace Stevens, renewed 1982 by Holly Stevens. Used by permission of Alfred A. Knopf, a division of Random House, Inc. Of Mere Being: Typescript, Huntington Library WAS 4205. Copyright © 1957 by Elsie Stevens and Holly Stevens. Used by permission of Alfred A. Knopf, a division of Random House, Inc.

Trumbull Stickney. "He said: 'If in his image I was made'": *Prometheus Pyrphoro: Dramatic Verses* (Boston: Charles E. Goodspeed, 1902). "And, the last day being come, Man stood alone": *Poems of Trumbull Stickney* (Boston: Houghton Mifflin, 1905).

Mark Strand. White; Orpheus Alone: *The Continuous Life* (New York: Knopf, 1990). From Dark Harbor: *Dark Harbor* (New York: Knopf, 1993). Copyright © 1990, 1993 by Mark Strand. Used by permission of Alfred A. Knopf, a division of Random House, Inc.

May Swenson. Question: *Another Animal*, in *Poets of Today*, ed. John Hall Wheelock (New York: Charles Scribner's Sons, 1954). Used with permission of The Literary Estate of May Swenson. The Lightning, Big-Hipped Nature; Each Like a Leaf: *Nature: Poems Old and New* (Boston: Houghton Mifflin, 1994). Copyright © 1994 by the Literary Estate of May Swenson. Reprinted by permission of Houghton Mifflin Company. All rights reserved.

Arthur Sze. The Unnamable River: *The Redshifting Web: Poems 1970–1998* (Port Townsend, WA:

Copper Canyon Press, 1998). Copyright © 1998 by Arthur Sze. Reprinted with the permission of Copper Canyon Press, P.O. Box 271, Port Townsend, WA 98368-0271.

John Banister Tabb. Nekros; Communion: *The Poetry of Father Tabb*, ed. Francis Litz (New York: Dodd, Mead and Company, 1928). Tenebræ: *Lyrics*, 5th edition (Boston: Copeland & Day, 1900).

Allen Tate. The Cross; The Twelve; Sonnets at Christmas: *Collected Poems 1913–1976* (New York: Farrar, Straus and Giroux, 1977). Copyright © 1977 by Allen Tate. Reprinted by permission of Farrar, Straus and Giroux, LLC.

Edward Taylor. from Preparatory Meditations: First Series; from Preparatory Meditations: Second Series; Let by rain; Upon a Spider Catching a Fly; Upon a Wasp Child with Cold; Huswifery; The Ebb and Flow; A Fig for thee Oh! Death: *The Poems of Edward Taylor*, ed. Donald E. Stanford (New Haven: Yale University Press, 1960). Copyright © 1960, renewed 1988, by Donald E. Stanford. Reprinted by permission.

Sara Teasdale. The Sanctuary: *Flame and Shadow* (New York: Macmillan, 1920).

Henry David Thoreau: Sic Vita; Music; Inspiration: *Collected Poems of Henry Thoreau*, enlarged edition, ed. Carl Bode (Baltimore: Johns Hopkins University Press, 1964).

Melvin B. Tolson. A Song for Myself: *Rendezvous with America* (New York: Dodd, Mead & Co., 1944). Copyright © 1999. Reprinted by permission of the University of Virginia Press.

Benjamin Tompson. A Neighbour's Tears: *Benjamin Tompson, Colonial Bard*, ed. Peter White (University Park: Pennsylvania State University Press, 1980).

Jean Toomer. Prayer; The Gods Are Here: *The Collected Poems of Jean Toomer*, ed. Robert B. Jones and Margery Toomer Latimer (Chapel Hill: University of North Carolina Press, 1988). Reprinted by permission of the Yale Collection of American Literature, Beinecke Rare Book and Manuscript Library, Yale University.

Frederick Goddard Tuckerman. Sonnets; "Not the round natural world, not the deep mind": *Poems* (Boston: John Wilson & Son, 1860)

Chase Twichell. Cloud of Unknowing: *The Snow Watcher* (Princeton, NJ: Ontario Review Press, 1998). Copyright © 1998. Reprinted with permission of the author and Ontario Review Press.

Robert Vasquez. Belief: *At the Rainbow* (Albuquerque: University of New Mexico Press, 1995). Copyright © 1995 by Robert Vasquez. Reprinted by permission of the University of New Mexico Press.

Jones Very. The New Birth; The Cup; The New World; The Created; The Origin of Man: *Jones Very: The Complete Poems*, ed. Helen R. Deese (Athens: University of Georgia Press, 1993). Reprinted by permission of the Houghton Library, Harvard University. The Cottage; Autumn Flowers: *Jones Very: The Complete Poems*, ed. Helen R. Deese (Athens: University of Georgia Press, 1993). Reprinted by permission of Helen R. Deese. Enoch: *Jones Very: The Complete Poems*, ed. Helen R. Deese (Athens: University of Georgia Press, 1993). Reprinted with permission from the Bryant-Godwin Papers; Manuscripts and Archives Division; The New York Public Library; Astor, Lenox and Tilden Foundations. Yourself, Night: *Jones Very: The Complete Poems*, ed. Helen R. Deese (Athens: University of Georgia Press, 1993). Copyright © 1993. Reprinted by permission of the University of Georgia Press.

Bill Wadsworth. The Authority of Elsewhere: *The Physicist Explains on a Cold Night* (New York: Breakaway Press, 2002). Copyright © 2002 by William Wadsworth. Reprinted with permission of the author.

Robert Penn Warren. Evening Hawk; Heart of Autumn: *The Collected Poems of Robert Penn Warren*, ed. John Burt (Baton Rouge: Louisiana State University Press, 1998). Copyright © 1975, 1978 by Robert Penn Warren. Reprinted by permission of William Morris Agency, LLC on behalf of the author.

Rosanna Warren. Hagar: *Stained Glass* (New York: Norton, 1993). Copyright © 1993 by Rosanna

Warren. Used by permission of W. W. Norton & Company, Inc. Cyprian; Antique: *Departure* (New York: Norton, 2003). Copyright © 2003 by Rosanna Warren. Used by permission of W. W. Norton & Company, Inc.

Edith Wharton. Terminus: *Edith Wharton: A Biography* (New York: Harper Collins, 1975). Reprinted by permission of the estate of Edith Wharton and the Watkins/Loomis Agency.

Phillis Wheatley. On the Death of the Rev. Mr. George Whitefield; To a Lady on the Death of Three Relations: *Poems on Various Subjects* (London and Boston, 1773).

Susan Wheeler. That Been to Me My Lives Light and Saviour: *Ledger* (Iowa City: University of Iowa Press, 2005). Copyright © 2005 by Susan Wheeler. Reprinted by permission of the University of Iowa Press.

John Wheelwright. Fish Food; Come Over and Help Us; Bread-Word Giver: *Collected Poems*, ed. Alvin H. Rosenfeld (New York: New Directions, 1971). Copyright © 1971 by Louise Wheelwright Damon. Reprinted by permission of New Directions Publishing Corp.

Walt Whitman. "In vain were nails driven through my hands": *The Uncollected Poetry and Prose of Walt Whitman*, Vol. 2, ed. Emory Holloway (Garden City, NY: Doubleday & Company, 1926). From "Song of Myself; from "Crossing Brooklyn Ferry"; As I Ebb'd With the Ocean of Life; When Lilacs Last in the Dooryard Bloom'd; As Adam Early in the Morning; Chanting the Square Deific; A Noiseless Patient Spider: *Leaves of Grass* (Philadelphia, 1891–92).

John Greenleaf Whittier. First-Day Thoughts: *The Chapel of the Hermits and Other Poems* (Boston: Ticknor & Fields, 1852). The Eternal Goodness: *The Tent on the Beach and Other Poems* (Boston: Ticknor & Fields, 1867). Unity: "Whittier's Uncollected Poems" in Samuel Thomas Pickard, *Whittier-land: A Handbook of North Essex* (Boston: Houghton, Mifflin, 1904).

Michael Wigglesworth. from *The Day of Doom*: Vanity of Vanities: *Poems of Michael Wigglesworth*, ed. Ronald A. Basco (Lanham, MD: University Press of America, 1989). Copyright © 1989. Reprinted by permission of the University Press of America.

Richard Wilbur. In a Churchyard; Advice to a Prophet; "A World Without Objects Is a Sensible Emptiness"; A Christmas Hymn; The Proof: *New and Collected Poems*: (New York: Harvest, 1989): Copyright © 1988 by Richard Wilbur. Reprinted by permission of Harcourt, Inc.

Emma Hart Willard: Rocked in the Cradle of the Deep: *Yale Book of American Verse* (New Haven, CT: Yale University Press, 1913)

C. K. Williams. The Vessel: *A Dream of Mind* (New York: Farrar, Straus and Giroux, 1992). Copyright © 1992 by C. K. Williams. Reprinted by permission of Farrar, Straus and Giroux, LLC.

Roger Williams. "God gives them sleep on ground, on straw"; "Boast not proud English, of thy birth and blood"; "They see Gods wonders that are call'd"; "The Indians prize not English gold": Roger Williams, *A Key into the Language of America* (Bedford, MA: Applewood Books, 1997).

William Carlos Williams. Burning the Christmas Greens: *The Wedge* (Cummington, Mass.: Cummington Press, 1944). The Gift: *The Collected Poems of William Carlos Williams*, Volume 2 (1939–1962), ed. Christopher MacGowan (New York: New Directions, 1988). Copyright © 1944, 1962 by William Carlos Williams. Reprinted by permission of New Directions Publishing Corp.

David Woo. Eden; The Ballad of Infinite Forgetfulness: *The Eclipses* (Rochester, NY: BOA Editions, 2005). Copyright © 2005 by David Woo. Reprinted with the permission of BOA Editions, Ltd., www.BOAEditions.com.

Charles Wright. Apologia Pro Vita Sua: *Black Zodiac* (New York: Farrar, Straus and Giroux, 1997). Copyright © 1997 by Charles Wright. Reprinted by permission of Farrar, Straus and Giroux, LLC.

James Wright. The Refusal; A Blessing; Saint Judas: *Above the River: Collected Poems* A Blessing:

Collected Poems (Middletown, CT: Wesleyan University Press, 1972). Copyright © 1972 by James Wright. Reprinted by permission of Wesleyan University Press.

Jay Wright. The Origin of Mary in a Cathedral Choir; Desire's Persistence: *Transfigurations* (Baton Rouge: Louisiana State University Press, 2000). Copyright © 1986, 2000 by Jay Wright. Reprinted by permission of the author.

Elinor Wylie. Address to My Soul: *Trivial Breath* (New York: Knopf, 1928). Copyright © 2005. Reprinted with permission of The Kent State University Press.

Louis Zukofsky. from "A"–12: *"A" 1–12* (London: Jonathan Cape, 1966). Copyright © 1978 by Celia Zukofsky and Louis Zukofsky. Reprinted by permission of Paul Zukofsky.

Notes

1.1 The Bay Psalm Book] The first book published in English North America, brought out in 1640 in Cambridge, Massachusetts.

3.5 Toleration] "Allowance (with or without limitations), by the ruling power, of the exercise of religion otherwise than in the form officially established or recognized" (OED).

5.5 Banks of *Lacrim* flood] A personification of tears (Latin, *lacrimae*).

8.30 In silent night when rest I took] A poem written after Bradstreet's home was destroyed by fire; it has often been published under the title "Some Verses Upon the Burning of Our House, July 10, 1666."

11.23 *Consideratus Considerandus*] The text of this poem is taken from Harrison T. Meserole, ed., *American Poetry of the Seventeenth Century*, which notes that although the poem is written in Saffin's hand in his commonplace book, it is possible that it is by the Earl of Rochester.

15.30–31 Fair . . . shameful end] See 2 Samuel 18.

16.21 *Omnia . . . Deum.*] All things pass except God's love.

17.3 *Preparatory Meditations*] Taylor conceived the poems in the two *Preparatory Meditations* series as a means to ready himself to receive communion. Begun in 1682, the *Preparatory Meditations* spans more than four decades of Taylor's life. Except for a few verses, Taylor did not publish his poems, and only in the twentieth century was his work discovered.

22.36 Michtam] Poem or song; the word appears in the titles of some Psalms.

23.1 *Let*] Prevented from traveling.

24.19 froppish] Fretful, peevish.

25.20 The Bare] The constellations Ursa Major and Ursa Minor (Great Bear and Little Bear).

25.20 Northern Blast] The north wind.

25.21 Torpedo like] In the manner of torpedo fish, rays that paralyze their prey through an electric shock.

27.4 Fulling Mills] A mill to clean, shrink, and thicken cloth.

35.7 bereaved Nine] The Muses.

35.12 *Maro's*] Virgil's.

35.36 *Tully's*] Cicero's.

45.3 *George Whitefield*] English Methodist minister (1714–1770) who made numerous visits to America and whose revivalist preaching drew large crowds during the first Great Awakening.

62.17 awful Jove] The statue of Zeus at Olympia, one of the Seven Wonders of the ancient world.

64.6 Taylor] Anglican clergyman and religious writer Jeremy Taylor (1613–1637), whose works include *The Rules and Exercises of Holy Living* (1650) and *The Rules and Exercises of Holy Dying* (1651).

70.1 Γνωθι Σεαυτον] "Know thyself," the inscription over the entrance to the temple of Apollo at Delphi.

80.12–13 the tablets . . . base] See Exodus 32:19.

81.12 marah] Bitterness.

81.13 Anathema maranatha!] See 1 Corinthians 16:22: "If any man love not the Lord Jesus Christ, let him be Anathema Maranatha."

83.23 *First-Day*] Sunday.

85.3 mete] A boundary or limit.

109.7 FROM *Moby-Dick*] Recited by Father Mapple in Chapter 9, "The Sermon."

111.6 *"Though . . . him."*] Job 13:15.

118.20 teokallis] Pre-Columbian Mesoamerican pyramid.

122.16 Paumanok] Algonquian name for Long Island.

184.8 *General William Booth*] English minister (1829–1912) and founder of the Salvation Army, whose leader is referred to as "General."

200.19–20 and rails . . . square:] H.D. lived in London during World War II.

217.8–11 *Similiter* . . . Trallianos.] Eliot quotes from a letter to the Christian community at Tralles (currently Aydin in western Turkey) attributed to Saint Ignatius, the first-century bishop of Antioch. The passage is from Chapter 3: "In like manner, let all reverence the deacons as an appointment of Jesus Christ, and the bishop as Jesus Christ, who is the Son of the Father, and the presbyters as the sanhedrin of God, and assembly of the apostles. Apart from these, there is no Church. Concerning all this, I am persuaded that ye are of the same opinion." (Roberts-Donaldson translation)

217.12–13 *And when . . . Laodiceans.*] Colossians 4:16.

222.24 Sovegna vos] From the words spoken to Dante by the Provençal poet Arnaut Daniel in *Purgatorio*, XXVI, "Sovegna vos a temps de ma dolor": "Think of me in my time of pain." The line is cited elsewhere in Eliot's poetry and criticism.

232.22–34 Sin . . . well.] Cf. the Thirteenth Revelation in St. Julian of Norwich's *Revelations of Divine Love* (c. 1393): "But Jesus, who in this Vision informed me of all that is needful to me, answered by this word and said: It behoved that there should be sin; but all shall be well, and all shall be well, and all manner of thing shall be well."

239.11 *Tetelėstai*] Greek, "It is finished," spoken by Jesus while dying on the Cross.

244.18 *Russian Cathedral*] The poem was originally entitled "St. Isaac's Church, Petrograd"; McKay visited the church on a trip to the Soviet Union in 1922.

247.3 *Luzzato*] Italian-born kabbalist Moses Chaim Luzzato (1707–1746) was threatened with excommunication by the Jewish authorities in his native Padua after he claimed to be receiving messages from a supernatural being called the "maggid"; he eventually settled in Amsterdam, where he wrote his major kabbalistic studies, and later went to the Holy Land, where he died.

255.9 John, founder of towns] Wheelwright's ancestor and namesake, the clergyman John Wheelwright (1592–1679), immigrated to Massachusetts as a Puritan in 1636. In part due to sympathies with the views of his sister-in-law Anne Hutchinson, he was soon banished, and in 1637 he founded Exeter, New Hampshire, then moved to Maine the following year. He returned to Massachusetts after the decree of banishment was rescinded.

260.3 Chladni] German physicist Ernst Chladni (1756–1827), known in particular for his pioneering work in the study of acoustics.

262.7 *Lachrymae Christi*] Christ's tears.

266.6–10 *Venient annis . . . ultima Thule.*] From Seneca's *Medea*: "A time will come in distant years when Ocean will loosen the bonds of things and the whole earth's surface will be open to view, and Tethys will discover new worlds; Thule will no longer be the outermost limit of the world."

266.12 Luis de San Angel] Collector of church revenues who advocated for Columbus' voyage in Queen Isabella's court.

266.18 Juan Perez] Rabidán friar who helped persuade Columbus to ask Ferdinand and Isabella to support his voyage, although they had rejected his previous proposals.

266.32 Chan] Title given to various dignitaries in the Near East and Central Asia, often spelled "Khan."

267.30 Palos] Spanish port from which Columbus sailed on August 3, 1492.

268.12 Teneriffe's] Largest of the Canary Islands.

268.14 Te Deum laudamus,] O Lord we praise Thee.

269.2–3 *To Find . . . Wrath.*] From Blake's notebook poem "Morning" (c. 1800–06).

273.8–9 *Music . . . system.*] From *Symposium* (187a–c), spoken by Eryximachus.

286.26 *Simon the Cyrenian*] The man who carried the cross of Jesus as he made his way to Calvary, according to Matthew 27:32 and Mark 15:21.

287.4 skin is black."] Cyrene was a North African city, in present-day Libya.

288.9 *Solomon Ibn Gabirol*] Eleventh-century Spanish Jewish poet and philosopher.

288.19 *Jehudah Halevi*] Spanish Jewish poet and philosopher (c. 1075–1141).

292.17 Yizchok Elchonon] Yitzchak Elchanan Spektor (1817–1896), chief rabbi of Kovno in Lithuania.

293.25 Paul] Zukofsky's son.

293.26 Prince Albert] A nineteenth-century frock-coat.

296.4 Celia] Zukofsky's wife.

302.7 *Horae Canonicae*] Latin, "Canonical Hours," the temporal divisions of the day governing prayer for Catholics and Anglicans.

302.8 "*Immolatus vicerit*"] See the Latin hymn beginning "Pange lingua gloriosi": "Dic triumphum nobilem / Qualiter Redemptor orbis / Immolatus vicerit": "Tell of the noble triumph, how the Redeemer of the world, himself a victim, was victorious."

302.9 PRIME] The first hour for prayer recitation, 6 A.M.

307.16 *Veritas sequitur . . .*] Cf. Thomas Aquinas' dictum, "Veritas sequitur esse rerum" ("Truth follows the being of things").

320.13 *Bahá'u'lláh*] "Glory of God" in Arabic, the name of the prophet and founder of the Bahá'í Faith, born Mírzá Husayn-Alí (1817–1892). In 1863, he declared his messianic purpose to a select group of followers in the Garden of Ridwan in Baghdad.

322.16–17 People of Bahá . . . slain] The 1979 Islamist revolution brought renewed persecution to members of the Bahá'í Faith in Iran.

335.23 the poet] English lyric poet Ralph Hodgson (1871–1962), who spent much of his life in Japan and, after 1940, on a farm in Ohio living in near-seclusion.

337.7 Fifth & Hennepin] In Minneapolis.

340.4 Azarias & Misael] See Daniel 1:6–21.

340.14 Germanicus . . . Smyrna,] Saint Germanicus, martyred in an amphitheater at Smyrna in the second century, was reputed to have goaded animals to kill him after they at first ignored him.

340.18–21 'Eighty & six . . . fire.] Second-century Christian bishop Polycarp of Smyrna was martyred in his eighties.

353.3 *Candlemas*] Feast day celebrated on February 2, commemorating the presentation of Jesus in the Temple and the purification of Mary.

364.14 *"A World . . . Emptiness"*] Cf. *Centuries of Meditations: Second Century*, section 65, by English poet and religious writer Thomas Traherne (c. 1616–1674): "Life without objects is a sensible emptiness."

366.6 Xanthus] The river Scamander on the plain of Troy; see *Iliad*, Book 21.

375.2 *Hath the rain . . . dew?*] Job 38:28.

387.6 Barbelo!] Gnostic name for the first emanation of God.

389.7 *Giovanni di Paolo*] Sienese painter (1395–1482).

447.9–10 "O hell . . . behold?"] Spoken by Satan in *Paradise Lost*, Book 4, line 358.

449.3 shochu] A Japanese alcoholic drink made from rice, barley, sweet potato, or other ingredients as its base.

449.31–32 Bless Masa . . . the crater] In 1967, Snyder married Masa Uehara on the rim of a volcano in Japan.

453.6 *Tsoai-talee*] "Rock-Tree Boy" in Kiowa, the name given to Momaday when he was taken as an infant to "Tsoai" (Devil's Tower National Monument in Wyoming).

459.6 "To do as Adam did"] See Thomas Traherne's "The Apostasy": "All bliss / Consists in this, / To do as Adam did, / And not to know those superficial joys / Which were from him in Eden hid, / Those little new-invented things, / Fine lace and silks, such childish toys / As ribands are and rings, / Or worldly pelf that us destroys."

462.25 Judah Halevi's] See note 288.19.

462.26 Ghalib's] Literally "conqueror," the pen name of Mirza Asadullah Khan (1797–1867), poet who wrote in Urdu and Persian.

463.13 *Apologia Pro Vita Sua*] Latin, "A defense of one's life," also the title of Cardinal Newman's autobiography (1864).

464.19 *Verona . . . Verona,*] "Verona made me, Verona undid me": cf. Dante, *Purgatorio*, V. 134: "Siena made me, Maremma undid me."

465.19 *Malocchio*] The evil eye.

466.7 *Perch'io . . . Toscana,*] The opening lines of a poem by Italian poet Guido Cavalcanti (c. 1255–1300): "Because no hope is left me, Ballatetta / Of return to Tuscany." (Ezra Pound translation)

475.18 "a deadly . . . robe."] Cf. Clytemnestra's speech after killing Agamemnon in Aeschuylus' *Agamemnon*: "My aim was so exact—I won't deny it— / that he could not outrun death, or fend it off / once I ensnared him in a deadly wealth / of robes, escapeless as a fishing net; / I struck him twice, and while he cried two cries, / his legs gave way." (Alan Shapiro and Peter Burian translation)

484.16 Elvin] Elvin Jones (1927–2004), jazz drummer who played with John Coltrane from 1960 to 1966.

485.6 Syeeda's "Song Flute"] Composition by John Coltrane, from his album *Giant Steps* (1959).

490.34–35 Gander base . . . flame] On December 12, 1985, a DC-8 aircraft crashed shortly after takeoff from the airport in Gander, Newfoundland, killing more than two hundred American soldiers.

493.3 *The Creation*] A retelling of the creation myth of the Acoma Pueblo people.

495.24 Shekhinah's] The female aspect of divinity.

496.9 "Even death . . . last"] From the Epilogue to Melville's *Clarel*: see p. 110.27.

513.24 LAURENCE HOPE] Pen name of Adela Florence Nicolson (1865–1904), English poet who spent most of her life in India. The epigraph is the opening line of her poem "Kashmiri Song."

529.3 *O-Bon*] Japanese Buddhist holiday commemorating ancestral spirits, marked by family reunions.

576.15 *brucha*] Blessing.

Index of Poets

Index of Titles and First Lines

The book is set in 11 point Dante, a face originally designed by Giovanni Mardersteig after World War II and based on his experiences with the popular book fonts Bembo and Centaur. This version of Dante was redrawn as a digital font for Monotype by Ron Carpenter in 1993.

The paper is acid-free Domtar Literary Opaque, which meets the requirements for permanence of the American National Standards Institute. The flexible binding material, Ultima 7, is a paper-based product protected by two acrylic coatings and manufactured by Ecological Fibers; the book is Smyth-sewn for additional durability.

Composition: Dedicated Business Services (New Market, IA)
Printing: Malloy Incorporated (Ann Arbor, MI)
Binding: Dekker Bookbinding (Grand Rapids, MI)